DESCENT INTO MADNESS

DEDICATION

To Michael Buday and Garry Rodgers
whose courage and dedication exemplifies the fine men and women
of the Royal Canadian Mounted Police.

DESCENT INTO
MADNESS
THE DIARY OF A KILLER

Vernon Frolick

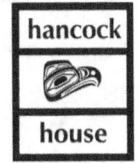

ISBN-10: 0-88839-026-2
ISBN-13: 978-0-88839-026-4
Copyright © 1993 Vernon Frolick

Sixth printing 2017, Black and White Edition

> **Cataloging in Publication Data**
> Frolick, Vernon, 1950–
>   Descent into madness
>
>   ISBN 0-88839-321-0
>
>   1. Oros, Michael. 2. Murder—British Columbia—Atlin.
>   3. Murderers—British Columbia—Biography.
>   I. Title.
>
>   HV6535.C33A84 1992   364.1'523'092   C92-091837-9

All rights reserved. No part of this publication may be reproduced, stored in a retrieval system or transmitted, in any form or by any means, electronic, mechanical, photocopying, recording, or otherwise, without the prior written permission of Hancock House Publishers.

Printed in Canada FRIESENS

Editor: Herb Bryce
Production: Lorna Lake

We acknowledge the financial support of the Government of Canada through the Canada Book Fund for our publishing activities.

Published simultaneously in Canada and the United States by

HANCOCK HOUSE PUBLISHERS LTD.
19313 Zero Avenue, Surrey, B.C. Canada V3Z 9R9
(604) 538-1114 Fax (604) 538-2262

HANCOCK HOUSE PUBLISHERS
#104 4550 Birch Bay-Lynden Rd, Blaine, WA U.S.A. 98230-9436
(604) 538-1114 Fax (604) 538-2262
Web Site: www.hancockhouse.com *Email:* sales@hancockhouse.com

Contents

Foreword 6
Acknowledgments 7
Chapter One 8
Chapter Two 16
Chapter Three 49
Chapter Four 58
Chapter Five 69
Chapter Six 88
Chapter Seven 115
Chapter Eight 123
Chapter Nine 136
Chapter Ten 141
Chapter Eleven 157
Chapter Twelve 167
Chapter Thirteen 199
Chapter Fourteen 206
Chapter Fifteen 227
Chapter Sixteen 266
Chapter Seventeen 279
Chapter Eighteen 291
Chapter Nineteen 301
Chapter Twenty 315
Chapter Twenty-One 334
Epilogue 356

Foreword

Originally, after the fatal shoot-out with Oros at Teslin Lake, I had no intention of writing this book. In fact, when Garry Rodgers and I sat in the Skeena Pub after he got back and discussed the details of his experience, the very idea that someone might write the story—glorifying Oros, sensationalizing the murders and trivializing Mike Buday's death—was repugnant.

Only those of us on the inside knew the whole picture. It was our case. Our special problem. No outsider would ever have access to the real story. The whole truth. The police investigation which commenced in Atlin on September 10, 1981, when Wiebe reported that Gunter Lishy had disappeared at Hutsigola Lake, grew from there, ultimately to span years and continents. The investigation even reached into the files of the FBI and Interpol, and tracked down witnesses and information no one else would ever find.

An outsider writing the story would have access to only the smallest part of the truth. But rumors were fierce: that Oros was a devil-worshipper and a cannibal, that he ran wild with a dog pack, naked but for animal skins, that he howled at the moon and ate raw flesh. Whatever was lacking could be filled in with imagination.

However, the private journals which he maintained faithfully from his early commune days in Taos, New Mexico, until his own violent death, chronicle a bizarre and frightening spiral into increasing madness.

The brave men who flew up to Teslin to confront Oros in his own territory are owed our gratitude. They were nearly all killed.

Later, when the events at Teslin Lake received international attention and we realized the story would inevitably be told—one way or another—I undertook to write it. As an insider.

Initially the idea was simply to report the truth to prevent a fictional account from filling that space. However, the more I became involved in the case, absorbing the details, the more I found myself drawn into it.

In the end I wrote the story because it deserves to be told.

Acknowledgments

I am pleased to acknowledge the assistance and kind support I received from Gerald Roach and Gloria Kupchenko, who encouraged the writing of this book, from Warren Wilson and Laurie Langford, who helped collect material and who edited numerous handwritten drafts, and, most importantly, from my wife Lynne, who put up with it all.

Chapter One

September 10, 1981: Oros was already well back from the shoreline watching from under the cover of the willows as the pontoons lifted off the surface and the plane was again airborne. The opportunity to kill the pilot had come and gone. Now that the plane was in the air, only a fluke shot would bring it down. Oros wasn't going to risk it.

Across the lake, like a dragonfly cruising a swamp for prey, it circled low over the forest searching the ground. After a few moments it returned to the lake and then passed directly overhead as it flew toward Oros' cabin. It was in range again. The high wailing sound of its laboring pistons assailed his ears but, though he kept a tight grip on his old rifle, Oros didn't bring it up to his shoulder.

Perhaps he should have killed the pilot when he paddled out to meet him on the lake; he knew that was his best chance to do it. Except killing him wasn't part of the plan. Besides, it's a damn sight harder to hide a plane than a body.

Oros' eyes burned with hatred as he watched. The pilot couldn't see him in the willows. But the green canoe was out there. From where Oros was hiding, he could see it clearly. Pulled up over the rocks, it was exposed as brightly as the moon.

For the hundredth time, his brain raced over his next step. He'd have to get rid of the canoe. They'd expect him to take it and travel north into the Yukon by water down the Teslin River and into the Teslin Lake system. Instead, he'd bury it and travel overland south past Zancudo toward the abandoned town of Sheslay. They'd never find him there.

As the plane flew over Oros' cabin, it rolled slowly into a steep bank and started a sweeping turn. Spiraling upward as though working an updraft, it continued to circle above the cabin, around and around, until, at 2,500 feet, it made one last bank to straighten out and then finally disappeared over the horizon toward Atlin in the west.

Oros stepped out from the dark green shadows of the swamp willow and stood for a long moment in the open air testing the space with all his senses. Any movement, any new sound, anything out of the ordinary to signal that the plane hadn't really left or that it hadn't been alone, and Oros would have faded away into the bush. But apart from some chickadees rustling nearby through the pine branches and the ever-present buzz of insects from the perpetual cloud around his head, the air was dead calm under the noonday sun.

It wouldn't be long before they'd be back, Oros knew. Yelling for his dogs, he broke from the trees and ran wildly toward the cabin with long, loping strides that covered the ground quickly. His steps were high, like those of a moose or a prancing spring colt, wired with energy. Oros thought of himself as past his prime but the truth was, there were very few people left in the country who could live and endure in the wilderness the way he had learned to.

Kila was inside asleep on Oros' bed when he called, and the dog got up to greet Oros at the door as he came in. Smoky walked in a couple of minutes later, his legs and belly caked in wet mud. There was one dog missing.

Knowing that they hunted together, Oros demanded quickly of Smoky, "Where's Toot?" This was no time for Toot to be off screwing around, Oros thought as he stepped outside to yell Toot's name again. He waited but there was no reply, only the subdued sounds of the forest. With a sudden growing realization that Toot was probably deliberately disobeying him, Oros' face flushed under his deeply tanned skin and his strong, large-boned hands closed into tight fists.

Nothing else moved. The two dogs that were there stood motionless, momentarily oblivious to the clouds of blackflies feeding on the hairless flesh that surrounded their eyes and from some open sores on their ears. Aware only of Oros, frozen in fear by his anger, they watched his every move and waited.

Precious moments were wasting! Oros was keenly aware of each second. He knew Toot was out there somewhere and probably close by hiding now that he was in trouble. Oros wanted to kill the dog! He yelled out Toot's name for the last time and then, cursing, took one quick look down toward the lake and reentered the cabin.

The cabin was only 100 yards from the shore of Hutsigola Lake. The lake itself was more of a shallow widening in the Teslin River than an independent body of water. The Teslin River was one of the tributaries feeding the Yukon River and flowed north into Teslin Lake, draining a large watershed of mountain streams and beaver swamps to the south.

Oros had planned to head north, to float downstream along this river for a few miles and bury the canoe under the sphagnum moss growing there overtop layers of ancient peat along the marshy river banks. Then to shake them off his trail, he'd travel back on foot, circle wide around his cabin and move south as quickly as he could following the swamps down past Zancudo. But Toot had just changed all that.

"Damn dog!"

Now he feared he'd have to hide the canoe near camp as best he could and leave a trail that Toot could follow. He knew that was dangerous. If Toot could follow, so too could they! Oros turned to the two dogs that sat there still watching him and cursed again.

He glanced quickly down the slope to the lakeshore, reassuring himself once more that the body wouldn't be found. It wouldn't. The water level was low but that didn't matter. Buried under the muck, beneath the water, in the lake, they'd never see it or smell it. It was safe. And when the water level rose again, it'd be even safer.

As Oros started to fill Kila's pack with dried meat and trail gear, a thin smile broke slowly over his face. He was running but he wasn't running scared! For the first time in years, he was standing up to them! He knew that as soon as the pilot returned to base and reported the German missing, they'd be hunting him again. But this time he was ready. If he wanted to stay out of sight in the bush, they'd never find him. Not in years. Not here, in his own country.

In the darkness of the dank interior, Oros knelt to the dirt-strewn floor to strap Kila's pack onto the dog's body. The load wasn't heavy but every pound helped and the dogs could carry ten pounds each. While Oros worked on Kila, Smoky stood off beside the dry sink set under the window and watched.

A breeze came up and some earth sifting down through the roof trickled onto Smoky's back, causing the dog to step aside and look up. It was an old cabin and Oros had tried to rehabilitate it, but there was no reversing the rot that had set in long before Oros ever came to Hutsigola. The first row of logs had become so punky with the weight of the cabin that they had disintegrated and the logs of the second row had taken their uneven place. Row by row, the cabin was dissolving, slowly and inevitably, from the bottom up. There was no saving it. Over the frame of the roof, boughs and branches had been laid to form a screen over which clumps of earth, moss, and sod had been liberally added. In addition, the roof now sprouted a miniature forest of its own, complete with saplings two inches thick and ten feet tall.

When it rained, the roof absorbed the moisture, soaking it in until, creaking and groaning under the tremendous weight, it threatened to collapse and crush the man and his dogs inside. Never dry, the odor of damp decay permeated the interior. From a distance, it looked like a mound of brush, a deadfall, and Oros sometimes had the feeling when he was entering it that he was climbing down, underground, into the earth itself. It was at those times that he loved this cabin the most, when he felt as safe as he ever could.

Smoky shifted his gaze back from the roof to see Oros hurriedly finishing with Kila. The scene distressed him. He knew exactly what the packs meant and that his turn was next. He didn't want anything to do with it. Pretending he had business of his own to attend to, he started to saunter nonchalantly toward the door. Oros halted his flight with a sharp command before turning his attention back to Kila's pack. With Oros once more seemingly distracted, Smoky's ears rolled back tightly to his head in determined but fearful rebellion as he resolved to escape. His head low to the ground and his tail curled up tightly under his legs, he started to slink out of the cabin to make for the bush.

But Oros was fast. Spinning around, he caught Smoky at the door. Lifting him by the thin skin of his hide, Oros boxed him soundly on the head. Smoky responded instinctively. Curling his lips back he gnashed at Oros' face, trying to bite him. Oros reacted with rage, almost losing control. Holding Smoky's head away from his own face, Oros punched him again and again until Smoky fell limp and started to whimper, dazed and in absolute submission. Oros dragged him back into the cabin and threw him down to the old, rough planked floor in the corner farthest from the door where a mound of ragged blankets revealed the dogs' usual sleeping place.

Smoky was, in fact, lucky that Oros didn't beat him to death in his present mood. It wouldn't have been the first time Oros had killed one of his dogs with his own hands. And for much less reason.

Of the three dogs, Kila was Oros' favorite. Kila was attached to Oros in a way the other two weren't and because of that, was dependable. Toot was the worst. Toot, he planned to replace the first chance he got. To Toot, it was all a game—playing wolf in the bush and trying to run down every animal he winded.

After Kila, Oros transformed Smoky into a pack animal and then it was his own turn. Because Toot had run off, he distributed Toot's load among the three of them, lifting most of it together with Toot's pack onto his own back. With his pack shouldered, Oros walked quickly across to his bed. He had built it himself with old planks and ax-hewn logs into a low boxlike frame and had set it into the corner directly across from the door so that as he lay in bed, he could watch the entrance. Into the empty space of the frame, he'd built a mattress up from the floor with branches and then covered them with strips of dried moss and armloads of leaves. A couple of woollen blankets, gray from long use, had been placed over the leaves and were tucked tightly down the sides of the bed. Over a roll of cloth he used for a pillow, Oros had built a narrow shelf into the wall where a coal oil lamp that dated back to the turn of the century sat along with some of the most precious books in his collection. He had found the lamp in the ruins of the abandoned settlement of Johnsontown to the north and used it sometimes for reading late into the night. With his eyes adjusted to the dark, he could see the books and, although he couldn't read their titles, he knew them all by heart. Some of them he had brought with him from Fairbanks years ago in what seemed so often to have been another life, and a couple he had carried with him even before the idea of moving to the north had ever entered his mind. *In Search of the Miraculous* and *The Fourth Way* by Ouspensky he had had now for years along with *Masked Gods* and *Book of the Hopi* by Frank Waters. In the beginning, when he was still free to leave the wilderness and enter the towns of Teslin and Atlin, he had acquired new books: *The Dangerous River* about the Nahanni River, *Nunaga: Ten Years of Eskimo Life, The Canadian Settlers Guide, Notes From the Century Before* about the trappers and prospectors who first explored the very wilderness where Oros now lived, and dozens of other paperbacks that each had their own meaning to him. He remembered buying *Death List* because the title had appealed to him then. It still did. It was one of his last purchases. Oros rolled up the sleeping bag that lay stretched out on his bed and shoved it under the flap of his pack behind his head.

They were almost ready to leave but, now that the time had come, he started to linger. Unsure of when, if ever, he'd return, the cabin was evoking emotions, like those roused by a parting of friends.

Oros reached down to a crate that lay alongside the bed within reach of his right hand when he was sleeping and lifted from it a holstered gun. It had been carefully stuffed between his clothes to be quickly accessible even in the dark. Feeling its solid weight in his bare hand, he tightened his fingers around the grip as he brought it up on a level with his eye and aimed it out the door.

Although it had been the German's gun, it had a feeling he liked and he knew that the .44 magnum which he held, a gun that could kill a grizzly, would easily kill a man. Returning the gun to its holster, he strapped it tightly to his belt. He was taking it with him.

From the shelf over his bed, he picked up the note he had written earlier and carefully tacked it outside his door. It would be the first thing they'd see when they arrived. Oros was pleased. He knew every detail counted and the note was a masterpiece of misinformation.

> To all who would enter here.
> I have gone on a journey but will return.
> Beware, this cabin and surrounding area have been sprayed by agents of the government with mind-altering drugs. The CIA, FBI and RCMP are behind it. Under the effects of these drugs you are not responsible for your actions. Make yourself comfortable but respect those who have gone before you.
> Sheslay Free Mike.

Oros liked it. It was as innocent as he could make himself.

If he had a choice, he would prefer to remain at the cabin. Already mid-September, there had been a few wet snowfalls melting on the woodpile in the mornings and a couple of nights ago, the faint, distant cries of geese were heard. Their honking calls, floating through the blackness between the stars were a portent of the imminent arrival of another long, dark, soul-crushing winter. Over the years since he arrived in the north, there had been so many dark winters of the spirit.

Oros had adapted well—better than he had ever expected to—but never so well that he ever looked forward to winter. At best, he was reconciled to the fact that it was inevitable. All part of the flow, like leaving the cabin. He had come to the conclusion that there were really very few choices even at the best of times. This time, he had no choice at all. Now that the pilot was returning to Atlin with the news that they had lost the German, Oros knew that very soon this whole area would be crawling with them.

Oros gently secured the cabin with a drop bolt that was raised and lowered by a cord that ran through the door to the outside. It was bear proof but he had learned that nothing short of death would stop these people. Beneath the handwritten note in the center of the door at eye level was a symbol that Oros had carved there years ago. It was a circle about three inches in diameter. At each of its four compass points, starting an inch from the outer edge of the circle, three parallel lines radiated out from the center for several inches. The middle line of each set extended another two inches beyond the two shorter lines which flanked it. It was Oros' own sign, his special mark: the symbol of the sun. Burning. (See page 36.)

Wherever Oros camped, he had carved it and now, after almost ten years, it was carved into the face of the earth across a vast wilderness territory. The sign had become well-known and Oros was proud of that. It was his gatepost, the sign that warned travelers they had entered into his territory—a country almost the size of England that Oros knew better than any other man alive.

Unlike the sun-sign, Oros' own name was a well-kept secret and few knew his real background. But there was one name he answered to and by which he was widely known. From the time he had first made his home in the abandoned gold-mining town of Sheslay at the confluence of the Hackett and Sheslay rivers, he had been called "Sheslay." And ever since that time, Oros signed everything he wrote, whether they were his private writings or the public messages he sometimes left behind on blazes he cut into trees, with either the sun-sign or the name he had taken for himself—Sheslay Free Mike.

Oros laughed, his confidence suddenly high, his mood almost buoyant. The sure knowledge that they would soon be on their way back to kill him wasn't as terrifying to him as it had been before. They had clearly underestimated him by sending the German in against him and the price for their mistake was the body that lay rolled in plastic and buried in the thick, black ooze of the lake only a few hundred yards from the cabin. The tide was turning. The old knowledge was that they were trying to kill him but the new revelation was that he could fight back. And win!

Oros turned away from the cabin and hurried down to the lakeshore where he shouldered the canoe up over his back. It was a tremendous weight to carry with the pack but he was exceptionally strong and his endurance, honed by years of hardship, would have left him uncomplaining even if his load had been doubled.

His back to the water, Oros entered the forest covering ground rapidly as he moved with his peculiar loping gait until weaving through the trees, he disappeared completely from sight. The two dogs, subdued and obedient, strapped tightly into their harnesses, followed, trotting close on his heels.

Toot, the white dog, would have to find his own way after them. If he could.

Chapter Two

September 12, 1981: A piercing, metal whine broke the deserted calm of the airstrip as preignition switches were thrown. Darryl Bruns' three passengers quickly joined him in putting on their headsets and immediately the deafening noise was reduced to a muffled hum. Connected to the earphones were adjustable wire bands that curved tightly around their right cheeks and ended near their mouths in miniaturized microphones. This allowed them to communicate freely with each other.

Their seat belts clicked in, Bruns glanced over his shoulder at them. In his life in the north, he had never seen men outfitted like these and he tried to keep the uneasiness he felt out of his voice. Noting their rifle butts resting on the pads between their feet, the black, stubby barrels pointing upward, he asked, "We ready?" Instantly, a passenger's voice rang like a charge through the system: "Let's do it!"

The pilot turned back to his instruments. The long, pendulous blade of the helicopter's prop started to rotate, slowly at first and then faster and faster until it became only a shimmering distortion of light against the rounded mountains.

Reaching for the radio controls, Bruns warned, "I'm switching to an open frequency, so we'll be going public." Then, adjusting a dial and speaking into his mike, he said, "We're on our way to meet you, Wiebe."

After a short silence, they all heard the clear reply through their headsets: "I hear you buddy. We'll be waiting for you."

The helicopter rose straight up off the tarmac over billowing clouds of dust as its massive blade sucked them up into the sky. It was an exhilarating experience of power, but their enthusiasm was tempered by the fact that their machine had one major liability—a well-targeted bullet could bring it down almost as easily as it would a bird, killing them all. The helicopter tilted ahead in the direction of its rendezvous.

While the helicopter was lifting off for the lake, four miles away, Corporal Bird walked anxiously down to the end of the dock where

Wiebe's single-engine de Havilland Beaver was tied. He stood facing into the cold wind that was blowing whitecaps across the lake. Beside him, the heavy plane rolled gently from side to side, bumping with dull, thumping sounds against the worn truck tires that had been cut into strips and nailed along the edge of the dock. The plane's wing tips arced widely through the air as the waves crashed unevenly into the pontoons, lifting first one, then the other. He grabbed the leading frame of the wing that hung out over the dock with one hand to try to steady it as he checked his watch.

Already eleven-thirty. Late to be starting, he thought, and hoped it wasn't too late. Lifting his hand to his forehead, he smoothed back his dark hair, blown out of place by the wind, and his black eyes studied the familiar shoreline in the distance. Across the lake, he could just make out the mouth of a short strip of water he recognized as the Atlin River which drained an eastern arm of Tagish Lake behind it. With the shallow-bottomed police boat he still had docked on the lake, he could run from here all the way by water to the southern tip of Lake Bennett from where the stampeders had built their first rafts after hiking over the Chilkoot Pass. He hadn't made the trip yet but he wanted to and he would, he promised himself, if there was ever enough time.

From the surface of the lake, his eyes studied the lay of the land up to the mountains that stretched away toward Skagway in a series of giant ripples. Only fifty-five miles away was White Pass, which looked down over that town. The forbidding plateau of bogs and black, gnarled trees was the easiest of those miles to cross. The rest was impossible. The overland route to Skagway lay to the north of here and then south through Carcross, winding and meandering around the mountains and glaciers that followed the lakes and river valleys.

It was impossible to live in this country and not wonder what it was like for those who had come before, on foot and by the thousands, to build these towns. Long gone themselves, their fading stamp upon the earth still remained. At the edge of the lake, not far from where Corporal Bird stood, was an imposing relic of that era: the *Terahinna*, one of the old sternwheelers that once ferried traffic from Carcross and Atlin to Whitehorse and Dawson. Its weathered timbers gray beneath the peeling layers of white paint, it rested majestically on a rocky beach, out of the water, on cribs made from railway ties stripped from long abandoned lines. Above the hill behind it was the community of Atlin, one of the last that survived, still struggling to pan enough gold from the nearby creek beds to make it all worthwhile.

Bird had found a special place for it all in his heart and imagination and he was proud of the town—fiercely independent but kind spirited—and of its history. Atlin was his post, the only one-man detachment left in all of British Columbia. His duty was to maintain the Queen's peace and here, where the people relied on him personally for their security and even the children knew him by his first name, he had discovered a real responsibility. Bird had no intention of ever letting them down.

He glanced at his watch again and cursed the delays that had kept them from going in to search for Lishy two days ago—just after Wiebe had burst into the small police office to report that Lishy had failed to show at the rendezvous at Hutsigola Lake. Breathlessly, Wiebe had told Bird that he had been met by another man instead—a man, who by his description, Bird knew could only have been Michael Oros, the wild man known as Sheslay Free Mike—and that this man was swearing he had been alone in the bush all summer, that Gunter Lishy had never been there.

The past two days had been a difficult and sleepless time for Bird, believing that Gunter Lishy's life had come to a tragic end and secretly convinced there had been a murder committed out there. Now, somewhere in his territory, haunting the wilderness, was a killer.

Bird breathed deeply of the cold air to calm himself. Mixed with its absolute freshness was the faint and not unpleasant odor of burned oil from the Beaver's engine.

'Well, the delays couldn't have been avoided,' he told himself. Not unless he had gone in alone to confront Oros—and he certainly wasn't prepared to do that. Then or now.

Not since the days of their antecedent organization, the Northwest Mounted Police, had there been a need for the kind of operation they had put together. In fact, the whole of Bird's territory, including the very lake they were flying into, was part of the legendary Sam Steele's jurisdiction during the infamous Yukon Gold Rush that had spawned Atlin as well as the several other communities that had been abandoned now for decades. But the rules were different now and even the provincial headquarters in Vancouver had agreed with the subdivision headquarters in Prince Rupert that men and equipment should be requisitioned for the search.

The extra men had arrived the previous day, within twenty-four hours of the call out but with the shorter days of fall, they had arrived too late to fly in. And now, with civilian pilots engaged for the operation, the briefing had taken much longer than usual, continuing from early morning until only a short while ago.

The team was already split into two groups and one of them, with three of the men, went off with one of the pilots to the airstrip to get the helicopter. Hearing some sounds behind him, Bird turned around quickly and saw the rest of the team filing out of the shack that Taku Air used as their water base.

Dressed in their combat clothing and carrying an assortment of weapons, some specially modified, they looked conspicuously out of place as they hurried down the path toward the dock; but Bird knew they were essential to the mission. If there was a shoot-out—and he fully believed Oros would not willingly surrender without one—they'd have to respond with fire. Although he had one of their bulky, bulletproof vests on under his shirt, he alone was dressed in the standard-issue RCMP uniform. They needed one man to play the role of a policeman and it fell to him, if everything worked according to plan, to expose himself innocently to Oros and try to make the arrest. His was the greatest risk.

Their departure from the shack meant that the helicopter had radioed in its take-off and Bird checked his watch again just seconds before the distant beat of the helicopter could be heard. The men quickly joined him on the dock. Wiebe, their own pilot, climbed in first, followed closely behind by Sergeant Jopling, who was in command of the operation. They made their way up into the cockpit and started the engine while two more men followed, seating themselves on the cold floor of the fuselage with their backs to the metal ribs of the plane. Bird stayed outside to slip the knots holding the plane to the dock. He waited until he could see David Wiebe's face at the window giving him the nod and then, jumping onto the pontoon and grabbing the struts, he pushed the plane away from the wharf with his foot. Wiebe opened the throttle and, as Bird climbed inside, the plane plowed away into the lake with a roar, spraying water backward over the bows of the pontoons.

Once in the air, the plane came up alongside the chopper. Then, flying side by side, they turned east, away from Atlin. They were heading at last, and in force, for Hutsigola.

The four men sitting comfortably in the warm plastic bubble of the helicopter's cabin had an almost unobstructed view. Leaning forward over their canvas seats, they could even look straight down as they flew below the upper levels of the mountains following the valleys. Bruns looked over to the Beaver, piloted by his friend Wiebe, and the two men waved to each other.

"Looked a little rough down there for fishing," Bruns said referring to the lake's surface. With the sensitive mike at his lips he could speak normally.

"At least I float," Wiebe answered over his radio, having to talk loudly and trying to sound lighthearted. "Hate to think what might happen to you if you tried to run your eggbeater through the water."

Bruns then saw Sergeant Jopling take off his headset and lean toward Wiebe. Wiebe looked back over toward Bruns, perched in his bubble, and said: "We're going to go off the air for a while. I'll reconnect in about fifteen."

"Fine," Bruns answered and turned his own radio off, allowing the men inside his helicopter to talk freely without having their conversation broadcast over the airwaves.

Inside the Beaver, Constable Connell turned around to watch the scenery through a small side window. All the creeks below them that fed down the narrow gullies along the sides of the valley's basin into Surprise Lake were being worked by a half dozen or more small gold operations. From the air, the tailings the miners were leaving resembled enormous earthworm furrows.

Connell yelled to Bird, "They making any money?"

"Yeah, some of them are," Bird yelled back, his mind preoccupied with other things.

"You see any of their gold?" Connell asked.

"No. They keep pretty quiet about it. Don't even come into town much except to get gas for their generators."

Connell turned to face Bird and, still shouting, asked, "You get any gold heists up here?"

"Not in recent memory." Bird answered. "There's nowhere to run to here, unless you go into the bush." In afterthought, he realized the 'unless' was in fact almost unlimited—to a person like Oros.

"How far is Skagway?" Connell asked.

"Four to five hours, fast driving—when the White Pass is open. They shut down the highway through the winter. Gets over twenty feet of snow," Bird replied, then shifted his body as Corporal Brewin's German shepherd stretched itself, rolling its back legs overtop Bird's. Connell turned back to the window to study the countryside again and Bird leaned over to talk to Brewin.

In the sunshine, Surprise Lake gleamed below them, a magnificent, elongated, liquid jewel. Its deep, turquoise-colored waters gave way to a brilliant clarity around the shorelines where the color in the more shallow water turned a vivid, nearly phosphorescent, emerald green. The deafening noise level from the engine that made verbal communication so difficult lent itself richly to private reflection.

"How well do you know this guy?" Brewin asked Bird. Sitting beside each other, the two men didn't have to shout, not loudly.

"Not well. I've seem him in Atlin once and a few times last winter when he moved into the government's highway's survival shack beside the road up toward Jake's Corner. I'd pass him on the road. But I only talked to him that once to give him directions."

"You really think he's dangerous?"

"No doubt he is to some people! Seems to have a thing for the trappers and outfitters in the Teslin and Sheslay river systems. He's raided their cabins, stealing their food, and left notes on their doors and along the trails they use threatening to kill them. The guy who stands the biggest risk is Fletcher Daye—one of the big outfitters who's based out of Telegraph Creek and guides into the area north of Sheslay toward Hutsigola. Apparently there's some kind of connection between them that goes back for years. Oros has left all kinds of notes in the bush saying, FLETCHER IS DEAD! and that kind of shit."

"Why hasn't something been done about him before?"

"Shit, I don't know! The guys who should be complaining about him aren't and those that do haven't got a case against him that we could take to court. Maybe the people who use that country have just gotten used to him."

"And what's his problem?"

"Who knows? Maybe there's something behind it or maybe Oros simply doesn't like anybody else being in his country. My guess is he's bushed. He's gone wild living alone. You know, even the Tlingit Indians from Teslin won't go down to the end of the lake because he lives in the area. Won't go near it!"

"Maybe they know something we don't?" Brewin suggested, his interest growing with the more he heard.

"There's some rumors he used to trap illegally and then unload his furs to a couple of the Indian families living in a little hole called Brooks Brook, up around the north end of Teslin Lake. Apparently that was quite a few years ago.

"The Teslin Indian band has all the trapping rights to the region. Their area extends down to the bottom end of Teslin Lake and then south of that past Hutsigola Lake. But they haven't touched it for years. You know what they're like, eh? We can't get anything out of them. It's almost as if they've got some superstitious fear of him. They don't even want to admit they're afraid of him—but they're scared shitless of the guy!"

"Why doesn't somebody quietly shoot him? Nobody's going to report him missing."

"I don't doubt there's a few people who've thought about it."

"I'll bet! What else you got on him?"

"Listen, I'm glad to have found that old warrant in the file for his arrest on the theft of the fisheries' boat. If we didn't have that, there's not much else we could pick him up on. There's a couple of reports on file of a man shooting from the ground at overflying aircraft—no positive identification but it had to be Oros. There's nobody else in that country. Now even the local pilots won't fly over the area unless they're above 5,000 feet.

"If he's really dangerous, why hasn't he killed anyone before?" Brewin asked. "Surely he's had all kinds of encounters with people after all these years!"

"Who's to say he hasn't?" Bird said. "We're not going to hear anything if some fellow traveling by himself disappears. There's all kinds of missing persons. But you're right, there's nothing we can prove."

"Anybody else missing from Atlin besides Lishy?"

"Only one on file is a young girl, sixteen. But we think she ran off to Vancouver. Nobody's heard anything from her for a couple of years. There's also some rumors Oros was seen one time at Telegraph Creek going into the bush with an Indian who disappeared on his way to Whitehorse and another one about an American hunter who went in from the Alaska Highway and never came out again, but they're only rumors."

"C'mon Bird! You're holding out on me. There's more to it, isn't there? Why has Vancouver ordered us in? You don't need this kind of firepower to search for a lost trapper or arrest some guy on a five-year-old theft warrant."

Bird didn't answer him for some time. The truth was that there really wasn't much more. Nothing concrete. But it was something far less tangible than evidence—real hard evidence that would stand up in court—that had convinced him there was something terribly wrong and very dangerous happening here. However, as much as the two men were friends, he was reluctant to discuss it with Brewin, or anyone else, until he had real proof. "I'll tell you one thing," Bird said finally. "Oros was pretty confident when he told Wiebe that Lishy wasn't around. So you want to know what I think? Oros knows exactly where the body is because he's hidden it! And I'll bet your dog doesn't help at all. Before we find Lishy, we'll have to get Oros! And that won't be easy. Oros is tough. Has to be to have survived here. And he's dangerous."

"Well, I'm glad you've got the job of arresting him." Brewin joked.

Jopling caught the tail end of their conversation through the open cockpit and turned back to address Bird, completely sharing the younger man's assessment that this was indeed a dangerous mission and concerned that Brewin's humor might be taken wrong.

"Peter, just because this is your area doesn't make Oros your personal responsibility. I don't want you getting out of the plane or exposing yourself to any risks until you're absolutely sure he's unarmed, right? All we're looking for is his help in searching for Lishy. Just play it by ear but don't you take any chances! When he comes out to the plane, if you can't talk him into coming inside to talk, try to get him to help you tie the plane to shore and then grab him until we can get out. Alright?"

Jopling had to shout to be heard and Bird missed some of what he said, but he didn't need any instruction on what to do—the operation was Jopling's responsibility though the plan was all Bird's, right down to the detail of using Wiebe and the Beaver to lure Oros into the open. Realizing that Wiebe wouldn't simply fly away, forever leaving Lishy behind, Oros would be expecting Wiebe to come back. When the Beaver returned, Oros should also recognize it as the same one that came in two days ago to pick up Lishy. And with the plane floating on the lake and only Wiebe visible inside it, Oros should feel safe enough to paddle out once more to get rid of it again with more lies. If all went well, they could arrest him without any trouble. It was a big if. There was a chance he just might shoot instead and, if he did, with five men stuffed inside the plane, things would be very hot.

Bird looked up toward Wiebe at the controls and wondered what he was feeling. He knew Wiebe hadn't hesitated when he was asked to take part in the operation, and in that respect they had something in common. They both felt responsible for Lishy's disappearance—Wiebe, because he had taken the German in and left him there, and Bird because Atlin was his post. Regardless of what Jopling had to say about it, the lives and safety of everyone in the district were under his care. And Oros was his problem.

"What do you know about Lishy?" Connell asked, breaking into Bird's thoughts and leaning closer toward him. In the cockpit, Jopling and Wiebe were in a deep discussion with their headsets on.

"Don't know too much about him—" Bird began but was cut off by Brewin jumping into the conversation.

"Jesus, Bird. You mean there's something you don't know about one of your townsfolk. You must be kidding."

There wasn't much time left before they'd be reaching Hutsigola but it was an unspoken practice to joke along the way rather than to raise tension levels by mulling over the risks. They were as well prepared as they could be. The two men liked each other and if there was any real competition between them, it was to see which one of them could appear to be the most casual about it all. Neither ever voiced his own fears aloud.

Bird looked at him and returned his grin. "He doesn't live in town. He's got a cabin on Fish Lake. You haven't forgotten that already have you?" When Brewin laughed but didn't say anything else, Bird continued, "Seems to be pretty much of a loner. We've got nothing on the cards on him in the office except he's registered as owning a .44 magnum. I checked his cabin yesterday with Brewin here, who seems to have forgotten, and we didn't find it. So he probably had it with him when he was dropped off by Wiebe. And if Oros got him, then Oros is probably armed with that as well. What was more interesting was a picture we found in his cabin. It was of Oros. Pretty strange because he only had two other photos on the wall, besides Oros', and those were of his closest friends in Atlin."

"Oh, ho! So they knew each other," Connell exclaimed.

"Apparently they met only once—at least as far as we can tell. And that was by accident in the bush. But Lishy knew Sheslay Mike's reputation and, I'm told, respected him for the way he was able to survive on his own. But who really knows, eh? We're gonna have to check it all out."

"How old was Lishy?"

"October the 1st, 1928," Bird answered from memory. Searching the cabin yesterday with Brewin before the rest of the team flew in, he had found some documents with Lishy's date of birth on them and had kept some of them for the investigation.

"Shit! He's an old man!" Connell said. "He could have died of a heart attack in the bush."

"That's right, and if we don't find Lishy's body we'll never prove he didn't. But he didn't. The man was healthier than you are," Bird yelled back.

Connell grinned, "That's pretty healthy, then," he said and then asked, "What was he, a trapper?"

"Yeah. You should have seen his place, though. He built it himself and every corner joint, every cut, every angle is perfect. The guy was a master carpenter. I've never been in a cleaner cabin in my life and I've seen quite a few. Not a speck of dust. Even the soap dish was clean. He must have dried off the soap every time he used it. The whole place was like that. Immaculate. A real perfectionist."

"Typical German," Connell said. And then Brewin, who had been sitting quietly beside Bird thinking, suddenly cut in and asked, "Peter, do you remember how many lynx Lishy had on those fur sale receipts we saw from last winter's sale?"

"Why?" Bird asked.

"Something you guys just said made me think. Shit and I've been helping on a trapline too. Anyway, it was around sixty wasn't it?"

"I seem to recall sixty. Sounds about right."

"Well?" Brewin asked expecting Bird to understand.

"Well what?"

"Jesus what kind of a bushman are you anyway? You know how many lynx sixty is?"

Bird looked at Brewin and then around at the interior of the plane. It had been stripped to carry cargo and the heavy belted straps that held drums in place during flights lay scattered across the floor. He was seated on some greasy bumper pads they had thrown over the pallets to cushion the ride and beside him were a couple of heavy-duty, war surplus gas cans which he studiously examined. Then slowly, he brought up his elbow to rest it over the top of one of them before he turned back to Brewin, who was waiting, and said, "It's not seventy!"

"No, it's not!" Brewin replied immediately. "But its close to three times more than I've ever heard any trapper taking in a season. And I mean a good trapper."

It was cold in the plane, the temperature of the air outside supported thick snow on the slopes on elevations lower than they were flying.

"So?" Bird asked. "Lishy was better than your best trapper. If he traps the way he keeps house, you can bet he's probably one of the best in the whole country. What's it prove?"

"Twenty lynx," Brewin said, "is a good take for a good trapper in a good season." He paused for effect. "Thirty, that's remarkable... Forty, absolutely incredible... And fifty? Why, that's unheard of. A fantasy of life in the days of the Hudson Bay voyageurs. Sixty is simply impossible!" And then he dropped his conclusion, obvious by now. "I don't believe that Lishy could have trapped sixty lynx by himself. I doubt he was working alone and I think he had a silent partner, someone who had to know the backwoods as well as he did. OROS! I'll bet you money they were working together. And that's not all. You know what else I just remembered? Any idea what lynx prices were last year?" Brewin looked at Bird and waited until he shook his head and then turned to Connell, who didn't answer him either. "Lots!" Brewin said. "The guys from Whitehorse were getting around 1,100 dollars for a good silver lynx and 600 for an average brown skin. Assuming Lishy knew how to stretch a hide, he should have made an average of at least seven fifty a skin and that, my friends, is 45,000 dollars. For his lynx pelts alone! When you double that for all his other furs, it's plenty of cash for a single guy with no expenses, eh? What the hell would a guy like Lishy spend 90,000 dollars on in a year? Where is that money?"

Bird stared back at Brewin blandly for a moment before speaking. "And it took you a day to figure that out?"

"I had other things on my mind yesterday," Brewin laughed. "But I'm not so touchy, my friend, that you can insult me easily. Nor do I consider that my timing in any way demeans my worthy contribution to the solution of this case."

"Oh, not my intention at all, I assure you," Bird said. "In fact, I think you might have something. If you're right, and Lishy was a greedy partner, then we might have our motive. Unless, of course, Oros has his own hefty stash of money squirreled away in the bush. In which case, perhaps Oros was greedy. Anyway, it's certainly an interesting angle."

They were getting close now and the conversation suddenly died away. Bird turned to look out the window on his side of the plane and watched the helicopter for a few moments. It was close enough to see that the men inside were involved in animated conversation. If Oros did start shooting from the bush, especially if he disabled the plane, the men in the helicopter were their only backup.

The plane was skirting closely around the side of a mountain face that continued to rise on above them into fields of deep, fresh snow that had ended the summer's view of the opaque blue ice of an ancient glacier. The wind, blowing in spirals around a high peak, picked up the snow from the glacier and swirled it skyward in thin sheets for hundreds of yards before releasing it to fall again where it collected in protected hollows away from the wind. The sounds of the aircraft engines echoed off the massive cliff faces that surrounded them on all sides and then rolled, vibrating downward along the slopes into the warmer valleys where trees still held on to their summer foliage in sheltered pockets.

Jopling said something to Wiebe that the men in the fuselage couldn't hear but they saw Wiebe tune in the radio channel and then Jopling speak into his microphone to the men inside the helicopter. The helicopter suddenly tilted forward and fell out of sight, descending rapidly toward the ground to approach a position it was to wait at under cover of a high rock face. Hovering. Out of sight and sound of their target. As the helicopter dropped down, the plane started climbing steeply to gain altitude. And there in the distance, shimmering on the horizon, was Hutsigola.

As soon as they saw it, the men rapidly checked over their equipment again, carefully sliding the actions on their short-barreled weapons back and forth with smooth, well-tooled precision; bullets were chambered, clips were full, ready to fire. Hanging from their belts on pull-away pins dangled extra clips packed with steel-jacketed military bullets that disappeared in double rows inside the long magazines. To test their own portable communications systems, they whispered into the thumb-nail sized microphones which were clipped tightly to their collars and listened through small receivers designed like miniaturized hearing aids that fit into one ear and left the other free to listen for other sounds. As the men went over their equipment, Jopling pulled out a set of powerful binoculars and carefully began a sweep of the country below for any signs of activity or smoke.

From the crusty edge of the swampy shoreline of Hutsigola Lake, the approaching beat of the Beaver's laboring engine could now be heard. Its steady drone drifted into the silent spaces of Hutsigola's dark backwaters like the memory of cicadas buzzing in the noonday heat of summer far to the south.

With a deliberate purpose, the noise continued, relentlessly growing nearer. And louder. Flying as high as the upper reaches of one of the region's Golden Eagles, the plane finally broke into view above the tops of the swamp willow. Swinging lazily against the blue of the sky, it drifted toward an old cabin that squatted root-like and dark on the west shore of the lake. Right over the cabin. Then out over the lake and beyond. To the forest on the far side. There, it banked gently, sideslipping to decrease its altitude as it circled back to the lake. Above the water, it veered gracefully to follow the north shoreline and to the west bank and then down the west shore.

Once again, it passed over the mound of living earth that almost completely hid the cabin beneath it from curious eyes.

It was a cautious approach, reminiscent, except for the noise, of a bird of prey. The plane's deliberate maneuvers gave the impression the pilot wasn't sure of the landing, was unfamiliar with the terrain, or was perhaps searching for something, hoping to discover it before he landed.

Once it had crossed the narrow ribbon of lake and was above the far bush, it made another turn and dropped lower. Approaching the water, the noise of the engine cut back. It was coming in to land.

Gliding with the power off and its flaps fully extended, the plane moved quickly toward the lake. Just above the water, the pilot lifted the nose and let it glide through the air. Approaching its stall speed, it settled itself down, pontoons first, to the surface where the water shot up in broad fans of white spray. Its energy dissipated, the plane settled deeper into the water as it plowed ahead, slowing gradually until, at last, it was free-floating, adrift in the center of the lake like a giant bird—exposed and vulnerable.

After the plane had settled, the wake reached the shore and cracked the skim of ice that remained in the shadowy protection of the weeds. From those weeds, the unmistakable profile of the pilot, Wiebe, could be seen sitting alone inside the cockpit.

The hands gripping the wheel were slippery with sweat and Wiebe consciously forced his grip to relax, letting one hand fall free to his lap but as his eyes scanned the shoreline, peering through the trees into the bush for any movement, his free hand rose unconsciously back up and clasped the wheel. Oros could be anywhere out there hiding and he wouldn't know it. But Oros wasn't in sight and he communicated that simple fact to the large man who crouched low, out of sight, at the door of the cockpit behind him.

"It took a while before he came out last time. Give him time. He'll come. Taxi around the lake. Make it look like you're back again looking for Lishy and do whatever you would do if you were." Jopling said, frustrated with having to rely on Wiebe to tell him what was happening.

Wiebe raised the trim, still set for landing, and edged the throttle open until the Beaver started plowing noisily through the water. He took the plane in toward the shore and followed it, keeping to the deeper water until they arrived at the point of land where forty-three days earlier he had last seen Lishy, alive. There Wiebe stopped, cutting the power to let the plane drift again.

It was this very spot, Wiebe remembered, that Lishy had agreed to meet him on September 10. Two days ago. Only, when he had landed then, it was a stranger with pale eyes peering out from a bearded face and long hair tied back in a ponytail who had paddled out five minutes later from the shore in a green canoe to ask him what he wanted. Wiebe wouldn't easily get the memory out of his mind. Dressed in clothing made from animal hides and stitched roughly together, with old patched jeans and black, army-type boots, the stranger had told him he'd been at the lake since early August and hadn't heard or seen a sign of anyone. He had even insisted Wiebe was mistaken. That he had gotten his lakes mixed up. That he was lost.

Wiebe studied the rocks of the point where he and Gunter had pulled up the plane to off-load Gunter's things and recognized the very rocks they had stood upon. They had unloaded a small mountain of goods there. Gunter had even brought in crates of prefabricated window frames, complete with their glass panes, which they had been so careful in handling. A whole planeload of supplies couldn't have just disappeared, although he could see they were certainly gone now. Along with Gunter. Wiebe's eyes traveled the length of the shoreline again as he waited nervously for that same canoe to reappear. Nothing moved.

Still, they waited. The engine idling, floating in full view, an invitation for Oros to come out of hiding and show himself on the water.

Behind him, in silence, Wiebe could feel the tension building as the minutes passed. If a hundred pairs of eyes were out there staring back, watching the plane from the concealment of the forest, he wouldn't know it.

Jopling didn't like the situation at all. If Oros were to shoot from shore, killing Wiebe, they'd all be in real trouble. He wouldn't have used Wiebe in the operation at all if he had had a better choice; but he didn't. Their own planes weren't available so they had to use a civilian and Wiebe was not only a good pilot, but, in these circumstances, he was the best possible choice. Jopling couldn't argue with the logic or the man. It was simply the use of civilians in a police operation that he didn't like. He looked back down into the fuselage at the men who made up his assault team. With their rifles and flak jackets, they were half-crouched, their backs against the inside wall waiting to spring into action if necessary. They were ready, as ready as they could be. But it was madness to be playing "bait"—crouching soundlessly, huddled together in the cramped tail of the small aircraft like fish in a barrel. If Oros started shooting, he could kill them all.

Still, there was no better plan. If Oros was as dangerous and as easily provoked as they feared, any other approach had even higher risks. They couldn't sneak up on him. And if they tried a straight coordinated landing with armed men leaping out of aircraft and running for cover, Oros would almost certainly react with force. Jopling wanted to avoid a deadly gunfight.

Jopling knew he shouldn't hold the plane on the lake much longer. If Oros was around and watching them, it seemed pretty clear by now he wasn't going to come out of hiding. But if they continued floating much longer, doing nothing, that would surely arouse Oros' suspicions. It might just provoke him into shooting.

One of the member's rifles bumped up against the frame of the plane with a loud ring as they rocked in the water and Jopling turned back to scowl at him as he weighed in his mind the merits of having

Wiebe go out on the pontoons to give Oros the extra reassurance that the pilot was alone and just trying to bring the plane into shore. But he quickly rejected it—Oros might only be waiting to get a clear shot off at him. Besides, Wiebe was only twenty-nine. Not that his age really mattered, Jopling countered to himself. After all, the other members were as young but Wiebe was a civilian and he had no right to risk a member's life, let alone a civilian's.

'Damn!' he thought. 'Where is that bastard?' And then, deciding quickly, he forcefully depressed the button on the plane's radio that he was holding in his hand and gave the chopper the order to move in.

Bruns had been in a holding pattern at tree top level a few miles west of Hutsigola out of ear shot. The moment he received the signal from Jopling, the helicopter roared ahead into life skimming the earth. As Wiebe watched from the surface of the lake, the helicopter came into view, flying low and at top speed, zeroing straight in to its designated landing, a clearing right beside the cabin. The moment it touched the ground, the three armed men inside burst out its doors and scattered, taking cover in the trees.

With the backup team providing cover for the plane, Jopling gave the next order to Wiebe, who quickly responded by running the Beaver to the rocky shoreline where he had landed Gunter. The pontoons grounded with a rough grating sound that vibrated through the hollow aluminum into the plane and the men inside rushed out, splashing quickly through the water to get behind cover.

Making their way carefully around the shoreline, they kept to the line of trees, aware that Oros could be anywhere at all. Joining the first group, they surrounded the cabin. Jopling advanced alone, cautiously, covered by his men. He worked around the cabin, ducking under the windows, until he reached the door. The men could see him pressed against the wall outside the door where he paused, studying something, before he reached out an arm and swung the door open and ducked back out of the way. Nothing happened. He waited a moment longer and then spun around through the opening and disappeared into the darkness.

Jopling reappeared quickly, his arms relaxed, his gun swinging over the ground. Again he stopped beside the door and called out to them.

"Look at this." he said, pointing at the door as they gathered around. There, tacked onto the door, high enough that the paper had some protection under the overhang from the elements, was the note that Oros had left. Jopling read it aloud.

"Some greeting," one of the men said.

"He was certainly expecting us," Jopling agreed.

"At least we know now what happened to him," another said.

Jopling looked at him and the officer explained, straight-faced, "The CIA got here first!"

A couple of the men laughed, relieved that Oros wasn't around. The sudden tension release had left them feeling almost giddy. "Hey, Bird! Could that German guy, Lishy, be working for the CIA?" another one asked.

"Gimme a break, will you?" Bird snapped without looking at him.

Jopling warned them again before they broke up to start the search to stay on their toes. "You don't want to come face to face with him in the bush unless you're ready for it."

Bird walked off, away from the rest, and stood to stare into the forest.

He could hear the men inside joking that Lishy had probably walked out on his own and was right now arriving in Atlin while they were stuck out here beating the bush for him. Now there was no real threat to deal with, they were enjoying themselves. As they examined Oros' cabin, they remarked on the strange things they found while they searched for any evidence that might link him to Lishy's disappearance.

Bird didn't share in the general relief that Oros had left. Instead, his disappointment was tangible. They were too late. He knew Lishy would never be seen again. At least alive. He could feel it. Something had happened here. There was a foreboding, almost a presence that Oros, wherever he was, had left behind.

Oros had gone but Bird knew it was no cause for celebration. Oros was around somewhere. Anywhere from a few hundred yards away and watching, to 100 miles and still retreating farther into the wilderness. But he was a master of the bush, at home anywhere in it. What it really meant was that any surprise they had to work with before was now lost. Now, if he didn't already, Oros would know for sure that they were looking for him. And because of it, he'd be ready next time, and even more dangerous to catch.

The threat wasn't over. It had just started.

Map of the territory in northeast British Columbia ravaged by Michael Oros prior to his death in 1985.

Gunter Lishy was the German trapper killed by Michael Oros because his fingernails were so clean that Oros didn't believe he was real.

Oros' Hutsigola cabin as it was in September, 1981 during the first search.

This March, 1982 photo of the Hutsigola cabin shows the huge snowshoes that Oros used leaning against the side of the cabin along with his toboggan. The cabin that Oros was building with Lishy's logs can be seen to the right.

This mug shot of Michael Oros was taken on March 5, 1982 at the Terrace RCMP detachment following his capture at Hutsigola Lake.

At the last camp on Big Island, Oros used spruce boughs for a bed. His fire melted a deep pit into the snow.

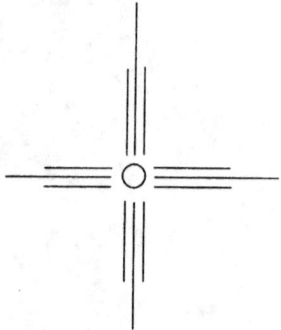

Artist's rendition of the blazing sun symbol that Oros used as his signature.

This aerial view of Teslin Lake shows the peninsula on the lower left and the delta of the Jennings River on the lower right. Big Island is north of the river delta.

Constable Haugen positioned himself on this peninsula to both intercept Oros and cover his team members.

This aerial shot shows Oros' sled, left on the trail at the location where Oros doubled back to locate his victims.

This view looking south southeast down Teslin Lake toward The Narrows shows the small peninsula near the end of the open water where Constables Haugen, Rodgers, and Buday lay in wait for Oros. The top photo on page 38 is a close-up of this peninsula and the photograph on page 37 shows the same open water and the peninsula from the opposite direction. The top photo on page 40 is of the same area looking from the north at a greater distance.

Teslin Lake looking south toward Hutsigola.

The sleds Oros left behind when he went off into the bush.

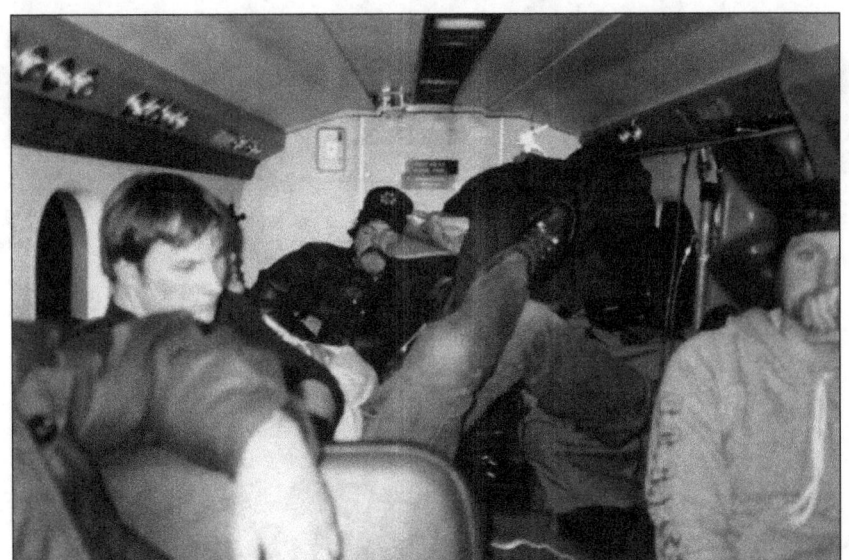

This last picture of Mike Buday alive, far left, was taken in the airplane on the flight to Whitehorse. The profile of the man immediately behind Mike Buday is Peter Robert. Dennis O'Byrne is at the back, with his eyes closed, and Deitmar Stiller is on the right. The picture was taken by Corporal Murray Dreilich.

Constable Mike Buday and Trooper.

This aerial view of the buildings at Hutsigola was taken in August, 1985 when Corporal Barry Erickson flew into Hutsigola to search the area one last time. It was then he discovered the bones of Lishy.

Oros' Hutsigola cabin in August, 1985—abandoned. The picture was taken when the bones of Gunter Lishy were discovered on the trail by the lakeshore.

By 1985, Oros had essentially completed the new cabin at Hutsigola. It is similar to his unfinished cabin at Sheslay.

Oros' boathouse at Hutsigola.

Oros' smokehouse at Hutsigola.

This photo like the one above it was taken in August, 1985 after the bones were discovered. It shows a storage shed near the smokehouse.

The clearings in the center of the photo are the location of Oros' cabin at Hutsigola. The line marks the trail along the shore to the spot where Lishy's bones were found.

Human bones were found along this lakeshore trail. The skull in the foreground was later identified as Lishy's through dental records.

One of Oros' high caches at Hutsigola which had been filled with Lishy's personal belongings and Oros' diary notes.

Lishy's shoulder bone with the bullet hole that proved he was murdered by Oros.

Constable Mike Buday and Trooper in formal uniform.

The cairn erected in honor of the memory of Michael Buday on the site of his shooting. "IN MEMORY—CONSTABLE MICHAEL JOSEPH BUDAY—ROYAL CANADIAN MOUNTED POLICE—REGIMENTAL NO. 33631—GAVE HIS LIFE IN THE LINE OF DUTY—ON THIS LOCATION, MARCH 19,1985—MAINTIENS LE DROIT"

The RCMP members who erected the cairn on June 6,1986. Front row left to right: Cpl. M. Dreilich, Supt. R. Currie, Bob Buday, Cpl. A. Girard, Cst. G. Rodgers, and Cst. J. O'Donnell. Back row left to right: Kamloops RCMP pilot Brian Dick, Sgt. F. Fawcett, Insp. H. Wallace, Cst. P. Robert, Sgt. D. Sunden, Cpl. L. Bretfeld, and Cst. G. McNevitts.

Chapter Three

September 12, 1981: South of Hutsigola, almost forty miles by trail, Oros was deeply troubled. He needed a place to spend the winter and he needed food. Only a couple of months earlier, the land had been washed in almost continuous sunshine, twenty-four hours a day. Daily now, the light was being overtaken by a consuming darkness. With the darkness was coming the cold. The high ridges were already under deep snow. Although the snow wasn't staying on the ground along the watercourses, that wouldn't last much longer.

Oros tried to put it out of his mind, to enjoy the day. Dawn had broken earlier into another Indian summer morning with light blue skies and the warmest weather in a month. He was sitting on some dry moss near a stand of small pines. His camp overlooked the deep, crystal blue waters of Gun Lake and his attention had been caught by a loon family that danced across the surface not far from shore. Rising up out of the water to run over the top of the lake, their cries to each other merged with the echoes that rang back from the surrounding hills into a melancholy tide of sound that flooded the land infecting it with their passionate energy.

Oros slowly stretched himself and then lay back with his eyes closed, listening with an intense rapture to their melodious, haunting music while he recounted other and better days when he had done the same thing with friends years ago and far away.

With his eyes closed, it came back to him so easily—those warm nights in Colorado. The memories had a misty, sentimental quality to them now as though colored with pastels but he could almost feel the freshness of the lush, early summer grass beneath his back and still hear the hushed murmuring of their voices as they whispered to each other, thinking it a sacrilege to talk aloud when the birds cried out. They slept as often as they could under the sky, zippered together in their sleeping bags, listening through the night to the chorus of peeper frogs along the shoreline as they made love, sometimes side by side with the next couple, laughing, whispering, dozing to wake sleepily and make love again reveling in the heightened sensuality of it all. By morning, they'd collapse, exhausted, and sleep in the sunshine until noon and then swim naked far out into the lake to restore themselves to the physical world. And then start all over again.

Oros let his mind drift back, indulging himself with abandon to the sweetness of the memories, until one of the dogs started whining with hunger and the images broke like a shattered bottle and brought his present situation back into sharp focus. Overcome with a great longing for the return of those days, he kept his eyes closed and tried to collect the scattered fragments to hold the mood a little longer. But they were gone. Sadly, he opened his eyes. It had been such a long time since he'd had a woman, such a hopelessly long time that even the fantasies about them that he worked up occasionally for relief were so transparently false that they only left him feeling more isolated and desperate.

The loons cried again and he rose slowly up on his elbows to watch them. He had grown accustomed to hearing the loons but he had never taken their company for granted. There was a secret brotherhood he believed existing between them in which their cries gave voice to the feelings of his own soul. Still brooding over the memories of lost love, he called out to them.

"When the lakes freeze over and darkness descends, you'll all go...know that when you do, you'll empty the earth itself of its soul, leaving me alone, a deadened shell to be ravaged by the storms of winter. Stay this year! Just this once! To turn winter back, and to keep us alive."

If they heard him, they gave him no sign and he watched them in silence. This day he perceived them to be close in another respect. Like him, they, too, were the innocent victims of dark powers. Confused by the capricious weather, they were performing their complex spring rituals like simple marionettes that had no choice but to dance when the strings were pulled. Yet there was some magic in it all and try as he could to hold this moment forever, he knew this day, like countless others, would soon fade in memory after they had gone and he would be left to suffer the emptiness of the land alone. Oros was dreading that day. Every fall, without fail, there was a feeling that died deep within him as the onset of winter slowly extinguished, one by one, the joys of summer life, finally crushing all hope beneath the all-consuming elemental struggle for survival. His heart failed him then until the deep winter freeze-up had completed its transformation of the land, turning even the memories of summer to distant fantasies themselves—and winter would once again be forever.

A bull moose in rut trumpeted suddenly across the lake breaking his train of thought. The hungry dogs, recognizing the sound of meat, jumped up excitedly and strained at the leashes, anxious to give chase.

"No goddamn way I'm going to let you bastards go off to run around the country and get spotted by some plane," Oros said, looking at them all without malice until his eyes settled on Toot and grew colder. Toot's whole body quivered with anticipation as he choked on his leash trying to break free. "Especially you, you mean mutt. I'm not giving you another chance to get us all killed."

He was still mad at Toot for having run off back at Hutsigola, but it seemed pointless to discipline the dog now. Toot had found them easily enough. Howling like a regular tracking hound in the distance, he had come up from behind them in the evening of that first day, creating a new threat to their security. Oros had tied down the other two dogs as soon as he'd heard Toot and circled back around to the trail on the downwind side to observe Toot's progress. Oros had to make sure the dog was alone and not being followed. From a safe spot, he had watched as Toot went by with his nose to the ground, tracing their scent. He waited there a long time before he felt reasonably sure that Toot hadn't given them away but he wasn't taking any chances.

He quickly rejoined the dogs and they took off again, covering ground as fast as they could. The trail to Zancudo ended abruptly at the edge of the swamps that surrounded the lake but they pressed on, wading deeper and deeper into the swamp until darkness forced them to stop. It had been a grueling pace for them all and Oros was exhausted when he made camp; yet he was unable to rest.

If the German's friends had the same ruthless determination the German had, then Oros feared they might just be on his trail, moving through the darkness, creeping up on him even in the swamps of Zancudo. The first night was a miserable time for them all, camped beside a shallow, mosquito-infested beaver pond in the center of the swamp where Oros had kept a sleepless watch.

Yesterday, starting at first light, they were off again, heading due south. Traveling hard, they had left the swamps behind and crossed the arctic divide in the afternoon, reaching the shores of Gun Lake in the Pacific watershed by nightfall. It was a milestone and Oros had slept soundly, waking in the morning to feel refreshed and hungry for the first time since he'd left Hutsigola. But now at a crossroads, he couldn't decide what to do.

Late as it was getting in the middle of the day, he still hadn't seen or heard any human activity. If they were searching for him, they either hadn't come out this far yet or they were doing it quietly. And, he questioned, if they were searching, would they continue to hunt him even through the winter? Oros pictured the sight of his own trail: great pockets of snow left trampled in a line behind him from the snowshoes and three deeper cuts in the snow left by the dogs. In the winter, from the air, he'd be an easy target to track. And from the ground, his enemies could run him down with snowmobiles as easily as wolves, bounding overtop the crust of deep snow, kill a floundering deer.

"Fuck! Well, what do you fellas think we should do? If we stay and if they continue to chase us, it ends everything!"

More than his own life, it would mean the end of his work.

"Everything will have been in vain if they kill me!"

Speaking his thoughts aloud gave him a greater power but the picture in his mind of those men ransacking his caches and destroying his records was even more depressing than the image of his own body half buried under a snowdrift, cold and dead.

"So many ifs. If I go, if I stay...." He turned to his dogs to ask them again. "What say you bastards?"

The dogs looked back at him with expressions so quizzical Oros laughed. Their mute counsel less than satisfying, he added, "We don't have to stay, you know."

He looked around the dogs at the trees of the forest, studying their girth and guessing their weight. Deciding quickly that they'd suit his purposes fine, he turned his attention back to the lake. From here, the waters of Gun Lake flowed down to the Nahlin River. In two days, if he wanted to, he could fashion a raft from the trees which would take them from these shores to the Nahlin and down that river to the point where it merged with the Sheslay to become the Inklin. From there, in three more days, they could be on the Taku. And another day or two after that would see them floating across the border into Alaska. The salt water of Taku Inlet just south of Juneau was one escape route no one would be watching. There were enough boats that motored out of Juneau to fish the Taku that he knew he could pick a ride on one of them into the city.

In ten days—with luck—they could be comfortably camped on the outskirts of Juneau, maybe even up the hill from the Red Dog Saloon with a view of the whole town.

Oros lay back down with his eyes open, staring up into the sky, dreaming of Juneau. The idea was certainly appealing. Lishy's friends would never find him there. Nobody would. And it would be a hell of a lot easier wintering in Juneau than alone in the bush, he thought. A hot bath, running water, candied yams, roast pork with applesauce, maple syrup and yogurt, fresh eggs and bacon, orange juice, even cream for coffee. The list of things he missed suddenly exploded in his mind as he transported himself mentally back to the port town he knew well. He could have a real bed again. With a mattress and clean sheets. They wouldn't starve in Juneau, either—although that was a real possibility if they stayed here.

"We won't need much money, Kila. Never did. And there's lots of work we can find. A couple of afternoons here and there helping the fishermen or working with the road crews will do us just fine." Oros broke out into a short-lived laugh and then turned to examine Toot critically. "The very first thing I'll do when we get there is to return you to the pound where I got you! I'll exchange you for another. 'Not quite what I had in mind,' I'll tell them. Something a little more obedient—maybe even a black dog." Oros laughed once more at the idea of giving Toot back. "Yes, it's almost worth the trip just to get rid of you. And it would sure serve you right if you never saw the light of day again."

Another thought crossed his mind and his broad face lit up. "There are women in Juneau, too. Real women. Not the kind that dissolve into sweat-soaked blankets smelling of stale earth and age when you embrace them, boys, but soft flesh...yielding, warm, and wet and loving."

The need suddenly brought out a pain deep within him and he closed his eyes, clenching them shut with such force he saw stars. Reminding himself he had to be realistic, he sat up stiffly, blankly staring out across the lake. Like everything else, its tranquility was deceptive. The notion of the trip—a mere ten days floating on a raft—was simple enough for the mind to grasp but the reality, as Oros remembered well, was another matter. The water was cold enough to kill after only a short exposure. Hardly enough time to swim to shore even in a flat lake let alone a swift river. And if they could stay afloat for ten days without the raft breaking up or sinking, there were always the snags in the river to face. Those were the most dangerous obstacles. In the milder weather closer to the coast, the trees grew larger and, their log jams were bigger and deadlier, constantly shifting around from flood to flood; there was no way to tell where they might be or to always get yourself in a position to avoid them.

Oros couldn't forget the time he was almost killed once doing the trip in summer, in the best conditions and when the rivers were in low water. That time, he and his dogs were floating with the currents that channeled them along the center of the river, far from both shores, and as they drifted around a bend, they were swept right into the middle of a snag. It had built up into the fast water from a sand bar in the center of the river and they ran right into it—with its mass of logs jutting out like a phalanx of spears waiting to impale everything that came down the river. The flimsily constructed raft he had was torn apart immediately, crushed against the big logs by the force of the river which slammed them into it. Oros had only enough time to grab his pack with one hand before he leaped clear, jumping free of the crash, to cling with both arms to a limb that stuck out above him. With his body in the fast, freezing water, which threatened to rip him loose, he had experienced the oddest sensations. Of heat! And great calm! The temptation to let go and sink into the warmth, to relax completely and give in, was as compelling as the rush of a climax during sex. He had been lucky. How he had fought it, he couldn't remember; but he had managed to hook a leg up over a log and then, raising his body from the water, he had crawled to safety. But everything else had been lost. The two dogs he had with him then were both killed instantly—disappearing under the surface and into the log jam without a sound to be heard above the roar of the river. When he finally made it into Juneau almost three weeks later, he stayed there for a long time before he was willing to make the journey back to Hutsigola.

"All things considered, if we go, boys, we might all be dead within ten days. Here, if we stay, I can guarantee you we'll live longer than that. But if we stay, we might all be dead before summer finds us. And if we did make it to Juneau, I can guarantee we'll see next summer. Except perhaps for your mangy friend Toot, here."

There was no easy solution. And he stood, instead, to survey the camp, once more putting the matter out of his mind.

All the packs were laid out on one end of his tarpaulin, the other end of which was folded back over them like a sandwich to create a floor and roof with enough space in the middle for Oros to crawl into. Beneath the packs, under the tarp, the earth supported a thick growth of peat. Soft and spongy, it was wonderful to walk and sleep on. Having passed a good night here, he was reluctant to move on. The dogs had settled down and he watched them for a while, envying the way they slept, curled up, pressed against each other. He had pushed them hard yesterday through some very difficult country and, though he knew they were still weak and hungry, they seemed so peaceful. Always at home under their skin, they hadn't even seemed to notice the snow or its significance when it had started to flurry several days ago.

His eyes drifted up away from the camp and out toward Hutsigola. Oros had learned to remain steady and unflinching hour after hour when he had to. While it wasn't necessary now, he nevertheless stood without moving, and stayed so still for so long that the dogs started to stir. He ignored them, his eyes fixed and unblinking on the distant sky. Pale blue, shielded from the light by his heavy brows, Oros' eyes had little color of their own and as the sky changed, they too faded from a reflected marine blue to gray. He blinked finally, breaking his concentration, and ran his hands through his long, sandy hair, over his scalp and then around his neck to his face where he scratched the skin under his beard to dislodge the blackflies which were still, in this late hour and season, vigorously determined to root themselves into his bloodstream. It would be easier, he thought, when he could build a fire again but, even at forty miles, he considered he was too close to Hutsigola to dare risk one. The smoke from a small cooking fire would be visible from a long way away. They could easily enough eat out of the packs for a few more days until they were in a safer place. Then he'd even consider letting the dogs run again.

His eyes focused back on the dogs. That was another problem. Four bodies were so much easier to track or to spot than one. He'd be safer without them, he knew, but he couldn't bear the thought of giving them up. Not to live in total isolation. Even if it meant his own ruin, he had to keep them—it was a matter of sanity—although he swore to do his best to minimize the extra risks their presence posed. None of the dogs liked being controlled and they had complained about it all day; but it was much safer, for the time being, to keep them tied down and out of sight. Against the dying green-browns of the earth, Toot, standing out as brightly as a mountain goat against a granite cliff face, was the biggest risk.

Oros had, in fact, almost always been careful with the dogs. Except when he used them to break trail for him through the snow, they traveled behind him so they couldn't alert anyone up ahead to his presence before he himself became aware of the risk. And, behind him, they covered his back. Nobody would ever sneak up behind him.

His eyes drifted irresistibly back to the sky above Hutsigola. Back and forth from the dogs to the sky. He hadn't much else of immediate importance to do or to think about. In silence, he studied the northern sky for any sign of smoke. Although the distant light had turned gray under the high cloud cover that was moving in, the air was still clear enough to see for miles and nowhere was there a trace of smoke. He felt a little relieved by that.

"At least they haven't put the torch to my cabin...yet." He fully expected them to. They had tried everything else. Nor would it be the first time they had tried to crush his spirit by burning him out. Though there was no telling what they were doing, he was convinced Lishy's friends were capable of anything.

Sure in his own mind that they were at that moment crawling all over his cabin, like a wolf pack tearing into a moose carcass, Oros shook his head angrily. The vision was made even more maddening by the fact that he was powerless to stop them. More than the present battle in his mind was the whole reality that lay behind it. The Ten Year War, as he had recently started calling it.

Thinking how fanciful and absurd it would have sounded, how absolutely unbelievable it would have seemed to him nearly ten years ago when he first planned to come to British Columbia, his eyes grew grim and his heart heavy. He would never have left Alaska to move to Telegraph Creek had he known then what it would lead to. But as bad as it was—and now that they had come out into the open to fight him, it was worse than ever before—it was only the latest chapter in a long history of skirmishes and battles between them. And now, now that he was so heavily involved, it was difficult if not impossible to break away, to turn his back on it all and leave for good. He had made a commitment years ago to remain and see it through knowing that if he didn't, nobody else ever would. And worse. If it weren't for him, nobody else would ever know.

The moose bellowed again from the bush across the lake, distracting Oros once more. If the conditions were right and they were farther from Hutsigola, he'd go after it. The meat would feed them all for nearly two months. Or he could, if he wanted to, call the old bull right into their camp. The fall rut was just starting and for the next few weeks the big animals, overwhelmed with the drive to breed, would come crashing in after almost any grunting sound he'd care to make. But they weren't low enough on meat to risk detection by firing a shot. There was plenty of game around and, when they really needed it, he'd get some. The land had never failed him. Not in ten years.

Suddenly, the dilemma Oros had struggled with all day was resolved. Almost without conscious effort, it had solved itself—the land. It alone had never failed him. Oros' mind was now made up. He could trust the land.

"Well, boys, we're staying."

Had he decided instead to leave, the thought that he could do it in greater safety by taking only Kila with him on the raft had occurred to him but he saw that as a drastic measure—something he'd do only if it really became necessary later on. It wasn't yet. His decision made, his mood lifted immediately and he started to break camp.

"What we need now is food." Not meat but the other staples he needed to survive. And he knew exactly where to find them. "To Sheslay," he said.

And then, he added quietly to himself, "Where it all began!"

Chapter Four

Christmas 1972: Oros had decided not to celebrate Christmas this year but, nonetheless, he was reflective on this, one of the longest nights of the year. He had been unsettled all evening, finding small tasks to occupy his time: bringing in firewood, splitting a large supply of kindling to place in the cardboard box beside the woodstove, stuffing woodchips and strips of rags tightly into the smallest cracks between the logs and, finally, leafing though his journals and thinking back to when he first came north in the spring of last year. He had started drifting to escape the draft, but, in that, he wasn't alone. A new tide had risen up out of the old social order, a phoenix, and he had ridden its crest from demonstrations to communes until the movement looked north to the frontiers of Alaska, and Oros had settled himself into Fairbanks.

His early plans had been law school and a practice in Colorado, and Oros still believed it might all have happened if it hadn't been for the war. In twenty more days he'd be celebrating his twenty-first birthday, and he knew it wasn't too late, if the fighting ever ended, to go back and start again. But he had already made up his mind that he wouldn't. He had different goals now.

He had quit school after his sophomore year and drifted from California to New England and back until the violence and destruction he witnessed at the commune in Taos, New Mexico, convinced him finally that only the open spaces of Alaska could provide him with the freedom he wanted.

Now, sitting alone under the dim yellow light of a kerosene storm lamp at the table in the center of the one-room cabin, he realized he was not sorry for anything that had happened. There were never any real regrets. Instead, as he saw it, with each change there was a new birth, a new person and a new beginning. There had been so many changes, in fact, that the person he was when he first quit school was more a stranger to him now than were his casual traveling companions. Oros enjoyed change, even though the cost was a life without roots and a personal history without continuity. Already, after only a year since his introduction to the north, Oros could hardly believe sometimes, without his diaries, that he had ever had a life before Alaska.

It was the diary, Oros' daily journals, that provided the only continuity in his life and he recorded everything in them—the people he met, their conversations, his experiences, his own thoughts and dreams, his fears and his hopes. Good and bad, he recorded it all. Apart from his diaries, he had few other possessions, the next most precious of which were his books. His favorite of these were readings in Zen and the philosophic works of men like Gurdjieff, Ouspensky, Kahlil Gibran, and Kafka. Each book had something different to offer him. Orwell's *1984* provided a vision of the future, Thoreau's *Walden* and *Civil Disobedience*, a study in life-styles. These he read and reread until, at times, the source of his thinking blurred and he was unsure if the ideas he had were his own or those of other men.

Something he had been reading sparked Oros' interest and he pushed heavily away from the table to get an earlier journal. Before returning to his seat, he threw another log into the old cast-iron stove and stirred some lentils that were steaming slowly in a pot off to one side. Stepping slowly over to the door, he carefully nudged the towel he had wadded into the space between door and floor with the toe of his boot where he could hear the winter air blowing in.

Sitting down, he pulled the lantern over closer to him to read from his old diary:

> The tides of memory of time-present recede with the crush of the flood of time-present. So much happens so quickly that I am rapidly becoming a confirmed addict of change.

It was a sentiment he no longer shared. He felt there had been enough movement in his life and what he now wanted more than anything else was a home, his own Walden. Earlier in the day, he had stood outside, gratefully drinking in the crisp dry air of the morning, and it had filled him with joy. Compared to New Mexico, Alaska was a foreign country. Far away. The real States ended at the forty-ninth parallel and here he was, north of the sixty-ninth, less than 150 miles south of the arctic circle. He loved it.

Oros found in Alaska a land, formed and influenced by powerful forces not altogether friendly, that southern man had missed or forgotten or perhaps even hidden from. The sheer enormity of the space alone scared some of the people he met, although he was confident he could live forever within it with ease. Traces of those who had come before him were left everywhere, rusting in the streams and rotting in the forests. In waves, they too had once come from far-off places to invade this land, squirming like spirochetes up the rivers in search of a receptive fertility. Most of them were crushed instead: and driven out.

Oros enjoyed thinking of himself as one of the first of a new wave of pioneers, although with a different vision, and was convinced and determined that he would never be broken. In this, his second winter in Alaska, Oros recognized that he was mentally well-suited to the isolation of the north and, with the vengeance of a long-time prisoner freed finally to return home, he swore he would always follow his heart and never leave. He knew now he belonged here—not at the cabin he was currently living in, or in Fairbanks, or even in Alaska—but rather in the north. If it were ever possible to experience and live a life of true freedom, it was here, in the vast, empty spaces of the frontier. Here, he could breathe as he had never before breathed. As the land itself breathed, with its own soul and consciousness. All that finally remained was to find his own special place in it all, and he was confident he would. It was an important decision, though; the most important, he believed, he could make in his life, and he wasn't going to rush it, knowing that sooner or later, in its own time, the place to make his home would reveal itself to him.

The truly pressing concern, he thought, in this, the winter of '72–73, was to memorize Japanese haiku poetry. They were the most perfect packages to carry around in one's mind, to bring out in idle moments to fend off unwanted thoughts. Oros had so far memorized dozens of them. The latest was one of Basho's, easy to understand and remember. He repeated it again, aloud as he turned to the window which was covered on the inside with thick hoarfrost that revealed nothing from the blackness beyond:

> How admirable,
> He who thinks not, 'Life is fleeting,'
> When he sees the lightning!

Oros laughed at the idea that life could be seen as fleeting. If anything, it lasted forever. Especially in the Alaskan winter. Time, he had plenty of.

As the wind whistled through the clearing around the cabin, whipping the lighter snow up off the ground and hurling it against the glass panes with delicate sand-crystal sounds, Oros ate his simple dinner of lentil soup beside the stove. The heat from the stove penetrated his body and produced a sensation of quiet calm and sleepiness. Although it had been dark for quite some time, it was only around five o'clock, Oros guessed; much too early to go to sleep. He returned to the table to read, stopping to copy a passage or record a thought his reading had inspired. Although his memory for faces, and even conversation, was uncanny, unless he deliberately memorized the written word or copied it out, it was soon forgotten. Of the poems he had memorized this day, there was one among them all, that he knew he would never forget:

> There is no place to seek the mind;
> It is like the footprints of the birds in the sky.

Oros tired of reading after a while and moved his chair closer to the stove, again opening the small metal door through which the logs were fed so he could watch the wood burning inside. Fragmented images of other Christmases, memories of faces and feelings, started to drift up from a forgotten past. When Oros realized what was happening, he stood up abruptly and, walking a small circle in the center of the room around the table, tried to focus his mind deliberately on his present life instead, thinking about the cabin and his new friends.

This was the third cabin he had lived in since coming to Fairbanks, but it was by far the best one and he was grateful to Neil for telling him about it. Oros liked to think about Neil and considered him to be his best friend—although, in truth, Oros was himself his only close ally and confidant. Until he had come to Alaska, Oros remembered having despaired of ever feeling real unity with other people. While friendship was a need he had desperately felt and had once actively pursued, he had only touched the lives of others for brief periods, in certain places, and they drifted apart again. He had previously experienced so much, so quickly, that as a result, he had been growing farther and farther away from others in what had seemed to be a hopeless spiral. But here, in Alaska, there was still a community of interests similar to his own to relate to. And more importantly, what was pleasantly surprising, the need for camaraderie was somehow less demanding of him and the people more tolerant of differences than in the south.

Oros thought back to the afternoon, three days earlier, he had spent at Neil's cabin, only a few miles from here. They had decided unanimously not to celebrate Christmas this year, as winter solstice had taken its place. For it, Bev had presented Oros with a kiss and a necklace that she had secretly made for him during the summer solstice. He had been pleasantly surprised. It was the only gift he had received this year—not that he cared for gifts, he reminded himself quickly. He hated the contrived commercialism of Christmas as much as the others but, still, now that the celebrations were over and he was back at the cabin and alone, he couldn't any longer stem the tide of memories that flooded out—those insistent memories of Christmases past that weighed so heavily on him.

So listening to the cold wind and feeling too far away from the rest of the world, he tried to take comfort in the usual way by taking up his pen to write down a little of what he was thinking and by reading again what he had written before. Oros saw his writing, one of his few insatiable appetites, as a great vessel into which he could pour his need for communication, drain off the energy of his psyche whenever he felt the desire. It was a constant pressure and Oros knew that as long as he had his journals to provide the outlet, he would never give up writing.

Outside, the noise of the wind was picking up. He could tell that it was shifting from the west to the north and wondered if a storm was coming. He started thinking about spring—when the ground would thaw and the sun shine for more than a couple of hours each day—as they all did when they were together, and then of the plans Neil, Bill, and Ben had for a project that Bill had thought up.

Bill's idea was to submit a proposal for a wilderness camp to the government under the Trade and Manufacturing Program for a free grant of eighty acres. Bill wanted to build cabins on the property, one on each corner and another in the center, and rent them out to urbanites seeking sanity. They could sell mental health. The three of them had spent the first two months of the winter discussing the details of the proposal, even getting into tentative building sketches and advertising lines for the national magazines.

Before Bill fell victim to the Alaskan winter, Oros had sat back, an outsider, listening to their discussions. He had wanted to join in but he hadn't asked to. And they hadn't offered him a part. Then, only a couple of weeks before Christmas, Bill's cousin wrote him with a job offer in Sarasota, Florida. Bill left immediately.

Thinking about Bill, remembering his good humor and solid nature, made Oros miss him. But Oros knew now that Bill was a southerner in his heart.

He shivered.

The stove was burning the wood too fast. Oros considered getting up to add some more but, even though the cabin was cooling off, he decided against it. It was the wind more than anything else that was to blame, sucking the heat from the cabin, stripping it off the walls outside. Oros just didn't feel like dealing with the physical problems right now.

Alaska wasn't for everybody, he knew, and in one respect, he was even glad Bill had left. It had opened a place in the partnership with Ben and Neil that he longed for. And they had asked him to join. Oros had agreed immediately. He even volunteered to take charge of the project himself. For Oros, it wasn't a winter's dream, a diversionary hook to hang thoughts of summer on until the spring. After years of drifting himself, the constant movement of people depressed him. They were too scattered, he felt, and drifting farther and farther apart. He wanted to resist that outward flow, to draw them in and bring them all back together again—all the friends he had ever had. The plan to get land fit in perfectly with his own private dream. What he felt was needed was a home base where everybody would be collected under one roof.

Oros closed his eyes, sitting back from the table, and smiled as he thought about it. It was the most ambitious dream he had. To build himself a home, a spiritual retreat, a meeting place for friends. Oros was confident enough in getting the land that he had set out to organize his own proposals for its use. He had spent the morning in the library yesterday researching the current state of literature on various subjects of food production and self-sufficiency. He had intended to work the entire day there, only they had turned him out to close early for Christmas Eve. Still, he had learned something and had come away with an impressive list of book titles and information sources—everything a person needed to know about self-sufficiency. Writing in small, precise print, he copied from the papers into his new diary the titles of fourteen books on beekeeping. Next were books on spinning, organic gardening, goat raising, mushroom identification, down production, and leather tanning. An address to obtain untreated, wild, American ginseng was written out in full. He laughed as he put an asterisk beside the next address, Population Planning Associates, 105 No. Columbia,

Chapel Hill, N.C. 27514 and then wrote and underlined, free samples of contraceptives. Next to beekeeping, books on housing structures occupied the most space, with everything from adobe construction to rammed earth homes, stone houses, log buildings, underground shelters, and dome houses described.

Oros looked the new list over and made up his mind to read most of the important ones before spring. There was lots of time. The very earliest they could start building would be April, he figured, and even then, the frost in the earth might make it impossible to lay down any firm foundations.

Oros looked up from his list and the bubble suddenly popped. He was cold. There was no denying the reality. April was a long, long way off. He put down the pen and focused his attention on his surroundings. The love and camaraderie he had been feeling slipped away and he was once again confronted with the bleak reality of the empty, cold cabin—warmed only by a dying fire and a flickering light from a single, burning wick.

There was no escaping it. He was lonely. Melancholy. Christmas was always a hard time. Oros had found four days of work at the post office helping out with the Christmas rush and had been quite surprised at the flurry of cards and mail that Christmas generated. In spite of his best efforts to resist it, the fact that he wasn't a part of the exchange depressed him a little. That was another cost of Christmas. Oros took up the pen again to try to work it out.

"Fuck, I hate Christmas!"

That helped a little. Enough to give him the motivation to get up and check the fire. The wood had burned down to a mound of white-gray ash that was smothering the coals and he threw in a couple of pieces of dry kindling before loading the remaining space with larger pieces of unsplit birch. Oros closed the fire door and, stepped back. He studied the stove with some dissatisfaction. It wasn't made for heating Alaskan cabins in winter but simply for cooking, and the firebox was just too small to keep any kind of fire going for any length of time.

He had filled the soup pot with water after his dinner and it was warm enough now to wash the dishes in. Using a cloth that was draped over the handle of the oven, he slowly wiped off the tin bowl that he drank his soup from and, dipping it into the water to rinse it off, leaned it up against the stovepipe to dry. The only other utensil that needed to be cleaned was the large pewter serving spoon, slightly bent around the edges, which he had found in the tall grasses behind the first cabin he lived in just after arriving in Alaska. With its handle intricately embossed and a unique smith's stamp on the backside, Oros guessed it must once have come from a grand collection and he felt not only a sense of history whenever he held it but also a bond with the unknown people who had owned it before him.

He stirred it back and forth in the water, scraping the sides of the pot clean at the same time and then, shaking it dry, laid it on the metal shelf above the stove with the other cooking utensils before walking quickly over to the door with the pot. Kicking the towel away, he opened the door, stepped through to the outside, and flung the water in a high, arcing stream along the side of the cabin. Then, leaving the pot on the floor inside the cabin and shutting the door, he walked briskly in short, pumping steps through the snow, following a path around the cabin which led toward the outhouse. At the end of the cabin, he stepped off the path and turned behind a corner of the building out of the wind, to quickly relieve himself there. He was shivering before he got back to the door, walking now into the wind which was driving sheets of the snow that had started to fall from out of the freezing blackness into his face.

Back inside, he went directly over to the stove, blazing now and swiftly heating up the cabin, talking to himself all the way.

"Shit! No wonder Bill left!" Oros said aloud as he held up his hands, still wet from the wash water and cold now, straight over the surface of the stove.

"I don't blame you for going! Shit, I'd go, too, if I had the chance to move to Florida or California. I'd even return to New Mexico if the offer was sweet enough!"

Although having just spoken the unspeakable, Oros stopped to consider it further and decided he was wrong. He loved the north. He wouldn't run away. He'd never leave. It was just the loneliness that Christmas had forced on him today that was causing him to react. After all, he remembered, he had lived in Colorado and knew winter before this and he had never really minded the snow. Christmas only made the darkness and the isolation seem more intense than it truly was. He'd get over it, he was sure.

Oros' thoughts turned to his friends, scattered over the whole continent, and to the last communication they had received from Bill. Bill had sent them a message, directed to Neil, via Tundra Topics, wishing everybody a Merry Christmas. They couldn't reply to Bill's greeting, even if anybody had wanted to—nobody knew his new address and, in fact, they didn't even know his real name. Oros was a little sorry about that, even though he knew it was safest to avoid addresses, and to use names like Bill and Ben and Neil. Oros didn't know any of their real names and had never asked. They were all refugees from the draft and as far away as Alaska was, it was still part of the States and they could be arrested here just as easily as anywhere else.

The name Oros used was Jim. It was something everyone was doing, even back home—using first name aliases. For a while, Oros had found it liberating.

Without a name, without a background, with no personal history, a person was free to be whoever he wanted to be. But lately, looking back, there was only a sea of nameless faces he had once called his friends, and he realized he'd never find them again and that, in part, it was the war that was responsible for keeping them apart, for causing the vacuum they all felt and the isolation that now plagued him. Bill was only the most recent of a long line of casualties.

It was the transience of it all that bothered him and he drew from his mind another haiku he had memorized, one that he considered fit the situation and proving that, at least in spirit, he wasn't alone:

> The skylark:
> Its voice alone fell,
> Leaving nothing behind.

He went over to a twenty-five gallon barrel in the corner of the cabin, where the warmth of the fire never penetrated, and filled a kettle with the clear water inside it. Placing it, sputtering, over the hottest part of the stove, he returned to the table and started to write again. He had recently joined a meditation group which had pirated a kind of creed-definition from the works of Robert Powell that he liked:

> Meditation, the cleansing of the mind from recurring torturing thoughts, is as important to mental well-being as hygiene is to physical well-being.

Oros paused for a moment to think about it. Not only was it true but it also worked. He didn't suffer from the distorted thoughts that had tortured him before. At least not the way he used to.

Everything helped, but it was mostly the influence of Alaska itself, the space, that Oros believed had cleared his head so much. It was all coming together, he thought. Slowly, slowly to be sure, but it was coming. Like the orgasmic explosion of spring after a long, long, long, dark winter, it was coming.

Oros laid down his journal as gently as if it were a new baby and walked to the window. The glass was solidly frosted over; the thin tracery of November's delicate white feathering had thickened to an opaque layer of ice, cold yet slickly wet to his passing finger. He cleared a spot by picking with his fingernails, then by rubbing the exposed glass with his woollen shirt cuff. Ben and Bev had been gone the entire day and still weren't in sight. If they weren't in the habit of staying away for days on end without telling him, leaving Oros to care for the cabin by himself, he'd have gone out to look for them. Outside, the tops of the trees were being flung wildly back and forth while beneath them, at ground level, the snow was falling almost straight down through the relatively still air.

The winds were amazing, he thought; they were the breath and the spirit of the land. Capricious and powerful, they could cut through any thickness of fur and wool turning thirty to sixty below zero, chilling a man's very bones, or could show in the guise of an arctic chinook, balmy, warm, moist, and full of the promise and flavor of spring, blunting the weather to a mild ten below.

Oros remembered thinking he knew winter before he had come to live in Alaska. Now he laughed at the idea of the Bing Crosby and Bob Hope winter—of sports jackets and singing in sleds and the snow that wasn't snow. Well, he certainly knew winter now. If you tried to sing "White Christmas" outside here at fifty below, you'd freeze-burn your throat and lungs. The frigid air was surely the worst drawback to living here. He knew he'd manage, but he didn't like it.

Oros returned to his table and the faces of his friends rose before his eyes again. Among them all, Neil's stood out with true inspiration and he wrote, "Neil is a real brother," a brother Oros never had. There wasn't anything bad he could say about Neil except perhaps that he didn't see enough of him. It was a badly abused word but he loved Neil. One day, after they had hauled and split three cords of firewood together, he even told him so. Neil, surprised by the ingenuous honesty of the younger man he knew as Jim, had smiled broadly back and said that he loved him too. No other man had ever said that to Oros and he treasured the memory of that moment.

Oros felt comforted thinking about Neil and described his conversations with him in his journal until late into the night. Oros wanted to be like him, but they were very different people and Oros knew he had his own course to follow, which might someday lead him away from Neil. Neil had already found his home, Oros realized. And Neil's urge to wander was gone.

Oros wasn't sure if he could say the same thing about himself, although he was sure that he had finally and completely fulfilled, exhausted, or purged all his urban desires, and, if he did not find peace, it would not be on account of living away from the concrete environments. He shook his head slowly and firmly as he spoke the words that committed him to his course. He would never return to live in a city. NEVER.

> For long years a bird in a cage,
> Today, flying along with the clouds.

Oros hoped that he would find his peace here. He would. He was sure of it.

Chapter Five

September 23, 1981: The wranglers worked quickly, strapping the panniers tightly to the frames on the packhorses and loading some supplies into them. The horses were big, calm animals. Percheron and Morgan crosses, they could carry 400 pounds each and yet were easy to ride. Steady and sure-footed, they were the best breed for this kind of country.

Fred Daye stood in the center of the camp watching the hands working at the corral and noted with satisfaction that they were almost ready to go. Everything seemed under control. He took a deep breath and expelled the air slowly through his nostrils. The heady odor of fried bacon emanated from the cookhouse. It almost changed his mind about having breakfast but he turned instead to the east and his eyes traveled slowly up the nearest slopes of Level Mountain, back and forth across the rising land where, toward the top, the morning sunlight was breaking. Below the light, the mountain appeared purplish gray with a soft haze that obscured finer details.

The tall, lean frame of his body became rigid. His black eyes were intense. He was looking for something. Something out beyond the camp.

One of the wranglers saw him and yelled out from the corral, "Hey, Fred. Should we tail them up now?"

The question broke his concentration. Fred thought for a moment before deciding the horses could be strung together at the last moment and replied, "No. That can wait 'till we're saddling up. Just make sure the diamond ropes are all tight. One of them slipped yesterday. We don't want to lose a horse."

It had happened before. The sight of a horse thrown off balance and then tumbling away, end over end, load and all, down a mountainside was a sight he didn't want to see again.

As the men called out to each other, their voices carried easily in the still morning air and drifted across the clearings of the camp out into the surrounding forest.

A burst of laughter came from the open door of the cookhouse.

The hunters were joking with the cook, complaining in good humor about the saddle sores they'd be taking back to Pennsylvania with them. Wealthy businessmen, they had had to book two years in advance to arrange a two-week hunt with Fred's father, Fletcher, and no minor physical discomforts were going to spoil it for them.

"Why don'cha just spread that grease around the camp and we'll sit here on our pillows and wait for them bears to come to us. Shoot 'em without even leaving the table."

The cook, a Tahltan Indian from Telegraph Creek, not realizing they were only kidding him, replied tolerantly: "You don't want to have grizzlies around the camp. They're smart bears. You make a mistake with one and it'll kill you!"

Fred next heard the laughter of the hunters as one of them told his friends, "Everybody's a big-game hunter in this country. Even the cooks."

That wasn't a fair comment and Fred frowned. People around Telegraph generally didn't hunt grizzlies. But everybody with any sense had a healthy respect for them; with a heart rate as slow as twelve beats a minute, even a heart shot wouldn't guarantee stopping one in a charge. And few locals were prepared to accept the risks involved for the dubious pleasure of hunting one. Far more dangerous than black bear, grizzlies were cunning and more unpredictable—especially when hunted. Then, the hunted quickly turns hunter.

Fred's first armed encounter with one happened quite by accident years ago. He was off in the bush with another hunter chasing after moose, not far from the camp. They stumbled on a grizzly rooting in the earth. They were close enough to it that he could hear the solid "thunk" of the hunter's bullet as his shot struck the bear in the right chest. Enraged, the animal attacked instantly. Its head close to the ground, it charged with its mouth open, trailing strings of white, gelatinous saliva. Its ferocity terrified the hunter, who cried out, turned, and fled for his life, leaving Fred to stand his ground alone. Unflinching, Fred brought his old 30-30 Winchester rifle up to his shoulder and rapidly fired shot after shot, as quickly as he could, into the hairy hump above the bear's head. The light, 150-grain bullets were next to useless in stopping the animal, as Fred knew they would be. Incredibly, however, only twenty feet short of reaching him, the huge bear lurched to a halt in front of Fred. Wheeling around, it ran away and disappeared into the forest. When the hunter returned, he found Fred calmly reloading his magazine, preparing for a new charge. It was this rare quality he possessed that was the determining factor in his father's decision to accept him into the business as a professional guide. For, as Fletcher explained simply to successive groups of hunters, "If you give in to fear, you'll die." Fred, however, traded the 30-30 for a 300 Winchester magnum.

Hanging suspended in the air from a game rack behind the cookhouse was the camp's bag to date: eight moose quarters, three Stone sheep, a goat, and the stretched-out skin of one very large black bear. Except possibly for the bear, none of the animals were Boone-and-Crockett trophies. Nor had the hunters seen a grizzly yet, but Fred was hopeful they'd shoot at least one before the party left. As he stood waiting for the hunters to finish breakfast, he wondered whether his father's presence would have added to the game taken. Still, Fred was glad his father wasn't in the bush. With the recent reports they had been receiving by radio from Eugene Edzertza at Atlin, they all knew Fletcher's life was at risk. If Oros had killed Lishy, then there was no reason he wouldn't kill again—and Fletcher was first on Oros' hate list. Until Oros was caught, it would be far better for Fletcher to stay away. Fred hoped a capture would happen soon. Fletcher was due back next week with the new party of hunters.

Fred turned his attention back to the mountain's slopes. He hadn't told anybody else in the crew, let alone the high-paying tourist hunters, of his concern, but Sheslay Mike was very much on his mind as he examined every detail in sight and reviewed what little information he had. Edzertza had called them nearly two weeks ago with the news that Gunter Lishy had gone into Hutsigola Lake and then vanished. The police were still trying to keep it confidential but there was no doubt that "Sheslay," as Oros was most commonly called, had killed him. Edzertza's next communication was more alarming. The police had landed at Hutsigola but Oros had escaped. Edzertza's best guess was that Oros would travel south. To Sheslay.

Fred turned in the direction of the old town of Sheslay, a few miles away, where he knew one of Oros' cabins lay; but seeing nothing beyond the trees, he turned again to study the mountain, from where a person could watch them without being seen. Somewhere out there, in the thousands of square miles of wilderness that surrounded them, Sheslay had eluded the police and was running wild. Fred wasn't taking any chances. Nobody was to be left alone in the camp. Even the cook was coming out with them each day on the hunt—an added service which the men found most agreeable.

"Freddie, we gonna see some real action today?" one of the men hollered out as the group came clamoring out of the cookhouse. "If we're lucky," he yelled back, adding under his breath, "or unlucky."

He wasn't afraid of Oros. Not personally. Given enough space, he believed, Oros would avoid a confrontation. Yet he couldn't be sure. And these recent events, together with the old problems, might have changed everything.

Preoccupied with his own thoughts, Fred didn't turn to the hunter who came first out of the bunkhouse and stood beside him, shoulder to shoulder, to look up into the alpine ranges of the mountains with him.

"You know Freddie, " the hunter said at last without taking his eyes off the country, "I've dreamed of this kind of space ever since I was a kid and, believe me, that's been a long time. Open country without a fence, a house, a road—for miles. It's all untouched, the same country that God created. Funny thing, now that I'm here, I'm almost as sad as I am happy because I know I'm leaving it all behind. And I don't want to. If I didn't have so many roots, if I were a young man again with a little courage to strike off on my own, I think this is the kind of place I'd like to spend a lifetime. You know what I mean? This place is really something special."

Fred smiled at him. The Americans were all like him, open-hearted and genuine. He enjoyed spending time with them. For most of the hunters, 10,000 dollars was pocket change yet they treated everyone as though they were all family. Unlike the French or the Germans who, arrogant and pompous, complained when their favorite European wines weren't produced at the table, the Americans understood and truly loved the wilderness.

"Freddie," the older man continued, "you know I don't give a good goddamn if I shoot a grizzly but I sure do want to see one—a wild grizzly in his own wild country—that would really mean a lot to me. God! That would really be something to see."

The two men watched the hills together while they waited for the other three hunters to join them. But instead of the hills, the mental image of a note Fred had found a couple of years ago nailed to a tree along one of the trails near the camp was what came into focus in his mind. Written in bold characters with charcoal, it contained only three words: FLETCHER IS DEAD. It was one of many they found over the years left in conspicuous places for them. Beneath the words was always the same symbol—a stylized, burning sun.

"If we don't find one today," Fred decided at last, "then we'll pack up and move up into the mountains, to an outpost camp close to the snow line.... It'll be a lot less comfortable than the base camp here but we'll have a better view of everything in the open country." They'd also be a lot safer out of the bush, Fred felt.

"Now you're talking. Look, I've got to see what's keeping those geriatric patients I been calling my friends...probably got themselves all tied up in their underwear."

Left alone, Fred walked down toward the horses scanning the forest around him with a watchful eye. The poplars were burning brilliant yellow in the sunshine and the earth had a cool, fall smell. A good wind would tear off the leaves and turn the forest gray and spiny like porcupine quills; but today the air was calm and the leaves would stay for a few days yet.

Behind Fred's back, only 100 yards away in the forest, Oros lifted his head slowly. Raising his chin up off the ground, he peered cautiously through the bush. Seeing that Fred was no longer looking in his direction, he rose up a little higher to get a better view, studying Fred's every move.

Fletcher wasn't anywhere around. That was a surprise. It was obvious that Fred was in charge instead. Oros wondered where Fletcher was. No doubt his disappearance was somehow connected to the German, he thought. He speculated that Fletcher might even have gone in to Hutsigola to search for the German.

Under darkness, Oros had crept into camp as soundlessly as the fog, listening with his ear almost brushing the walls of the tents. As daylight approached, he retreated into the cover of the bush. From this distance, the features of each man would be recognizable—easy targets if he chose!

It had been a long wait but his patience was rewarded. Counting the men as they arose, he knew not only how many were in the camp but he also learned that they'd all be going out on the trail. The camp would be left empty. He had been prepared to raid the camp at night, when they were asleep, but this was far better. He'd have the camp to himself.

Waiting for the men to clear out, Oros watched Fred with particular interest. They hadn't always been enemies. As Fred helped the cook pack supplies for lunch, Oros was surprised to see how little Fred had changed since he had last seen him. In fact, he hardly looked any different than he did when they first met in Sheslay almost ten years ago. The sight of Fred working in the camp brought out old memories in a flood of mixed emotions.

Everything had seemed possible then, in the beginning. Fred was his own age and when Oros had started construction on his first cabin, little more than a root cellar only a couple of miles from the Daye Camp, he was sure then that they'd become the closest of friends. He'd never forget that it was Fred who first took him up into the mountains above Sheslay to explore the country on horseback. Even more endearing, Fred had the same kind of easygoing confidence that Neil had possessed. Secure in his own definition and relationship with the world, Fred had already "arrived" while Oros was still searching. It was a quality that Oros had felt attracted to and, in part, it was Fred's presence, the existence of the Daye Camp and Fred's vision of the country around Sheslay, that influenced Oros' own decision not to return to Telegraph Creek but to make his permanent home here.

His face suddenly grew grim as he remembered his first year in Sheslay. Yes, he thought wryly, high times were certainly had by all then. It had seemed such an idyllic place, a paradise, Sheslay in the summer—until winter came and turned it into a living nightmare.

Oros dropped from his elbows, pressing himself flat into the earth as one of the men who had swung up into his saddle looked directly toward him. With the rifle breach beside his face, Oros gripped it tightly in his right hand and listened to the sounds of their voices. If they came toward him he'd have no choice but to start shooting. He waited for the shout of discovery to be given; but nothing happened and he raised his head again, slowly to peer through the weeds. Nobody had seen him. The sounds of the men talking and laughing drifted through the forest, rising and falling in volume as they prepared to ride off. With the ground close to his nose, Oros smelled the mustiness of decaying vegetation, the early rot of leaves wilted by killing frosts and tubular stalks gone soft and mushy.

Finally the men saddled and began riding away. With Fred in the lead and the hunters behind him, the crew followed in a long line with the packhorses. The sound of their voices grew more and more distant, then faded away. The air was again still and quiet.

Oros waited a little longer and then stood up. The front of his body, in contact with the ground, was soaked right through to the skin and covered with bits of debris and slimy plant growth, which he absently brushed at with his free hand. Except for a few dying poplar leaves that clung tenaciously to their branches and trembled in a breeze almost too light to feel, nothing else moved in the clearing ahead. Inching forward, one step at a time, his eyes constantly shifting back and forth, his ears straining to pick up any sound, he skirted the clearing, stepping from tree to tree to keep his outline obscured. Carefully he worked his way to the trail they had left by and listened there. Everything was quiet. They were gone.

Knowing they wouldn't return until dark, a confidence spread over him, relaxing his body, and he laughed. "Time to go shopping, ol' buddy." he announced to himself cheerfully. Strolling boldly out into the open, he headed directly for the cookhouse.

Having lain in hiding all morning watching the routines of the camp, it felt good now to be master of the place. He had started his life here in Sheslay at the Daye camp from the inside looking out. Then, he had felt only wonder and awe at the immensity of the wilderness that he found himself in. Now, it was that same wilderness which had become his home. He found it somewhat ironic and disconcerting to realize he lived almost as one of its wild inhabitants. On the outside looking in. The thought that more than his perspective had changed disturbed him but he quickly put it out of his mind. It didn't matter, he told himself. He was free to come and go as he pleased. There were no boundaries for him. And he was hungry.

The screen door swung shut behind him with a crash and, inside, he quickly stripped off his clothes to hang them over the backs of some chairs beside the still-hot stove. With the smell of bacon even stronger in the kitchen, he checked the pans first, hoping to find the grease left behind to fry some bread in, but they had been cleaned off already. Taking one of the mugs off the rack where they were hanging, he drained the rest of the coffee from the pot and sat down at the table with a loaf of bread and a large tin of strawberry jam. Grinning happily, he put his bare feet up under the table on another chair and, with his own knife, cut thick slices off the loaf and smeared them with mounds of jam. The coffee was strong and, from the bottom of the pot, a little grainy, but it was hot and full of flavor. As he ate, he groaned unconsciously in pleasure. It had been such a long time since he had eaten this kind of food. Even the crusty bread was a treat after months of pan-fried bannock. Inside the big cooler, he found a box of meat and returning to the stove, threw a couple of pork chops into a frying pan big enough to accommodate ten eggs at a time. Slicing up some cold, boiled potatoes, he added them to the pan and then opened a can of beans and poured them over the top. While he waited for it all to cook, he carried a five gallon pailful of peanut butter to the table, and with a slightly dated issue of the *Economist* someone had left at the table, settled himself down for the feast of the year.

It felt good being inside a real camp again. Here was a link with the outside world: peaches from Summerland, oranges from California, bananas from Ecuador, and news of the international economic climate. Oros laughed heartily. He owed it all to Fletcher. Among the camps, Fletcher's was his favorite. Even if he hadn't known it so well, if he hadn't helped build a part of it, he would still have found it attractive. Fletcher kept it stocked like a grocery store and Oros had been a regular "customer" here for years—raiding Fletcher's food stores ever since that first winter in Sheslay.

Taking a handful of plastic bags from his packsack that he had picked up from his Sheslay cache last night, he began filling them with the staples he'd need: flour, sugar, rice, oatmeal, tea, cornmeal, powdered milk, dried fruit, lard, dried beans, salt, and a dozen other products that would keep through the winter. In the past, he'd always been careful to take only a little from each bin so as not to disturb the appearance of the pantry; but the need now was greater than the risk of discovery afterward and he stuffed each bag. Before he left the cookhouse, he wiped off the frying pan and his dishes, putting them back where they had been before, smoothed over the contents of the bins, replaced their lids, and brushed off the table. Satisfied there was nothing obvious that would attract attention to his visit there, he left. Closing the screen door and bolting the bear-proof door behind it, he walked quickly over to the bunkhouses.

There was more than food on his shopping list. He needed ammunition. He had less than 200 bullets left for the .303 and most of those were cached with his furs at Hutsigola. If he was to survive over the winter and feed his dogs, he'd have to shoot a lot of moose. And it was the .303 that did all the important killing. It seemed more unlikely but he was also hoping to find some .44 magnum bullets for the handgun. He hadn't enough to waste them on target practice and he wasn't familiar with shooting it. As a result, the revolver's usefulness was limited, but as an emergency, short-range weapon, it was a lot quicker and easier to handle than the rifle. More ammunition for it would make it invaluable.

Inside the guest cabins, the beds remained as they had been left, with the sleeping bags zipped open and bunched up. He had more bags than he needed and he ignored them. From a wash table, he pocketed a tube of toothpaste and dental floss as he examined the toiletries the wealthy hunters had brought with them: expensive colognes, aftershaves, skin creams, and pills of all kinds. A large box of hemorrhoid suppositories made him laugh before he turned to inspect their duffel bags. In an inside, plastic-lined pocket for dirty clothes, he found a heavy woolen shirt which he stuffed into his own pack. In the same pocket were four pairs of thick woolen socks. The sight of them suddenly made him angry. In the duffel bag beside them were eight more pairs. With the tags still on them, they were all brand new. The thought that these people were able to change their socks every day, that they had probably never had to wash a pair in their lives, infuriated him. That these people could come here and kill the game for sport, for trophies, and then fly out again, never experiencing hunger or pain the way he had, tempted him to leave them a message they'd never forget. It was a temptation he resisted. He couldn't afford to make any mistakes now. Taking only their dirty clothes—the clothes they wouldn't miss—he left the rest intact. Nearly all their things were new, as though they had purchased everything just for this one trip. Even the extra guns they brought with them, which he removed from their cases to examine, were factory clean, without a scratch or a sign of wear anywhere. None of the ammunition for the guns they had taken with them was of any use to him and the two rifles they had left behind were both wider-bored guns than his own .303. A .340 Weatherby magnum and a .338 Winchester magnum, these were weapons that could bring down an elephant. With no .303 bullets to be found, he considered taking one of the new rifles with its ammunition instead but quickly discarded the idea. He didn't need another rifle and he couldn't carry the extra weight. He'd have to make what ammunition he had count until he could get more. He would. There were other outfitters' camps he could raid. Beside the rifles were a couple of shotguns and he took a box of birdshot. Even though his closest shotgun was in Hutsigola, the shells would come in handy in the spring when the ducks returned.

By noon, he had all the new supplies safely back in Sheslay. Keeping only the perishables and as much of the dried goods as he and the dogs could comfortably carry, he stored the rest in his secret caches—steel drums, buried in the earth, their tops flush with the ground. When their lids were secured, they were nearly waterproof and, covered with dirt and branches, the best concealed of all his caches.

Oros was sitting on the floor of his own cabin. The dogs were rested, their packs were full, and they were ready to go; but Oros couldn't tear himself away from his cabin yet. Stretched out on the dirt floor with his back up against his pack Oros was staring at the ceiling. Except for the frame of a cot, the room was empty.

"It's almost finished, Kila!" he said quietly, looking about him. "All that's left are the windows and the floor and it's done!"

He tilted his head back, facing up at the high, cathedral-domed ceiling. "God, that was a bitch! I never thought I'd finish that. But just look at it! And it's dry too." He was filled with pride as he spoke. The ceiling was made from logs, raised one at a time over the height of the walls. There were six walls. The design for the hexagonal cabin was one that he had first worked out in 1973, modeling it after the tepee. The ceiling logs were laid around the corners of the cabin, one on top of the other in a spiral, higher and higher, until there was only a small hole left in the center of the cone-shaped dome which he plugged with branches and mud. Now, years later, the roof was still solid and dry.

This wasn't the first cabin he had built but it was by far the best one. His first effort was a conventionally designed hut he had raised quickly with a flat, adobe-styled roof. Like a prairie sod hut made from logs rather than turf, it was warm inside and had served him well. Until it burned down.

Somebody who didn't want him there torched it. He had left it on a winter's morning to check his beaver traps and when he returned, a few hours later, all that was left was a smoking mound. He hadn't known who had done it but he guessed why and it had been a turning point. He was sure it was intended as a warning. To drive him out. But, challenged, he responded as he always did. With resistance. If they wanted him out, he'd stay. And if they wanted to fight, he'd fight.

In the spring following the fire, he had started construction on the hexagonal cabin. Building it to last a lifetime, he found it had proceeded more slowly than he had planned and he had been forced to erect another temporary shelter for the following winter. Since then, there had been other cabins, other shelters, scattered across the vast territory he lived in, but this one remained closest to his heart. Now, almost ten years later, it still wasn't finished; but he hadn't given up hope of completing it. More than a symbol of his resistance, it would be the fulfillment of a dream to finish it. Even if he could never live openly in it, he wanted to see it complete—to keep faith with that early vision, so full of promise. It was meant to be the retreat shared with friends that he had dreamed of in Fairbanks. And he'd never forget that it was the dream of building this cabin, of having a permanent home, that had kept him going through the horrible darkness that descended on him that first winter—after the hunters had all left, after Fletcher had flown back to Telegraph Creek forty-four miles to the south, after the bush had been emptied of its life, when he had found himself alone in Sheslay with the snow falling, absolutely alone.

Thinking back, he still couldn't understand why he hadn't left for Telegraph Creek when he'd planned to and when he still had the chance, before the snow had sealed him off in Sheslay. Oros shook his head at some of the evil memories that still plagued him from that first winter.

There was still so much he didn't understand. And so many more disturbing experiences since then.

Standing up, he walked around inside his cabin with steady, measured paces, studying the walls and remembering each log. It had taken so long to build and had never been lived in. He had worked on it every year whenever he had some time and wondered now when he'd ever have the chance to work on it again. The cabin was a thing of his own creation, as personal as his own thoughts. The fact it remained unfinished bothered him deeply.

He would like to stay. But it was too obvious a place. They'd be watching the cabin. And it was too close to the Daye camp to be safe.

Turning away from the cabin and the abandoned town of Sheslay that lay through the trees around it, mostly buried out of sight in the earth, he walked quickly to the bank of the Hackett River. There, he suddenly stopped again, staring down at the ground. Remembering. With the toe of his boot, he kicked a small lump of earth over, exposing the dirt clinging to the roots of the wild flowers. Dark and fertile earth. Already the little clearing was covered with young poplars that grew up from the furrowed ground. It had been his garden. The garden that had produced such abundance. Now, no one would ever guess it hadn't always been wild. With his head bowed low, he walked over his old garden. On the other side, he stopped again to examine a few charred logs that were almost completely buried and overgrown with vegetation. His expression hardened at the sight, changing from sorrow to anger, and he looked up quickly in the direction of Fletcher's camp. Stepping around the remains of his first cabin as though it were a sacrilege to walk over it, he climbed down the bank of the river to its gravel bed. Exposed by low water, the shore was hard packed and dry, with no obstructions. Walking rapidly with wide, sweeping steps, he followed it downstream, putting the cabin and his early dreams behind him. With the dogs following closely behind, they were soon miles from Sheslay.

Arriving at a large pool in the river, he set his rifle down, took off his pack, and edged gingerly out along a narrow beaver dam that flooded a small tributary creek draining into the pool. From the dam he jumped onto an adjoining beaver house, where two poles planted in the water in front of the house rose up above the dam. Grabbing a pole in each hand, he yanked them hard, pulling them out of the muck bottom, and raised them heavily up over the house he stood on. Halfway down the poles, secured by two metal rings attached to them with chains, was a connibear trap. Oros had set it last night. Now he laughed with delight upon seeing it. He had caught a beaver.

Oros held the beaver by one of its back legs and swung it heavily over the heads of the dogs to tease them. They went wild. Hungry since leaving Hutsigola, they jumped up with gnashing teeth to pull it from his hands. Oros kicked them back down roughly.

Quickly skinning it out, he tossed meaty chunks to each dog, and watched, amused, as they fed. Half wild things themselves, they snarled over their portions, jealously guarding their meals. Gulping down fistfuls of crushed bone and flesh, they coughed and gagged in their haste to be full.

Catching the beaver had driven Oros' confidence up so high he started laughing. If all else failed, he'd survive the winter by trapping. Even if he had to kill two of the dogs to make the meat last, he'd get by.

His own philosophy had changed so dramatically since that first summer in Sheslay. Where once he'd believed in the existence of an absolute harmony, a unity of all life striving toward perfection, he knew now the hard reality of an uncompromising environment. The land provided but it took, too, and the competition was fierce. It all distilled down to one simple truism—eat and be eaten. Kill and be killed. And none surrendered willingly.

The floatplane which drifted over them a couple of days earlier was still on his mind. Even though it was quite high, he had been out in the open with the dogs when he saw it and he was sure it had spotted him. Having decided that pursuit was now likely to occur from the south as well as the north, he felt he had to keep moving. Now that he had some supplies, the urgency that drove him to Sheslay had abated. For the immediate future, they could survive on the trail. He would like to have returned to Hutsigola, to prepare for the winter, only he knew that was impossible. But Sheslay being as far south as he dared travel, they set off north again, in the direction of Hutsigola. Keeping a safe distance off the Telegraph Trail, they followed the Sheslay River instead until, when the light became too dim to travel much farther, he led the dogs away from the water and into the cover of the bush to make camp for the night.

While darkness obscured and then obliterated the outline of the treetops against the sky, he built up a small cooking fire from dry sticks. It was the first fire he had dared to burn since leaving Hutsigola two weeks ago. With an old cast-iron pan, he started frying the beaver's liver in some of the fat he had scraped off the inside of the hide. Sitting back on the edge of his tarp, he took out his diary to enter some notes by the fire's light as he savored the aroma of the meat cooking. The liver was the best part of the beaver, its flavor more delicate than that of beef, it texture finer, drier, and more palatable. Fresh plums and coffee followed. With his mood soaring, Oros rolled a joint from some old papers and a little bag of Stikine home-grown he found in his Sheslay cache and then settled down to enjoy a night filled with more promise than any since he had left Hutsigola.

Kila came and lay down beside him and Oros rewarded the dog's loyalty by scratching his head. With the warmth of the dog's body pressing through his clothes against his groin, Oros felt the beginnings of an arousal.

"Well Kila, you're lucky you're a male." He spoke quietly to the dog as he continued scratching it. "If you were a female, I think I'd try to fuck you. Although, on second thought, unless I get some other action you may not be safe by spring."

Oros turned abruptly to Smoky and Toot, lying curled up together a short distance away, and yelled their names. "TOOT! SMOKY!"

The dogs were instantly alert, anxiously watching him. Sounding as stern as he could, he warned them, "You bastards decide you're too horny to save it any longer, I'm giving you notice right now. You do it to yourselves, but just keep away from Kila."

At the mention of his own name, Kila too started whining and got up pacing around the camp as though to discover the cause of the commotion. The other two dogs, locked in eye contact with Oros, didn't move.

"And don't you guys start thinking of pulling a gang rape when my back's turned either," he said to them. "I'll know. And so help me, you'll pay for it, you queer bastards. Now go to sleep and dream of bitches."

When Oros turned away from them and started laughing, long and hard, the dogs, released from his attention, relaxed and lay down again. Taking off his boots, he crawled into his roll between the canvas, breathing deeply of the air, tasting it through his nostrils and delighting in its fullness.

He was happy. The successful raid on Fletcher's camp gave him an intense satisfaction. The familiar smell of his own odor mixed with the sweet musky mildew of the cool, moist earth under him and the tangy, turpentine-pungent fragrances of the pine produced a sensation of great closeness with the earth. The clouds were breaking and a few stars peeked out from behind them. With the end of the daylight, the blackflies had taken cover but the mosquitoes had come out to replace them. The mosquitoes were harder to deal with than the blackflies. At least the blackflies were quiet.

Kila started whimpering and then growled but he was only asleep, already dreaming his dogs' dreams.

"Kila!" Oros called and the dog woke up.

"Quiet!" he ordered and the dog fell silent again.

Oros marveled at how tough the bugs were. The temperature was starting to fall below freezing but, in spite of that, the mosquitoes were still full of drive. He hated them with a passion but he couldn't help himself from admiring their tenacity. Always ready to die for blood! 'They're a good example for me,' he thought, only half jokingly. 'The best thing about winter is the absence of bugs. Maybe the only thing,' he corrected himself, considering what was ahead. 'This could be a hard one,' he feared. 'They'd never find me in the summer; but in the winter, they'll track me through the snow. The safest thing to do would be to lay in enough stores to hole up until spring; but even with the new supplies, that's impossible. Winter is seven months.'

He wondered what was happening at Hutsigola. His worst fear was that they'd go on a rampage. But if they did, he promised himself, they'd be sorry.

"Oh, Christ, will they be sorry!"

At least they're not invincible, he thought. And the German would make them think twice now about sending people into the bush after him. Oros thought about the pilot, the only living witness, and realized again, in retrospect, that it had been a mistake to paddle out to meet the plane. But at the time, it was a risk he felt he should take. He had to find out who they were. He had to know if the German was alone. Because he had shown his face, it meant they were onto him and would be hunting him again. But it also gave him valuable information. Now he knew for certain the German wasn't alone. The German had been dropped off. And, too, he knew they would be hunting him. They wouldn't catch him by surprise. So it wasn't a total mistake. Their own mistakes were even worse. There was some satisfaction in knowing that. Their biggest mistake was to have used the German at all. That was really stupid. As if he wouldn't remember. Their drugs had done some things to him—his eyesight was failing, for one—but his memory for faces was intact. He never forgot a face. Never! It was the German's mistake and it had cost him dearly.

Oros well remembered his first meeting with the German. He was camped on the old Telegraph Trail, fifty miles or so from Tahltan by Egnel Creek, a mile from the Sheslay River. It was a trail camp like the one he had set up here, he remembered, only with the tepee. The man had stepped so quietly out of the trees that the dogs had failed to give any warning until Oros himself, sensing the presence of another, spun around to discover the German standing there. Right in the camp! The dogs, taken by surprise, had reacted instinctively and put up a show; but Oros knew they were cowed by him. He himself froze, staring horrified while the German, smiling, played it so cool. Thrusting out his hand, he had walked right up to Oros! Oros even remembered his name, Gunter. From Atlin, the German had said, which Oros just knew was bullshit. He felt it so clearly. But the German had him and there was no use fighting it. Oros played along with him instead. He even shook Gunter's hand and managed to smile back, although he didn't introduce himself. He didn't have to. Gunter knew who he was.

"You're Sheslay. Sheslay Mike," he said, and Oros nodded.

"Well, Sheslay Mike," Gunter said, "I've always wanted to meet you. You got the pot, I got the tea." And with no further encouragement, he rooted out a tin of loose tea and proceeded to make himself comfortable in Oros' camp.

Thinking back over it, even the memory shook him up. Gunter could have killed him then. And there was nothing he could have done to save himself. He wasn't going to be caught like that again, he promised himself. Gunter was good. So good that he almost fooled Oros. Almost. After Gunter had sat down, he explained that he was a trapper and, when they talked about it, the German was believable enough.

He looked to be an old man and Oros, wanting to check the German's pack, lifted it to move it aside. Gunter had bounced in with that pack on his back as though it were stuffed with down. Oros, suspicious at first that it was, was surprised to find that it weighed close to seventy pounds. It was believable enough that the German could be a trapper. Even his traps, which Oros asked to examine, were real enough and, he observed, well-seasoned. In fact, all the details were good. Almost perfect. They talked about the trails, the fords, the game and trapping, and Oros had to concede to himself privately that Gunter's knowledge of the country was better even than his own.

"Why haven't we met before?" Oros asked fairly.

Gunter explained that he ran his lines out of Atlin east along the trail to Terrahina Creek, up to Gladys Lake, across to Hall Lake and then down toward Teslin Lake and south to Hayes River. That was his area. He said he understood that Oros spent most of his time south of Hayes River and, under those circumstances, it wasn't surprising they had never met before. Oros didn't answer him. How could this man know everything about him, while he knew nothing of the German?

What the German said made good sense but it was just too good. When he talked, it sounded like he had learned his information from textbooks. It was missing the animation of a man whose knowledge is gained firsthand. Still, Oros remembered, he might have believed Gunter if it weren't for the one most significant detail which gave him away in the end—Gunter's fingernails. They were clean. They were the nails of a businessman. Of someone whose hands don't touch the earth. Don't get dirty. Their rounded tips were white, unbroken, and without a trace of dirt under them. He said he had walked down the trail from Atlin, 150 miles to the northwest, and was on his way out to Dease Lake through Tahltan.

More bullshit! Oros knew. Nobody walks 150 miles through bush, alone, with a seventy pound pack, without getting dirt under his nails. Nobody! Oros was sure then that Gunter, or whoever he was, was neither acting alone nor with an innocent purpose in coming into Oros' camp.

Oros didn't know what to do. He had imagined them to be well-trained but Gunter was better than he feared in his worst nightmare. He hadn't heard the engine but the German could only have flown in. It might have glided silently in, the last mile with its engine off, watching the smoke from his fire; but however it came in, there was a plane out there somewhere and Gunter was not alone. He could only conclude that they wanted to be sure they had him before they closed in on him.

When Gunter was repacking his tea to leave, Oros considered jumping him, but Gunter never turned his back to him and Oros' ax was across the camp, twenty feet away. Even his rifle was out of reach. Although Oros was only half the German's age, there was an agility and confidence to the way the German moved that ruled out a hand-to-hand fight. And Gunter was armed. The .44 was strapped to his hip.

Suddenly then, without warning, Gunter had pulled out a small instamatic camera from an outside pocket of his jacket and, in one motion, stood, raised it to his eyes, and pointed it at Oros. In that instant, Oros recoiled, reeling backward. Clutching a length of cord he had been holding, he started to rise up when Gunter asked, "Do you mind if I take your picture?"

The memory of that moment still drew beads of perspiration over Oros' face. So deeply was Oros lost in that time past that when the wolf howl drifted over his camp and stirred the dogs, he heard in his mind only their stirrings on that earlier occasion. Their timing was perfect. Gunter was playing with him then. Absolutely exposed and powerless, he stared back at the German, who watched him through the camera lens.

Gunter didn't wait for any reply before the shutter snapped with a loud click. Oros remembered best the face behind the camera, the German's face grinning madly at him. He'd never forget it. It seemed to Oros that all the German wanted was a souvenir before the execution. A modern scalp.

"Well," the German said immediately after taking his picture, "I've got to push on."

Gunter hoisted his pack up over his shoulders and fixed a tumpline across his forehead. Just before he disappeared down the trail, he turned around to look back and their eyes met, locking for a long moment. Oros could feel that Gunter had penetrated through them into his soul and was thrilling at the fear he found there.

"Maybe we'll meet again," Gunter called out. And then he was gone.

And as soon as the German was clear out of sight, Oros threw together his own things and fled.

If he took to the high country along the treeline over the open granite faces, he would have fairly flown; but pursuit was easier there, too, and so he chose to follow the series of bog swamps and shallow lakes that ran north toward Hutsigola, keeping to the worst of the country. These were the swamps that kill dogs and drown caribou and Oros remembered the hell he went though inching his way forward, fighting the muck that sucked him down trying to pull him under and the deadfalls, huge tangles of trees piled and thrown together like match sticks from spring floods, that he crawled through tearing his clothes and cutting his flesh as he portaged the dogs, one at a time, on his back over the worst of it. It was summer then and the nights were brighter than the days of winter. Clouds of flies followed them for days, sapping their strength and driving them mad until he couldn't tell any longer whether it was night or day. He just pushed on and on and on until, in the end—the dogs long past exhaustion and nearly dead, his own face swollen from bites and crusted with blood—delirious and barely conscious, he was unable to move any farther and simply collapsed.

God, it was awful, he thought, remembering it all.

He opened his eyes and tried to focus on the night sky to rid himself of the memories, but he still saw only the summer sky, bright and dancing in the heavens where there should have been darkness. He closed his eyes again and cursed angrily, shaking his head roughly to bring himself back. He could feel the night's chill on his face and the spongy ground beneath his back; but when he opened his eyes again nothing had changed. The sky was still bright in the dead of night.

Colored lights, silently exploded into long fingers that stretched thousands of miles in an instant around the globe. Suddenly he realized what he was seeing and relaxed.

"Ah, my friend, you had me fooled," Oros whispered.

The clouds had cleared even more and above them the aurora borealis was dancing in the upper atmosphere. Silent explosions of light that rippled through the frigid air of space with a visual warmth that comforted even as it excited the senses.

Oros lay back, stretched his arms out of his bag and crossed them under his head to watch the show. As he exhaled, his breath frosted but he was glad now of the temperature. Thinking of Gunter Lishy had disturbed him so deeply that his head under his tangled hair was burning with the heat of his own steaming sweat. He wouldn't think of Gunter any more tonight. He didn't have to. Gunter could do nothing to him now. In fact, he thought, that was cause for celebration and his dancing partner was already on the floor, burning with desire and wild energy. Only she was thousands of miles away and cold as ice.

Chapter Six

February 1973: Bev in her tight jeans straddled the wooden seat of the high-backed wicker chair. Her arms crossed along the top of the back, she rested her chin on her hands and studied Oros' naked body in the subdued light of the coal oil lamps as he washed in front of the stove from a shallow soapy basin at his feet. She liked the look of his hard, muscled body and the way he moved so easily. Thinking of him as a living sculpture, an aesthetical pleasing form, titillated her unfocused desires. As he bathed, he seemed to her to concentrate all his attention on the simple task of getting soap under every bit of dirt and sweat that had accumulated since the last bath a week ago, leaving her free to enjoy the show he was offering on whatever terms she—his sole audience—wished.

Bev had been reserved this cold February night, mostly sitting quietly watching him. He was flattered by the attention but apart from trying to amuse her, he had done nothing to find out what was bothering her, preferring to wait for her to tell him in her own time. He had no warning, no indication at all, how important this night would be in his life; but not knowing spared him for a while to enjoy an evening he would long remember. For his part, Oros was convinced his life was finally taking form. The meditations and his Zen reading had worked to clear his thinking to the point that his own writing, reflecting his more careful thought, had never been as poignantly descriptive and lucid. And physically—except for a short period just after reading Jethro Kloss' *Back to Eden* when he thought he had aluminum poisoning and vowed as a result never to cook with aluminum again—he was feeling healthier than he had in a long time. Since Christmas he had grown closer to his friends, too, particularly Ben and Bev, here in the cabin, and Neil. They were so much a part of his life and figured so prominently in his future plans that he wondered how he ever got by without them.

On this cold, quiet evening, listening to the ticking of the stove and watching Oros wash, Bev wasn't thinking of sex. At least not at first. They had all seen each other often enough in the nude. Even had there been some modesty initially, living together in the same one-room cabin over the past few winter months would have dispelled most of it. As it was, they were never much concerned about nudity and bathing had been a public event for everybody for as long as they had been together. Ben and Bev were even relatively free in their love-making—Ben bluffly saying he wasn't going to deny himself because another man was in the same room. Oros tried to appear discreet and casual about that. Regardless of what he thought privately, he didn't want any friction or disputes to arise between them which might ultimately threaten to disturb his own place in the very unit which had given him both a home and a necessary solitude.

He would have been surprised to know that there had been times when Bev was making love to Ben in their bed that she was thinking only of him—lying alone in his own bed across the open room and listening in the dark. More than once as she imagined him growing excited by the sounds of her moaning desire and cries of ecstasy, she had climaxed to the vision in her mind of his own enraptured face—the vision and his silent presence in the room sharply heightening the experience she was in fact having with Ben. They had never been physically intimate but this night while the opportunity was once again presenting itself, Bev had other things on her mind, more pressing concerns that she wanted to discuss with him, yet she was unsure of how best to approach the subject.

Oros had sat facing Bev, on the edge of his bed, an old, metal framed, army cot with a thin rubbery mattress, and had stripped down, tossing his clothes with a high-handed abandon as he removed them, one article at a time, onto a bench at the foot of his bed which he and Ben had built together, using unpeeled spruce saplings. It was a crude looking thing but, together with some other furniture they had made with similar materials, it served its purpose in helping to fill their cabin.

The two of them were alone—Ben had gone off into the city for two days with some undeclared business—and Oros was in an exuberant mood. Leaning back across his bed to pull off his jeans, he had been laughing: "You know, I can't get over that interview with Nixon's mother, where she says she remembers Dick best for the 'oh, so careful way he always used to mash the potatoes.' I see the spuds getting bigger and bigger and Nixon riding a masher the size of the Empire State Building to flatten them. And rivers of gravy. Lakes of melted butter. Be a good title for a book, don't you think: 'The Mashed Potato Presidency?' Or maybe, 'The Gravy Years.'"

"Let's not knock him too hard," Bev said. "He's stopped the war!"

Oros sat upright to take off his shirt. "There's something strange behind that. Only a week before Christmas Nixon was pounding Hanoi with all the B-52s in the air force. Remember we were talking about it at the party at Neil's? And we all figured the fighting would never stop? And then, just a couple of weeks ago—out of nowhere—we hear the Paris Peace Accords were signed and the war's supposed to be over. Shit, I'm not going to believe that until we're all out of 'Nam. I think Tricky Dick's just trying to pull another fast one."

"No, it's true! I talked to mom last week by phone and she said they're already coming back. Apparently there's all kinds of celebrations going on around the country. Ben said some of the people here are going back, too, now that the draft is over."

"Well they're stupid then," Oros said. Naked, he leaned down to reach under his bed and brought out a pair of worn sneakers to put over his bare feet. "Uncle Sam isn't forgiving any of us. They've already said we'll continue to be prosecuted even though they say there's no war left to fight now."

"You'd go back if it was safe, wouldn't you?" Bev asked. Oros stood up, wearing only the running shoes on his feet, and Bev saw that he had the necklace which she had given to him at the winter solstice party, around his neck. She tried to concentrate her focus on the necklace as he stepped closer to her toward the stove beside the table where he was warming the large bucket of rinse water, but her eyes kept slipping down, lower, to his loins, breaking her train of thought as she struggled with her question. "You only came up here because of the draft, didn't you? So you can go back now—I mean, if it was safe."

Oros carefully poured out some water into a basin at his feet then replaced the bucket on the stove before he answered her. "Bev, I guess it was the war once. But not anymore. Even if everything was forgiven, I'm not the same person I was before. In fact, everything's changed. People are different than they were ten years ago—really different! People have a different will than they had and now that the war's over, if it is, they're going to be searching for real alternatives, for new insights and values. We're right where we should be to show them the way; you know that. There's a new revolution coming, something really big and we're going to be part of it. Right here."

As he was talking he had dipped a washcloth into the water and wetting his body first, he started to soap himself thoroughly. With nothing more to say on the subject, he closed his eyes and began singing loudly, pretending he was alone inside a shower stall, while he took particular care to wash those parts of himself that tended to sweat most profusely, all the while dripping soap and splashing water all over the floor. Bev hadn't heard him, the sound of his voice when he spoke trailing off in her mind as the distraction of his naked body grew.

Still holding the cloth, he stopped, apparently finished, and then, turning toward her, he came directly over to stand almost toe to toe in front of her. With a merry, boyish expression on his face, his eyebrows high, his light eyes twinkling, he said, "I guess if I don't come right out and ask you to wash my back, you're not going to volunteer for it, are you?"

Rivulets of water, white with soap bubbles, ran down his chest and collected in his navel before spilling over in a stream into the narrow, pencil line of hair that began there and grew more thickly lower down. Bev was acutely aware of his genitals, close enough to her fingers wrapped around the top of her chair that she would brush him if she opened up her hands, and she reacted, blushing, suddenly embarrassed by her own immediate response to the intimate physical closeness. Caught off guard and flushed by the unexpected rise of a powerful desire, she tried to hide her feelings, taking both his shoulders in her hands as she rose to her feet and turned him around away from her to face his back.

"You're dripping water all over the floor!" It was all she could think of to say and he laughed in reply.

"Does it matter? Does it really matter?" he asked and he turned his head around to look at her with his eyebrows upraised again and a superior smile on his face.

She put two fingers carefully into his cheek and gently forced his face back as she replied nervously and inappropriately, "Don't be mean!" But she swung her leg out around the seat and, pulling the cloth from his hand, walked over to the basin as he followed closely behind, quietly amused. She still didn't intend to do anything more physically intimate than simply wash him and he had no real expectation of making sexual contact with her—but he was enjoying himself immensely.

Plunging the cloth into the water, she lifted it out with deliberate recklessness, spilling water everywhere and slapping it hard up against his back, she started rubbing him vigorously while he hummed happily with his eyes closed, his head back, his feet slightly apart, reveling in the feel of her hands running over his body. As she washed him down lower, he detected a subtle change in her touch. Taking her time, she exercised greater care, pressing more softly in slow, sweeping motions. Finally, she finished and tossed the cloth down into the basin.

"Adam never had it so good," she said and slapped him lightly on his rear. Oros turned around then to look at her with a broad smile spreading across his face and Bev stepped backward. Something about his expression evoked in her a feeling of age as though—while she was in fact only two years his senior—she was witnessing the hopelessly vulnerable expectation of youth in love. Having seen the look before in her life, she smiled back, shaking her head at the same time at her own betrayal, which drew an unknowing grin from him in response. Walking to the stove, she lifted up the heavy bucket and, holding it by its wire handle with both of her small hands straining under the weight, she jerked her chin up toward the door saying: "Outside, lover boy! Time for you to remember where you're living. You'll think twice about California after this is over."

"You just better be quick about it." he said, asserting himself with a threatening tone as he went to stand shivering by the tightly closed door. Wearing only his wet running shoes and the necklace, his body was already steaming in the cooler air away from the stove. On the other side of the door, the temperature was twenty-eight below.

"Have I ever let you down before?" Bev asked, replying rhetorically, but she wondered as she spoke whether he thought she ever had. She hoped not. Not now—now that she was leaving him forever.

"Here goes!" he yelled as he whipped open the door. Screaming as loudly as he could his imitation of a wolf howl, he ran outside to stand near the entrance. They had all loved to cry out in the night, exhausting their lungs, knowing there was nobody to complain. It was one of the few freedoms the space provided that they all agreed upon.

Familiar with the routine, Bev did not immediately follow him out but stood within the relative warmth of the open doorway watching the mists working around his body and waited for him to tell her when he was ready. The moment his hot, wet body entered the night's crisply frozen air, it was enveloped in a vaporous cloud of fog of its own making, dense enough to obscure his outline as he stood in the light of the open doorway. As much of a shock as it was to suffer these extremes of temperature, it was the closest any of them in Alaska had been able to get to the rich sensations of a sauna and snow bath, and it produced the same exhilarating, skin-tingling qualities that made them feel so physically alive. Although thoroughly enjoying himself, Oros was now screaming out a constant stream of sound that was more like the agonized cries of a bound Prometheus than of a man free from pain, but it was only part of the ritual and Bev laughed to hear the total abandon with which he gave voice.

"Oh, shit it's cold!" he yelled at last. "Do it now! Quickly!" He clasped his hands behind his neck and held his elbows up to expose his soapy underarms to Bev, who giggled as she stepped out to splash water, steaming like molten rock, from out of the galvanized bucket over his body, aiming at the areas that showed the greatest need.

"It looks to me like you need to be cooled off a little," she said as she playfully ran her fingers under his testicles, cupping them quickly in her palm before she slid her grip lightly the length of his erect penis.

"Oh God, no!" he yelled the moment her touch broke off. "Don't stop. It'll freeze and fall off, I swear!" And then, hooting loudly, he laughed. He loved to bath outside. Whatever the temperature, he always felt better for it afterward and, tonight, it was so far proving to be even more worthwhile.

"Well, we don't want to lose it that way, do we?" she said laughing. Upending the bucket overtop his head, the rest of the hot water washed in a sheet over his body, carrying away all traces of soap. "Okay, that's it. Into the house," she ordered. "You're cleaner than a whistle."

Spinning around on the ground, steam rising in thick clouds from his naked body, still running in warm water, he marched from the smoking but rapidly freezing puddle where he had been standing, stiff-jointed and deliberately robotic as though he were a creature of the ice, half frozen himself, back into the cabin and directly over to the stove.

"I've got to thaw out," he said, trembling his voice. "Look how stiff I've become!"

Bev followed him in, closing the door behind her and laughing continuously. It had taken less than thirty seconds to rinse him off outside. "It's not that bad," she said consoling him, pretending to take him seriously. "Come here and I'll dry you off...if you can still move?"

"I'm thawed!" he quickly announced, immediately compliant. "Back to fluid motion...except for this little bit of me here," he added looking down as though in surprise toward his crotch as he explained, "which seems to have gone into shock and is locked in place." He was only too glad to have her touching him. It had been a long time since he had had a woman and he was aching for the intimacy of the release.

"You should be ashamed of yourself! Reacting like this with an old friend!" Bev said referring to his sudden sexual arousal. But she stood up close to him, reaching for his face above hers, and started drying it for him tenderly. When she finished with his eyes, he opened them and looked directly into hers for an instant before she averted her gaze.

"Hold your arms out," she ordered and he lifted them straight toward her while she wiped them briskly. Working her way up his arms to his broad shoulders, she stepped in between them close to his body and with her warm breath falling on his chest, she placed the towel against it, covering the sparse growth of hair he had there and, holding the towel with both hands, rubbed him in a circular, massaging motion as she dried him off, lower and lower.

His back to the stove, he watched, unbelieving, until all he could see was the thick black hair of her head hanging in long, waving rolls over her face and across her neck as she bent over to wipe his taut stomach muscles. His nerves jerked across his stomach in involuntary spasms to the touch of her fingers which lightly brushed his skin. He closed his eyes again and smiled, filled with the delights of a totally absorbing sensual experience. His back, warmed by the fire, was hot enough that a thin film of sweat slowly developed under the water droplets and then, collecting in the hollows alongside his spine, ran down them in gentle trickles while his chest still tingled from the numbing sharpness of the biting air and the blood that was now rushing up to the surface with the pressure of Bev's hands behind the towel. His face, too, was growing hotter with anticipation, hoping he wasn't mistaken but unsure enough of himself and the situation that he didn't dare touch her or speak for fear of breaking the spell. Ever so slowly, he lowered his arms to his sides. His feet, still encased in the wet running shoes, were painfully frozen, but he didn't care. Hot and cold at the same time, it was the combination of physical sensations that he loved and that drew him closer and deeper into the moment until nothing else existed except his body, his intense, uninhibited desire, and the woman who had now gone down to her knees in front of him.

Rubbing his hips and his thighs, she moved even closer, but he was aware only of her delicate breath on his penis as she exhaled deeply before the warm wetness of her mouth closed over it.

He groaned quickly in relief and happiness, impulsively reaching his hands around her head bobbing smoothly back and forth. Entwining his fingers though her hair, he tried to hold back the orgasm which was building rapidly inside him. Driving with its own energy, too powerful to resist, he went with it instead and clutching her head tightly to steady her rhythmic motion, he began plunging himself forward into her with a wanton force as he moaned loudly, consumed with the intensity of the feeling as, having drawn together all the vigor within him, it burst out in one long sustained rush—flooding into her.

Suddenly empty and weak-kneed, he broke out into laughter, embarrassed by his lack of control. Leaning down, he raised her to her feet and kissed her softly on her lips to reestablish contact; but she couldn't look at him, feeling both foolish and, with her own desire not the least abated by his quick climax, transparent and exposed.

"It's your turn," he said calmly, smiling with the new control he had over her as he confidently put his hands around her waist and, slipping them up under her heavy woolen sweater, slid them to her full breasts where he stroked her nipples with his fingertips. Bev stood before him, passive and unresisting. Puzzled by his meaning, her eyes darted quickly to his and then away again, but she didn't say anything.

"Bath time," he explained eagerly. "I want to wash you down now."

"Oh, no! It's too cold. I don't need a bath anyway...."

Still embarrassed, her voice trailed away. Oros let his hands slide down the yielding softness of her slightly rolling waist to rest them over her hip bones, just under the top of her jeans, and pulled her closer. Then, bending low enough to see up into her downturned and unsmiling face, he grinned broadly at her, trying to bring her out again.

"Hey listen! You're not going to tell me 'that's all' are you?... I mean, after bringing me out here to this place, plying me with drugs and alcohol, and then taking advantage of me like that when my pants were down, I expect a little consideration! You're an evil woman if you think it's right for you to take like that without giving anything in return."

When Bev laughed finally, he added quickly, "Ah, I knew you weren't that kind of a girl. C'mon, lift up your arms, I'll be real quick about it."

"I'll bet you will," she said smiling, having made up her mind at last to go along with it.

"I meant with washing you," He added with a raised voice, exaggerating his true reaction.

"I know that's what you mean," Bev explained, slightly amused but not entirely convincing.

"Okay?" he asked, carefully now, changing the subject.

"Okay," she replied softly.

Both naked, Bev watched him working as he hurried about the room quickly filling the bucket for her bath with fresh water and placing it on the stove before stuffing the firebox with kindling to get the blaze as hot as he could and she felt glad in her heart that she was leaving him with this little bit of happiness.

Later, buried under the thickness of two unzipped sleeping bags, Oros was supremely content. Within the narrowness of his bed, he lay on his side close to the wall, pressed up against Bev's body. She lay on her back with her hands behind her head staring up at the flickering shadows on the ceiling cast by the lamps, both of them listening to the late-night dedications of songs on Ben's portable, battery-operated radio. It was the only piece of twentieth century technology in the cabin, none of them laying claim to even a watch. Oros liked it that way. Even in his diaries, he had stopped using dates since Christmas and had burned the only calendar they had. Outside, stuck into the snow, was a spruce pole which he could see from the door. That was the only calendar he needed—when it fell, spring would have arrived. Oros called it his seasonal clock and that, together with possibly a sundial, were the only instruments to measure time that he wanted.

"There's a timelessness here," he said to her whispering. "Right now, in this cabin, with you. I feel like this night will never end but will go on forever, indefinitely, endlessly...as though we've somehow transcended time or maybe we died and this is heaven."

"Sounds horrible!" Bev said. "To be imprisoned forever in darkness and ice!"

Oros watched the motion of her thick lips as she spoke. There was a husky quality to her voice, a slight raspiness which he loved to listen to. "No, its wonderful!" he insisted fervently. If eternity could be like this—this moment captured forever—I'd want nothing more from life. Ever!"

Bev raised her head off the pillow to look at him and then said, "You're crazy." Joking with him and filled with goodwill, she was stung by his reaction.

Oros had been caressing her stomach, rolling her loose skin between his fingers and sliding his hand back and forth down between her legs and then up to her navel; but he suddenly pulled away from her, jerking himself up stiffly onto his left elbow.

"Why are you calling me crazy?" he asked drily, his voice taking on a distant and flat tone as he detached himself from her.

"Well, I'm sorry! Shit, it's just an expression. I didn't mean it.... You know what I think of you!"

His voice was still cold. "No, I don't!"

"Well, do you think I'd be here laying beside you if I didn't care about you?"

Oros felt somewhat appeased but the caustic quality of his tone remained. "Sure you would!" he answered. "You're just a horny bitch!"

Bev's reply was quick but without any malice. "And you're a horny bastard!"

Oros paused for a moment and he laughed. "Yes. I am!... You're absolutely right.... Let's do it again."

Bev let her head fall back to the pillow and she sighed deeply. "Oh, no! Michael, why do you do this to me?"

"Because I love you...you ready?"

Bev looked at him and shook her head. In spite of herself, the expression on his face made her smile. He was so eager. "Not right now," she answered. "I'm still tired...let's wait a bit, it's so nice just laying here. I like what you were doing with your hand, don't stop."

He lay back down resting his head on his elbow and took her wide, dark nipple into his mouth, sucking on it until it stood out taut on its own, hard between his lips, while she murmured sounds of contentment.

"Now?" he asked, teasing her.

"Not yet," she said and then asked, "Can you hear the wind?"

It was impossible to miss. Oros had been listening to it all night. Blowing in under the door with a steady whine, it was also gusting down the chimney with dull, popping sounds as the cold, heavy air pushed against the hot air rising from the fire, almost threatening to blow the stove pipes off and forcing at the same time more smoke than usual into the cabin. He didn't mind the smell of smoke inside. Even when it was dense enough to cloud the air, it only produced a mild, heady sensation of rich thickness which he liked.

"Yeah, I can hear it," he answered, burying her nipple in his cheek as he rested his face on her breast and stared over her into the room with a fondness he felt for the space. His earlier mood had been completely restored. "It's the sound of the purple darkness, frozen outside, that makes this cabin and our fire so precious," he explained to her in a dreamy voice as though half asleep. "The smell of your body, the touch of your skin is like the earth to me—wholesome and alive. You're Eve, mother of the earth, and I am Adam, the only man, and the two of us are all alone, surrounded by an endless night in a vast, vast plain of emptiness...there is nothing out there...everything that exists is right here. You're draining me of more than my seed, woman. You're taking everything that's made me a hollow, wanting man and have returned me to the Garden of Eden where I have no more pain and no desire."

"You're not a hollow person," Bev said, misunderstanding him completely. In fact, although she sometimes considered him childlike, he was more complex than she could understand.

He laughed. "I meant incomplete," he said kindly. "This night I feel I've reached Nirvana—you've made me feel complete."

"You're really happy?" Bev asked, still unsure.

"Truly and completely," Oros answered honestly.

"I'm really glad I could do that for you. You deserve to be happy," she said, feeling the serenity of success and, excited now, ready to receive him again.

They made love slowly this time, wordlessly working into each other's bodies as the endless winter's night grew deeper. When they finished, Oros reached over to the floor under his bed and brought out the old metal snuff box to roll some joints from its contents. It had been grown locally and wasn't very strong. They had to smoke a lot of it to feel any effects.

"This is Rene's dope, isn't it?" Bev asked as she took the joint from Oros after he lit it.

"Yeah, he told me it's been specially bred to increase horniness."

"You're NOT ready to do it again?" Bev asked incredulously.

"You just wait till I finish a few of these," he answered.

"I don't know...smoking Rene's dope...we might end up like him... he's pretty weird. I think he's been here too long. He's bushed."

"Yeah," Oros agreed, "he's a strange dude, alright. Told me he harvested over eight pounds from that little greenhouse of his...said he figured it was almost enough to get him through the winter."

Bev giggled. "Shit! I'd need a lot more than dope to get me through another winter here."

"You've got a lot more than that." Oros laughed as he pulled her hand under the covers to lay it over his penis, limp and still wet from their sex.

She jerked it away, ready to make a reply, but changed her mind, thinking instead that finally this was a good time to approach the subject, now that he was in a relaxed mood.

She tried to sound nonchalant. "Michael, you ever think of going back home?"

"I am home, silly chickadee. Where do you think we've been living all along."

"You know what I mean. Really home. Back down to the States."

Oros laughed at the question as though it was ridiculous. "To where?"

Pretending it was just an idea, Bev asked, "Your mom's in Kansas, isn't she?" And when he nodded his head absently, she continued. "Then Kansas. Or back to New Mexico...or Colorado. You said you were happy there. Or even maybe California."

Oros was silent for a long time before he said, "What if I get caught? You know I was locked up once before...and I swore it'd never happen again. I'd die if I ever got locked up."

Bev was surprised. "You never told me that before. What happened?"

Oros shook his head, not looking at her. "Nothing! Never mind, it's not important. Anyway, you read Obi's letter yesterday. Marcia's parents tipped the FBI about Paul's real name and they got him. I don't want to go back and live in fear of getting picked up."

"Who's going to inform on you?" Bev asked, disappointed by his reaction. She didn't really believe he'd leave and go with her but she had to ask him anyway. It was the least she could do.

"That's not the point," Oros insisted without any explanation.

"Ben's not afraid to go back," she said provokingly.

"Listen!" He raised his voice as he turned to her, feeling insulted and angry. "I'm not afraid of anything! I'm just happy here! I'm never going to leave. Okay!"

Oros lay back down and they both fell silent, Oros listening to the radio's sounds mixing with the warm crackling of the fire and Bev hearing only the cold wind blowing outside. After a while, Oros became aware of the distance growing between them and, waiting until after the song on the radio finished, he asked, "What are you thinking?"

"Oh, I was just wondering if I'll see Tony again...now that the war's over, I guess he'll be coming back to the States too."

"You still care about him?" Oros' eyebrows came up in complete surprise. Bev had never said much about Tony and, in consequence, Oros simply assumed she never thought about him.

"I don't know...sometimes I don't...then sometimes I do."

"Well, what'd you marry him for?"

Bev wasn't sure herself. "I don't know...maybe it was stupid." She had done a lot of things she couldn't really explain. They just seemed right at the time and she'd do them. "Can you believe I lived my whole life in the San Fernando Valley and never saw a Mexican? So the first one I saw, I married. Just cause he was different from everybody else, I guess."

Oros wasn't impressed with her answer. Now that their own relationship had come so far, he wanted to learn everything he could about her and how she thought of things. Mostly, he had only wanted to talk about himself before. Not about his life but his ideas.

"Why didn't it work out?" he asked.

"Shit, I don't know that either. I thought it was all good...and then, just after Brandy was born, he left one day and never came back. He never said nothing, just left! I had no idea what happened to him. Then I heard he was in Nam. The asshole went and joined up. He wasn't even drafted! I guess he just had to get away."

Oros passed the joint back to her and watched her face glowing in the light of its tip. As she drew in a deep lungful, he exhaled his. Speaking through the smoke which came out in gusts with his words, his voice, rising as he spoke, froze Bev, so completely bitter was the sudden enmity that possessed him.

"You'd be lucky if Tony was killed," he said coldly, speaking with real malice and a deep loathing. "The stupid bastard deserves a bullet in his fat face!"

"MICHAEL!" Bev yelled his name at him, so strange was it for her to hear him talk this way. She had known him as such a reserved person, almost shy but always filled with caring. In the shadowy light of the lamps, even his face had taken on a distorted appearance, which frightened her. But her cry had done something and he changed again, looking back at her blankly.

"You got no call to say such things," she scolded him as one would a child. "That was an awful thing to say. Nobody deserves to die. Especially not him—he's my husband."

"He deserted you," Oros said simply, as though that were reason enough.

"People leave each other all the time," she argued, still frightened. "It's normal. Lots of marriages don't work. We all make mistakes. If it was his mistake to leave, it was mine for marrying him. And his face isn't fat either! It's lots thinner than yours is!"

Oros wasn't listening to her. Removing the joint from her fingers, he knocked the ash off the end with the tip of his fingernail and took one last drag from it before mashing it into a log of the wall beside his head.

"I made a mistake once, too," he said finally in a secretive, confidential tone.

"What's that?" Bev asked, glad the subject had changed and mildly curious.

"I didn't go to Woodstock," he answered.

"Oh, shit! That's hardly a mistake!"

"It's not?"

She knew he was acting now, pretending to have been struck by a revelatory discovery, and laughed. "No, it's not!"

"Well that's a relief," he said. "It's bothered me for years, thinking it was a mistake."

Bev barely resisted the impulse to call him crazy again and, grateful for the humor, asked, "So why didn't you go?"

Oros lit up another joint before replying. "We were living at Erie at the time and I knew the parking would be a nightmare. I hate crowds."

"And you're sorry you didn't go?"

"Nope, never had any regrets." He grinned at her, holding the joint tightly between his teeth with his lips drawn back.

"Oh, you ass," she yelled and punched him on the shoulder he had close to hers.

"Ow!... No wonder he left you!" He laughed but stopped when she told him it wasn't funny. "No, it wasn't," he apologized. "I'm sorry. I didn't mean it."

"Where's Erie, anyway?" she asked.

"In Pennsylvania. Right on the lake...halfway between Buffalo and Cleveland."

"What were you doing there? I thought you always lived in the west."

"No. My folks moved out there for a while too. We moved around quite a bit."

"You're lucky to have done so much with your parents. I've never been anywhere except California and here."

"I'm not lucky," Oros said seriously. "You want to know something I haven't told anybody?"

Bev couldn't tell if he was joking or not. "Not if you don't want to tell me," she replied playfully.

"I do. I want to be right up front with you. I don't want to keep any secrets from you anymore."

"Is this a true confession?"

He ignored her question, determined to tell her. "I don't have a father."

"Oh, right! Bev said. You just growed up, did you?" She was smiling.

"I never did."

He looked so serious that Bev considered it but she still didn't believe him.

"Michael, you talk about him all the time. You even brag about him."

"It was all bullshit," he explained, not looking at her at all. "That guy I mentioned is just some dude who came along afterward. My real father is some prick I never met. He fucked off on mom when she was pregnant...he did the same thing to her Tony did to you.... It's the same fucking drama over and over. That's one of the reasons I always liked you. Sometimes when I look at you, I think of mom and how it must have been for her when I was a baby."

Bev took it all in slowly and then asked, self-consciously, "You must think I'm really awful then."

Oros was genuinely surprised. "Me? No. Why?"

"For leaving Brandy with my mom and taking off on her too."

"No." Oros paused, searching his own feelings. "I never even thought of that. I just figured we had something important in common."

"And what do you think of your real father?" she asked, thinking he might give her some insight into the feelings Brandy might have when she grew up.

Oros laughed but it wasn't at all a friendly sound. There was a recklessness to his moods, an uncontrolled venting of his feelings that she hadn't seen before and which she didn't like at all. She had only this night witnessed an undercurrent of hostility he had kept so well hidden before. She watched him anxiously after he laughed. As he took another long drag off the new joint he had, she wished he'd stop. She was sorry now they had smoked any of it.

"So you see," he said at last, voicing a deep secret, "I really am a bastard!" And then he laughed, a strange and disturbing laugh, before he laid his head down on the pillow to stare up at the open peaked ceiling. Remembering.

"What do I think of him? Good ol' dad?" He stopped to take another lungful off the joint before continuing slowly and calmly as though telling a story about someone else. Long time ago, I used to think that I wanted to meet him. To get to know him and be his friend, if not his son. I was just a kid then but I used to dream about him, wondering where he was, what he was doing, who he was. Sometimes I'd imagine he was really rich and he'd find me and we'd do all kinds of incredible things together. You know what I mean?"

"I guess so," Bev replied. "I guess that's what all kids think when they're missing a parent."

Oros laughed a horrible laugh again. "That's a funny word, missing. He wasn't missing me. And when I got older, I stopped missing him too. I still wanted to meet him, though. Just once. To see what he looked like, to see if we were the same kind of people—so much is in the genes. But after that, I didn't even care about him anymore. I still wanted to find him but only 'cause I wanted to kill him...Ha! I used to dream about killing him. I'd look at people on the street his age who looked like me and wonder if they were him and I wanted to kill them all just to be sure I got him."

Oros flicked the ash off the joint and after taking another drag, passed it over to Bev without looking at her. "Fuck, that bastard really got to me!" She took it from him and then quickly dropped it on the floor beside her, carefully so Oros wouldn't notice. Absorbed in his own thoughts, he was barely aware of anything else and he continued.

"But now I don't give a fuck about finding him anymore. I'm through searching for him.... I only hope he's already dead and rotting somewhere. If not, and I run into him, I'll kill him.... Where's the joint?"

"I finished it," Bev lied, hoping there'd be no more but she said nothing as he rolled out another one from his can and lit it. "How many of those do you have?" she asked.

"Enough to keep us for a week," he replied, passing it to her. His tone was normal yet Bev couldn't believe after having just said those things about his father that he could sound so complacently calm.

"No, I've had enough already. I don't want to get really stoned tonight. I've got to talk to you about some things."

Bev felt she couldn't put it off any longer. She had to tell him and get it over with but she wanted him to understand and agree with her that it was the best thing to do.

"What's that?" he asked.

She looked at his face and decided she couldn't tell him right out. "What do you think of me?" she asked instead to approach the subject indirectly.

"You're Eve," he said without elaborating.

"Honestly, I want to know. What kind of a person do you think I am?"

Oros raised himself up to look at her and grinned, misinterpreting her question as an offer of a new kind. "You're the moon goddess," he said. "Mother and lover that natives worship at night under the full moon to keep the earth fertile. You're the free spirit of the pioneer's wife. We're going to do everything together from now on, living our own lives, simply, in the woods away from the kind of material madness that's possessed everyone else. You're the kind of woman we need here to start a new society...and, if you really want to know how I feel about you, I'll tell you...you're perfect for me. Perfect!"

It wasn't at all what Bev wanted to hear. Instead of Oros agreeing

Alaska was no place for her and that she should leave, he was telling her how much he wanted her to stay. She certainly didn't share his feelings. Bev had come to hate Alaska and couldn't wait to leave.

"I don't mean that," she said nervously, looking pained as she tried to explain. "You just told me how you feel about your father leaving you and I've done the same thing to Brandy. I'm no better than he is."

"Of course you are!" he said quickly, wanting to reassure her. But she shook her head at him and didn't return his smile.

"No, I'm not. Really, I'm not. I know it. I hate myself for leaving her. You know I haven't seen my baby for so long now, she won't even recognize me when I get back. I have to go back, you know."

Oros' face lit up suddenly with the idea of a child joining their group. It would be a real family with children around, he thought, and said, "Why don't you bring her here?" He made it sound as though the idea was novel, the solution, a simple one.

Bev's face reflected the horror and disgust she felt for it as her own carefully guarded feelings washed out in a torrent. "HERE? To this shitty little cabin? What's she going to do here? Stay locked up like a prisoner, like the rest of us, and play on this filthy floor? Or is she supposed to play outside in the snow? Christ, she'd be dead in an hour! At home she lives in a good house and plays outside all the time in the yard where it's clean and warm, and she's with good people. Shit! What's she going to do here? Sit on the edge of the bed and watch me fucking Benjamin? Or you? Never! I'd never bring her to this kind of place!"

Oros put his hand to her cheek stroking it gently and asked softly, "Why you being so hard on yourself. You're not to blame."

"That's bullshit! Of course I am. I'm her mother." And then as she realized there was genuine concern for her showing in his face, she softened her own tone and told him as plainly as she could. "Jim, I've got to go. You know that, don't you?"

But he didn't get past the name. "Why'd you say Jim? I thought you were going to call me Michael whenever we were alone."

"Oh, it's not important," she said, suddenly tired.

"Yes it is," he insisted.

"Alright Michael, I forgot...but I can't stay here any longer. I've started to hate myself. I only meant to come for a couple of months and I've been away for over a year. It was supposed to be a holiday, you know. I got so fucked up at home, I had to get away to straighten out my head."

She quit talking when she realized that incredibly Oros was still smiling and waiting to speak.

"Doesn't that prove it to you?" he asked. She raised her head and stared at him without answering, so he continued. "You're not fucked up now, are you? California fucked you up; Alaska healed you. You came here for a holiday and you stayed. This is where it's at. You're sitting on it and you didn't even know it. You're home. You belong here."

She shook her head sadly. Somehow, he was still missing the point. She knew it was her fault. She wasn't being very clear. Bev had hoped he'd understand and accept her decision but he was resisting her, thinking the issue was still open.

"Michael, this has never been my home. I don't like Alaska. Being here has made me realize how much I had back home. It's just time for me to leave now. We all have our own lives to live."

She spoke with such conviction that Oros, for the first time, began to see that she was serious about leaving and a creeping level of desperation started to show itself inside him as he struggled with the idea that she, too, might go away and leave him. The way everybody else had. There was a pleading quality to his voice when he spoke. "You can't go back! California's crazy! You can't leave here. You and Ben are just about the best people I've ever known. You know I love both of you. You're my family; we're a unit. You can't break it up. I don't think I could live without you."

"Michael, please don't tell me that." Bev felt close to tears. "Besides, I don't believe you. You got along pretty good before we came along. Remember, I read all your journals."

"You're the only one who has. I never let anyone else see them before."

"Well, I'm sure you'll get along just fine without us."

"But I don't have to." Oros suddenly sounded sure of himself. As he spoke, his voice strengthened with conviction, absorbed and inflated by the message his own words were carrying.

"Remember you told me we'll probably always be doing something crazy, really spectacular? Well, I've always believed that, too. Our involvement in a super-project of some kind is inevitable. And it's true! Bev, this retreat we're going to build is it. I know it. It's going to be the start of something new. Something really big. It'll be the model for hundreds more. Bev, we're right at the beginning of a new era. Everything's pointing to it. Even Neil said so. Things are so fucked up, the country's going to explode unless there's a release. And we've got it. We're going to build it together, you and me and Ben and Neil. Why this is more important than any of us, than all of us put together. Bev, this is what we've been waiting for all our lives."

Bev heard him out and when he was finished, she felt sorry for him. Whether or not he really believed what he was saying, he was deeply mistaken if he thought the rest of them were still interested in his project. She always knew it was only a lonely man's dream.

"Michael I'm leaving!" She said it as straight as she could.

But he wasn't hearing her. Filled with his own visions of their future, he carried on, convinced she'd be swept along with the magnitude of it all.

"You can't leave now. There's too much to do here. The work will..."

Bev interrupted him bluntly. "Michael! Listen! I've been trying to tell you but you're not listening. I'm going home, Michael. I've already made the plans. I'm leaving."

Oros was struck dumb. The effects of his smoking increased his confusion. He had heard her clearly enough but the meaning was an impossible one and it numbed him inside, scrambling his thoughts. The greasy, unburned fumes lifting off the flames of the coal-oil lamps in thin, black streams had permeated the cabin with their acrid odor and he could taste the bitterness it left in his mouth. He felt a terrible weight crushing down on him with the slow realization that he was going to be left behind. Abandoned and alone. He could see from the look on her face that she wasn't joking. It was going to happen. All his mouth could form was the one most important word.

"When?"

"As soon as Ben can make the arrangements. That's why he went into the city—he's booking our flights."

"Ben's going too?" Oros' voice was completely flat—drained of everything. He couldn't imagine them both leaving. Slowly sitting up in bed, he stared down toward his feet, feeling genuinely empty and hollow now. "But this is your home," he said weakly.

"Michael, it's never been my home. You know that. This whole thing's just been a big trip for all of us, and it's turning into a bummer. We don't belong here anymore...and you don't either!"

Oros sat stiffly, immobilized, and she decided she should ask him now, knowing how terrible it was to feel left behind when people you loved moved away.

"Michael, we want you to come with us. Ben's going to stay with me at mom's until we can find our own place and you can stay with us too, if you want, until you get settled."

In the dim light of the lamp beside the bed, she watched his profile. The line of his mouth had hardened and his eyes were blinking rapidly as though to hold back the tears, causing her own to well as she tried to raise his spirits with an enthusiasm in her voice that she didn't really feel.

"We'll have such a good time. God, it's been so long since I've walked over a hot beach, I can hardly remember what it feels like. We'll go to the beach all the time...you can take up surfing. Shit, I bet you'd be a real good surfer. You'll love Brandy, too. We'll take her on picnics up into the mountains and to the beach..."

She stopped talking when she realized it wasn't having any effect on him; and when she tried again, she couldn't sense his feelings at all. He was so completely distant. She knew he loved the north but as much as she had tried to relate to it the way he did, she couldn't. There was nothing in Alaska for any of them as far as she was concerned. Only wilderness—empty bush for hundreds or thousands of miles—desolate, barren, devoid of life.

"Michael," she said, her voice heavy with the urgency she felt, "there's nothing here for you, either. It's been fun but it's over, Michael! It's time to go home.... You should be with people. You need people! You shouldn't be alone.... Will you come with us?"

She waited anxiously for his answer having exhausted everything she could think of to say. Until tonight she had thought she understood him pretty well, certainly better than anyone else did, but he had surprised her all night. He wasn't reacting at all the way she had expected.

His head jerked, lifting up, and started to turn slowly toward her, pivoting mechanically around on his neck until he was looking directly at her, over his shoulder, with an expression filled with loathing and suspicion. He had, earlier in the night, spoken with a feeling she never knew he possessed, but the tone and level of absolute disgust it had now was completely foreign and it terrified her as she lay naked and exposed beside him.

"So that's why you were asking me if I wanted to go back? You want to destroy me, don't you?"

She knew he meant it literally. He was looking at her as though she were an animal, something dangerous to be destroyed. "No! No, that's not right! I don't ever want to hurt you!"

"And what the fuck are you doing here right now?"

"I stayed behind to say good-bye. I didn't want to leave without telling you."

"You mean this was all a good-bye?" His face had changed again and now showed only anger. Bev could feel the relief wash over her. She understood anger and although it was hard for her to deal with hostility or rejection, there was at least a familiar face and mood glaring at her.

"I just wanted to give you something before I left."

"So you fucked me!"

"Michael, please..." she said as the tears welled up in her eyes again.

"While I'm telling you how happy I am with you and how this is our home and about all my plans here, you're preparing to leave. And you figure that'd make me happy!"

He yelled out his last sentence at her, ignoring the tears that were flowing freely down her cheeks, as she stared back at him, red-eyed and desperate, realizing the warmth of the evening was gone and everything good they had had together was crumbling apart.

"Well FUCK YOU!" he screamed at her. "No wonder your husband left you...you're a fucking bitch playing mind games!"

"Michael please," she pleaded, "I only wanted to say good-bye nicely.... I only wanted our last evening together to be good...and you were so happy..."

Oros turned his back to the wall to get as far from her as he could and watched the tears drop from her jaw to fall on her breast as she lay propped up on her side facing him. This distance from her restored some of the strength which had drained out of him and he began to react more calmly, his control returning.

"I don't need your charity—your fucking charity. Go fuck someone else who wants it."

"I'm sorry, honestly I am. I didn't want to hurt you.... I never did.

I hate to think of you being left here alone. I thought maybe you'd come with us..."

"What do you think? That I'm not strong enough to survive on my own?"

"No. I just thought you'd be better off away from here."

"Bullshit! You think I won't survive here, don't you."

"No, Michael, I don't."

"You're lying. You do, don't you?"

"YES!" She yelled back, unable to keep her feelings inside her. "Yes! I'm afraid for you! I wanted you to come with us. You need people. You can't live like this. Nobody can. Michael, you're changing. You've already changed and I don't like it. Everybody can tell. Something's happening to you here—you've gotten colder and colder! Christ, why do I have to tell you? Can't you see it? This place is doing something to you."

Oros sat silently on the bed against the wall listening to her, and when she finished, he smiled broadly at her. The thought that she had broken through to him flashed in her mind and her mouth was already turning up into a responsive smile when he struck out at her violently without any warning. Catching her in mid-section, kicking hard with both his feet, the force of his blow drove her straight off the bed and spun her body in the air. She landed heavily face first on the rough floor and continued rolling, twisting herself into the covers that flew off with her.

Oros' breathing had become shallow and labored with a nervous reaction of his own but he still had his voice under control. Sure in his assessment of the situation—abundantly clear to him now—the self-critical smile that had come out was fixed firmly on his face. He understood finally that it was all a mistake—a hideously massive one—that he had made and he silently criticized himself for it. He should never have trusted her. It was a mistake he had made before too. He should never trust anybody.

"No!" he said slowly, speaking toward her prostrate form on the floor. "It's not me—it's you. You're a deceitful little bitch. I thought you wanted to work with me...to build something together. But you don't. You don't want to build at all, do you? You want to destroy. You're into destruction. That's what you've been trying to do all along...win my confidence to destroy me. To turn people against me." Oros pushed his arms down into the bed, lifting himself up to impress upon her with greater force the magnitude of the act she had committed. "That's a dangerous head-game to be playing for little girls—fucking dangerous."

Bev hadn't heard a word he said. As she lay sprawled out on the floor gasping for air, Oros waited silently for her to regain her senses. He glanced quickly around the room, seeing everything in a new perspective now. It was a little more chilling than it had seemed only a short while ago, less cozy, more stark. But at least it was his and he knew he could trust it.

Sobbing loudly and still gulping in air, Bev rose slowly to her hands and knees, balancing herself, and then rocked back from her hands to sit up on her heels. A trickle of blood running out her nostrils had smeared across her face and, now that she was upright, started running into her mouth. Her body convulsing from the shock, she turned her head to look at Oros, who immediately propelled himself forward, away from the wall, to grip the edge of the bed tightly with both hands, leaning over it with his face projecting into the room.

"Don't stop there, bitch! You're halfway to the door. Keep going! GET OUT!" He spat his words at her and Bev, not comprehending, cringed backward peering at him through watery eyes. "You think I need you?" he asked. "I don't need anybody. You want to leave so badly? You hate this cabin? Then LEAVE! Right now!"

Bev's clothes were draped over the end of Oros' bed and she realized in a frightening flash that he meant for her to go out without them. Desperate not to offer him the slightest provocation, she stopped crying and froze, holding her breath.

"Go! Fuck off! Get out!" he screamed at her.

Instead, she gripped the covers tighter to her body, clutching them to her nakedness as she prayed to herself that his anger would pass and he'd leave her alone. But Oros reacted instantly, understanding her actions.

"Oh no! Don't wrap yourself in my blankets! Take them off!"

She didn't move. The idea that the eye contact alone might be keeping him going suddenly struck her, but she couldn't tear her eyes away.

"Don't you understand me? I said drop my sleeping bag and get out of my cabin!"

Naked, in temperatures close to thirty below outside, she'd die, and she cried out, convinced her own life was at stake, "It's not your cabin! It's…"

But before she could finish, Oros vaulted off the bed, landing on his feet beside her and grabbed the sleeping bag. He ripped it from her and threw it to his bed. Then, as she tried to scramble away from him, he lunged after her, catching her by the legs, and started to drag her toward the door while she fought back, kicking and yelling desperately—but uselessly—for help. Oros wasn't a big man but he was well muscled and was far larger and more powerful than Bev. Roughly yanking open the door, he had to step away from it to let it swing around him and, as he did, he moved in closer to Bev, giving her the opportunity, with her knees bent, to kick out at him with both feet as hard as she was able. Caught off guard, Oros stumbled, releasing his grip on her and reeling backward out through the open doorway. Leaping to her feet, Bev ran to her own bed, jumped on it, and curled herself into a tight ball, too frightened to even look at him as she pleaded with him to leave her alone.

"Michael, please don't do this. We're friends. Please don't. I'm begging you, please don't. Please! Don't hurt me. Please don't." All the while she was cringing in fear, expecting to be torn from her bed and thrown out into the winter's night to die. It was all so terrible, she dissolved sobbing, unable even to speak anymore.

A few minutes passed and nothing happened. Gathering up her courage, she stopped crying and turned on her bed—to see Oros still standing in the open doorway, naked, glaring at her. In the light against the blackness outside, each breath expelled from his lungs, freezing into crystal clouds like hot smoke blowing from a dragon, made him appear ghostly white, almost demonic. The cold air swirling around him had filled the cabin and she started to shiver with tiny convulsions that began at her hands and then spread over her entire body. The sight gave her no comfort and she waited in wordless terror for him to move.

Spellbound, she didn't hear the radio until Oros himself drew her attention to it. "They're playing your song," he said sarcastically, and then she heard the Beach Boys singing, "…make you feel alright and the northern girls with the way they kiss, they keep their boyfriends warm at night…. I wish they all could be California girls…"

Closing the door, Oros walked over to his bed at the far end of the cabin. There he stopped and, with his back to Bev, said, "That's the kind of shit you want to go back to, then you go. I'm not going to stop you." Without looking at her again, he dressed quickly and marched out into the night, slamming the door behind him.

Bev pulled the covers up, crawled under them, and hugged her legs tightly to her chest, trembling from fear and the cold. Alone and suffering the abject misery of a powerless victim, she tried to think of a rational solution but she quickly disintegrated, and wept uncontrollably. All the repressed negativism she felt for Alaska, the people here, and for Oros flowed out in a great gush, concentrating and attaching itself to the physical reality of the cabin which was imprisoning her—seeing it now as a monument to isolation and despair, a death trap and a tomb.

Fearing that Oros would return and renew his attack, she didn't move. Then an hour later, she had to do something. The temperature inside continued to fall steadily as the fire burned out. Cautiously sliding out of bed, she got up, intending to add some wood to the stove. However, as she moved in the empty cabin, walking quietly on her toes toward the wood stacked near Oros' bed, she heard the wind howling around outside and felt suddenly exposed and vulnerable again. With a creeping sensation that made her skin crawl and her hair stand up over her body, she could feel the presence of Oros close by—somewhere, just beyond the door waiting for her, listening with his ear to the frame or, much worse, watching her through the window. Convinced now that his face was there—pressed up against the glass panes—she forced herself to stare at the floor. She didn't dare look at the window—if he was there, it would be even more terrifying than the horrible picture she had in her mind. Without touching the fire, she ran to Oros' bed, gathered her clothes, rushed back to her own corner and, hurriedly dressed, expecting Oros to burst in as she was doing it. Then, pulling on her boots and parka, she crawled back under the heavy covers. Finally, feeling more secure, she closed her eyes and prepared to wait for dawn. In the morning she'd go, she promised herself, and never return. Ever.

Hours later, the door slowly opened and Oros entered. Standing with his back against the closed door, he listened to the sounds of the cabin while he recalled all the times he had spent here that had been happy. In the subdued light of the coal-oil lamps that still burned, the space felt warm and friendly to him and he wondered sadly how anyone would choose an urban environment over it. The radio still played but he paid no attention to it. Apart from the older songs, there wasn't much he liked to listen to that they ever played. The sound that was more important to him now was the sound of Bev's breathing as she lay fast asleep in her bed. It was a sound that had become comfortingly familiar to him. He was a light sleeper and there had been so many times he lay awake at night or had woken from sleep and listened to her delicate snoring. He couldn't believe he'd never hear it again. Lying on her side facing the outside wall of the cabin, there was enough room beside her for another person. He stared at that space, wanting to curl up beside her, to feel the warmth of her body, to smell her womanliness, to hold her tightly and never let her go—if only until dawn.

The thought that he would be alone was indeed frightening. Bev was right about that—he needed people around him. Only it was an impossible need to fill. His life had taken on its own course and there were so few people, if anybody now, who wanted to share it with him. It never seemed to matter much when he was busy. Or when he was outside, when the movement of his body through the forest and the sense of super-reality he experienced in nature gave him both meaning and reward enough. It was only afterward, at night, in the cabin, with only his own thoughts to keep him company, that he broke down and despaired. Not knowing how he'd adjust, he didn't want to think about it—there'd be plenty of time for that later.

Quietly, so as not to wake up Bev, he bent down and took his boots off at the door. Crossing the room in his stockinged feet, he carefully built up the fire, starting from scratch, and then put on a pot for tea. Pulling the woolen toque off his head, he tossed it over to his bed and then, draping his coat over the back of a chair, sat down on it, exhausted and depressed. Burying his chin in his hands, he sat, statue-like, his eyes riveted to the corner of the room where Bev lay sleeping, until the sound of boiling water which threatened to wake her, mobilized him.

Deep into the night, his tea untouched and cold on the table in front of him, he opened his diary and tried to seek solace within it. Hours later when he fell asleep in his chair, it was still dark outside—so dreadfully long were these endless nights—and when he woke again to darkness having slept through the short daylight, she was gone and he was all alone in the numbing emptiness of the north.

Chapter Seven

October 2, 1981: A sudden, violent thrashing in the bush nearby, not fifty feet away, brought Oros immediately to his feet, ending a restless and fitful sleep. His adrenaline soared and he gripped his British .303 rifle, a more powerful weapon than the .44. Oros quickly slid the safety back, readying the gun for shooting. Facing the threat, he started walking backward, careful of his balance in the dark, trying to get away from it, to give himself more room. The dogs were up and excited. Toot, growling fiercely and straining on his rope, was ready to go in after it, while Smoky and Kila, far more bush-wise, were both hanging back, ready to run for their lives.

A dead silence. Only the blood rushing in his ears and the grunts and whines of the dogs. From the blackness of the night, it too was waiting. Standing motionless. Listening. Maybe smelling them out. Oros stood, his feet slightly apart, the rifle up to his shoulder, sighting along its barrel at the bush in the direction of the sound. Smoky and Kila confirmed his initial fear that it was a bear. The only other animal that could make a noise like that was a moose; but Smoky would follow Toot into the blackest night to chase a moose. Right now, he was cringing in fear. Even if the other two backed Toot up in a fight—and it was obvious they had no intention of doing that—the three dogs were still no match for a grizzly; even a young one would easily kill them all. Oros hoped it was a black bear rather than a grizzly; they were more easily intimidated.

"HEY BUDDY!" Oros yelled into the bush. "It's only me and my dogs! I got nothing here you want! Fuck off and leave us alone!"

Off to his left, 100 feet from where he had heard the first sound, the bear roared. It had circled soundlessly around more than ninety degrees! Oros' hairs stood up over his body at the sound and he trembled as he waited for the charge. It was a grizzly.

"Damn you! Go away! We got nothing you want! Go away!"

If the bear was going to charge, he'd do it soon. The roar was usually the final stage in a stalk. Peering into the darkness, he couldn't see fifteen feet. There wasn't enough light even to shoot by. Realizing he was now standing between the grizzly and the dogs, he quickly changed his position to get behind them. That way he might get in a second shot—while the bear was dealing with the dogs. He might even be able to save himself.

"We don't mean you no harm!" Oros yelled, but he tried to put some softness into the tone of his voice to convince the bear of his good will. "Go on your own way! There's no food here for you to eat!"

Oros was familiar with the big bears and knew that, while they were unpredictable, they threatened more often than they charged. They weren't stupid enough to risk injury to themselves unless they had to. This one may only have been passing silently in the night and decided, simply curious, to check them out. Or, winding them, it may have been caught off guard, frightened, and was now just bluffing them, trying to scare them off.

As he waited, nervous sweat welled up over his whole body. Minutes passed. Still nothing happened. Slowly he began to relax. He had been through this whole thing before many times and the bears had always bluffed him. So far. He lowered the barrel to point toward the ground, his arms tired from holding it up, although he remained ready in the instant to shoot if there was any need. Over the sound of the dogs' own heaving breath, he listened as well as he was able for any sound that the bear was moving, coming closer, circling farther around, or leaving. He knew one of their favorite tricks was to circle around 180 degrees after roaring and then charge in from the back while their prey was looking ahead. He kept his eyes on the dogs, especially Kila and Smoky, relying on their hearing and their sense of smell to alert him to any change in the bear's location; the dogs' attention remained riveted on the spot the grizzly had roared from. Unless they were mesmerized by the roar, they weren't giving any sign of the bear's movements. Another fifteen minutes and all three dogs lay down, again convincing Oros that the danger had indeed passed. More cautious than the dogs, he waited another fifteen minutes before he felt safe enough to return to the tarp to sleep.

Awake before first light, he had to fight with himself to crawl out of his bag. Kila had wormed his way closer to Oros during the night until the dog's head and upper body were lying over Oros' legs. Oros didn't mind. Kila radiated heat and Oros had slept a lot better because of it. Usually the dogs slept together, huddled in one lumpy mass, but Kila had been sticking closer to Oros than the other two since they'd left Hutsigola. Oros remembered that he was to keep a closer watch on Toot. Rather than becoming more civilized by Smoky's example, Smoky was growing more wild, adopting Toot's reckless and carefree attitude. He thought briefly about splitting them up for a while by keeping Kila between them, but that would mean tying them down whenever they camped and there was enough to do without having to bother himself with lessons for them. 'The snows will come soon enough,' he thought, 'and then they won't be wandering off to make their own tracks unless they're forced to.'

Oros was finishing his oatmeal breakfast when the sun broke over the horizon with its deep golden light. Facing it, he closed his eyes. The rays still had some substance to them and he enjoyed the feel of it as it lightly probed his skin. That wouldn't last either. Soon enough it would turn to an almost colorless pale yellow with no more warmth than the lights which danced every night now in the sky against the blackness of space. The snow was already building up in the higher elevations and moving down lower into the valleys every week. In the mountains, you could watch winter descend.

Oros slowly dipped his cooking pot into the water at the edge of the small lake they were camped beside and watched the fingerling trout that rushed in to get at it. As he held it under the surface, they bumped into it, hopelessly trying to suck some nourishment from the steel. The idea that they were hungrier than he was cheered him. Feeling benevolent, he crumbled up a left-over piece of breakfast bannock and tossed it out over the surface. The trout went wild, thrashing the whole surface in front of him in their frenzied feeding.

Oros suddenly shook his head sadly at the thought that he had just done another stupid thing. It seemed as though he were making more mistakes lately, that they were more frequent. But he wasn't keeping track. He didn't want to. It could only be bad news—the rate that the drugs were consuming him was accelerating, eating away his body and his mind.

He bent down, picked up a handful of sand, and threw it angrily into the water, scattering the fish, before turning to the dog which had followed him down to the lake to watch greedily as Oros threw food away.

"Sorry Kila," he said, meaning it. The fish could survive months without food. The dogs, which had been trying to feed on plants for the past several days, wouldn't last another week.

Oros tossed what he had left to the dog, who picked it out of the air in one wide-mouthed, eager gulp, and then walked back up from the lake to the fire and slid the coffee pot away from the heat. The rich smell of its coffee filled the air around him and he breathed deeply of it, savoring its delicious aromas. He had, at least, lots of coffee left.

He'd set out the connibear traps for beaver every day for the past week in different swamps but he'd caught nothing. He started worrying that his luck had turned. Without meat, the dogs were slowly starving. He still hadn't decided either how or where he was going to get through this winter.

It'd been nine days since the raid on Fletcher Daye's camp at Sheslay and winter clouds, heavily pregnant with snow, lay draped over the land in a smothering embrace much of the time. As he moved north, each step taking him closer and closer to Hutsigola, Oros tried to plan out his next move.

Unless he got back to Hutsigola, where his main caches were, it was going to be a very difficult winter to pass on the trail. It wasn't time yet, he knew, to go back there. It was still too soon. And there were other cabins, at least a dozen he could think of, that would be much safer to winter in. Only he was already set up in Hutsigola. He found it hard to change plans that had taken months to organize. Even thinking about it caused him terrible stress. He desperately wanted to act rationally but the ideas that came to him were confused and tortured, and he gave up finally in disgust and anger. Easier not to think. Well, he didn't have to, he knew. He could rely on his instincts instead. To feel into them for the right decision.

Oros was proud of his instincts. Living alone in the wilderness for so long did more than tune his senses. Gradually, over the years, a new face, almost another personality, had emerged to assume more and more control over his actions. Oros had felt himself changing but was glad of it when it happened. His earlier life had ill-prepared him for the bush. But since then, primal forces surfaced to help him cope. They had become so integral to his lifestyle that survival and escape were second nature to him. He could act on them automatically now, without reason. The truth was that he trusted his instincts more than he trusted his own mind.

Reading his own instincts, buried somewhere deep within him, was like mining for revelation. It was an intuitive search for direction, more fruitful usually than the Tarot, although he relied on the cards as well. When his instincts and the Tarot both pointed in the same direction, he'd trust his life to the decision. But the Tarot hadn't been reading clearly the last few days either. He didn't want to force the decision, believing that the answer would present itself to him when it was ready, but he was quickly running out of time. The dogs would be dying soon if the situation didn't change.

Well, he argued, he wouldn't go back along the trail he had just come up. The Coast Range was to the west, 100 miles away. But that route dead-ended in an impregnable wall of ice. If it were spring, he'd move east. Although he had no caches to the east, the land there was open, wild, and friendly to him. But without supplies, he knew he wouldn't make it through the winter. There was only one direction left. North. Along the very trail and route he was already on. North. Toward Hutsigola. Everything pointed that way. Still, he didn't like it. It was as if he were being drawn back to Hutsigola by forces beyond his control. As though Hutsigola itself was drawing him back, calling him home. He fought with the decision that was imposing itself upon him but there was no really good reason why he shouldn't go back, except, of course, that it might still be too soon. They might be waiting for him. Watching the cabin. And if they were, he'd be walking right into their trap.

Sooner or later, there'd be a fight, a real bloodbath. He was sure of it. And even though they were now one man short, he knew he could never hope to kill them all. At best, he could pick them off slowly, one or two at a time, but the day would come, no matter how many he killed, when they'd overwhelm him by numbers alone and that, he believed, would be the end of him. He wasn't afraid of dying—far better even to die that way than by their slow poisoning—but he was determined that they should pay dearly for his life. And when it came down to the battle, he'd always promised himself, he'd be the one to choose the setting.

After a few short hours on the trail, unmotivated to hike farther and uncertain where to go in any event, he stopped to set up camp near Tedideech Lake. Although they had moved quietly all day, they hadn't seen any game bigger than a squirrel, and he missed his chance to shoot that. The dogs were now one day hungrier than they were yesterday. The need to get meat was critical. Already they had to rest every hour through the day. Another two days without eating and the dogs would give up altogether. It was a chilling thought and Oros quickly promised himself he wouldn't let it happen. There was at least one guaranteed source of food for them that he'd use before they all died. Toot. If he had to, he'd feed them Toot.

The day was ending as it began, with Oros entering events into his journal; but he soon gave up and put the book away. There was no sense in recording mistakes and misery.

With his canvas shelter set up and his bedroll laid out for the night, Oros' own energies, not the least abated by the day's short hike, kept him on his feet pacing wide circles until well after dark.

As he paced, mulling over his life, adrift in the open spaces, cut off from his base, he felt exposed and unprotected. Threatened, his instincts took over. Rising automatically from within him to dominate his feelings was a desire to destroy the threat. To fight back.

He had supplies enough in Hutsigola, food for them all, but they had forced him out. They were keeping him away. They were starving his dogs, tormenting his life. "Damn! Those horrible, horrible people! THEY were doing it all! But they'll regret it. God, they'll be sorry for fucking with me."

Over and over he cursed them.

With his anger pumping through him and spilling over, breaking out like the hot flow of a summer storm over Teslin Lake, the dogs, dozing lightly, stirred and whined when he broke the silence, sometimes speaking quietly as though to himself and then raging wildly in the still evening as though his enemies stood before him.

"You think you can break me, you bastards?" He yelled into the night, his breath condensing, like smoke in the cold air.

"Never!" He screamed.

Continuing more softly, "You've never done it. And you never will!"

A surge of pride came over him, firing his eyes and quickening his pace.

"That's one promise I'll always keep faith with—never to let myself be broken. And I won't."

"Fuck them all! They'll never break me! Never! Not Sheslay Free Mike! I'm free...after all these years.... As free as the wind!"

Oros laughed then with a rough, raucous sound. He loved to think of himself as the wind, capricious and volatile, unseen yet omnipotent.

He was almost floating, having taken himself so high, but suddenly from the pinnacle, his perspective shifted and his mood, following it, plummeted and grew dark with anger again.

'Yes,' he thought soberly, lifting his head and turning his eyes toward the north. 'I've gained freedom...but at what price? To be driven from my own home and hunted down like an animal?'

He couldn't think about it rationally. But he consoled himself with the thought that a person needed more to survive here than rational thinking. After all, it wasn't a rational environment.

He tried to recall a poem he remembered having read in one of his early journals about the mind being like a bird, but he was unable to. That depressed him a little. There was a time not too many years ago, he recalled clearly, when his mind was open and sharp, filled with discovery, philosophy and ideas. Not anymore.

Oros had felt the deterioration setting in some years ago. It wasn't dramatic but it was steady. His brain was eroding and his own thoughts were sometimes suspect. There were truly bizarre visions his mind conjured up now. And reactions he never had before. And feelings, terrible ones....

A low rumble in the distance drew his attention and he stood up quickly. The dogs too, hearing it, woke up again and started to whine.

"Quiet!" Oros yelled and the dogs fell silent. It was the sound of a distant explosion.

The sound hung in the air for long moments as Oros listened, every nerve suddenly keyed. Slowly, the rumbling sound trailed away, leaving behind only the dry whisperings of the shallow wind across the land.

Oros relaxed. It was nothing. Only an alpine avalanche, far away, echoing through the mountains. They were in season again with the weight of new fallen snow clinging precariously to an ice-slippery layer of harder snow.

Later, while the northern lights played overhead, with the temperature dropping, he gave in finally to the irresistible urge that remained undiminished within him, succumbing to the pressure it exerted—to keep going the way he had been going. North. That was the way of the flow. Back to Hutsigola.

Well, he reasoned, he wouldn't walk into his camp until he was absolutely sure it was safe. And he could trust his instincts for that. If it was hot, he'd feel it.

He relieved himself of the rest of his lingering doubt with the thought that he didn't have to stay at Hutsigola. If need be, he could make it a short stop only. Just long enough to resupply before pushing on. In fact, there was another cabin he could use farther north on Teslin Lake if he decided that Hutsigola wasn't safe enough to stay in yet. But he had decided—he was going back.

It was a milestone. The decision was made.

'They want to drive me off? I'll stay. Fuck them. Fuck them all.'

Then, turning to the sky and shouting out his anger toward Hutsigola, he screamed, "Bastards! You'll never break me! You can't keep me away!"

Oros stopped suddenly in front of the dogs, his only sentient audience, but although he could see them clearly and had gained their attention momentarily, he wasn't aware of them, focused instead on the dream of freedom. It had always been his most cherished dream, the one that had lured him here. To the north. To this land. It was its greatest promise—to attain true freedom.

'And I've done it,' he thought.

"I'm free! You bastards!"

"I am the wind that blows strong and eternal across this land. I am the spirit of the north. I am Sheslay Free Mike!"

Oros raised up his arms straight out from his sides and started spinning himself around in circles.

Waving his hands through the air to touch the ethereal substance of the space itself, stirring it like a propeller while he repeated, chanting, over and over, louder and louder:

"I'm free. I'm free! I'm free! I'm free! I'm FREE!"

Chapter Eight

April 1973:

> The high dawn's haze
> cracks the night,
> seeping into the spaces between the stars,
> coloring them out.

Oros had been on the road already for two weeks since he had left Fairbanks and most of the distance crossed had been on foot.

Within twenty-four hours of raising his thumb to the trickle of traffic leaving Fairbanks, Oros was sitting high off the ground in the comfortable cab of a large truck watching the guard-rail which blocked the highway at the border draw nearer and nearer. Beside him the driver noisily geared the truck down and prepared to stop his rig for the border inspection. Sitting parked beside the customs' shack on the Canadian side was an Alaskan State Police cruiser. The sight of it unnerved Oros, although he kept his body under control and tried to appear calm. The truck rolled up to the window and stopped. He needn't have worried. The Trooper stayed inside and the customs' officer was mostly interested in knowing whether they'd seen any game on the road.

As they squeezed under the sign that hung over the road and crossed the boundary marker, Oros' heart started pounding with joy.

He'd done it!

Out of the States and into Canada.

It was a major step. The most important decision he could ever remember having taken—crossing the border into the Yukon.

The Yukon!

Canada!

He had repeated those words like a magic incantation, over and over in his mind a hundred times since then. And still, two weeks later, Oros couldn't get over it. He'd really done it. He'd left the States. Everybody had talked about getting out. To Holland or Mexico or Canada. All talk. But he had actually done it.

He had escaped. Not even the military could touch him now. He was free!

Alaska had seemed like a foreign country but Canada really and truly was. Here, the light seemed a little different, the dawn a little sharper, clearer as it rose to illuminate a new and foreign land.

That first day, as he walked the streets of Whitehorse, down to the banks of the Yukon River by the old White Pass and Yukon Railway station, Oros was struck by the contrasts between old and new. He was deeply attracted to the former. As he examined the pilings of long-gone warehouses which had once lined the sandy shores of the still frozen river, an idea he had been mulling over for a couple of years suddenly crystallized into a coherent theory: man had drifted away from the natural order of things in an attempt to set up a new order. So total was the new order, he reasoned, so all encompassing and pervasive was it, that it was now difficult even to conceive of the natural one—the one that had existed since the beginning of time. Time being dictated by the demands of a technological economy, and space and motion being defined by the parameters of science, modern man had become dislocated, cut off from real roots. Tension was the result of the disharmony.

In this new life, he wanted to achieve harmony. To seek reunification with the natural world. Peace would follow. He was sure of it.

In Eden, space had been defined by the distance a man moved under his own muscle power; time, by the rhythms of his own body and those of the land. Since he was heading for Eden, he decided that there was no better time to start than the present. He was moving through two worlds, leaving one and entering another, and for the transition itself to have meaning—a rite-of-passage for the rebirth—he'd have to rely on natural limits.

One step at a time!

For the rest of the way from Whitehorse to Telegraph Creek, he'd walk. That was the human pace.

And so he left Whitehorse on foot. Waving at the occasional vehicle, whose driver honked, he declined to ride with any of them. But now, two weeks later, he was reviewing those same arguments. Unaccustomed to the physical strain of the march, he traveled alone under the weight of a heavy pack and slept within earshot of the highway in the depths of the as-yet-unmelted winter's snow. His muscles throbbed, his bones ached, his hands were raw with the cold and, worst of all, the balls of his feet and toes were painfully blistered. Still, it took little effort to keep his spirits buoyed and he rationalized the pain he was suffering as necessarily incidental to the process of rebirth.

Riding would spoil everything. Apart entirely from physically getting to Telegraph Creek, the trip itself was a spiritual odyssey—the old life slowly draining out over the miles he walked, to be replaced in full with the fresh visions of this new country stamped into his soul.

Besides, he thought more soberly, he didn't want to arrive too quickly—not while the reality of Fairbanks remained so heavily in his heart. He had resolved to leave Alaska months ago, after Bev had betrayed him and left with Ben. Except for Neil, the family he had known there was gone but, still, there was the comfortable familiarity of Fairbanks and the security of the few friends who did remain that might have been reason enough to stay. Several times since leaving, moments of doubt had turned to panic. Almost everything had been left behind and all he was taking with him for comfort was his vision and faith. He had staked everything on this move.

There would be no more after this one, he promised himself. Whatever happened, he'd make it work.

Writing in his journal, Oros sat beside the highway with his legs stretched out in front of him toward the fire. A pale wash of pink color, underlying thicker bands of deeper crimson, was working its way up the eastern canvas of the sky. Without taking his eyes off the new light, he reached forward and poured himself another cup of tea from the pot set into the ash along the fire's edge and considered what he should do. He had planned to march every day, covering as much distance as he could, but with his feet swollen and blistered, he was in no hurry to pull on the boots that had eaten into his soles and to start walking again.

He lifted one bare foot up close to his face to examine it. The blisters had all popped and the enveloping skin had torn away, leaving patches of raw flesh, pink and wet underneath. Even where the blisters hadn't eaten into his soles, where the skin was intact, it was soft and thin. Almost feminine, he thought. Then, stretching his legs out again, he lay down over the top of the tent he had collapsed for a groundsheet and laughed at his own self doubt.

It didn't matter. He was a free man and time was his to spend at his whim.

"The point is not to get there as quickly as we can," he explained to the dog, Krish. "We prefer to walk. Don't we girl. And don't you disagree with me, either!"

Yesterday they had left the Alaska Highway at the junction of the Cassiar Road, where they turned south, and started walking toward Dease Lake. They were nearing the home stretch now.

Since crawling stiff-jointed and numbed out of his cold and damp sleeping bag to build a fire, he had passed this morning by studying a well-worn map that lay spread open beside him on the tent.

For the hundredth time, he examined the solid black lines that represented roads. There were so few of them. One of them, the Alaska Highway, roughly paralleled the border between the Yukon and British Columbia. Another, the Cassiar Road, a dirt track, ran south from the Alaska Highway 500 miles into northern British Columbia, half the height of the province, to spit itself out at the Indian Reserve of Kitwanga where, touching pavement again, it finally met up with another road, the Yellowhead Highway, which crossed through the center of the province from east to west.

On both sides of the Cassiar Road, all the way south to the Yellowhead, lay unbroken wilderness. Vast expanses of untamed, rugged, and wild country. Over all those hundreds of miles, there were only two towns: Cassiar, a mining company town of a thousand people, seventy miles south of the Yukon border; and Dease Lake, a mere road stop, eighty miles south of Cassiar, with a population of 400 souls.

There was another line, an even thinner one than the Cassiar Road, that snaked west from Dease Lake for seventy-two miles. It followed the deep canyon walls of the Stikine River halfway back to the coast, where it ended at an even smaller dot with the name Telegraph Creek printed beside it. It was there that Oros' attention was absorbed.

"There's our new home, feet." Oros said, trying to imagine the reality that the dot represented. "Only a few more days and we'll see it in 3-D, eyeball technicolor. The end of the journey. The wanderlust devil defeated at last."

Surrounding him were mounds of snow that still covered the land to an average depth of two feet. The country reminded him constantly of Montana and he leaned back, inhaling the air deeply.

"Just look at this country, Krish. It's so beautiful! This place is like paradise—and it's so empty! There's nobody here. We got it to ourselves, girl. Amazing it's so empty..."

Feeling a little lonely, Oros picked up his journal, flipped it back to February when the decision to leave Alaska wasn't fixed yet, and started reading.

> How quickly Alaska has emptied of people. A real freak out. Still it feels pretty close up here—see the same faces all the time. Melancholy finally gone. With everyone else. No real longing for spring yet which is a good sign. The rules as well as the conditions are different here. I didn't realize how cold its been until I went out to visit Neil. -35! Definitely prefer not knowing.

Almost every page written then had at least one reference to Neil. Oros missed him but he was thinking less and less of Neil as the days went on. Neil, like everyone else, belonged to the past now and, even before Oros had left Fairbanks, their friendship had cooled considerably. If it hadn't, he might never have left. It had started at Vide Bartlett's party, Oros remembered. As he thought back over it, he rummaged through his pack until he found a sealed plastic jar, from which he removed a garlic clove. Licking the oil off his fingers, he popped the clove into his mouth to fight back the cold that had been sapping his energy these past few days.

Oros liked thinking about the party and had written down as much of the conversation at Vide's party as he thought worth remembering. Now, as he reread it, the memory of that one afternoon he had spent at her home filled the morning for him as it had done so often before. In the hallway of her house, he had seen a photograph of her standing with Lyndon Johnson and Lady Bird, and he could still feel the sense of greatness he had felt just being with someone who had lived as much and as well as she had. In the stillness of the forest's edge, beside the deserted roadway, absorbed in this own thoughts, Oros laughed aloud as her comment about Nixon rang again through his mind: "The first time I met him, I knew he was a dangerous man!"

Oros continued smiling, thinking how much he liked her, as he removed a small pot from the fire in which he had been boiling rice and dried cereals for breakfast.

"I'll have to start eating meat again pretty soon," he said, looking at the pot as he set it into the snow to cool off. "It'd be too much to expect of people in this country to put up with a vegetarian when everybody eats meat." From his pack, he pulled out a string of dried beef jerky that Neil had given him earlier in the winter and, cutting off a small piece with his knife, added it to the garlic he was still sucking on in his mouth.

They had sat around Vide's after a dinner which he'd thoroughly enjoyed. He remembered feeling self-conscious and acutely aware of the smell of his smoke-saturated body in the stately atmosphere and refined presence of that great lady. Vide talked about her late husband, Bob, and of his efforts to have Alaska admitted into statehood in '59 and of the politics at the senate afterward. Oros listened attentively, enthralled by her as she told of growing up in Dawson City in the Yukon, of moving to Alaska, and of her life in the north. Of all its good times and hard times. She later brought out a book of poetry by Robert Service and read to them "The Squaw Man," "Athabaska Dick," "The Shooting of Dan McGrew," and a dozen others which filled him with visions of the world of the men who had come here before him. They had seemed a people more worthy than modern man—reckless, daring and brave. They were chasing dreams with a spirit of freedom and abandon not seen since.

So powerfully did Vide read that the descriptions brought tears to his eyes. Here was a world Oros knew instantly, a world in which he belonged. But he had arrived a hundred years too late to faded images and dying memories.

Oros wasn't sorry when Neil changed the topic by bringing up a *Time* article on a Norwegian town that Michener wrote about in *The Drifters* which suffered the same kind of winter blues from darkness that Fairbanks did. They, too, passed the winter in dreams of summer, Neil said. And then, as though on cue, everybody started unloading their sunshine fantasies while Oros recovered quietly from the shock of hearing words in poetry that had so completely penetrated his own private dreams. Their fantasies of Gulf Stream waters, Caribbean breezes, Amazon jungles and Israeli beaches bored him until Vide spoke up, adding her own simple wish—to drive slowly across the country from New York to San Francisco. "Just to see it in all its glory one more time before I die," she explained.

Oros remembered the silence that followed, nobody too sure what to say. And then Neil spoke up, volunteering then and there to take her. Oros had thought it a grand gesture and was even proud of Neil for making it. But when they discussed it privately a few days later, he was deeply shocked to discover that Neil had been serious.

It cut the final cord holding him in Fairbanks.

"What could be more important than fulfilling a dying person's last dream?" Neil had insisted.

It was a terrible revelation for Oros, for the first time realizing that even Neil wasn't committed to Alaska. The discovery had made Oros sick. Like all the rest of them, Neil's plans were only so much talk. "So much for home and friends?" Oros had asked cynically as he probed Neil's motives. Given the chance, Neil, too, would leave the north without a backward look. They even argued about it. Neil insisted there was no cause great enough to command his following and Oros argued the distinction between principles and causes. In the end, Neil accused him of being too esoteric, which Oros recognized as Neil's polite way of telling him he was full of shit. Oros felt a rift open with the realization that even Neil's friendship—the greatest Oros had ever shared—was only transient. And shallow.

Oros flipped through the weeks following Vide Bartlett's party. He had stopped using dates ever since Christmas when the focus of attention on a particular date seemed so artificial and redundant. He still wasn't using them but conceded he would start again once he got settled into Telegraph Creek. To keep the record straight.

A lot of what he wrote then made little sense to him now, although, at the time, he knew that every word counted. The words, however, completely failed to express the anguish he'd felt when writing them. It had been an utterly terrible time.

> Another soul lost. So many have gone leaving me here. Bill, Sola, John, Owin, Paula, Relta, and Joan and David, Bev and Ben, and now Ann. And winter has barely begun. Rene is living confined to his mind, dropping drugs. Drifting out of touch. Waiting teary-eyed for the ladies of the night. Singing hallelujah and praying to the Lord. Ready for a trip through the Looking Glass. Only a flickering lamplight. The glow fading. Beyond these walls the dog barks. Cresting the hills. The stars we mean to touch. Imploding. Blinking, unbelieving at the beauty of ice crystals. Smeared sight. Stay with me. High and low. There's a lifetime still to go. Faith, hang on.

As winter deepened and the storms raged, he continued to deteriorate. Dramatically. Abandoned first by Bev and then Neil. Alone through the rest of the winter in the cabin, staring out at the endless night from which nobody would come to relieve his loneliness, he had clung to his sanity as to a tattered piece of cloth, hanging on with physical effort against the onslaught of winter. Day after day, week after week, red-eyed and vacant-hearted, he'd kept faith with the single desperate belief that spring would bring salvation.

Oros laid the diary down and, with the large pewter soup spoon he'd brought with him from his Fairbanks cabin, he started eating breakfast straight from the pot while the dog looked on hungrily.

"Well, just me and you now, Krish. Alone again."

The silence was awesome. His hands close to his face, he examined them with a detached kind of interest. They were tougher than his feet but they, too, were soft. That'll change, he knew.

"This is it. Here we are. Sitting in the snow with a raw throat. Coughing and picking at scabs." Oros laughed. "Hardly paradise, is it Krish?"

Breakfast finished and the dog fed, Oros packed up his camp. Wading through the deeper snow in the ditch, he lifted himself heavily out on the roadside and stamped his feet to knock the snow off his legs. As he walked, he massaged the tips of his little fingers to relax his heart, which had started to pump fiercely with the sudden exertion of the march. The weight on his back from the old Trapper Nelson pack crushed his shoulders and new pains developed in his feet. Beside him, Krish walked easily, the soft padding sounds of her feet barely audible, and he tried to meditate on the rhythms to distract himself from his own discomfort.

For a long while, they walked along with only the sounds of their footsteps and their breathing breaking the absolute stillness of the pink dawn when a loud croak startled Oros from his reverie. Looking up, a raven was making a pass at him. It was a large bird and as it flew, Oros could hear the rushing sound of air streaming over its feathers as its wing tips cut through the quiet, cold air and the creaking of its joints as it beat its wings. Now flying up the road ahead, it wheeled in the air and flew back toward him. As though it, too, was glad for the company in the deserted space, it studied him with keen eyes before greeting him with another croaking call. Oros lifted a friendly hand to the bird.

To his surprise, the bird appeared to understand, for it dipped a wing quickly as though in parting and then wheeled away from the road to disappear out of sight over the trees. It seemed so intelligent that Oros toyed with the fanciful Indian belief that the raven was the reincarnation of a long dead Indian brave, a master woodsman who had been given the reward of flight for a devotion to the wilderness he now lorded over.

Oros was happy. "If I am granted one wish, when my body finally nourishes Mother Earth, may I be reborn a raven."

His body warmed with the exertion of the walk. He was even sweating lightly. The air temperature, although it hovered around freezing, felt refreshingly cool.

"Yes, I'm here to be reborn—not to touch the earth and run. Alaska was crazy with winter—everybody sneaking away physically or slipping away mentally into fantasies of summer. Or worse...."

The thought of the deceit made him momentarily angry.

"They're all so fat-oriented. Comfort and security.... Fuck them!... All that really counts is now. The present. This moment forever."

A haiku poem came drifting into his mind and he focused on it, relaxing as he did:

Sitting quietly, doing nothing,
Spring comes, and the grass grows by itself.

Feeling uplifted, Oros started to sing a spiritual he had heard over the radio and memorized. His voice, ringing out loudly and clearly, drifted off into the vastness of the space. Words and phrases, bouncing off towering cliff faces came back to him as echoes, faint and delayed.

Swing low, sweet chariot,
Comin' for to carry me home.

I looked over Jordan and what did I see,
Comin' for to carry me home;
A band of angels comin' after me,
Comin' for to carry me home.

I'm sometimes up, I'm sometimes down,
Comin' for to carry me home;
But still my soul is a-Heaven bound,
Comin' for to carry me home.

Swing low, sweet chariot,
Comin' for to carry me home.
Oh, if you get there before I do,
Comin' for to carry me home

Tell all my friends I'm comin' too,
Comin' for to carry me home.

Toward evening, after several rests through the day, they came to a flat area miles long, perhaps once an ancient lake bottom. The forests covering it had been burned over. Salvage attempts to recover the still-standing but blackened timber gave the area the appearance of having been ravaged by all the destructive power of man and nature combined. Apart from the burn, Oros continually marveled at how similar the country was to Montana. The sparse growth—stunted trees in sandy soils—of the Whitehorse region had given way south of Teslin, where he had left the Alaska Highway, to larger trees and firmer ground.

At the base of the first hill after the flats, he came upon the first sign of human habitation he'd seen all day. It was a fire burning beside the road. He stopped to warm himself and took out his metal canteen to melt some snow, while, from the corner of his eye, he studied the cabin set back in the trees away from the road. As unobtrusively as possible, he watched the two faces pressed to the cabin's window. After a few minutes, nobody having come out of the building to greet him, he walked carefully up the snow-packed trail from the fire toward the cabin.

Before he reached it, the door swung open quickly and two heavy, middle-aged Indian women squeezed themselves into the doorway, blocking any view he might have had of the interior. When they stared stone-faced and failed to respond to his greeting, he got right to the point.

"I'm looking for a place to camp for the night and was wondering if you know of anywhere a fellow could stay?"

The women eyed him with obviously fearful suspicion. Oros couldn't blame them, realizing he must look a peculiar sight in the circumstances.

He hoped for an invitation to spend the night under their roof, but he quickly changed his mind. He was starting to choke. Even from a distance of ten feet, the cabin emanated terrible odors. The air, cooked by the red barrel heat of a blazing wood stove in the tiny cabin, was wafting out the open door in hot, nauseating waves.

It was a trapper's shack and the pungent rot of drying animal skins mixed with a dozen stale human odors to fill the air. His senses reeled. The larger of the two women answered coldly with a plain "No!"

Holding his breath, and his laughter, he bowed graciously and left quickly.

"Well Krish," Oros said, when they were out of hearing range and back on the empty highway, "I guess you blew it for me. Your long fangs must have scared those old crows shitless. Although I think I should kiss you." And then he laughed, glad they hadn't invited him in.

Miles past the cabin, he came upon a road marker—the thirty-six kilometer post south of the Alaska Highway. Although he had only covered twelve miles all day, he pegged his tent into the snow beside the marker, fluffed his sleeping bag to improve the loft and untied his boots to let his feet air. He then prepared a simple dinner over a small fire of crackling spruce branches: frozen rose hips and some highbush cranberry he had picked along the roadside, granola and wheat germ with powdered milk, sunflower seeds, almonds, dried fruit, and a small piece of kelp.

Dinner over, he set his pot back on the fire, melting fresh snow for some peppermint and alfalfa tea, and brought out some of the books that weighed so heavily on his back. Without them, the trek would have been much easier, he knew, but they represented more to him than mere reading material. Here were the journals, his diaries that he had started years ago—his most precious possessions. Here, too, were the books he had identified with, that formulated his philosophy and had given him meaning and motivation. Some of them he had carried with him even before Taos. Those he would never part with. Separating Shunryu Suzuki's *Zen Mind, Beginner's Mind* from the rest, he slowly read from it aloud to Krish, who had settled herself close to him beside the fire.

After only a few minutes, Oros closed the book. There was no point in reading. He couldn't concentrate. Instead, he stared into the flames, wondering how hot it would have to be to burn and not to leave the ash that always remained like memories of the past.

"We must never look back, Krish. Whatever we do, we must be completely committed. There is only ahead. The past is gone forever. There is only now, this moment, extending forever into eternity."

But in spite of himself, as soon as he crawled into his sleeping bag after noting up the day's events in the journal, his thoughts returned irresistibly back to Fairbanks and the events which had led to his leaving.

He first heard of Telegraph Creek from Telegraph Creek Bill who he'd met at the Howlin' Dog after Bev and Ben had moved south. Bill had described Telegraph Creek in glowing terms and extended an invitation to Oros to come and visit. He agreed for the sake of being polite but had no real intention of ever going. At the time, he still had other friends—most notably Neil—and for them, and history, he had determined to stay. But the rest of the winter changed that. Night after night, watching the moonlight on countless millions of powdered ice crystals, he became unsure whether it was all horrible or absolutely beautiful. Alone for too long, he started to go crazy with cabin fever. When the temperature dropped below sixty and the trees cracked from the cold, splitting the lengths of their trunks, and thirty below started to feel mild by comparison, his sudden lonely laughter turned frequently to tears and his wretched sobbing to hysterical laughter. Perversely, he savored each new moment of eroded control, until all he felt was the outrushing of uncontrolled emotion and the matter of sanity became a real struggle. Finally, when even the effort of eating became a monumental task, almost beyond his ability, he seriously considered leaving.

The decision to quit was as much a desire now to flee Fairbanks and the States as a reaction to the darkness of winter, the social isolation, and the loss of friendships. But it was later, that the final decision was made. The direction revealed. It was after Neil had dropped over and rescued him. Like an angel of mercy, he had burst through the door, as he had done so often before, filled with good cheer and carrying a pack stuffed with food and books. The books had done it. Detailing other people's hardships, they helped put things back into perspective for him. By comparison with some others, his life was a royal romp—he, at least, had a warm roof over his head and food to eat. And, by coincidence, one of the books, by Edward Hoagland entitled *Notes from a Century Before*, concerned the exploration and early settlement of British Columbia—the very area around Telegraph Creek that Oros had an invitation to visit.

Halfway between Fairbanks and Montana, Telegraph Creek seemed the perfect compromise. As a result, he sat down one day and wrote off fifteen letters to everyone listed in the "contact" section of the *Whole Earth News* magazine who lived in British Columbia. He remembered laughing as he did it, thinking of it as the "back-to-the-earth-lonely-hearts-club-column," and his own response nothing more than a fantasy to build the escape from winter around. Although he followed up the correspondence he received back from his letters with days in the library researching everything he could find on Telegraph Creek, he fully expected it all to pop like a bubble when the spring weather finally broke. But then came Vide Bartlett's party and his falling out with Neil. From the pit of darkness he found himself in afterward, he promised himself he'd escape the very first chance he got. And he did. Weeks later, as soon as the light changed, he packed his things quietly, said good-bye to his few acquaintances and with Krish at his side—the dog Neil had given him after Bev and Ben left—he set off for Canada.

Oros had been fueling the fire as he lay half out of his sleeping bag and now that it had gotten quite dark and his backside, away from the heat, was freezing, he stood up to relieve himself next to the fire. In the distance, far away, he heard the high, barking yip of a coyote and, looking up, saw thin lines of dim color, the start of an aurora borealis warming up to dance beneath the diamond sky.

The night was full, leaving no room for other places. "God, Alaska seems so far away. It was just like one long drug trip, eh Krish? And even now, now that it's over, it's still hard to get a real grip on any of it."

He dropped to his knees and searched in the dark through his pack. Feeling the smooth, cylindrical form of his flute, he brought it out and put it to his lips, adding a long, melodious note to the night.

"Maybe I should stick to playing with my bamboo flute," he said and laughed, perfectly content. "What difference does it really make?" And then, remembering a quote he had memorized from Alan Watts, he answered his own question with it:

> We eat, excrete, sleep, and get up;
> This is our world.
> All we have to do after that—is to die.

Krish fell asleep, her head on Oros' lap, to the lullaby of the bamboo flute which played soulfully long into the night.

Chapter Nine

October 3, 1981: The sky started to drop snow before he fell off into sleep and the wetness running off his face woke him later in the night when, shivering in his summer sleeping bag, he called out to the dogs. They came to him and curled themselves around and over his bag, sharing their precious heat with him. He slipped quickly into a deep and dreamless sleep and woke after dawn feeling completely refreshed and respirited for the first time in weeks.

His hunger added an edge to his energy and he set off for the Nahlin River, eating a fast cold breakfast on the trail to save as much daylight as possible for traveling, now that he had settled on their destination. They were going home.

With the days shortening rapidly into longer and longer nights, light was becoming another precious commodity.

He reversed the usual order of procession when they set off by having the dogs walk ahead of him through the still falling snow. There was more of a chance they'd scare off any game they came upon by barking or tearing off after it before he'd have a chance to get a shot away, but they'd also warn him of any people up ahead or traps on the trail now that he was getting closer to home. And, more immediately, their breaking trail for him through the snow-covered brush saved him from getting soaked to the skin. Yesterday's torments were gone, purged by the fresh snowfall, and he rejoiced as they traveled. They covered ground as quickly as the weakened dogs were able. Their packs, empty of all fresh food, were light and the air, even with the wet snow, had a sharp, sparkling crispness to it that cleansed him as he breathed it in. The air, the breathing—in and out, in and out—and the pace, with shorter but firm steps, rhythmic in their repetition—right, left, right, left—were intensely satisfying. There was a calmness to the space that their movement enhanced, perhaps by contrast of action, and they reveled in it. It was their first heavy snowfall, and Oros was happy.

By midday, they reached the south bank of the Nahlin River and there, on the bluff overlooking the water, stood a young mountain goat. Driven down off the higher elevations by snow, it watched them, standing still long enough for Oros to get a shot off.

The bullet caught it in the shoulder, high, near the spine, knocking it over. Its legs kicked wildly a few times and then it was still. Dead.

Oros yelled in relief.

They were saved.

That night, the cycle of a perfect day was completed.

Utterly content, a large portion of fried goat tenderloin inside him, a hot cup of rich boiled coffee in his hands, and his feet up on a rough sawhorse beside the stove, it was a day that had fulfilled its promise. The smoke that seeped from the cracks in the stove's iron plating clouded the cabin in a gray, steamy murkiness that was hard to breathe and irritated his eyes, forcing them closed. But the weight of the meal, the smoke, and the heat made him feel too lazy and sleepy to care. If it weren't for the weather, he would have preferred to have remained outside sleeping under the sky, but the wind was gusting, blowing sheets of hard ice crystals through the air to sweep the earth, and he was at least warm and dry. The cabin was an old one. One wall had come down and the roof had caved in over it, creating a closed-in, lean-to space.

Over the years, he had stayed here on occasion and, like the other cabins scattered throughout his territory, and the trails themselves, he had once tried to fix it. To keep it from rotting away entirely. It was a responsibility he had felt almost from the beginning, to care for the relics of the old world, to keep open the trails built by those earlier bushmen, the trappers, prospectors, and traders. To keep faith with them through their works. He had patched the remaining roof on this cabin as well as he could and had slipped some rough, ax-cut spruce planks into the open window frames to keep out the weather. He was pretty sure this cabin was one of the old "line" cabins built in the days when ambitious men tried to link New York with Paris by building a telegraph line to stretch more than halfway around the world, across the Bering Strait. There were old cabins all along the Telegraph Line Trail. Some in better shape than this one, others worse. Some were mere mounds of moss-covered timbers. There were so many cabins Oros couldn't save them all. As he sat, relaxed, listening to the wind howling, he decided to carve an inscription into the wall and composed several in his mind. The best one he came up with was a variation of another he had used on a cabin farther north, by the Teslin River rapids.

> This cabin has been refurbished by the Sheslay Historical Foundation for use by free men and their friends only. Rednecks beware!

He found a certain satisfaction in leaving messages, a historical continuum, a communication with those who had been before and those who were yet to come. Mostly, though, it was the assertion of *being* that a message represented. It broke the sense of utter and absolute isolation, an isolation more acute than most men had ever experienced—and fewer still could live with. Most of the cabins bore at least one inscription—the name of an earlier inhabitant, a date—some kind of message. But this one had nothing, at least nothing he could find, and he had looked everywhere. It could have been obliterated. The rot had gotten into the logs and they were crumbing away on all exposed surfaces. Oros looked around him and tried to imagine what kind of scenes this cabin had held. It might also have been an early trading post, a collection center for furs from the Teslin watershed to the north. From here, one could easily float a raft down the Nahlin River until it spilled out into the Taku which, in turn, emptied itself into the sea south of Juneau. He himself had done the more difficult trip by raft from Tatsamenie Lake along the Sheslay and then into the Taku to the sea.

Then too, it could just as easily have been an early prospector's cabin. Or an outpost from the boom town of Laketon on the west side of Dease Lake, 100 miles to the east. If it dated back to the times of Laketon, it could be 120 years old. Although thinking about it, it didn't seem possible. Like Johnsontown, Surprise, Porter Landing, Sheslay, and the others, nothing had remained of the community there that had been home to thousands long before the rush of 1898 to the Klondike. Even the stone jailhouse in Laketon, which had seen prisoners led from its cells to the gallows, had crumbled back to the earth. Until the second war when the Americans built the Alaska Highway through British Columbia and the Yukon, all ground traffic had been by foot, dogsled, and boat. There had been a lot of traffic over these trails and past this cabin for almost a hundred years. It all stopped forty years ago when the highway was built. So he knew there was really no way to date the cabin accurately. Anywhere from forty to a hundred years could be right. Cabins never aged the same way. And sadly, without an inscription, the cabin had no real history. It was just there. A cabin on the north side of the Nahlin River.

Oros changed his mind. There wasn't much sense in putting his name, let alone a detailed inscription, to a cabin without history. And, for the cabin, it was already too late to start a new life. And the fire was warm. Too warm to move away from into the clammy darkness that filled the other spaces.

Oros poured himself another cup of coffee, examined with satisfaction the skin of the goat he had stretched out to dry on the wall behind the stove, put his feet back up close to the open firebox, and closed his eyes again, dozing contentedly. It was a good hide. A high-elevation member of the antelope family, this goat had been pushed off the mountaintops by the deeper snows covering the alpine and had already grown its full winter wool. Turned inside out and joined to one or two more hides, it would make a splendidly warm winter cape.

The weather outside grew uglier by the minute, ushering in a howling storm. As snow blew in through the makeshift windows, Oros edged a little closer to the fire. The storm could rage forever, for all he cared, as long as they had a shelter and meat. Nobody would be hunting for him in this weather. Tucked in under the storm in a forgotten cabin in the center of a land inhabited only by himself, feeling full and warm, nothing seemed impossible at this moment. The sweet fragrance of the goat's meat, fried in its own grease, was still lifting off the pan on the stove near his nose. The pan, too close to the heat, was still sizzling, but he didn't move to slide it away. Instead, he contemplated idly whether he should throw another piece of meat into it for himself, whether he could even eat another piece.

Oros was pleased. The desperate need for food had abated with the killing of the goat. Hutsigola was close now, only two days' hard hiking, four or five if they moved cautiously, stalking the trail, watching for traps. The meat would last that long. He didn't know what would happen next, what they would find when they got home. But for the moment, he didn't care.

The sounds of the dogs feeding acted like a narcotic on him. Wild sounds like the rumble and roar of distant thunder breaking with the sharp crack and snap of anger flashing momentarily then subsiding almost to a calm and then rumbling again softly, far off—it was all one sound, whether from the feeding of dogs or the movement of rolling clouds, the sound was the voice of nature. To Oros, it brought back memories—of thunderstorms in Kansas. With eyes closed, listening to them, they were easy to see rolling in across the land, low, hugging the earth, shadowing it under their boiling, black turbulence. That was a long time ago, he thought slowly, calmly, without wanting to disturb the memories. Another lifetime really. Before he had fled to Alaska even and was taken in by Neil. So long ago, it was all more a dream than reality.

He had learned so much and had changed so much since then. In fact, he had changed so much he was another man now. With an entirely different vision.

Chapter Ten

April, 1973: Moon of the Long-necked Cranes: The blisters on his feet worse than ever, Oros relented in his plan to walk all the way and accepted a ride with a truckload of friendly drunks, who insisted he was mad to walk when he could fly with them. They were right. Within a couple of hours, he was in Dease Lake.

After a few days there, meeting people and making connections he felt he'd need later, with his feet greatly improved, he set off on the last leg of his trip to Telegraph Creek. Some of the people he was meeting now, he had already heard spoken of, so small was the community in the north. And some had already heard of him. The local talk was of a stranger coming who had walked all the way from Whitehorse. Oros was flattered. The land, too, was becoming familiar to him. He walked the final stretch of dirt road from Dease Lake to Telegraph Creek through stands of birch and poplar that encroached upon the shoulders. The road passed through low swamps, and over high alpine country carved out of lava rock, and hugged steep cliff faces towering above the raging Stikine River. It was all a series of internal visions to him, of mental constructions brought to life. The country, the landmarks, the odd building, even the taste of the air—it had all been described to him over and over in varying detail until, without ever having been there, he could have passed himself off as a longtime resident. He soaked up information with the capacity of a willow stand soaking up moisture after a long drought, storing the minutiae in his log.

Against the advice of several of the Dease Lake residents, he hadn't acquired a rifle to carry on the walk in. A weapon, he believed, only invited confrontation. Far deeper than his belief that eating flesh was unhealthy and immoral, bearing arms was a sin against nature. He'd never own a gun. And if he ever had one, he could never use it. In any event, he hadn't run into any wildlife larger than marten, although there were fresh bear tracks everywhere. Of all sizes. Whenever he came upon them, he stopped, examined them, and then with Krish sniffing the air, looked carefully around in all directions.

He had been told about the climate changes and was expecting them, but the experience itself filled him with great delight as he walked westward from Dease Lake toward Telegraph Creek. The difference in a distance so short was remarkable. Slogging through slushy snow at Dease Lake, he was now sinking into the mud of the rutted road as he neared Telegraph Creek. And the occasional clearings next to the road were nearly ready for planting.

It took Oros three days of walking on the Telegraph Creek Road before his final destination appeared in the distance ahead. With a surge of nervousness that washed over him, he stopped on the road and pulled out his diary to record the momentous event:

Arrived the 11th day of April, 1973! Telegraph Creek! At last!

The clinging muck of the thawing earth, the skunky smells of wet land recently freed from winter, and the heavy mists that hung like a burlap canopy over the smoky village when he arrived gave it a distinctly other-worldly mood, as though he had stepped back in time to a lost but familiar place. The only two obvious links connecting the tiny community to the outside world were the tenuously constructed road that he had just come in on and the bizarrely incongruous satellite dish near the Department of Highways compound. Television in twenty-eight channels from all over the continental States.

Standing at the edge of town, Oros was in a state of utter exuberance. As the highway widened to become the main street, he followed it, walking slowly, studying everything he passed with intense interest. Past the satellite dish and the Highway Department's yards, he walked by the Indian Band Office and community hall, the post office, an old repair shop, the school, and some new houses. At the Co-op store—its windows boarded up tightly against vandalism but its front door propped wide open with a chair for the spring air—the road, a muddy strip through the village, curved sharply and dipped down into a narrow gully that ran into the valley bottom of the Stikine River. Here, as he made his turn and began his descent, he entered the old town. Around him on both sides of the road, built on the slopes of the riverbank, old log houses still stood—some occupied, others mere ruins, abandoned after the gold rush had no further need of them. Steep yards were built into the riverbanks and were terraced with field stones. The terraces created walkways and steps of narrow gardens. Old boardwalks rotting and buried under a near century of growth meandered across empty fields and into woods. The streets and buildings they once faced were long gone, stripped for their wood and burned. Weathered, gray picket fences surrounded a few small, turreted buildings and a steepled church raised entirely with locally milled timber and boards.

Lower down, large cottonwood trees growing along the shore leaned precariously out over the river, which flowed in a creamy-brown frenzy. Bloated with the spring melt, the river was undercutting its banks. Flat-bottomed, aluminum-hulled riverboats, drawn up out of the water alongside larger fishing skiffs on wooden rollers, were being made ready again for the coming fishing season. Here and there, dogs barked from leashes or followed closely behind, snarling or simply curious, trying to sneak in a sniff at Krish. Oros kept her on a tight leash close by his side while he wandered slowly about, staring at everything.

For the first time in his life, he experienced the reality of a dream he had long held dear—here was a place he belonged! As he surveyed the townsite, he imagined himself living here, or there, and the advantages and disadvantages of each spot. Never before had he been presented with so many agreeable choices and his mind spun with the headiness of it all. But, although he reveled in it, they were only playful notions, for he didn't really want to live right in the village.

On the far side of the river, a long stretch of open clearing on a narrow, flat terrace, thirty feet over the water's surface, was all that was left of that portion of the old town which had once had a population of 10,000 and had spilled across both sides of the river. Nobody lived there now. He eyed it keenly and it held up favorably as a possible homesite for him. Close enough to the village to smell its rich woodsmoke, which hung heavily in the air, and yet distanced by the barrier of the river, it was as private as a man could ever want. It would do, he thought happily. But there were better places yet. And even more to see. The road, he had been told, continued on for another sixteen miles downriver from Telegraph Creek where it ended, finally, at the abandoned town of Glenora.

Glenora had been an American town on Canadian soil, the end of the line for the river sternwheelers that ran up the Stikine from Wrangell. A sister town to Telegraph Creek, it too had a population of 10,000 in its day. There wasn't much left of it now except for some pilings along the shore, a steel beam here and there rising from mounds which had once been old buildings, and a graveyard, wild and grown over under the forest, that still held up a few granite tombstones, most of which belonged to wealthier Americans like the colonel who had worked the shipping line and died there in 1903. But, most promising of all, there were what some of the locals he had met termed hippies—he hopefully termed them real brothers—who were living along the Glenora Road. American refugees from the war.

Mostly, they kept to themselves, he was told, and had their own community. Nobody knew exactly how many there were. Their numbers seemed to fluctuate but there were more than twenty of them. More than enough, Oros figured, for the kind of close community he wanted. And they had found the best part of the country. Just as the climate grew more temperate from Dease Lake to Telegraph Creek, so did it continue to become more moderate farther downriver. Glenora was even closer to the coast. There the rich volcanic soils along the wet riverbanks supported almost tropical gardens. On the higher land away from the water, cherries and plums grew under near perfect conditions. And too, in the sandy soil of the mountainsides, patches of marijuana supplied most of the households, the plants growing quickly in the long daylight hours of summer.

Here, where the salmon spawning up the Stikine turned its tributary creeks crimson with their bodies, here where the Tahltan Indians had lived off the land in settled communities for 6,000 years, as they still lived in Telegraph Creek, he knew with an excitement that sparked his nerves and quickened his breathing as he thought about it, that this was it. It had everything. Even a natural economy based on the land and its seasons. It was an economy that he was sure he, too, could tap into and live from. A salmon a week, cranberries and huckleberries and blueberries by the tub, and a few beehives for honey, would do nicely for a start. Maybe even a small orchard, he mused, dreaming happily about the possibilities of really achieving his dream of a self-sufficient home.

From Glenora, and indeed from Telegraph Creek, the 140 mile run to Wrangell could be made in a day by a small boat, in less than four hours in one of the bigger river jet boats! A few Alaskans from Wrangell, he was told, had erected summer camps along the river west of Glenora where neither the State Troopers nor the Mounties ever patrolled and there they held wild, raging parties that lasted for days.

Oros sat on the edge of a stone wall, looking west down the river in the direction of Glenora and Wrangell, and laughed as he remembered a conversation he had with an operator of a road grader. Working the Telegraph Road, the man had shared some of his coffee with him from a thermos.

"Them American hippies," the man had said, "living out the Glenora Road are a pretty queer bunch. Graded that road there myself a number o' times and met quite a few o' them before we stopped grading there...ain't gonna do no more down that road. Ain't no money and too damn expensive to maintain a road nobody got any use for...except them hippies. Folks here never see much of them and don't have nothing to do with them either.... If I was you, I wouldn't get tangled up with them folk at all."

Following that advice was the furthest thing from his mind. In his imagination, as he sat on the wall staring downriver, he saw himself up in the forward bow of a fast boat on the run down to Wrangell from Glenora for supplies: the sunshine gleaming off the water as it sprayed in broad fantails off the stern, the warm, summer air blowing through his hair as the forests of poplar, saskatoon, dogwood, willow, alder, birch, and cottonwood flanking the river and filling the air with their sweet fragrances whisked past, a cold beer in his hand, some good homegrown, and friends laughing and sunning themselves naked.

Little wonder, he thought, that they never came out to Telegraph Creek or Dease Lake. Even if they survived the grader operator on the road, the river run to Wrangell is faster, smoother, and safer than the drive to Dease Lake. And he knew, having seen both places, that compared to Wrangell, Dease Lake was only a dirt stop.

In Fairbanks before he left, Oros had believed that he'd have to find work around Telegraph Creek to raise the capital to buy his land. But now that he'd arrived, he found the country not only naturally pristine but also that it was far from the guardians of regulation. He didn't have to buy anything. He could squat, like everyone else, wherever he wanted, and there'd be nobody to complain even if they knew he didn't have paper title.

Ah, he wanted to shout for joy. To yell out his happiness with all the power of his lungs. Instead, he contented himself with scratching Krish and assuring the dog that the long hike was over. The wandering was all in the past now.

"We've arrived, old girl. We're really here. Fuck, I can't believe it! And it's better than my wildest, craziest dream.... It's too much! It's got everything. If we can get used to eating meat again we'll never go hungry again either. Salmon steaks, moose, bear, caribou, even wild goats and sheep.... If you were a cat, I'd plant you your own garden of catnip; but I'd guess you'll settle for salmon won't you? Shit, I can't believe it! Imagine, a whole community of brothers and sisters living way out here. I'll bet they can teach us a few tricks about self-sufficiency.... No wonder everybody was splitting from Fairbanks—with places like this to live. And what a place for our friends to visit. They'll be so jealous when they get here and see our home on the river, we'd better start thinking right now of marking off our property or we'll be swamped with our own squatters. You're going to have to learn to bite balls, Krish. When news of this place gets out, it's going to be crawling with urbanites seeking sanity."

And then, laughing, he stood and stretched, breathing deeply of the moist air while his eyes scanned the countryside. Eagerly, he absorbed all the details in the broad lay of the land but concentrated his gaze to the west, toward Glenora, where a range of snow-covered mountains could be seen periodically rising above the ground fog. Now that he had arrived, the pressure he had felt, the urgency of his actions, slipped away and he was content just to be here and in no hurry to start anything—except new friendships. People were now the number one priority. Once he had established himself with the community and knew more of the country, he would then pick out his own special spot. Deciding on the location for his home was one of the most personal decisions he believed he could make and one with the most important criteria rooted deeply in his psyche. The decision to make his home and the exact location of that home was as much mystical as it was rational. Perhaps even more so. It could wait. A decision that would govern the quality of his life for perhaps even the rest of it, could not be pushed, and wouldn't be, he decided finally before he turned away from the river and started to walk back up the road toward Bruce and Jim McGregor's place.

Oros had met the McGregor brothers in Dease Lake a few days earlier and had spent the happiest night he'd had since leaving Alaska with them and one of their friends, Scott. That first night, Scott played the congo, Bruce the guitar, and he the flute. And then, after the music, they'd sat up until dawn with Bruce discussing the philosophy of Lao Tzu. In Bruce, he'd found a true soul mate, and he hoped their friendship would be a long one.

It was the McGregors who showed him how to rig up a carrying system for Krish so that the dog could at least take some of the load off Oros' back. It was so obvious and simple, he was embarrassed by the fact that it had never occurred to him before to use Krish as a pack dog. Until Dease Lake, she had been company only. Now, she carried nearly ten pounds on her back all the time. And that was weight off his back. Even more importantly, the simple fact of working the dog radically changed the way he perceived her. No longer was she simply a living pet that he was responsible for like a caged bird that provided him some basic company and entertainment. Her whole status had changed. There was a real friendship between them now. Carrying her own weight, she was more a partner than a pet. They were a team. There was a sense of balance in the new relationship he hadn't felt before, a bond as man worked with beast for a common goal. In fairness to the dog, though, he concluded, the goals were his and the dog more a servant than partner. But far better that, he argued—resisting the voice of his conscience which had at first made him feel guilty for the new roles—than to suffer the reverse. In retrospect, he realized that he had been the dog's slave, carrying its food on his back while Krish romped freely and at will, chasing squirrels up the trees all the way from Fairbanks.

Since that night, Oros had reexamined all the old values from dogs to people. And now, as he walked along the muddy spring road, the new ideas coalesced into a new vision. In Fairbanks, all his friends had talked about being the new wave of pioneers, reading the books, talking the fantasies, developing the philosophies, mirroring each other's lifestyles. But, with new insight, he realized that it wasn't real at all. None of it was. It was just talk. The revelation that it was all a game was a new one. As he walked through the very real village of Telegraph Creek, the perspective it gave him made him see things so much clearer than ever before. Here, all around him, were gardens and greenhouses. In Fairbanks, the only real garden any of them had had was the greenhouse Rene tended for growing pot. And as much as they talked of scorning the cities, there they lived right on the very fringe of one. Just far enough away in the woods to give the illusion of having adopted a different lifestyle but, in reality, close enough to pass away the hours of a day in its bars or libraries. None of them lived off the land. And the only labor any of them pursued was in search of odd jobs here and there to make enough cash for a beer or the price of a one-way ticket back to the cities in the south.

The more he looked at it, the more contemptuous he felt the whole lifestyle was that they had lived in Alaska—as false and hollow as the urban-commercial work they pretended to abhor.

As critical as these new revelations were, they were liberating, and as he walked through the village, carefully placing his steps to avoid the worst of the mud, he felt as though an early spirit had been exhumed within himself and filled with the breath of new life. In response to every face that looked his way, he shouted out a greeting and waved cheerfully.

"Shit! No wonder I wasn't happy there!" he said, thinking aloud about Alaska. "I was fooled by the talk, the false camaraderie. Like Taos, where the people talked love and peace but were really into hate and destruction."

Oros was truly happy. Here, finally, as he had witnessed not by their speech or philosophy but by their deeds and their very lives, he had come to a society such as he had always wanted. Here were people who were self-reliant. Here, they still lived on the earth as man had for thousands of years, close to it in spirit and body, understanding its seasons and moods.

Oros hadn't abandoned his ambitious dream of building a wilderness retreat to provide a natural base for his friends to work from—his "sanctuary for sanity." That was one thing he had taken with him from Alaska. Although his faith in the people who expounded them had been shattered, his commitment to the old philosophies themselves hadn't been shaken. With new partners if he could find them, or alone if he couldn't, he swore to fulfill his promise. All he wanted now was a place to start building.

Oros was sure that nothing would go wrong anymore.

The very next morning, Bruce and Jim suggested a change of plans. They wanted him to leave Telegraph Creek immediately. The McGregors ran the Hyland Ranch, a big-game hunting camp located twenty-five miles north of Telegraph Creek on the old Telegraph Trail. They had to fly in supplies and do some repairs after the winter. The work would only take him away from Telegraph Creek for a week or so.

There was an appeal to it that Oros found hard to resist, a short-term job and a chance to see the country from the air. He would have preferred to stay and explore the country between Telegraph Creek and Glenora, to study the soils and the run-off, and to look for a place for his own roots, but he had already decided that building friendships was his first priority and the McGregors were people he wanted to know better. Besides, he reasoned, he wouldn't be gone long. A week and he'd be back. If there was anything he had a lot of, it was time. A week couldn't hurt.

Heavily loaded, they flew close to the ground, studying the trails and looking for game. They were all crowded into the cockpit of the de Havilland Otter, with Oros kneeling over the trim for the best view of the country he could get. He had, of course, heard the Telegraph Trail was still visible but the sight of it below them winding through the low country, following creeks and rivers, skirting lakes and rock faces, thrilled him. From the air, it looked like a game trail, the ground imprinted from the weight of thousands of footsteps that followed each other in a line a yard wide that stretched northward from the village of Telegraph Creek.

"It's still in use around here," Jim explained. "We use it to get in and out of our camp and to hunt from. So does Fletcher Daye. We keep it clear but even where it's overgrown farther north, you can still see it."

Oros was beside himself with excitement. Here, almost lost and forgotten, was one of the very trails those heros of old created. Here were their very footsteps. Their lives were still imprinted upon the land.

"Where does it go?" Oros asked breathlessly, leaning forward in the cabin over the controls to search for it as it stretched away across the undulating land, rising and falling in front on them.

"Right to the Klondike. This was the poor man's highway to the Yukon goldfields. Can you imagine the trip that was?" Jim asked and Oros nodded his head.

"So this trail was made in '98?" Oros asked, thinking of Jack London's stories.

"No. It was used then. But it's much older," Jim answered. "The Tahltans probably used it to trade before the white man ever got here, but it's at least as old as the old towns. There were gold seekers up here long before the Klondike rush and they founded a few towns around here. There was a big town called Laketon on the west shore of Dease Lake which is gone now. Hotels, saloons, a Hudson's Bay trading post, a large police detachment, even permanent gallows. Anyway, one trail ran from here to there and another from there to

Johnsontown on the east side of Teslin Lake at the mouth of the Jennings River. The place has mostly disappeared now too. This trail under us runs north for about 100 miles and then splits at the Nahlin River. One branch runs north from there and into the watershed of the Teslin River and ends up at the southern tip of Teslin Lake. From there, the connection with Johnsontown and Teslin and the other old settlements up in the Yukon was by water. All big lake boats. The other branch I mentioned runs northwest to Atlin and that one's still pretty clear. In fact, they were still using it in the 1930s to run mail in the winter by dog team from Telegraph Creek to Atlin. Apparently a good team could make the 200 mile run, heavily loaded with supplies, in twelve days."

Oros was fascinated, even envious of Jim's knowledge of the country. But the names were starting to become familiar to him. It would take time, he knew, but he'd learn the country. Everything there was to know about it.

"Anybody use them anymore?" he asked.

"Dog teams?" Jim asked.

"No. The trails."

"Nope. Apart from our place and Fletcher's, there's nobody near them. Except maybe for the occasional trapper or private hunter out of Atlin, there's nobody else out in this bush. This is it, man! Just what you see. Trees and rocks and swamps and mountains, all the way to the north pole. There's not a soul living north of here until you get to Teslin in the Yukon. You came through there on the Alaska Highway. Remember?"

Oros remembered, mildly insulted by the suggestion that he might not.

"Well," Jim continued, "except for Atlin, we're all alone up here. Hey, Bobby?"

The pilot agreed laughing. "That's right. This is the end of the world. The edge is just up ahead, beyond the horizon. You go any farther from here, boy, and you fall off. Lost forever over the edge."

They landed on New York Lake, a little mudhole barely large enough to take off from. While the plane made several trips back to Telegraph Creek to ferry load after load of supplies to the lake, Oros and Jim sorted the growing pile and erected weather guards over it. In the late afternoon, when the plane flew away for the last time, taking Bruce back to Telegraph Creek, Jim and Oros were left alone in the bush, with three tons of supplies. Bruce promised to return in a few days if he could, to walk out with them back to Telegraph Creek. Oros was looking forward to that—a two-day hike on the Telegraph Trail back to Telegraph Creek. In the meantime, Jim and Oros quickly settled into an easy routine. By day, they hauled supplies on their backs from the lake to the camp a few miles away. In the sunshine, even over the wet snow that remained as deep here as in Dease Lake, the air was warm enough to strip down to the skin. But the moment cloud obscured the sun, blocking it out even for a short time, they were plunged back into a deep freeze that sent them scrambling madly to get on their double shirts and parkas. The feed sacks for the horses were the hardest things to move. Floppy and weighing 100 pounds each, they strained the imagination of the two men hauling them in outdoing each other with inventive curses.

In the evenings, Jim sat quietly reading and left Oros free to contemplate his future. His permanent status in Canada was a matter he wanted settled as soon as possible, knowing that, as unlikely as it seemed that Canadian Immigration would ever find him here, he didn't want to be put at risk of being deported to the States should the situation ever arise. It became obvious to him then that he'd only resolve that worry by getting his Canadian status as soon as possible.

The night they finished the packing, they celebrated by making giant, pan-sized chocolate-chip cookies. The week had passed too quickly for Oros. McGregor's camp had worked some magic on him, transforming him from an outsider to a resident. He couldn't remember when he'd felt so much at home. He found the routine of the camp so congenial after a winter of such suffering that he hated to leave. Jim too, after a week spent hauling heavy supplies, was ready for a little leisure time. When he suggested, between mouthfuls of cookie, that they might just as well stay on a little longer at the camp, Oros jumped at the chance.

Oros felt a little guilty about the decision but it was only April 17. A few more days wouldn't change anything. He had lots of time. In fact, he had all summer ahead of him and there was still snow on the ground. There'd be lots of time to do everything.

They had been at the Hyland Ranch for nearly two weeks when the wolves arrived. It was just before dawn when Oros awoke to their howls outside the cabin. Without thinking about it, Oros was out of bed and dressing as quickly as he could when Jim said sleepily from the darkness, "If you're getting up, you'd better let the dogs inside and hope your bitch hasn't run off for a little strange action."

The wolves had indeed come for the dogs and Oros found them pressed up against the door in terror. When he opened it, they nearly fell over themselves in their haste to get safely inside. With his sleeping bag unzipped and wrapped around him for warmth and his bare feet in his cold boots, Oros stepped quietly outside and stood a short distance from the cabin to listen to the wild night. There were a number of wolves brazenly running about the area and, from time to time, one of them would howl, a long, mournful cry that thrilled him, sending shivers over his skin and causing his blood to course hotly through his body.

Like spirits come to greet the newly alive, they howled and ran around him so closely he could hear their feet padding across the frozen ground.

Exhilarated, he stood in their midst, eyes closed, without fear. They seemed to be performing for him, urging him to take that final step and join them, to cast off all restraint and touch the primordial spirit they embodied.

When the eastern sky cracked a line between heaven and earth to reveal a new alabaster dawn, the wolves slipped away into the forest.

Just above the horizon, the narrow crescent of the moon could be made out against the brightening blue of the sky and Oros quickly christened it. "The Moon of Long-necked Cranes."

Oros licked his finger tip and pressed it up into the air toward the new sun, in greeting, as a golden eagle drifting on the currents sailed into view. It was another good omen.

The second week came to its end. Like the first, it too passed quickly. Too quickly. He wasn't ready yet to leave. Instead of wearing off, the magic that had seeped under Oros' skin was now stronger than ever, compelling him to stay.

Unlike the deadly slow days so recently passed in Fairbanks, the days spent at the Hyland Ranch blended together into one long, pleasant afternoon. Happier than he'd been in recent memory, Oros said nothing at all to Jim about leaving when the time came. And then, grateful for each day, like a gift from a kindly god, he and Jim, in silent conspiracy, drifted into the third week.

Each day passed like the others. Putting off the decision to go back to Telegraph Creek for another day. And then another. And another.

Oros telling himself it was the way of the flow. Things would come together. It would all work out.

Each day the sun rose earlier. Days lengthening into summer. Living each new day as though it might be his last, Oros squandered his opportunities. One day at a time. And then the days turned to weeks.

Oros might have gone all summer without having had any insight into the effects the isolation was having on him and on their relationship, if it weren't for the dramatic way it revealed itself to him. It was an experience he knew too well.

It happened at night after they had bottled eighteen quarts of home brew he had cooked up. Oros was studying Jim's detailed topographical maps of the Telegraph area for a home site.

"The area around Alkali Lake looks good to me. You know the spot?" Oros asked. "Looks about eight miles from Telegraph?"

"Sure do." Jim replied.

"What's the water like there?"

"Got some nice-sized trout in it. Warm enough for swimming, too, in the summer."

"Ah, swimming!" Oros exclaimed. "That's something I really miss. Sure would be nice to settle near the lake or maybe right on the lake itself. Anybody else living there?"

"Probably some," Jim said. "One guy for sure I know about, name's Sam. He's a white trapper—lives somewhere around Six Mile Creek, which is the same general area."

"What's he like?" Oros was already thinking Sam might be a good contact to make. A trapper could teach him a lot about the bush. He wasn't prepared for Jim's response.

"Don't know much about him. What he does is his business, eh?" Jim said and then paused as though struggling to say something that he had been avoiding but had to be said. "Like most of the people here, keep things to themselves. You know what it's like in a small town, eh? Everybody trying to know everything about everybody else? Well, lots of the people came here to get away from that kind of shit. Like yourself. They want their own lives and don't want nobody getting too close."

Oros was shocked to hear it put that way. He didn't feel he was like that but he didn't want any open disagreements with Jim so he kept his reaction to himself.

"Well, I'll be careful not to cross him," he offered. "You know wherever I set up my camp I'll be careful about it. But don't you think if I set up near the lake, that wouldn't be crowding Sam or anyone else? They'd be over a mile away. That is, if I even like the area after I explore it."

Jim thought for a while before he spoke and when he did, Oros wondered whether his words had a deliberate double meaning. Whether they were a subtle warning. He thought so but he couldn't tell for sure.

"There aren't too many people in the whole Stikine Valley. And people are sensitive here to what you do. Even with all the space, one new person is a significant difference."

There, the conversation ended abruptly. Oros became aware of a coldness between them, a void that he felt hadn't existed before. Although he tried to ignore it, the situation had a disturbing similarity to his relationship with Neil.

Later that night, as Jim sat reading under the light of the propane lamps and listening to CKVN, a Vancouver radio station they had found which only came in after dark but didn't wander constantly, Oros lay in the dark on his bed in the loft upstairs. He had excused himself early and retired, trying to keep Jim from discovering the disturbing thoughts he'd been having. For the first time since he'd arrived at the Hyland Ranch, he felt unwelcome. And if he wasn't wanted, he wanted to leave. As soon as he could. To get away from Jim. To get back to Telegraph Creek. He had already wasted so much time.

There were other feelings he was having, too, and in a chain reaction, they started spilling out. Some of them were triggered by the songs the radio was playing downstairs—songs that brought memories of good times that were gone and lost forever, making him want to cry—and some of them just crystallizing out of the deep isolation he was suddenly feeling.

In the darkness, the images floated up white on black. Faces of people he once knew. Places he'd been. Times from the past. His mind, in turmoil, started spinning. Dizzyingly. And still the images came. Faster and faster. Accelerating out of control. Spinning him away.

Oros blinked his eyes, trying to clear his mind. But the images burst instead, like spore from a global puffball, melting time and space. Swirling about in an uncontrolled fury, around and around, the lip of the swirling maelstrom, a kaleidoscope of fragmented memories in the light of sunshine and beneath them, slipping away into the pit, was a black hole of nothingness, sucking everything down into its widening maw, sucking the very air from his lungs, choking the life from him.

Oros couldn't breathe. Soaked in sweat, he was fighting for his very life. For his sanity. In desperation, he leaped from the bed and lit the gas light with trembling hands. The room, brought into focus by the light, superimposed itself over the images which still spun with a frenzy in front of him like a waking nightmare he couldn't run from. Oros shook his head to drive them out of his mind and began talking to himself quickly. The sound of his own familiar voice, whispering, added to the physical reality, building on the little stability that the light provided. Clutching at the sounds of his own voice, he dragged himself away from the edge of the hole he'd been sinking into. Slowly, gradually, the images faded, then stilled. And, finally, he was whole again, back in the room, breathing hard and sweating profusely from the terrible exertion it took to regain control.

Minutes passed and he continued to calm down. Listening, all he could hear was the constant hiss of the burning gas and the radio playing quietly below him through the floor.

By the time he had his journal out in front of him, everything had returned to normal and he wasn't sure, what he should write. He didn't want to think about what had just happened let alone write about it and, now that it had passed, it didn't seem important anymore.

One thing was clear, though. He'd been in the bush too long. It was time to get out. To go back to Telegraph Creek. Soon. Before it got even worse.

He sat down heavily on the edge of the bed, listening to the music that floated up through the floor under him and with a heavy heart started writing in his precise and meticulous print.

> Strange melancholy. Listening to the radio.
> Memories of other places
> And other times
> A sea of faces I'll never know again
> Stretches off into a distant past
> Such a heavy sense...resisting the darkness inside me.

Oros put away the journal and lay back down on his bed. It had been a long time since he'd had such a frightening episode of eroded control. And he didn't like it. It wasn't a good sign. Isolation always seemed to make the feelings worse and there was a strong message in it for him. Bev had been right about one thing.

He couldn't live alone. It was time to leave. Before it was too late.

Chapter Eleven

October 10, 1981: Oros sat under the shelter of the roof staring out through the open door frame at the falling snow. As it touched the black, mirrored surface of Disella Lake, it disappeared instantly, swallowed up by the dark void or transferred into another dimension by the Disella Looking Glass.

Oros had stayed at the cabin at Nahlin Crossing until the sixth feasting on the goat while he scraped its hide and restitched his boots and the dogs' packs. With the dogs' strength regained and his own confidence higher than it'd been in weeks, he had set out finally for Hutsigola—only to run into another storm after a couple of hours on the trail. They had arrived at this cabin yesterday, after two miserable days fighting the storm and camping in the bush.

His eyes traveled along the shoreline of Disella Lake, resting at the spot, now covered in fresh, falling snow, where, not long ago, he had buried the puppy, Lola. Although he'd had Lola for only a few months, her death was still painful to him. He remembered her as a good dog, one that he would have preferred to Toot.

He hadn't wanted to hurt her, he remembered. In fact, he had slept with her ever since he got her. Oros shook his head sadly. Lord, he had been made to do terrible things.

The memory of it was as vivid in his mind as it was when he filled pages of his diary with it.

He had passed the summer in the bush southwest of Sheslay with the dogs, living on berries and salmon. Until late July, everything had gone well. Until he had decided to head north, back to Hutsigola. The bugs were bad all summer but they got even worse every mile farther north they traveled until, finally, to escape them, he detoured up a mountain with the dogs. After a few bugless but hungry days camped near the snow line in the cold, breezy mountain air, they climbed back down into low country, determined to push on to Hutsigola. But when they entered a large burn, Oros experienced one of the worst bug-infestations ever. The mosquitoes swarmed in clouds over them and the blackflies bored into their flesh at every opportunity, causing blood-scabbed and itchy welts to rise by the dozens. The dogs, reluctant to move forward, had to be kicked and dragged ahead. It was in the burn that Lola, the puppy, had collapsed. Oros looked her over carefully and saw that she was very sick but, at the time, the only thing he could imagine that could have done it to her were the bugs. She was a mass of bites.

Now, as he sat calmly at Disella Lake and reflected back, Oros thought she wasn't sick from the bugs at all but had been reacting to the poison the sneak-arounds had sprayed on the bush. Although she had been a healthy dog when he found her in Teslin, he figured Lola had succumbed first because she was the smallest. Thinking about it, he remembered she'd actually been sick even before the worst bug attacks. It was early August when they'd entered the burn but it was in July that she had gone from an energized bundle of life to a lethargic lump of complaining fur.

Of course, the poisons would be more concentrated in the burn, he reasoned. In a living forest, they'd be absorbed and dispersed more rapidly. Lola had merely gotten worse in the burn. She was so bad, he remembered, that he had to tie her onto Toot's pack, forcing Toot to carry her until Toot went lame under the extra weight.

Oros shook his head at the memory, grateful at the moment for the wintry weather which had finally killed the bugs off. But back in early August, the sun's rays, burning for days through cloudless skies, had produced a dry, acidic heat that rose in fluid waves off the ground and seemed to inspire the insects to multiply their own number a thousandfold. Oros remembered that his own nerves, over-taut with the prolonged stress, had been ready to snap when they stumbled on a small and unnamed green lake. At the time, the oasis had seemed to be a gift from the gods. On seeing it, Oros stripped down and, rushing out into the lake, submerged himself in relief up to his nose in the shallower water along the edge.

They had stayed beside the pool for several days, until Toot and the pup recovered sufficiently that Oros thought them fit to travel again. He had been in the process of packing up the last few things from their camp when, suddenly, out of nowhere, a small plane drifted over them to land on the lake.

Oros had tied down the dogs immediately and belly-crawled to the shore to a secure hiding spot to see what was going on. The plane was floating with its power off, drifting quietly on the water on the far side of the lake. Oros snuck around the lake through the bush and got as close as he could to it.

When the two men inside got out to stand on the pontoons and examine their surroundings, Oros had raised his rifle and taken a quick bead on the one he figured was the pilot, then, silently but furiously, debated with himself whether or not to kill him. He was an easy shot; the man was standing in full view not 100 yards away. In fact, Oros was pretty sure he could kill them both before they could get away and if they were on foot, he would have done it, he knew. But an aircraft was too formidable. The plane meant they had an organization behind them. Although they were both old men, he had no doubt that these two were both sneak-arounds. There was no other reason for them to be on the lake. They were probably torture-druggers too, he thought, using the aircraft to spread their poisons.

He wanted desperately to kill them. It wasn't often he had this kind of opportunity. Still, he didn't press the trigger, knowing that if he killed these men, others would be down on him immediately.

Instead, with his own fears riding heavily on his shoulders, he quickly gathered his things and fled. Running hard, he quit only when it was too dark to go any further. Convinced the presence of the plane meant the bush had recently been sprayed with "torture-drugs," he was frantic to get as far from the infected areas as he could, knowing that if he didn't, he would soon be reeling in waves of pain. Already he could feel his skin crawling—the beginning signs.

He was making camp for the night and unpacking some of his things when he discovered he'd lost his knife. It was the long-bladed hunting knife he'd used for the past couple of years. Realizing the knife could only have slipped its sheath when he was crawling around the green lake watching the sneak-arounds, he decided to go back. Whatever the risk, he needed that knife.

The entire next day was spent in an exhausting trip retracing their steps back to the lake. And he was right. He found his knife on the shore where he'd lain in hiding. The plane was gone and, after recovering his knife, he scouted the entire shoreline around the lake looking for tracks or anything else out of place. But there wasn't a single sign that the men from the plane had come to shore. That was ominous. It confirmed his belief that the men had been sneak-arounds. Anybody else would have come to shore. There was no other reason for landing.

With the fear rekindled that he was in the center of a recently sprayed area, he once again fled from the green lake as though his life depended upon it. Exhausted and threatened, his temper on a hair-trigger, Oros was in no mood for disobedience from the dogs. When the pup balked at climbing onto a hastily constructed raft Oros had thrown together to get them across a deep river and then tried to run off into the bush to hide from him, Oros snapped. Lola was slowing them down. Her disobedience was threatening their lives.

Catching Lola by her hide, Oros lifted her up by the skin and started punching her with his fist. Over and over again he struck her. Even after she lay limp in his grip.

Strapping her unconscious body to Toot's back, they pushed on. The creepy-crawly feelings that shot across his skin like electrical currents had gotten worse. And his vision was starting to blur, although whether from his own exhaustion and lack of food or from being poisoned, he couldn't tell. To make matters worse, after only a few hours of carrying Lola, Toot suddenly went lame again and collapsed with the weight on his back. He could still travel on three legs but not with any load. Rather than risk Smoky or Kila also going lame, Oros lifted Lola up to his own back and, after carefully covering her body with the flap of his pack so that only her head lay outside, cradled against his own ear, he set off again. His own muscles were now getting rubbery. He saw this as another symptom of the poisoning, one which finally confirmed to him that the men he'd seen were, in fact, torture-druggers and, worse, that they'd gotten him again with their drugs.

While the pains he suffered multiplied, he continued to carry Lola on his back, constantly reminded of her suffering by the noises she made in his ear. When finally they stumbled off the trail safely at Disella Lake, the relief Oros felt in having finally escaped was shattered by the overwhelming grief when he lifted Lola out of his pack only to find that she had died quietly while he was carrying her.

By dawn, as Oros faithfully recorded Lola's death in his journal, his grief had focused itself into a burning desire to hurt them back. He wanted to avenge Lola's death. To kill the people who had killed her. Blood for blood.

He set off soon afterward for Zancudo Lake, arriving there, after two nights on the trail, on August 20. As always, Zancudo was a milestone, being only a short day's hike from Hutsigola.

Although two nights had passed since burying Lola, the penmanship he displayed that night, sitting by the fire at Zancudo and writing by its light, remained so disturbed it was barely recognizable as his own.

Anxious to get back, Oros had left Zancudo early in the morning, expecting to arrive at Hutsigola by midafternoon. From Zancudo, the route home was an easy one. Connecting the two lakes was a trail, largely overgrown but still passable, that had once been a well-used track in the days of the gold rush. No one used it any more, except for Oros. As familiar to him as the trails that circled Hutsigola Lake, Oros considered it all part of his private territory, his home ground.

Oros had just cleared the edge of the swamps surrounding Zancudo, to a point where the trail took on its first real form, when he suddenly stopped cold in his tracks. Ahead of him, running like a highway straight for Hutsigola, was the trail. But it wasn't the overgrown and crowded footpath it was when he had left it. It had been cleared right out. Oros bent low to examine the stumps, and then the sawdust that lay about. The trees and limbs that had been cut away had all been dragged off to one side. It was now wide enough to drive a car down it, or at least a snowmobile.

Farther on, he came to the remains of a small fire that had burned on the trail and he examined that too. It was all fresh. Everything. The cut brush, the sawdust, and now the ashes. The sheer boldness of it all was terribly disturbing.

With his gun at the ready and the dogs firmly tied down, he set off cautiously along the trail to find the answers. Although he tried to keep his head clear and his thinking in order, his emotions were in turmoil and his thoughts were scrambled.

Upon the heels of Lola's killing, they had now invaded his own sanctuary.

Nothing was going to stop him now.

Knowing every tree and stump in the bush around the cabin made it especially easy for him to creep right in close without being seen. There, beside the cabin, not twenty yards away, was a man bent over a portable field mill. As Oros watched, the man ran his chain saw along the edge of a small log and then added the board he made from it to a large pile of lumber he'd already cut. Nearby was the man's tent. Beside that, his cooking fire was still smoldering. Around it, in an area the size of an acre, the trees had all been cut down. In their place there was now a stumpy field.

Oros' eyes slipped past the man to a pile of supplies drawn up on the shore and covered by a tarpaulin.

The man was moving in on Oros! In 1,000 square miles of wilderness, he was building a cabin in Oros' yard!

Oros would have shot him instantly, only he wasn't sure the man was alone and he didn't want to kill him only to be surprised by others. As he had done so often in the past, Oros lay behind cover and watched. Until he was satisfied. And then he killed him.

Oros fired straight into his back.

The force of the bullet knocked the older man face forward, spinning him bodily into the ground. Shot through the right lung, he took a few moments to die.

Oros spent the next several days cleaning up the mess. Covering Lishy's tracks and hiding his things. The German had come in with a mountain of supplies. Not only had he set up a portable camp, completely outfitted with food, fuel, and cooking ware, but he also had brought in the tools and prefabricated parts to build himself a permanent cabin—everything from double-glazed, premade windows to roofing tar paper. Oros was shocked by the activity. In the short time he had been at Hutsigola Lake, Lishy had felled, peeled and cut to length all the logs for the new cabin. Beside the logs, in neat stacks, were more boards cut than he'd need for the roof and the floor combined. With everything ready to be put together, Oros guessed, Lishy would have had the cabin up and finished in only a few more weeks. It amazed him. As far as building a home was concerned, this German had almost done more in the short time he'd been here than Oros had been able to accomplish in almost ten years. The thought of it made him angry. The inequities of life always bothered him.

For the next couple of weeks, Oros did little else but hunt and fish to feed himself and the dogs and to put up meat for the winter. Apprehensive about the consequences of having killed Lishy, he stayed close to Hutsigola to keep an eye on things, armed and ready for a fight if it should be necessary. He had killed Lishy on August 21 and then worked at a furious pace for a couple of days to conceal that fact; but as the days that followed slowly passed into weeks and still nothing happened, he began to believe that Lishy might have been working alone and that there'd be no consequences at all. Being safely home, too, had helped calm him down as much as did the regular routine which followed, which involved the constant washing of his clothes and body in the lake to dilute and rinse the poisons out of them. Physically too he was feeling much better and, toward the end of the month, almost normal.

By September 10, when the plane flew in, Oros was as ready for it as he could ever have been.

Thinking back over it now, he wasn't sorry he'd paddled out to talk to the pilot. He had to find out if the plane was connected to the German. And finding out that it was had set the course for him since then. Remembering his own flight from Hutsigola, he was reminded that he had felt like killing Toot and promised himself once again that he'd replace the dog, the very first chance he got.

Well, he thought, luck had been with him. Things were falling into place. He'd been to Sheslay and back and the weeks had passed without mishap. So far.

He had earlier checked the pup's grave and was heartened to see that it hadn't been disturbed. Now that winter had begun and snow was covering the frozen earth, it would be safe from discovery until spring. He had prepared the German's body even more carefully. If the dog's grave had gone undetected, so too would the German's.

Beyond the frame of the doorway, the falling snow had gained momentum. Coming down in sheets, it was obscuring the surface of Disella Lake. Early for winter, Oros thought. He brought his hands up to his mouth and, cupping them together, blew his warm breath through them a few times until the feeling came back to them.

Tomorrow, he was going to leave for Zancudo Lake, whatever the weather, and the next day would get him home. He was worried about what he'd find this time. He had no way of knowing what had happened after the pilot left Hutsigola a month ago with the news that they'd lost the German. Oros was convinced that they—the other torture-druggers and sneak-arounds—were capable of anything. And although he was hoping they hadn't touched his things, he was afraid they might have gone on a rampage and destroyed everything.

As he wondered what was happening at Hutsigola, Oros flipped through the diary in his hands. His worst fear was losing the diaries.

Oros had believed long ago that his life would somehow bring inspiration and meaning to the world. He didn't believe that any longer. In fact, there was little enough left of hope even to inspire himself. He still believed his life was a mission. But it was one with a secret message far removed and more ominous than any he had imagined years ago, even in his darkest hours. Oros felt that the onus of this secret had fallen solely on his shoulders and although the burden of his task crushed him with despair at times, he nevertheless embraced it completely. Whereas in the past he had lived and then recorded his experiences in his journals, more and more he was living now only to record his experiences. The journals were now more important than his own life. They would outlive him, he was sure, and would take his message to the people.

All that mattered now were the journals.

Although his passion for writing had not diminished over the years, he was less verbose than he had once been. The narrowness of his existence, its focus, the social isolation, the rigors of his battles had all taken their toll in limiting the field of his expression. He now used words in their full literal meaning and with strict economy. He had started his most recent journal only three months ago. He had most of the last seven years of his writing cached near Hutsigola. His fear that the people hunting him might find those hidden diaries tormented him. He simply could not bear the thought of losing them. They meant everything to him and his last great goal was to somehow get them out, to have them published. They were his proof of what had happened to him, of what was happening. He had it all written down, every incident recorded and documented. In thousands of pages.

Oros had no doubt the sneak-arounds were after his diaries. The diaries were his only records and if he died, if they were successful in killing him, the diaries would be the only evidence. If they got their hands on the diaries and destroyed them, they'd win everything. He well remembered having had some stolen from a secret cache he had near Swift Lake, a few years ago. Six or seven, he guessed. That had been one of the worst losses he could remember.

Since then, he had gathered seven more years of evidence to indict them. All of it written down. Every new event, another piece to locate and place into the jigsaw puzzle that spanned years.

It all fit together. The fights, the torture-drugging, the sneak-arounds, the German. Even the killing of Lola. It hadn't always been as clear to him as it was now.

Now he knew that it was their voices he'd been hearing all these years—those furtive voices that called out to him so often from out of the blackness of the darkest nights. Laughing at him. Taunting and tormenting him. Time after time, over the years, he'd taken up their challenge and fired his gun off into the forest, hoping to hit them. At times he even chased after them, running wildly through the bush in search of them.

But they had always eluded him. Even in the dead of winter, in the deepest of snow, he'd never found a thing. Not a trace. Not once. It was a frightening prospect—that they were so good they didn't leave any signs behind.

Yet he always knew when they were out there. He'd wake in the mornings to terrible sensations of poison painfully wracking his body and know with the certainty of his own agony that the sneak-arounds and torture-druggers had once again spread their poison over everything. He knew they were trying to kill him. The torture-druggers who spread the poisons even told him so. From loudspeakers strung through the forests, they sometimes broadcast their messages of death to him at night.

Oros now believed that, at first, they had only wanted to scare him, to drive him out of the forest. But he had stayed. And so they changed their tactics. Now they wanted to kill him. And slowly or quickly they were doing it. He already had a dozen physical symptoms he could attribute to the drugs, symptoms that had been recurring over the years, from swollen and aching testicles to blurred vision, depression to bouts of acute lethargy. He had it all written down, all carefully documented in the diaries. And because of that, he had no doubt that they wanted his diaries. In them, he had also recorded the events that exposed the conspiracy. It wasn't all clear to him. In fact, most of it seemed totally incomprehensible. But there was one truth he had distilled from it all that kept him committed to fighting them for as long as he was able: everything bad that had ever happened had happened because of them. Everything.

Their killing Lola was only the last of a long history of crimes they had committed against him. More than spreading their poisons, those netherworldly people who moved like mists through the forests, spying upon him and taunting him, had also kept others away. They had spread rumors about him on the outside so nobody else had ever come to the forest to make their home with him. They had cut him off from friends, isolated him in the forest. They had destroyed his Eden and collapsed his dreams.

They were destroying the wilderness. To drive free men from the country and back to the cities where they could be forever and completely controlled, these people were poisoning the earth. And, because he knew what they were up to, he knew they'd kill him too. The first chance they had. Oros hoped that it wouldn't be soon, but things had recently escalated and he wasn't sure what to expect next.

Ever since he'd killed the German, he had been trying to figure out what the other sneak-arounds would do next and then plan his own moves. He wasn't having any luck, though. It was like trying to see through a solid mountain wall. Even the Tarot was reading with mixed messages.

Still, he reflected, the German had died easily.

Easier than a dog, he thought, and then, relaxing, laughed at the idea. He was happy. The realization that he could in fact kill them, that they died even easier than animals, made him feel giddy. Finally, after years of running from them and hiding, of living in fear of their poisons, of being tortured by them, he realized he could stand up to them. And win. He didn't have to be afraid anymore. He had the power of life and death.

Chapter Twelve

May 5, 1973: Moon of Mosquitoes and Rushing Creeks: Oros didn't return to Telegraph Creek. As often happened, daylight brought relief and a change of heart. Although, when he emerged finally from his room, he was still shaken and pale from the eruption of his psyche.

Perversely, he was now fighting his need to leave as though the exercise of free choice existed entirely apart from his own emotional and psychological needs. More than anything, he wanted to be free and that meant control over his decisions. He felt that leaving was running away. And that, he wouldn't do. Desperate not to give in to fear, Oros rejected the wisdom of leaving, stubbornly refusing to acknowledge the real significance of his own experience.

Determined now to stay at the Hyland Ranch until the natural flow of things returned him, at the proper time, to Telegraph Creek, he drifted back into the easy routines they had established.

After a few more days, the nightmare experience as well as the plans he had made that flowed from it, had passed away. Almost from conscious memory.

Although constantly aware of the need to leave, to find a place to set up his own home, he was nevertheless reluctant to go. At least here he had a place to sleep and food to eat. All he had to look forward to at Telegraph Creek was work. And there was too much of that to be very enthusiastic about.

As the days that followed blended effortlessly into weeks, Oros did nothing to disturb the balance. When the time came to move back to Telegraph Creek, he'd know it. It would happen naturally.

Finally, with the spring bloom maturing into early summer, the translucent quality of the forest that invited penetration gave way to a darkening opacity that surrounded them with an impenetrable and chilling isolation. Peering at the forest from the sanctuary of the clearings around the camp, Oros at last felt that the time had come to make a move. To leave. To return to Telegraph Creek and build his own home.

Jim had other plans.

It was a quiet day, with the occasional raven breaking the calm with its hoarse call and a few chickadees chirping like insects here and there.

Jim raised the dripping toilet plunger out of the drum of steaming water and turned to Oros, sitting on a stump with his feet up on another log.

"What say you, we go visiting?" Jim asked. It was immediately obvious to Oros that Jim didn't mean Telegraph Creek.

"Oh, sure!" Oros said sarcastically. "Why don't we just send out invitations and hold a party right here?"

"No, I'm serious," Jim explained. "Let's hike up to Sheslay and visit Michael."

Oros raised his eyebrows. After weeks in the McGregor camp alone with Jim, nothing had ever been said about anyone else living in the bush. And north of them, too. He had assumed there was nothing north of them for hundreds of miles. Only an empty, unbroken, and hostile wilderness.

As Oros thought about it, Jim dropped the plunger on the ground beside the fire which burned under the large drum and then, gingerly picking the clothes one at a time out of the water, he fed them carefully through a handwringer. Oros leaned over Jim to see the color of the water as it left the clothes. As soon as he saw it, he laughed. But Jim wasn't pleased.

"Fuck, I can't believe it!" Jim said. "How many times do I have to wash my fucking clothes before they're clean? Look at them. They're still filthy!"

The water pouring from between the rollers ran down along the grooves of the sloping tin shelf to the edge where it spilled off the table in gray and dirty streams to the ground.

"Oh, well," Oros said cheerfully. "Cleanliness is such a relative and subjective thing anyway."

"Shit! Three times is enough. If I had a washing machine, fine. I could let it run for a week. But I'll be damned if I'm going to stir them around in this barrel anymore."

"I wouldn't," Oros said encouragingly. "Mind you, they didn't look bad to me even before you started."

"I'd rather they were cleaner than this but without a washing machine up here, this hand washing is for the birds."

"Ah, the seductive lure of technology.... Pretty soon you'll be wanting to eat Pop Tarts and Instant Breakfasts."

Jim ignored him and critically examined the pair of jeans he had just cranked through the wringer.

"Who's Michael?" Oros asked after a few moments.

Apparently content with the results, Jim smoothed out the creases in his jeans and draped them over a wire clothesline before he answered. As he spoke, he continued to pull clothes from the barrel and fed them into the narrow gap between the rollers which he cranked noisily with the handle.

"Some dude who lives by himself up in Sheslay. Used to be a town there, a day's walk from here. Not much left now. Even the old ruins are pretty much gone. Anyway, the trail goes right through the old townsite and that's where he lives, right on the Telegraph Trail about fifteen miles from here, farther north. He's American, I think. One of your kind."

Oros winced but didn't say anything.

"How long's he been out here?" Oros asked.

"About two years," Jim replied. "He hasn't come into Telegraph since last July, though. Been out in the bush all alone since then."

Oros whistled. The idea of living alone for so long was impossible to grasp. He himself had spent close to ten days alone—the longest time he had ever spent absolutely alone—in his cabin in Fairbanks the past winter and that was long enough. Things had started to happen to him in those ten days that were spooky. It wasn't an experience he ever wanted to repeat.

"You think he's still alive?" Oros asked seriously.

"If he's not, he won't have left much behind," Jim joked. "He's got a reputation for real basic living, and I mean real basic. I guess living up there you got to. It's too far to walk from Sheslay to Telegraph for food—ninety miles round trip—so I figure he's probably pretty wasted by now. Unless he's figured out a way to live off snow.... Should be a gas to drop in on him anyway."

Oros' mind was reeling. There was a kind of *deja vu* in Jim's whole description. "Michael." They even had the same name. Unlike the people in Fairbanks, here was a brother with the same spirit he had. Someone he intuitively felt had been inspired by the same dream he had and who had come out here before him, two years ago. It was mind-boggling. Family! Here! Thousands of light years from home. Only fifteen miles away.

There was something compelling about it: unfocused, impossible to articulate, and almost mystical. He had planned to go south, to return to Telegraph Creek but now, without hesitation, he agreed to go north, deeper still into the forest. To meet a real brother living alone off the land, he'd go to Sheslay or anywhere else ten times distant that offered so much. Like a window into his own future, the experience was too irresistible to pass up.

Had he had any inkling of where it would lead, any insight at all into the deadly trap he was putting himself into, Oros would have fled back to Telegraph Creek, firmly placing himself as close as comfort allowed to the people he knew best. But he had none. There was no way of knowing that this journey would ultimately lead him to his worst nightmare—abandoned and alone at the beginning of a long, frightening odyssey in the wilderness. Instead, with the lengthening days of summer, optimism was boundless. He still believed there would be time for everything and everything would fall into place in time.

They began the hike a couple of days later, a journey deeper into the very forest that, by its alien impenetrability, had convinced Oros there was something to be said after all for living in an environment of people. But their spirits were high. With the smell of adventure in the air, the trail open and well marked, it was a joy to be out feeling the rapid pulse of the land in the early summer heat. Around them, late-blooming trees were still bursting their buds and the sunshine filtered to the ground through a thick wash of color, splashing light into countless shades of green and yellow. Flowers and wild grasses lined the way, scenting the air with their sweet fragrances. Here and there, Jim stopped to examine tracks in the earth and to point out the distinguishing features between wolf and coyote, marten and fisher, squirrel and weasel. The deep impressions of a grizzly bear needed no explanation and even Oros, who had yet to see one in the flesh, knew the animal which had left them had to be a giant among its own species. In immediate response to the fresh tracks, the two men raised their voices in nervously exaggerated conversation and then broke out laughing as they took off running, trying to outdistance each other.

Coming upon a spruce grouse clucking slowly across their trail, Oros waved at Jim to freeze. Bending low to the ground, his fingers closed around a smooth stone which he drew back over his shoulder. Then, with well-measured force, he threw it with all his skill at the small bird. The sight of the stone bouncing harmlessly off the ground far behind the bird sent Jim into a fit of hysterical laughter.

"Jesus Christ your aim's lousy!" Jim roared.

"I wasn't trying to hit it," Oros lied. "I was trying to scare if off so you wouldn't kill it with your mindless rifle. I was just feeling benevolent."

Jim shook his head and laughed. "What crap! For someone so recently weaned off a vegetarian diet, you're rather anxious to make your mark on our local fauna."

"Just trying to fit in," Oros said more honestly.

"Then you'll have to get yourself one of these," Jim said, raising his rifle. "You won't get far throwing stones." And then as though to prove his point, another grouse appeared, which Jim shot immediately, neatly taking its head off at forty feet.

Jim quickly skinned the bird, tossing the feathery bundle aside, and then gutted it. From the corner of his eye, he saw Oros pick up the bird's skin and tuck it away into a corner of his pack.

"What are you taking that for?" he asked immediately.

Embarrassed at having been caught, Oros couldn't look at him. "I'll use it."

"For what?"

"I'll find some use for it," Oros insisted.

Jim burst into laughter again. "I'll bet you're one of those people who collects things, aren't you? Paper bags and rubber bands, too?"

Oros didn't know why he had kept the bird's skin, only that it seemed wasteful somehow to leave it. And sad.

The crop of the grouse was full of highbush cranberries, which grew in abundance everywhere over the low ground, the fall berries, bitter and slightly fermented, still clung to the branches. As Jim pointed out different things about the forest, which now seemed so vibrant and welcoming in the sunshine, Oros' perspective shifted and he thought of it again as a veritable Garden of Eden, the abundance of edible plants and animals apparent everywhere. As the grouse had done, he too stripped the berries from the branches along the way, popping them into his mouth as they traveled north along the old Telegraph Line Trail toward Sheslay.

Seen from the distance when they broke into the open clearings at

Sheslay, Michael's cabin was a strange-looking affair. Standing only a few feet high, it was in fact dug down into the ground; the clearance inside was barely enough to allow a man to stand upright without hitting the flat-timbered roof. The walls were log, though, and the heavy door, latched and bolted, was obviously meant to keep out bears, as were the tiny windows set on each side of the narrow building.

To their surprise, Michael wasn't home, although the smell of the cabin spoke of recent and prolonged habitation. Michael's absence disappointed Oros and when Jim suggested that they might as well wait for a couple of days to see if Michael returned, he never even considered it before he agreed.

Going with the flow. One step at a time, Oros was sealing his own fate.

They slept that night amid the ruins of Sheslay. Existing once at the confluence of the Hackett River and Egnel Creek, there was little left of the original settlement of Sheslay. The forest had swallowed up most of the cleared land and all that remained of the original buildings were low mounds like the lumpy ground of an abandoned and overgrown graveyard. Even the history of the town had been forgotten. Whether its roots were an Indian community, a trading post, a gold town, or an early pioneer settlement, nobody could say anymore.

They awoke late in the morning, surprised this time by a party of hunters moving quietly through Sheslay on horseback. Seeing a group of armed men, Oros was immediately apprehensive; but Jim broke into a broad grin and, waving at the lead rider, rushed to greet him.

It was Fletcher Daye, a big-game hunting outfitter who wintered near Telegraph Creek. With him were a group of American hunters from Pennsylvania after spring bear. Jim made the introductions and although Fletcher paid little attention to Oros, he seemed genuinely pleased to see Jim, immediately offering to hire him on as a guide for the rest of the spring hunting season. Just as quickly, Jim agreed.

Oros' face flushed in alarm. In one instant, everything had changed. The bomb had dropped. Fletcher's next words didn't come too soon. In a state of rising panic at the thought of Jim suddenly mounting one of Fletcher's horses and then riding off, abandoning him, alone in Sheslay, Fletcher's invitation to Oros, spoken almost in afterthought, to join the camp, was gratefully accepted.

Fletcher's base camp was a collection of canvas-covered cabins, woodstoves, and log buildings several miles from Sheslay. There, Oros settled in, bunking in with the wranglers and the other hands Fletcher had working for him.

After weeks of being alone with Oros, Jim was obviously pleased to be in the company of old friends and left Oros to his own resources.

Spending a few hours each day doing odd jobs around the camp for Fletcher, Oros didn't miss Jim's company either. He had a lot more to think about. New interests had developed. Although he found little in common with the other men in Fletcher's crew, Fletcher's own son, Freddie, was different.

Oros saw qualities in Freddie that he wanted to possess himself and, although they were the same age, he quickly developed a kind of hero worship for Freddie.

A few days after he moved into the Daye camp, Freddie took him along on a scouting trip into the mountains on horseback. Climbing steadily, they broke out of the trees an hour from camp and, after another mile of low and patchy ground cover, Oros, breathlessly excited, found himself transported to a land he had thought was gone forever. Like the prairie foothills, the earth leveled out into wide, sweeping stretches of alpine meadows that flowed in giant ripples across the country from peak to peak, the valleys between them sometimes dipping down into the forests. Wading marshes and streams and circling snow-filled basins, Freddie scoured the country for information on the sheep and goats they'd be hunting in the fall while Oros galloped along beside him. It was more exhilarating and beautiful than anything Oros had ever experienced. Deeply moved, he was grateful to Freddie for having been given the opportunity to be a part of it.

Studying Freddie almost as much as the alpine country they rode through, Oros saw in Freddie's bearing the embodiment of the spirit of the land—wild, powerful, commanding, and confident. Oros hoped that, over time, he too would be transformed, like Freddie, into a creature of the wild mountains. At home anywhere. With the soul of the land mirrored in his eyes. Like a god.

Oros also continued to be intrigued by the stories of Michael and when the news of Michael arrived in camp one day—a hunter having spotted him moving in the forest a few miles from the Daye camp—Oros' nerves tingled with an unusual and excited anticipation. To Oros, Michael was a mysterious figure, a traveler like himself, but a man on his own mission, living all alone in the immensity of the wilderness. Like Freddie, Michael possessed an irresistible attraction for Oros—he had sailed forth over waters that Oros had yet to venture into. And he had returned. Oros wanted to get to know him.

After that first sighting, Michael was observed more and more frequently. Most often he was spotted out in the open, circling wide around the Daye camp, like a wolf, avoiding other people. But Oros deliberately and painstakingly sought him out. Hiking the four miles to Sheslay whenever he could, he took every opportunity to try to make contact. Eventually he succeeded.

A difficult person to find, Oros discovered Michael was even more difficult to befriend. And, like the taming of a wild bird, he accomplished it slowly and with patience.

After a year in the bush with no outside contact, Michael had developed a protective kind of suspicious hostility toward strangers; but gradually, Oros won his confidence. And when he did, they became friends.

As he intuitively knew he would, Oros found he had a lot in common with Michael.

Although not as warm and friendly as Neil or Jim, Michael had something the others in his life all lacked. Michael was a man of action. He lived his dreams. And although Oros admired Freddie, it was all from a distance. With Michael, it was different. More human. Michael could read right into his mind and from him he had no secrets. Fellow travelers, they were true soul mates.

As unlikely as it could ever be, here, in the wilderness of northern British Columbia, Oros found the brother he had always wanted.

From the beginning, as their friendship grew, Oros started gravitating away from Fletcher's camp closer to Michael's world and his vision of things. And although Oros observed a tension between Fletcher and Michael, as though they each resented the presence of the other in the area, Fletcher never tried to stop Oros from going off to visit Michael, nor did he raise any objection when, later, Oros started taking Fletcher's food to him.

As Jim had said, and Oros found out, Michael did indeed live simply, his main source of food being a small illegal trapline he was running for beaver along the Hackett River. Setting aside the pelts and the beavers' valuable oil sacks, Michael showed Oros how to cut the meat in strips and then hang it, red and raw, high up off the ground to dry slowly in the shaded air without smoke. Once dried, the beaver jerky kept for months, he explained, and a man could live on it through an entire winter, as he had. To Oros, who was still trying to justify to himself the killing and eating of wild game, the mere sight of the dried strips of blackened, raw meat turned his stomach, although he did his best to conceal that fact. These, after all, were the secrets to Michael's survival.

When Oros pointed out that the meat, though dry, was still raw and that smoking it might be better, Michael explained that smoking didn't actually cook it and that originally it was only to keep away the flies.

"And, as a matter of fact," Michael added, "all the flies do is lay their eggs on the meat, and since maggots are quite edible, the whole fuss is really quite stupid. You know, the Pueblo Indians used to cultivate maggots in fly gardens to eat as a main course. Once you get used to them, they're really no different than eating frogs' legs or mushrooms."

Realizing that Michael meant the maggots and that he was talking from personal experience, Oros fought back the nausea while Michael continued relentlessly.

"Look, you want to live out here, you're gonna have to change your thinking!... Like, nothing they teach you prepares you for this."

The end of the spring hunt was marked by the cremation of one of Fletcher's horses, which had gone lame and had to be shot. It was one of Oros' first funerals and he helped pile brush up over it until the flames burned twenty feet high.

In the evening, Oros returned alone to the funeral pyre, now a glowing mountain of embers. Low flames licked up around the horse's legs, which had somehow turned to point up to the sky. Its blackened hide, a burned and crispy shell, had cracked and gasses were hissing out of the fissures. Its head was thrown back into the coals and the heat had burned off its lips exposing its teeth which grinned horribly up at him from the bed of glowing embers. From out of the deep, gaping eye sockets streamed twin pillars of creamy smoke, draining its very brain matter into the night.

Oros stood mesmerized by the thing which had died so easily but was now refusing to burn away, sputtering and smoldering as though in final outraged resistance.

From out of the evening's shadows, one of the American hunters came over to Oros and stood, his back to the fire, directly in front of

Oros. Completely oblivious to the rank inferno behind him, he politely asked Oros what the date was.

Dumbfounded, Oros stood mute. Backlit by the fire, the man's face was obscured in shadow.

It was only when the hunter, growing impatient, next asked what day of the week it was, that Oros understood the question. And then, comprehending slowly that the man was serious, he rapidly lost control. The horse, grinning wide-mouthed at him over the man's shoulder, seemed to share the humor. Sliding down to his knees in an uncontrollable fit of laughter, Oros clutched at his stomach to hold himself together and crashed over on his side, laughing hysterically.

When he finally regained enough composure to answer, the man was hurriedly walking away and Oros had to shout after him that it was "The Moon of the Burning Horse!"

Fletcher had no plans to keep the camp open after the spring hunt and Oros expected all along to leave the bush with the rest of the men when they pulled out. Oros wasn't at all anxious about it. There was still plenty of time to get everything organized before winter. Especially around Glenora. The winters there were a hell of a lot milder than at Fairbanks, he knew.

Oros had every intention of leaving. And he would have gone. If that were the way of the flow. Only it changed. Again.

In the spring, when the earth was still frozen, Fletcher had cut and dragged out of the bush enough logs to expand the camp with some new buildings. And now that they were drying out, he needed them peeled. And he needed someone to do the work. Or two men.

During the burning of the horse, as preparations were being made to shut down the camp, Fletcher offered the job to Oros and Michael. Peeling at the rate of three logs a day, working every day, the job would last them a month.

They accepted and Fletcher closed up the camp.

The first plane flew the hunters out with their trophies of bear hides and wolf skins. An hour later, on the second flight, Fletcher, the cook, and the other guides were gone, leaving only Freddie behind with the wranglers to take the horses out overland.

Oros rode with Freddie a short distance back along the Telegraph Line Trail, lingering until the last moment before he said his final good-bye, shook hands firmly with Freddie, and jumped off.

A lone figure standing motionless on the trail, Oros watched silently as Freddie rode off, leading the packhorses on the long trail to Telegraph Creek. When they passed finally out of sight, he turned and slowly made his way, by himself, back to Fletcher's empty camp. Not without some doubts, Oros had decided to stay behind. Alone.

Although Oros had been spending more and more of his time with Michael, he had continued living in the camp, eating his meals there with the rest of the men, sharing their humor and some of their hardships. It wasn't his society of choice but it was comfortable enough, and he felt he had fit in. But now that they were gone, now that the cookhouse was boarded up and the corrals were emptied of horses, the silence that remained was terrific. And frightening.

Oros struggled with his doubts, trying to resolve them. He desperately wanted his own home. And he had, after all, deliberately left Fairbanks early in the spring to allow himself plenty of time to get established in Telegraph Creek before the next winter closed in on him. Yet now, here he was squandering that time wandering around the wilderness. He had to get back to Telegraph Creek as soon as possible.

On the other hand, he had been happy here. And happiness had always been such an elusive and tenuous thing. While it lasted, it wasn't to be forsaken before its time. And, too, he had a warm place to sleep, a real job with pay, Fletcher's food to live on, and so much more yet to be learned from Michael. And Michael. He alone was reason enough to stay, Oros told himself. In fact, Michael was the main reason for staying. They had become true brothers and friendship was more valuable than property and security, he knew. And lastly, he argued with himself, the summer had really only begun. There was lots of time. A whole new life was just beginning. It would be a real mistake to christen it with guilt. Peace and tranquility were the goals.

In the bloom of early summer, with endlessly long days under deep blue skies, the lifestyle had seduced him as completely as any woman could have done. For the time being, he had no desire to leave its consuming embrace and saw nothing sinister in his decision to stay a little longer.

Nighttime, however, presented an entirely different reality and a new set of arguments. The nights were too frightening. And there were no consoling arguments that could make them more bearable. It took only a couple of nights alone in his tent at Fletcher's for Oros to pack up and move to the clearing in front of Michael's boxy little cabin.

He didn't want to be alone anymore. He wouldn't let that happen again.

The days that followed began wonderfully. When the sun touched the tent walls at dawn, he'd awake to the fresh smell of morning air filling his lungs. Emerging into the sunlight from under his tent's flap, he'd crawl through the dewy grasses that grew up in the field to his knees and do his exercises under the rising wall of Sheslay's Level Mountain, stretching and arching himself through the splash of color from the fireweed and lupines until Michael joined him for breakfast. Log peeling followed and lasted until noon, when they'd break for a lunch of fresh Hackett River trout, fried beaver, or bear stew, with beans, bannock, and canned fruit kept cold in the river. The afternoons they left free to wander about, fish, read, or sleep.

Exploring alone one day, Oros discovered an old bridge that crossed the Hackett River. On the other side, two small, man-made clearings survived and beyond them, farther from the river, he found a third little meadow, which was dominated by a little knoll that rose up from its edge to preside over the clearing. From the top of the knoll, a ridge line started that meandered away, climbing higher and higher until it broke into the alpine and then continued on until it joined with the mountain's peak.

There was a quality to this spot, to the third, hidden little field, to the knoll reflecting sunshine back down to its private pasture, to the ridge which united the river bottom and the mountaintop in a perfect harmony. Oros found it irresistible.

Drawn to the place, he returned again and again in the afternoons to wander around in the small clearings or lay daydreaming, his back against the earth, staring up into the sky, watching the clouds sliding their bellies over the higher rocky outcroppings of the mountains. Usually he took his flute with him, which he'd play from the top of the knoll, sending notes rippling away into the surrounding forest below. The knoll commanded a view above the trees in all directions and Oros quickly discovered that it was also a favorite spot for wolves, a fact attested to by their fresh nightly droppings.

Three weeks passed. The summer ripened. Day after day, Oros examined his deepest feelings, searching for signs of self-doubt, for guilt at remaining, for anxiety at being so far from Telegraph Creek but, surprisingly, there were none. Instead of his anxiety increasing with the passage of time, he was feeling increasingly calm each day.

More peaceful, in fact, than he had ever felt before. At first, he didn't question it, intuitively feeling right about his decision to stay a little longer in Sheslay.

There was something here. Something special that touched Oros deeply. And then, finally one day, it all became clear to him.

He was perched on his knoll and, from that vantage point, he was suddenly struck by the truth of the fact that he was happy. Truly happy. As though his inner mind knew before his conscious one did what was better for him and why. The decision not to return to Telegraph Creek with Fletcher's men began to take on prophetic qualities.

All the issues he had been struggling with crystallized with the startling flash of revelation. Rushing down the knoll, he dropped to his hands and knees in the meadow and started clawing excitedly through the grass roots with his fingers to get to the soil.

It was good. Dark, rich and full of life. That confirmed it.

"Here!" Oros yelled to Krish, who had followed him and stood curiously by as he dug in the earth.

"This is it!" he shouted wildly.

It was all so obvious, now that he saw it, that he couldn't understand how he had been so blind. Deliriously happy, Oros laughed. It was the same thing he had criticized Bev for, he remembered. She was so preoccupied with thoughts of being somewhere else, she didn't even know where she was. And he had fallen into the same trap. He had been here for weeks, all the time thinking about Telegraph Creek, without ever realizing that he was already home.

He'd already arrived!

Oros lay down on the ground and rolled over it, feeling it with his whole body. It felt wonderful.

"Right here, Krish, we'll have our first garden. Whoooyeee!... Our very first garden.... Shit!... Krish, this is it! We're home! Home!"

Oros started dancing with joy, looking all around him at his new home. Everything he saw suddenly became very personal. The ground was his now. The soils were his. For better or worse, although, by the color of them, he was sure they'd produce anything he wanted to grow in them. This clearing, the trees surrounding it, the knoll, the ridge to the mountain, the mountain itself, the views, everything his eyes settled on was included in his world. Everything was now his.

It was more than he had ever thought possible or dared to hope for. Without enough money to even own a cemetery plot in the city, here the Garden of Eden was left empty, abandoned and waiting for takers. Oros laughed deliriously again. The decision was made. He was going to stay.

Now that he had a home, his optimism knew no bounds. For the first time in his life, he could begin to build his life up around the dreams he had carried with him since Taos. With roots and a home, he was suddenly convinced that they would all be realized. The transience that had always marked his life would now be a thing of the past. The loneliness and poverty that a life of drifting had led to were over.

And this was only the beginning.

Grandiose plans were laid in his mind for the lodge he would build for his home.

"Krish, we've got to have a big house. We'll need enough room to entertain a dozen guests at a time."

Oros had always planned to have a garden and quickly decided that it would be the first thing he'd do.

"We'll have a really huge garden, Krish. One which'll give us all the fruit and vegetables we'd need to last for a year of feasting. We can grow fat here, old girl. And we can do it without ever having to buy anything packaged and processed and sold in supermarkets again.... Krish, we're free!" Oros was giddy with unbridled optimism.

"And we'll stay clean with a sauna by the river." He knew the spot, near a pool he could plunge into when the build-up of body heat would make the frigid temperatures of the river seem temperate.

"And an icehouse. Krish, we've got to have an icehouse to keep the meat fresh through the summer."

Visions filled his head, of wild game, of moose and bear and caribou hanging in his icehouse; of jars of preserved wild cranberries, huckleberries, and blackberries; of racks of smoked salmon and grouse; of sacks of potatoes, turnips, carrots, and other vegetables. The thoughts intoxicated him, sending him higher and higher with their headiness.

The only wrinkle was the isolation. Sheslay was a lot farther from Telegraph Creek than the Alaskan cabins he had lived in were from Fairbanks, a two or three-day walk just to get out. In good weather. What it would be like in the winter with the short days was hard to say. But certainly a lot more difficult.

Still, after quickly considering it, he dismissed the fear.

He'd have two homes.

Sheslay would be his main home. His summer home. But he'd build a winter place in Telegraph Creek. A cabin somewhere along the Stikine between Telegraph and Glenora. Whenever he needed to get out, if he needed to, he'd make sure he had a place to stay in Telegraph Creek. But he wouldn't even be isolated in Sheslay for long. Already Sheslay had two citizens. More were sure to come. As soon as the word was out, as soon as he was set up, he'd be beating back newcomers and guests. What he'd found here was the perfect "sanity-retreat" he and Neil had talked about before. Why, even the American hunters, those wealthy urban businessmen he'd met at Fletcher's, talked about living out here—and they were the old world. The new world had more conviction. And courage. They lived their dreams. And now that he'd arrived, the silent scout of the new generation, the wave that had carried him first to the communes of Taos and then from the desert north to Alaska would next break over this forest. He wouldn't be alone.

Fantasizing conversations at great gatherings of brothers and sisters, the music of their conversation, the movement of their bodies, sex with women eager for the intimate touch he offered, Stikine homegrown by the drumful, food, cheeses, and smoked fish; sex with small-breasted Indian girls, sex with large-breasted earth goddesses, flesh, warm and willing, inviting and receiving; fantasies without end, of relationships and friends, transported him away for the rest of the day as he lay dreaming in the wild flowers at the base of the knoll, his eyes half closed, his face smiling, his lips moving soundlessly, his shirt open to the sun, which cooked him lightly with its rays on this long summer afternoon. Paradise.

When Oros told Michael of his plan to stay and build a home nearby, Michael threw a party for him and even made an impromptu little ceremony by presenting Oros with the gift of a gun. Oros' first rifle.

"It's only a .22," Michael explained somewhat apologetically. "But you can get used to carrying a weapon and practice with it. It'll kill squirrels and grouse."

When Oros protested that he didn't know how to shoot a gun, Michael replied prophetically, "You'll learn."

They continued to see each other most days. Drawn by the routine they'd established previously and the job they were both committed to finishing, they'd turn up pretty well at the same time every morning at Fletcher's camp to peel the logs. Oros had thought that Michael would be grateful to have a neighbor nearby and it was with initial surprise and then growing dismay that he realized, after only a couple of days, that Michael didn't really want anybody living near him.

With the passing of each day, their relationship inexplicably grew colder and more hostile. Avoiding any substance, their conversations became increasingly strained, and then ceased. After that, Oros' feelings for Michael also changed.

With a regularity that revealed the depth of his anxiety, Michael began checking on Oros unexpectedly several times a day. Showing himself, he'd stand for a moment, at the edge of the clearing, his hands on his hips, breathing hard with obvious agitation, and then turn without a word and stalk away, leaving Oros to wonder how he had offended his friend so deeply to have turned against him so completely.

The work on Fletcher's logs was done in almost total silence now, but the end was in sight and neither man wanted to be the one to acknowledge the magnitude of the problem by confronting it or quitting.

Having moved his tent out to his own site by the knoll, Oros' sense of isolation was deepening. While a summer rain drenched the earth and beat against his tent, he sat cross-legged on his sleeping bag inside trying to fight off the creeping melancholy by writing a letter he had been mentally composing for a week. Using the back of Pacific Evaporated Milk can labels to write on and, with the smallest script he could manage, to save space on the waxy paper, he spent almost an entire day penning the first in a long series of letters to girls he had once known.

Describing little more than the natural beauty and bounty of Sheslay, the letter was calculated for its effect. He didn't want to have to ask a woman to join him. If one came, she had to come on her own and not because he wanted her to come. He didn't want to start any relationship like that. Owing her. He lay in the dampness of his sleeping bag for hours that night thinking about it. He didn't want a woman who only loved him but a woman who loved the same things he loved. Only then would he have a relationship which would work.

In the morning, there was ice in the bucket outside and while Oros was bent over it picking at it curiously, Krish suddenly rushed off into the bush, barking frantically. Ahead of her, Oros heard the sounds of a large animal crashing heavily through the brush. Instantly, Oros rose to his feet. With his heart in his throat, he stood immobilized in fear as the wild animal came crashing closer and closer, right toward him. From the sound of the breaking bush, it had to be large and powerful. Oros suddenly felt weak and vulnerable. He prayed it wasn't a grizzly but he was fearfully sure it was. Desperately hoping that nothing would happen, there was nothing he could do but wait. If it wanted to kill him, there was no one to save him. And if it did, nobody would know. As it came closer, Krish's barking became a sustained and hysterical protest.

Only ninety feet away from him, it finally broke cover. The sheer size of the animal, so near, took away the relief he would otherwise have felt. It was a big bull moose. With long, loping strides, it crossed the tiny clearing in seconds and then was quickly gone, crashing off into the distance in a straight line through the forest, leaving Oros still shaking from the rush of adrenaline. In those few moments, paradise had just revealed its dark side to him.

Suddenly, the good will of other living things wasn't something he could trust his life to. Dressing hurriedly, he ran from the tent to the log pile at Fletcher's camp, willing to put up with the tight lips and the hostile and furtive glances that Michael treated him with for the simple need of human companionship.

Michael wasn't there when he arrived, breathing hard, but the mere fact the camp was there and that it had once held people calmed him. It was civilization, a human oasis in an alien forest. Quietly, Oros settled down to his work of peeling logs.

Michael arrived a couple of hours later. Oros saw him coming but was sufficiently composed by then to pretend not to notice him.

Walking directly up to Oros, Michael stood beside the log Oros was working on, and glared at him. Still not wanting to acknowledge him, Oros kept his eyes averted.

"What the fuck do you think you're doing?" Michael screamed, his voice filled with menacing hostility.

Oros looked up in surprise. Michael's face was flushed with anger —and he was carrying his rifle, Oros noted. Not the small-bored gun for squirrels but the high-powered rifle. The one that could kill big game. He was clutching it in front of his chest with both hands as though he was afraid of something and ready to use it.

Increasingly uneasy in Michael's presence, Oros now saw him as unpredictable. Unstable. And dangerous.

The knuckles of his hands white clenching the rifle, Michael yelled at him again.

"Don't think I don't understand what you're doing. You're trying to move in on me! You're trying to steal my scene, aren't you?"

Michael was on a hair trigger. His body jerked convulsively. Oros was sure that if he answered, Michael would completely lose control. So he said nothing.

"I know!" Michael screamed. "I know what you're after! You want to get rid of me and move into my cabin don't you?"

Oros looked at him, wide-eyed, as Michael continued ranting.

"I don't give a fuck if you want to live out here. You can do whatever the hell you want to do. But just keep away from me. Don't come sneaking around my place or causing me any trouble, you understand?"

In case he wasn't being clear enough, Michael pointed the rifle menacingly toward Oros' feet while his nostrils flared hotly. Waiting.

Finally, Oros replied quietly, "That wasn't my intention."

"It sure looks like it to me!" Michael yelled and then, threatening him one last time to stay clear of his cabin, Michael stalked off quickly, still tightly gripping his rifle.

A few days later Fletcher's logs were finished. After that there was no reason to see Michael anymore and no chance to mend the rift. In the days that followed, the anxiety Oros had felt before about Michael intensified tenfold. In the silence and absolute isolation of Sheslay, the sense of being watched, of being followed about and spied upon, grew like bacteria in festering flesh, poisoning his peace.

Nor was the new fear without real cause. For Oros now spotted Michael every few days, sneaking about through the bush around the knoll in a secretive and frightening way. And he was always carrying his rifle.

Afraid for his own life, Oros began moving his tent, changing its location every night to hinder an attack by Michael. And as unnecessary and foreign as it had at first felt, he kept his own .22 rifle close at hand. The very weapon Michael had given him became a comfort.

By day, perched on top of his knoll like a raven on a fence post, Oros kept up a watch for Michael. Although Michael remained hidden, the smoke from his cabin always rose like a beacon over the forest top. The day it stopped signaled a change in the situation. Oros was instantly afraid and alert. If Michael's fire wasn't smoking, Michael wasn't there. And if Michael wasn't there?...

By first light next morning, Oros was on his belly hiding in the shadows of the forest surrounding Michael's cabin as he scouted the little clearing, looking for signs of Michael. Nothing. Only the silence and emptiness of the forest.

That evening, from the top of the knoll, he waited for signs of smoke from a dinner fire but as the sky blackened with the night, still no smoke materialized.

Under cover of darkness, Oros moved his own tent farther into the bush. Farther away than he had ever slept before. Two more days passed before Oros decided to investigate more closely.

Michael's cabin was open. Inside, everything Michael could easily carry and which was of any value was gone. The cabin was empty.

Michael had fled.

With the disappearance of Michael, Oros' mood soared again. The threat gone, the Garden of Eden was instantly restored to its natural, pristine character. Instead of being crushed by the isolation as he had always been in the past, he was buoyed by a new euphoria. The forest was his alone.

Writing in his journal, he explained, "Alone longer than ever before. Feel surprisingly good. No homesickness at all. What can I say. I'm home."

Riding the crest of summer, Oros had completely forgotten how short was its bloom. Forgotten, too, were the lessons he'd learned in the eternally long nights alone in Fairbanks. He didn't want to remember those. They were too terrible.

There was another pleasant surprise awaiting Oros after Michael left. Michael's cabin. It was a real windfall.

Michael had left almost everything behind, from pots and pans to a stove, bed, animal traps, and skinning boards. Stripping it of everything Michael had left, Oros delighted in the richness of its varied treasures as he examined his new possessions in minute detail. Inspired by his new tools and supplies, Oros passed ten more days building a high cache near his own garden to store his new property. A log cabin in miniature, it was raised six feet off the ground for security from animals. It was the first building he had ever put up and, although it had its flaws, it was dry and sturdy enough to support all the gear he had together with his own weight. Most importantly, it had all been done with his own hands, natural materials, and the techniques he remembered having studied from books for another project he had planned on doing over the winter—it seemed like centuries ago—in Fairbanks.

Still living out of his tent, he had considered moving into Michael's cabin, and would have if the roof had been higher, but being constantly stooped over and banging his head while inside it, he wanted a space he could at least stand upright in. It was crazy, he thought, to be in the middle of one of the greatest wilderness spaces in the world and then to live so squalidly, doubled over in a coffin. There was no delaying any more. He had to build himself a real home.

Oros wanted to start on his hexagonal cabin but he knew he had to start more realistically with a modest structure. Something he could build quickly. The hexagonal cabin, his dream cabin, could be built after that.

As Oros labored to build his own shelter, he tried to reconcile himself to the exhausting effort it entailed with the thought that this cabin would someday be converted into a big sauna for him and his friends to use and that he would then appreciate all the work he was putting into it now. But his resolve failed daily as he woke up every morning with his fingers raw and his hands cramped from the hours spent peeling off the green bark.

There were other problems, too. He had lain such grandiose plans that the mere thought of the effort required to fulfill them exhausted his will. The euphoria which had carried him for so many days after Michael's departure had been completely consumed.

Chewing on a dry piece of kelp that Neil had brought up to Alaska from California two years ago brought back keen memories of Neil and California. Of friendships and hope, sunshine and people, of beaches and palms, of saltwater and ice-cream, of cars and cold beer, and long hair blowing back from convertibles on freeways, of all the things that Sheslay didn't have. Fantasies of women, of flesh on flesh, nearly drove him insane, as old desires reasserted themselves.

Try as he could to focus on the reasons he left it all behind for the open spaces of country, he still felt the isolation deep within him. Although he fought it off as best he could, rationalizing the need for company as a conditioned reaction which he could overcome in time by positive thinking, it was a copy of *Oui* magazine which he found at

Fletcher's that plunged him into the first real crisis of isolation he'd experienced since arriving in Sheslay.

> It seems nothing short of madness to be settling into the wilderness seventy kilometers away from the nearest village. And that with no single women either!

Gradually, Oros began to seek solace in fantasies, keeping company with himself out of necessity, wandering the human paths of Fletcher's deserted camp, reading aloud every magazine he could find there and writing down everything he felt. As though seen through a telescope, the worldview he now held had a fixed focus on the narrow plane of his own reality. And, as he had during the isolation of Fairbanks, Oros again took refuge in his diary.

> Added some fresh greens to my lentils tonight—roseroot, fireweed, and riverbeauty. Dark and overcast again. Drizzling. Mixed feelings about this whole trip. What am I doing here? And why? But the answers are always the same. This is where I belong. I am here as part of the cosmic flow of my life.
>
> If I had stayed instead with the other game, I'd be lost now in the emptiness of graduating from law school. My life is here. In Montana, I didn't hunt and wouldn't eat meat because I wasn't in touch with the cycle of life and death. But now, here, I live on equal terms with all living things. Eyeball to eyeball. And die as easily. There is no help in a crisis. No one to call. No one to run to. No easy escape. Only my own two hands and feet to trust—and my instincts. My greatest goal is my desire to slow down, to quiet unwanted thoughts. With my mantra, I meditate on unity—striving to lose my ego—an end to the barrier it creates between me and the oneness of all creation.

As the days passed, his moods fluctuated like the weather, gray and turbulent one day and clear and blue the next.

> At night darkness creeps in like a living thing. Sucking the very breath from the land, until the stillness is overwhelming. Alone. The silence ringing in my ears. I keep the fear at bay by singing or whistling. Even the silliest songs. If only there was someone else in the bush, even a mile away, it would help. But knowing there's nobody in most directions for 100 miles and even Telegraph Creek is a forty-four mile walk leaves me with a different kind of feeling. Scary.

> Walked past Michael's empty cabin yesterday and instantly, when I saw it, I felt the grip of a powerful loneliness again. And fear.
>
> Mosquitoes for company. I'm torn between hating their torment and respecting their will. They have as much right to life as we do.
>
> Digging up the earth, I wondered again what am I doing? How can I live here? In Sheslay. Alone. I don't want to be afraid but when Krish barks and the bush roars or thrashes, the tremors run through my body. This is still the best place to be and I hope it works out but I won't stay without a good gun. Maybe the fear is part of the experience of all living things.
>
> The maggots, too, have now become a part of my life. I found them in all my meat. They were especially thick in the cavities of the beaver heads. Exposing the meat to the sun and wind helps. The maggots seem to need a moist home and fall off if it's dry.
>
> My mood lifted yesterday. Working in the garden, surrounded by flowers and perfume and color—red, white, yellow, blue, green, and gold. And hummingbirds. In the evening, the light that set on the peak of Kaketsa washed it in bright pinks and reds. Glorious. Feels like home.
>
> Trying to take it slow. One step at a time. When I question what I am doing here I always come to the same answer. This is where I belong. The cosmic flow has brought me here. To live one-to-one with all life.

As much as he could, he was trying to learn to live off the land, and as Michael had warned, it meant a radical change in his thinking.

> If I had stayed with the old trip I'd be graduating from law school instead of experiencing the life cycle of maggots. They are in all my meat. At least they don't bite. A small mercy. And they brush off easily. Can't say that for the mosquitoes. Or the deerflies! More than once had to run to take shelter from them. A guy can only take so much!
>
> There are moments of sheer terror. When the bush roars my legs get weak. Am I mad to live way out here? Alone in the bush with no neighbors for miles. And miles. I need a gun. A real one.

From the magazines Oros found at Fletcher's camp, he rewrote portions of articles he liked, incorporating the sentiments they expressed into his own philosophy, or merely taking comfort from sharing common thoughts with others. One quote by Saul Alinsky from the March '72 *Playboy* was raised to prominence above all the rest by being written in bold print and underlined. It reflected the fundamental tenet of a new and growing creed. One which would one day occupy a central theme not just on paper but in his mind and soul.

> People don't get opportunity or freedom or equality or dignity as an act of charity; they have to fight for it, force it out of the establishment.

As the gloss of summer dulled with increasing periods of overcast skies, obscuring mountaintops and the stars, Oros worked more and more often in the rain. Soaked through to the skin, cold, hungry, and heavy-hearted, he examined his little garden, watching the rain build up into muddy puddles in the hollows of the furrows.

Oros had moved into Michael's cabin until his own shelter was complete and when the rain came down in sheets, he stayed inside, the door open, staring bleakly out. It was dry in the stuffy little room but the oppressive darkness and low ceiling quickly drove him back out under the open sky in everything but the hardest rainstorms, deepening his resolve to finish his own little cabin as soon as possible.

By late summer, men started trickling back into the bush to reoccupy Fletcher's camp for the upcoming fall hunting season. As though awakening from a dream, his contact with people brought him instant relief. The effect was profound. The despair and depression he'd been experiencing with the isolation at Sheslay suddenly disappeared and his moods once more soared.

Convincing himself now that the fears he had been so recently consumed by were groundless and fleeting, he set to completing his own cabin with a burst of newfound energy. When he moved in to take occupancy of his first real home, he was ecstatic. It was all coming together.

Isolation was not really a condition of life in Sheslay, he wrote. It was merely a state of mind. As transient and fleeting as the footprints of the birds in the sky. And, if he ever felt isolated in Sheslay again, Oros told himself, all he had to do was walk out and talk to a few people. Go visiting. That was the solution.

Oros had somehow forgotten that the farthest he lived from the city at Fairbanks was an hour and a half. Even in winter. And that had been too far! Yet now, in his euphoria, he wasn't the least daunted by the fact that Telegraph Creek lay a full three days from Sheslay. And that in the summer. When the trails were open. And a man could walk about. Oros thought he knew isolation before Sheslay. But he had forgotten the hardest lessons. Indeed, he had done everything he could to drive them like devils out of his mind.

The high point of Fletcher's return to Sheslay was the load he brought in for Oros. Jim Harris from Fairbanks had arrived in Telegraph Creek over the summer with all the property Oros had left behind in Neil's care: snowshoes, dried foodstuffs, honey that Bev had got from her mother and left behind when she fled, books—a whole boxload of them, some of which he hadn't read yet—clothes, and, most exciting of all, mail. The very first mail he'd received since leaving Fairbanks.

Savoring the letters, he read them slowly, line by line.

He had sent out a lot of letters over his last winter from Fairbanks to people who were listed in the contact section of *Mother Earth*. Although he didn't know them, writing to real people broke the loneliness he felt and he never really expected his letters to be answered; but here, in this mail, were a half dozen replies. The first one he opened was written by a woman calling herself Braham, to whom he vaguely remembered sending a letter. He couldn't remember anything about her or even what he'd said in his letter, so was quite surprised to discover that, after one letter, she was already proposing a trial relationship. He guessed his must have been a good letter, or else she was a mighty desperate lady. Her offer was even sweetened with detailed descriptions of a hundred-acre property she owned near Victoria along the coast where they could live. The proposition was certainly interesting. The property and the poetry of her phraseology made her sound like landed gentry and Oros tucked the letter carefully away, to be reread later, over and over again.

From old friends and new friends, there were other offers that came with the letters. One of them, to go north back to Fairbanks. Another to New Mexico. Others to California. Oros read each of them, sweetly contemplating the different realities that lay behind the offers.

As he read the letters, he toyed with the notion that if things did get rough for him, he could always leave Sheslay and winter outside. There were a great many places he could spend the winter, and he enjoyed the freedom a large number of choices gave him.

That he would, in fact, find himself still in Sheslay, all alone to face the winter with no options left to him, was something he never believed possible. Not in his worst nightmares.

Another letter offered Oros a place to stay on balmy Saltspring Island near Victoria. Oros read the offer with equanimity. The transition from isolation and despondency to human contact and peace was so rapid and total. The moment he was back with people again opportunities and choices were thrown at him. Life was once again so rich and varied that he could take for granted the opportunities he had without ever considering any of them seriously.

The trap in which the empty forest had imprisoned him was purged from his mind and in its place remained the simple vision of the land itself—a picture of calm godliness. Of purity and tranquility.

The salmon run had started crowding all the back eddies and tributaries with the powerful fish. The weather was warm, the nights unthreatening, the salmon delicious and plentiful, and, in a tightly sealed package from Fairbanks, was enough of Rene's low-grade, homegrown to last him till Christmas. Oros rediscovered paradise.

Over the summer, Oros had been making lists of what he'd need, and now he had the chance to review them with the men running Fletcher's camp. From one of Airport Bill's catalogues, he wrote out a mail order form for an army surplus .303 Lee Enfield rifle. Bill's arguments for it were simple. Moose and bear were plentiful but as substitutes for beef and pork he'd need a gun to kill them with. The .303 was cheap to buy, built to last, fired reliably, took any punishment, would kill moose and bear, and was common enough that ammunition for it was everywhere.

In addition to bringing down meat, which he found himself actually enjoying again, there was also the matter of self-defense. After several weeks alone in the bush, he now realized it was a problem that was real enough.

Oros wrote the gun down on his list in neat print. It was the first item there, topping the list. Next were ammunition, oil, and cleaning rods.

The list of necessaries followed: 150 pounds of powdered milk, 100 pounds of flour, 200 pounds of oats, 200 pounds of wheat, 20 pounds of wheat germ, 200 pounds of honey, 100 pounds of sunflower seeds, 20 pounds of sesame seeds, and ten pounds each of lentils, turnips, onions, and carrots. Next were treats. Molasses, coconut, lecithin oil, dates, margarine, alfalfa, vinegar, brewer's yeast, figs, apricots, pumpkin seeds, walnuts, and almonds were all items he could live without but they would make life eminently more enjoyable.

Apart from food, the list of household items and tools was short: mouse traps, nails, spikes, a hammer, pens and notepads for writing, rope, a toothbrush, a sledgehammer, glue, a cold chisel, saw blades, tin snips, a scythe, fishnets, conibear traps, two axes, five stainless steel dishpans, two swede saws, three long saws, a lantern and lamp glasses, ten gallons of kerosene oil, a gaff to hook salmon, envelopes, a meat grinder, long underwear, boots, a block and tackle, a stove, and, last but not least, guitar strings.

Relying on Fletcher's good graces, Oros prevailed upon him to help. The Indian Co-op in Telegraph Creek had some cigarettes, chocolate bars, assorted chips, pop, and some canned and dry goods but they weren't much good for his needs. And the general store in Dease Lake was no better.

The expeditor that the outfitters used was in Dawson Creek—850 miles from Telegraph Creek. One way. The round trip from Sheslay was over 1,700 miles.

"A hell of a walk to go grocery shopping," he noted humorously in his journal.

It wasn't necessary, however, for Oros to do the trip himself. Leaving his order with Fletcher, Fletcher made contact with his own expeditor, who had the goods flown into Telegraph Creek. From there, the packhorses being herded in empty to the camp for the fall hunt, were loaded up with Oros' supplies and driven in to Sheslay where they were dropped off. One ton of food and supplies. Home delivered.

Oros was deeply grateful. Fletcher even absorbed the shortfall on the cost of purchasing the goods and flying them to Telegraph Creek, offering Oros some work around the camp again to pay him back.

Oros found himself liking the country and its people more and more.

Like Fletcher and Freddie, Oros preferred the American hunters to the Germans and the French. It wasn't just the language that made communication easier but the philosophies that guided their lives. Although they were all wealthy, the Americans treated him as an equal, including him in their conversations if he was near and sharing their visions with him. The Europeans, treating him like a servant, ignored him and were openly rude.

After a summer of silence, Oros enjoyed all conversation now, and often sought out the Americans to engage them in conversation.

Trading experience and revelation with each other, they consciously competed for the relevance of their lives. To Oros, listening and talking, the conversations were liberating, touching the heart of the most important questions of life. A quest was revealed in them all. A search for a better way to live life. They were all passengers on the same wave which was washing over everything. None of them completely happy with what they had, none of them fulfilled, all of them were still searching. Quietly helpful or hostile, no one was indifferent. They had all been infected by the same corrupting idea—that there was more to life.

But among them all, he believed that he was alone in making a commitment to the vision he believed they all shared. Oros talked about Sheslay. Not the isolation, the loneliness, and the despair but the abundance of natural food, the purity of the wilderness, and the liberation of complete independence. He had his place in it all. With the goal of unity, he would become one with the land.

The hunters encouraged him. Politely apologizing that they were themselves individually too dependent upon the old world to pioneer another way of life, they nevertheless told him that, with courage, they might stay too, that they too believed in his dream.

Oros felt renewed by all this contact. His faith was boosted by it to a certainty of conviction. Secretly, but stronger than he'd felt it in months, was the conviction that his was a real vision, a prophet's life, which would bear fruit, be recognized and glorified. His was a new way and he was the light. It was a glorious feeling. He was the pioneer and his footsteps would show all of them the way.

His work at Fletcher's finished when his debt was paid, Oros had less reason to spend his days there and, alone at his cabin, he watched the snow falling on Kaketsa. At 6,175 feet the mountain rising over Sheslay was already starting to feel the weight of winter!

To cheer himself up, he baked a cherry pie and returned to the draft of another letter he'd been working on to a woman he knew before Fairbanks. It had to be just right. The content had to be positive. Nobody would come if he scared them off with horror stories. When he finished it hours later, he read it critically over and over to himself; but it held up. It was good. The offer was indirect but clear. If she liked what she read, she'd come and join him. He certainly didn't want anybody who was going to sit around and bitch about the comforts she was missing.

Beside the lantern on the table was a neat stack of letters he had written to other women. Oros added this new one to the pile, reminding himself that he had to give them to Fletcher to fly them out.

Darkness forced the close of his day. There were candles and kerosene in his supplies but artificial light was a special luxury to be saved for emergencies and special occasions. Oros crawled into his sleeping bag. Calling Krish to him, he wrapped his arms around the dog and listened to the rain pounding down on the flat roof. The low, cramped cabin was heavy with the smell of the dog's body but he hardly noticed it anymore. Not at all tired, he blinked his eyes, but the night was so total there was nothing to focus on and no change whether his eyes were open or shut. Having spent idle days with the weather beating down on them, his body, accustomed to a daily routine of hard labor, refused to relax.

Lying awake in the darkness, a welling of feeling, the desperate gnawing pains of melancholy, started deep down in his stomach and rose to engulf his heart, pounding desperately against the blackness, which, threatened to snuff out its beat as completely as a storm takes out a candle. He had felt it all before, although never as powerfully as he had of late. In Fairbanks, it had been milder, the pain belonging to another time, almost another person. It had come on then after he'd been alone for only ten days—the longest he had ever been alone before. The pain had started to eat him away then, too, just as it was now doing, unraveling his nerves and threatening to explode him into a thousand pieces if he moved. The only relief was to lay absolutely still, tightly curled up into a ball, to resist the sinking spiral that tried to spin him into the depths of a maelstrom from which he knew—if he ever slipped in—he'd never get out again.

Oros made it through the rest of the night by meditating on his mantra of peace and harmony. Dawn, when it finally came, brought instant relief. In the sunshine, the world was filled with color and promise, and the determination he felt at night to leave, to escape from the bush, dissipated as naturally as the dew.

Hummingbirds were in his garden and the early light on the peak of Kaketsa washed the mountain in iridescent pinks and reds.

Oros sat before it with a book of Japanese poetry and memorized a Haiku that he felt said it all.

The rain falls so easily.

Daily the nights grew longer. And colder. But still he remained in Sheslay, having convinced himself finally that he was the pioneer and that others would come later. The great gatherings of brothers and sisters would still take place, he was sure. And they would be centered at Sheslay. Around Oros himself.

Oros reveled in the fantasies that he wouldn't be alone for long.

Perversely, he decided that isolation was not the real problem. Rather it was the fear of isolation. Fear itself was his worst enemy. And, once he identified it, Oros resolved not to give in to it. Ever.

Nightly paralyzed by fears now and daily tranquilized by the increasingly familiar routines, he squandered his days, stubbornly committed to the decision he had made. Unable anymore to think clearly about anything, his moods rocketed out of control.

August 31. The tears of a lone candle fill the plate. Alone again. My money all spent. Everything recedes until there is only the present, the long moment, forever. Harmonica tunes linger mournfully in the still air. Sheslay has known this mood before. But it offers little comfort.

A spider drops from the ceiling onto the paper and scurries away as the dog, frightened, barks outside. Something moving through the night has scared it. Me too.

The night-hawks cry out against the purple-blackness.

How long must I wait for you? Do you hear my heart beating?

As winter drew nearer, the days continued to shorten until, finally, a darkness prevailed out of which there was no escape.

September 1. Flickering candlelight. Ate a huge feast tonight gathered from the land. A salad of turnip greens, boleta mushrooms, and onions. Carrots and salmon. Found a huge one today trapped in my fishing hole. A tree crashed over the bank into the river and traps them as they float downstream. All the food I can eat for the picking. This one hadn't been dead too long. Hardly any rot on it at all. At any rate, it was sure good tasting and we didn't throw up afterward. A wonderful moon breaking over the black horizon. Wolves will be wild tonight.

September 6. The isolation here is an immediate and constant thing —even though with hunting season on again I've seen four separate groups of people moving through the bush in the past week. All hunters.

My first contact with people again after such a long time was different than I expected. It felt good to be sure, but it was no big thing. And now its been a few days since I've seen anyone again and I don't mind at all. Is that scary? That I can go for so long alone and not be affected.

September 10. Eating salmon every day from the Hackett River. They die after they spawn and their bodies, useless to them, nourish us. We share their bounty with the bears. Tracks of huge animals—grizzly bears—along the same bank I find my fish.

The moon is looking out for us over the night. Bright enough for a moonlight walk through the willows. Except for the bears.

Woke up a couple of times to find snow covering everything but it didn't last. It won't be long though. Already Kaketsa and Level Mountain are under snow which will stay there until next summer.

I play music each night before bed. Flute or harmonica. Feeling better all the time. I'm slowly adjusting to being alone. It even surprises me how easily I've gone back to eating flesh. Thinking about friends a great deal of the time. Sometimes I lie awake all night, too excited to sleep, remembering conversations, imagining new ones with friends here in Sheslay. That would probably sound sad to Mom but she hasn't been here. I've now set a new record for living alone without seeing a single person, and I still feel great.

It was over two weeks before Oros made another diary entry. Longer than he had ever gone before without writing. Like a radio signal powered by a dying battery, his journal entries grew shorter and weaker. Until they ceased altogether. For a long time.

September 26. I heard voices again. Same ones I heard last time. Laughing. Is it possible? I wondered. The hunting party returning? But I didn't find anybody. And I looked. Everywhere. I stopped searching only when I found I was shaking. Haven't heard them since. Almost positive they were people. Had to be. They were laughing, only I couldn't hear what they were saying. Their voices were muffled. Nearby, too.

Took a chilly bath in Salmon Creek (the Indian name for the Hackett). Took no time at all. Found a salmon that I'm roasting now. Had decided to stop eating salmon but this one still looked so fresh, I couldn't pass it up. Also had a couple of its raw eggs. Just to try them. Very fishy.

Strange dream last night. Mom showed me a newspaper story about Victor and Wendy and some other people who had killed a large number of policemen. What was really weird was that I knew all the details even before I read the story. Victor and Wendy had been arrested and were sent up the river for life. It was a real bummer. I wanted to help, but what could I do. Seemed to me that they had fallen into the trap I'd be in if I had stayed in the city. Very weird.

My mind is so clear, I can almost touch the images I think of. It's like being there. In San Francisco, with the speed of thought—the lights and people, the concrete and glass, the noise, the fumes, the movements, and the details are so real. Even as I sit here surrounded by natural silence.

I feel great. Not lonely at all, though I still think about friends all the time. Feel very at home. I've gotten used to being alone.

Families lived here once. On foot, off the land. They are still here in spirit. Clutching a line through time for sanity. A trail out, the escape route from here to Atlin and on through there to Carcross and Skagway, so far away, there is a flicker we share.

The legends remain but not much else. Peeling logs for my new cabin and keeping back tears. One day, I will look back on all this, read these notes and laugh, but now, now is all that counts—this moment which stretches off forever.

I dreamed of her picking wild strawberries but there are only flies buzzing in the field, so I hide my dreams.

I am alone with Krish. Just the two of us.

Today. And tomorrow.

It can't go on like this—new approach is needed to adjust to this place—so beautiful and yet so difficult alone.

Another dead mosquito.

Please children stop the suffering.

All seems chaos as night floats down, smothering us in its embrace, laughing and crying. We carry on. One step at a time.

Who is there to understand? Keep faith lonely trapper!

September 28. I'm really getting scared of being alone—so much so that I'm likely now to seize the very next opportunity that comes along to get out.

September 29. Heard people talking today. Just outside the cabin. Krish heard them, too.

REAL LIVE PEOPLE.

Went out to meet them but there was no one there. Nothing.
But there were voices.

LIVING PEOPLE VOICES.

Not the whispering voices we hear every day in the wind, blowing through the trees and washing down the river but REAL VOICES. BREATHING PEOPLE.

It's true.

Oh please, Mother Mary, tell me it's so.

October 29. I dream forever. Tripping into the void. Still here, as weird as ever. I walked over, at last, to Fletcher's camp with my letters to mail but it was empty. They've all gone. The season's over. To save paper, I stopped writing so now I have only empty pages and vague memories of what has been. A month since I last wrote. A month. I've never done that before. What is a month. Just a word.

Outside the door winter rages while snow falls so softly.

    Sleet falling;
        Fathomless, infinite
            Loneliness.

Time is so indefinably amorphous, moving inexorably onward, carrying us into the future.

I sit and watch the door waiting for Neil to visit. He's been gone so long.

November 2. I can't wait much longer.

Where are you?

Chapter Thirteen

January 29, 1982. Atlin RCMP Detachment: Bird rocked back on his chair and stared out the window beside him. The sun was hanging low, hugging the earth, its rays so pale he could examine it without blinking. The light was one of the reasons they hadn't gone in after Oros yet. There were hardly enough hours in the day to get into Hutsigola, get Oros, and get out again before darkness. That and the force's political duties. The last time he had everything set to go, the police plane that was to bring the team up from Prince Rupert was ordered at the last minute to fly south instead—to take a senior officer from Ottawa around Vancouver Island on a sight-seeing tour!

A gust of wind picked up a ball of dry snow and rolled it like a spinning top across the frozen surface of Atlin Lake.

A small, single-engine plane cut its power in front of the detachment and glided down to the ice to land on skis, the air turbulence around it whipping the powdery snow away in great rolls. Bird watched as the pilot threw a warming blanket over the engine cowling to keep the oil from freezing and then hurried to his shore cabin to get indoors. It was bitterly cold.

Bird liked these pilots. If this one had made a pass by Hutsigola Lake, he knew he'd get a call from him soon reporting on his observations. Ever since they'd spotted smoke back at Oros' cabin before Christmas, the pilots had been going out of their way to check on it and keep Bird informed of Oros' whereabouts.

Everybody wanted Oros out of the picture. And the sooner the better. In the dead of winter, Bird knew Oros wasn't going to leave Hutsigola and he was pretty sure they'd get him next time they went in after him; but the politics still irritated him.

Bird turned back to the Interpol file on his desk and poked it to the edge as though he wished it'd disappear.

He cursed softly. Instead of simplifying things, the new facts complicated everything. With the Interpol information, a good lawyer would kill their case against Oros.

There were so many questions about Lishy and they had so little information that he had contacted Interpol not only to trace Lishy's next of kin to advise them of Lishy's disappearance but also on the off-chance they might somehow shed some light on the situation. The report he got back, sitting in a file in front of him, only made things more curious than ever. Interpol knew him, all right. They had their own file on the German. Except theirs was a closed file. Closed almost fifteen years earlier on an official finding that Gunter Hans Lishy was dead. Bird was stunned when he'd first read it. Officially, in Germany, Lishy had been dead since 1965.

The rest of the report supplied the details. Born into German aristocracy, Lishy had entered the war on the eastern front in 1944 at the age of 16. Captured by the Russians, he spent nearly two years behind barbed wire where he was starved and tortured by Russian female guards for being German, a male, and an aristocrat. His freedom purchased with western currency, Lishy was ultimately saved. But not before he was deeply scarred. Hating women, war, and uniforms, distrustful of all state organs, his life in Germany was a constant state of fear and anxiety anticipating the outbreak of World War III against the Russians. Then, suddenly in 1957, he disappeared. Heir to a personal fortune, the considerable wealth of a reduced family focused into fewer hands, his mysterious disappearance sparked an intensive search through Germany. Interpol became involved when the search became international. But it was all futile. By 1965, he was presumed dead by order of the German courts and his estate passed on to living relatives.

Bird knew the rest. The prisoner had not died in 1957 but had gone into hiding. With a new beginning he started a new life. In Atlin. As remote from world affairs as one can get.

The information put a new complexion on the case. Lishy, not unlike Oros, lived the principle of independence and self-sufficiency. Perhaps that was why Lishy had put the picture of Oros on his wall. For both of them, their almost fanatical independence was the means by which they minimized contact with the outside world. There was indeed much more that these two men had in common than anybody thought before.

Bird pulled the Interpol file back from the edge of the table and flipped through it without reading it again. He didn't have to. He knew what it said. And it didn't help his case. Given Lishy's history of disappearing and the fact that he was even previously declared dead, there would have to be pretty strong evidence that Lishy didn't just up and go again, leaving everything behind without a word to anyone, as he had done so many years before. Maybe even having left all his stuff beside Oros' cabin with the perverse thought in mind that the authorities would conclude by it that Oros had killed him? While he secretly slipped away into yet another new life? With the thousands of dollars he must have made and saved from his trapline, he certainly had the funds to start up again some place else. Bird was well aware of the fact that Lishy's money was never accounted for. So it was just possible that Lishy may have run again, setting up the whole thing so nobody would ever try to trace him. Bird rejected the idea outright. It was possible, too, that dogs could grow wings. He knew it hadn't happened that way. Lishy wasn't hiding anywhere. He was dead. Really dead this time. And his body was concealed somewhere around Hutsigola Lake. Bird was sure of it. But, without producing it in the flesh, he knew that there was just enough truth in the other argument that a jury couldn't reject it. And if they couldn't, they'd have to acquit him. Every unanswered question was a reasonable doubt which would let Oros walk. And there were plenty of those still left.

In light of the Interpol file on Lishy, an earlier FBI response to his inquiries about Oros also had new significance. The FBI reported that Oros had been treated in 1967 by Dr. Beck, a psychiatrist in Topeka, Kansas. Apparently, Oros was admitted to the psychiatric ward of a hospital there as an involuntary patient after having suffered from some kind of attack.

Bird found the doctor living in Eagle, Idaho, and on the off chance she might still remember the case, he had phoned her. She did.

Oros had come into her care for only a few days, she remembered, and then explained that it would have been longer except that Oros had escaped and was never returned. As Bird already knew from the FBI records and an RCMP computer check, this was probably the only time that Oros had been locked up against his will.

And he obviously hadn't liked it.

"Is he still alive?" Beck had asked. Interested.

"Yes. We're looking for him right now," Bird had replied, not wanting to give her any details until he had all the answers.

"That's a surprise!" she'd said. "He was a very disturbed young man, you know. Angry. Very angry. I don't recall any final diagnosis I made…. In fact, I think he ran off before we could be certain of one, although he was suffering from paranoid delusions. You see, he believed that people were poisoning him, drugging him. He may actually have had those kinds of experiences in one of the communes he was living in. There were indications of a lot of drug use there and they got quite violent in the end. Amazing, as I talk about this, how much comes back to me. He was really a different kind of case for me. In some ways, he was so typical of the young people then. Filled with idealism. But in others, he was so different. I've often wondered what had happened to him. How curious that you called."

"You said you were surprised he was still alive?" Bird had asked, directing her to the issue he thought more relevant.

"Oh, yes. Aggravating his condition or his attitude—I'm not sure which it would have been—was a really deep hatred for his father. He was illegitimate, you see, or maybe abandoned by his father, I forget which, when he was an infant. And he blamed his father or rather the father figure for everything bad that had ever happened to him. I remember thinking that he was quite capable of killing a symbolic father. You know what I mean? A figurehead, a political leader, a father-figure type. Anyway, he was definitely headed toward a collision course with destruction as his goal. Frankly, I'm surprised he's lived this long."

Thinking about it in his small detachment office, Bird believed that Lishy could have been seen as a symbolic father by Oros. They were the right ages to be father and son. They had the same general temperaments, the same interests, the same fears of persecution by the state. They were both living simple, solitary existences. They had both fled their native countries to seek refuge in the Canadian outback. They were both fearful of war but obsessed with it. If they had ever sat down and talked about their backgrounds to each other, they might well have found they had a lot in common. Oros might have seen in Lishy the father he never had.

But would he kill him because of that?

There were some other people Bird had found and talked to. Each with his own story to tell. There was a reason behind every killing. A motive. And unless Oros confessed, they'd have to build a theory for the motive on their own based on what they knew. Each new set of facts, every insight he could get, helped define the theory.

The obvious key to Oros' motive lay in Lishy's move to Hutsigola. Why Lishy started to build a cabin on Oros' doorstep might well provide the clue for the killing. It was unlikely the two events were unrelated.

Lishy might have known the old cabin on Hutsigola legally belonged to an old Indian living in the Yukon, but even if he didn't know Oros had taken it over and claimed it as his own, once he'd landed on Hutsigola, he wouldn't have missed the signs. The blazing sun symbols were everywhere. And Lishy, who dared to track grizzly while they were stalking game, didn't misread the bush. Even a cursory glance into the old Hutsigola cabin would have told anyone who'd heard of Sheslay Free Mike that here was his cabin.

No. To stay at Hutsigola and build right next to Oros couldn't have been a coincidence. Bird liked the sour partner theory. If they weren't strangers but were partners, that would explain a lot. Why else would Lishy have kept that photo of Oros hanging up in his own cabin when the only other photo he displayed was of Peacock, perhaps his closest friend?

But Peacock said it just wasn't possible. Gunter never mentioned meeting Oros except that once, on the trail, when they had shared tea and he'd snapped Oros' picture.

"So why hang Oros' picture?" Bird had asked.

"Well, Gunter respected him," Peacock had explained somewhat reluctantly. "He respected Oros' reputation."

Everyone from Telegraph Creek north to Teslin and west to Atlin knew the name "Sheslay Free Mike." Oros was already becoming a legend but his was a story which kept most people out of the Teslin Lake system rather than attracting them. There were stories that he hunted people and ate their flesh, that he howled at the moon and ran wild with the wolves. Gunter didn't believe the stories. But he knew that no man had ever lived that long in the wilderness and survived. Ever. Except Sheslay Mike. Oros had something. And Gunter thought he understood what it was.

"They both had tremendous abilities in the bush and Gunter probably figured they'd get along. They had a lot in common, that's all."

But it was Peacock's final argument that convinced Bird. And it was an obvious one.

"If Oros was Lishy's partner, Lishy wouldn't have built a cabin there at all. He'd rely on Oros to trap the area. And he certainly wouldn't have cut a skidoo trail from Hutsigola to Zancudo. That trail was for Lishy to trap from, not Oros."

One thing in particular that Lishy liked about Oros' reputation was that it kept the Teslin Indian band out of the area. The Indians had all the trapping rights but, superstitious and afraid of Oros, they hadn't trapped the area in years. They wouldn't even venture into it. Lishy knew it wasn't legal for him to run his own traplines through the area but nobody else would ever know. Except Oros.

A homosexual relationship? Bird had thought that too was possible. The Interpol records explained why Gunter never married. And the diaries they had found, when searching the Hutsigola area, spoke often of sexual encounters Oros had in his dreams with boys as well as women.

Chuck Fipke, a B.C. geologist, put that theory to rest. Chuck and Gunter had known each other for years, having once worked together in the Yukon for a few months. He had even worked Gunter's trapline with him on and off for a few years and had learned something of Gunter's bush skills as well as his sex life. Chuck remembered Gunter starting the story with a question, like a puzzle. "How does a man get a woman whenever he needs one?" The answer was a little like trapping. With bait and understanding of behavior.

"Anytime he needed a woman," Fipke explained, "he'd drive up to Whitehorse and cruise the bars with a forty ouncer in tow until he picked up a woman ready to do anything for a party. Afterward, he confessed, he always felt so sick about it and so disgusted with himself he wouldn't drink for another six months—until the hormones built up to a point he couldn't stand it anymore and he'd do it again. Every six months. No, Gunter was strange but he certainly wasn't queer."

Fipke also cleared up another question that had been nagging at Bird for months. Lishy's trapping record. It was so good it was unbelievable. But Fipke had worked Lishy's line with him and knew his record. And he remembered a winter when Gunter Lishy trapped twenty-three wolverine. In one winter. A Canadian record. Better than any Indian trapper had ever done. In the bush, Gunter really was a superman.

"I mean he was very competent," Fipke said, greatly understating his real opinion. "And he wasn't antisocial."

On that, Fipke and Peacock agreed. Most likely, Lishy simply wanted to have a neighbor out in the bush and believed that Oros would be grateful for the company. After all, it was only a trapper's line cabin he was putting up. A place to stay while on the trail. He'd only be in there a few days every once in a while over the trapping season. Not long enough or often enough to bother anybody.

Lishy might have been an innocent, getting himself in deeper than he'd realized when he got out of the plane at Hutsigola, but Jamie Stevens had a different kind of story to tell about the German.

Stevens, the local game warden, was on Edzertza's trapline one winter day. He and Edzertza had been traveling by skidoo all morning, stopped for a quick lunch, and then were off again. When they stopped for a break in the afternoon, Lishy burst out of the bush beside them, his big .44, which he always carried, drawn and pointed at Edzertza. Believing the two men were "checking up on him" and that Edzertza had been encroaching on his line, Stevens felt Lishy was right on the edge, ready to kill—for an encroachment on his trapping rights. As Stevens talked him down, he also realized that Lishy had been watching them all day. Although he'd been on snowshoes and they were on snowmobiles, he'd kept up with them through the bush all day. He had even watched them when they stopped for lunch and knew exactly what they had eaten. He was that close to them. Silent and hiding in the snow. Stevens had never seen anything like it.

What it all boiled down to was that Gunter Lishy had more than one face. In the end, Bird was left with two conflicting theories, each one equally compelling.

Lishy might have been moving in with good intentions, expecting to make friends, only to be surprised by a homicidal maniac. Or he might well have expected Oros to react the way he himself did when he figured another trapper was encroaching on his territory. Feeling tougher than Oros, he may have intended to push Oros out, the way a stronger bear drives out a weaker one. And not caring how violent it got, either. Who'd look for Oros if he disappeared?

As Bird knew, a good defense lawyer would create that argument before a jury just as well as he could. And with that theory floating in the air, even a dead body wouldn't prove the killing was murder.

Unless there was actually a bullet hole in the back, they'd never be able to convince a jury it wasn't self-defense. Like the shoot-out at O.K. Corral, Lishy drew first but fired last.

Everything boiled down to Oros. Only he knew what really happened. If they could make him talk. Or if his diary for August and September was found, they might still solve this case.

But they had to catch him first.

Chapter Fourteen

March 1, 1982: Oros lay back on his goatskin bed listening to the CBC radio station out of Whitehorse. He had picked up the radio in the fall during his raids and to save the batteries, he used it sparingly, turning it on only once every couple of days to listen to the news. At night, with the antenna strung out over the top of the roof and up to a treetop, he could even pick up an American station once in awhile, although he preferred to listen to the Whitehorse news. Ever since he heard his own name on the radio in connection with the disappearance of the German trapper Lishy, he couldn't know enough. All they ever said, though, was that there were two men missing—Lishy, believed dead, and Oros, who was believed to know something about it but had disappeared into the bush. "The police are still searching for him," the news report concluded, suggesting the story wasn't over yet. But that was a long time ago and he hadn't heard his name mentioned for months now.

Oros had returned to Hutsigola in mid-October to discover the area deserted. But as he had feared, it had been ransacked. The cabin and most of the high caches around the lake had been stripped. They'd even found the cache on the east side of Hutsigola. One of his safest caches. The chain saw and gas he'd taken from the German were missing, along with all the roofing sheets and tar, nails, and wedges. The hammer and his lantern were missing, too. The loss of the lantern was particularly surprising. He'd had it for a couple of years already and they still took it! The spare sleeping bag was gone—the good one, the down one the German had used—they had stolen that too. Everything. Even the spare ax.

Oros had raged over the losses for weeks. He wasn't feeling sorry for himself. He was just mad. Furiously mad. And in his anger, he wished the people who had done it were still around. Promising himself he'd show them what it meant to rob Sheslay Free Mike, he spent so much time hunting them that the winter was almost full blown before he'd settled down enough to concentrate on replenishing his supplies by raiding the cabins and camps to the north along Teslin Lake and the western edge of the Kawdy Plateau.

And now, now that he was reasonably secure, the anger, one of the few constants left in his life, burned like embers. Soft and quiet but extremely hot.

Now that they had invaded his house, violated his personal space, the list of people he wanted to kill grew from names of individuals to whole categories of people. All government men—undercover and uniformed—paratroopers, police, fisheries officers, game wardens, the pilots, guides, and trappers. All the antihippies, the straights, and the rednecks. They would all have to die.

By far the worst pain was the loss of his diaries. It was so devastating, so personal, so total that they might as well have cut out his heart. The diaries were stored in two caches which they had found. All the evidence he had collected. Ten years of writing. Everything. And they got it all. Without them, he was no better than Kila or Smoky. Just another animal scratching out an existence alone in the wilderness. The diaries were his last link to an organized society. They were his roots, his personal history, his past and future. They were the record of his voice speaking out against what they were doing and what they had done.

All he had ever wanted to do with them was to get them out. To have them published. To let everyone read for themselves what THEY had been doing here. What THEY were still doing. What THEY had done to him. He only wanted to warn people. To let them know that there was another way, a better way to live than the way they had been living.

He had it all written down. Everything. And now it was all lost.

In the beginning, when they burned him out of his first cabin in Sheslay, he was sure they only wanted him to conform. To accept their will and leave Sheslay. To abandon the forest and his dreams. Only it backfired on them. The fire had strengthened his resolve to stay. And to fight back.

Since then, their purpose and tactics had changed. No longer content merely to drive him out of the forest, they were now determined to destroy it all. To poison the forest and kill him.

It didn't make sense to him, what they were doing or why, but they almost always came in for him at night, with darkness their closest ally, tormenting him and torturing him with their drugs. Sometimes as he peered out with terror and rage at the shadowy forms that flitted through the blackness, he fired at them. Shooting when they called out to him. When there was a voice to give direction. Whispering secrets about his death—that he was already dying. Calling to him.

But the worst part of the voices was always the laughter—a deep, wild laughter. Almost inhuman. A horrible and terrifying sound. Even when there was more than one voice heckling him with complete abandon, they were always from the same mouth, many voices speaking with the same sound—the voice of evil incarnate, personifying absolute madness.

Mercifully, the voices were quiet last night.

Just as well, he thought. He didn't have enough ammunition to waste it firing at sounds. Even with all the shooting he had done in the past, there were never any traces left behind of THEIR presence in the mornings. No bodies. No blood. Not even a single footstep. Ever. Even in fresh snow.

It was bewildering.

Oros turned off the radio and lay back down in his bed. They hadn't mentioned him or the German tonight, which was a good thing. No news was good news. In the darkness, he closed his eyes and listened to the ice popping out on the lake. It was very cold outside. So cold that the ice, already a meter thick, was freezing even thicker. As it expanded with the falling night temperatures, it shattered along pressure lines, with each side of the crack heaving and rubbing against the other. Some of the cracks split through the ice with a sound like a sonic boom and went from shore to shore. The noise reverberated in the calm water under the ice the way distant thunder continued to rumble after the first earsplitting crack. It was pleasant lying in bed imagining the sounds of a hot summer night's storm, imagining it was that other season—when there was light and natural warmth and the smell of living things in the air. Summer was the time for living. And winter, the time for dying.

Damn it was cold, he thought, guessing it must be close to fifty below outside. He didn't want to admit it was cold. Not even to say the word. He refused to allow himself to think negative thoughts. Negative thinking wouldn't contribute to his peace of mind. Even to acknowledge negative feelings was to give them meaning and power. And cold had such bad connotations. It was a negative absolute that left no room for hope or anything else. Like dead. It was too final.

Cool, on the other hand, was relative. Nowhere near as bad as it could get. Cool was anywhere between warm and cold. Oros smiled to himself. Yes, he agreed. Cool was much better. It was cool outside. In fact, he could safely say it was quite cool outside and that didn't sound bad at all.

Having listened to the six o'clock news in the darkness of the night, it couldn't have been much later than seven when he fell asleep. With the short daylight, he spent most of each day inside his sleeping bag, sleeping as much as he could to pass the time. He awoke to darkness, unsure at first whether he had just dozed off for a few minutes or whether he had slept through the night. It was impossible to tell. More than once, he'd slept right through the short day and then wondered where the light had gone. It was so much easier in the summer when he could tell the time any hour of the day by the light conditions alone. Judging by the way his body felt, he had indeed slept for a long time. At any rate, he wasn't tired and guessed it was morning, or what would be morning if it were summer. But there wasn't much point in crawling out of his bag in the dark. There was no wood to burn anyway, as he'd burned everything last night. Usually he only gathered one day's supply of wood at a time, dragging whatever half-dried wood he could find into the cabin and chopping it up as he needed it. Without a fire burning, the cabin was too cold to stand around doing nothing.

"Hey, Kila, you lazy bastard. WAKE UP!" Oros yelled. Kila and Smoky both jumped to their feet, growling in the dark, expecting some trouble.

"What time is it?" Oros demanded of them, but they only whined back from the darkness. Oros broke into deep laughter and then pulled the bag tightly around his head before ordering them back to sleep. They wouldn't. Instead, they stood by the door complaining so insistently that Oros, cursing, decided he'd better let them out. The last time he kept Kila in when he begged to go out, the dog had exploded, sending excrement all over the place. It was pretty funny at the time but the cabin was foul with the smell of it for a couple of days, until it dried out. Moving quickly across the frozen floor, he whipped open the door, speeding them out with his foot, and rushed back to his sleeping bag. Even that short exposure to the cold caused the soles of his feet to go numb and the skin of his body to pull tight. With the fire out, it was close to twenty below in the cabin. Maybe colder. Not cold, he corrected himself again. Cool. Very cool. The dogs wanted back in but he ignored them. Until it was light outside or showed some real signs of morning, he wasn't going to move again. It might only be four o'clock.

Oros had lost Toot after returning to Hutsigola. They had gone north to check his fur and gun cache on the west side of Teslin Lake, near the Hayes River, far from Hutsigola. The sneak-arounds had missed it. There were other caches Oros had scattered throughout the wilderness that they also missed but this was one of his most important ones. Stocked with tools, ammo, furs, traps, and a couple of spare rifles he'd collected, this one cache alone could keep him alive.

Taking the beaver hides, stretched out, dried and stacked like brittle cardboard, his two lynx pelts, one of them a silver lynx caught by accident in a muskrat trap, and four, slightly ratty, marten pelts, they worked their way north to a cabin across the lake from Johnsontown where they'd found a new canoe. With the canoe, the rest of the trip to Brooks Brook to trade his furs for some supplies was a quick in and out and everything went smoothly—except that Toot had run off when they touched shore near the tiny village and never came back.

Thinking about Toot. Oros realized that Smoky was a better dog without Toot around and it didn't seem that any of them really missed him at all, although he had to admit Toot was the best trail breaker in deep snow that he'd ever had. Even the worst dogs were always good for something.

The wind gusted a little outside and the cabin creaked. Under the weight of a meter of snow on the roof, it was a surprise the cabin held up at all. From the outside, the cabin was more like an icehouse than a log building. The snow that slid off the roof had built up on the ground until it had piled up in places and met the snow on the roof in one continuous and unbroken mound of snow. Under the shadow of overhanging snow, the windows let in virtually no light and the cabin was darker than it had been all summer. Only the entrance was clear, the overhanging roof kept the snow away from the door.

Still curled in his sleeping bag, Oros planned his day. There was nothing pressing to do. Lying just outside the door at the edge of the cabin under the protection of the overhang was a large piece of meat. Almost a whole quarter. Enough to last a few more days before he'd have to hike back to the bull and cut more off it. He'd been lucky with meat this winter. The bull was the fourth moose he'd killed so far. And he still had some of the cow left. That, he was saving for himself. Her meat was far more tender than the bull's. And the dogs seemed to enjoy chewing on the old bastard anyway, he thought.

The small trapline had brought in some meat, too—several marten and almost twenty muskrat. They were good for a change. Roast muskrat. He left the martens for the dogs. Skinned out, they looked too carnivorous to eat—like big squirrels with small weasel heads and sharp teeth. Their skins were good, though. Prime pelts. But he had decided against adding them to his fur cache this winter. Better he make use of them and enjoy a small luxury than for someone else to have that pleasure.

It was a crude looking affair, the marten robe. He remembered reading that there was a trick to sewing fur coats but he couldn't remember the details and he hadn't figured it out for himself yet. Well, it was coming along alright anyway, he told himself. A few more pelts and it'd be done. He could work on the robe today. Later on maybe. If he felt like it. The snowshoes needed some work done on them as well. Big seven-footers, they were his own design. The snow was too deep and powdery to use the shorter ones that all the factories made. He had carefully drilled holes through the frames with a small awl and then stitched the webbing in place with moose gut. The only problem with them was that the strapping kept breaking apart and constantly needed to be redone. The sleds were in the same condition. Their harnesses, made from green moose hides, were also rotting away. They'd need to be restitched before he took them up the lake to haul back another heavy load of meat from the old bull; but it was too cool for any heavy work and hauling the sled through four to six feet of powdered ice crystals wasn't easy. Besides, they didn't need the meat right now.

The only other big project he had, apart from getting firewood, was the new octagonal cabin he was building, sixty feet away. The idea to build it had come to him last fall after he killed Lishy. And once he'd got back to Hutsigola in the early winter he had started on it. He would have preferred a six-sided cabin but the German had cut the logs too short for that. Before the snow had stopped him, he'd got most of the walls up. They were already eight logs high. Three more and it'd be ready for the roof. Only he had already used up all the logs that Lishy had cut. And he didn't much feel like chopping down more trees. That was more work than he needed.

Besides, he didn't want to finish the cabin too soon or close it in.

It had to air thoroughly first. The sneak-arounds had poisoned the logs. They were so heavily covered in the torture-drugs that working with the logs, just notching them and raising them into place, infected him badly. He still didn't know if the drugs would break down naturally but it seemed safer to leave them exposed to the air and let the weather wear them down before he did any more work on the cabin.

Oros reached an arm down to the box beside his bed where the marten robe lay and stroked its silkiness. When his hand brushed the cold, wooden grip of Lishy's .44 magnum, he let it linger there, his fingertips lightly outlining the feel of it in the dark. The pistol grips were firm as he slid his hand around them and squeezed. A good feeling. Sliding the gun slowly back out of its holster, he swung it out of the box and then let his arm hang freely with the full weight of the powerful handgun pulling like an anchor.

Raising his arm up over the bed, he held it, straight-armed, pointing toward the door at an imaginary intruder. The rifles had to be aimed. He never had much use for handguns before but this one could be fired instinctively. He carefully slid the gun back into its holster in the box beside his bed. It was a nice little bit of extra security—having the weapon there fully loaded and ready for the quick draw. If THEY ever rushed in here and tried to get him when he was sleeping, or if the fighting ever got down to close quarters, the .44 would pay off handsomely.

There were some other guns around, one by the stove, another leaning up against the wall right beside the door, another hanging on two hooks from a tree in the bush forty feet behind the cabin where he dragged most of his wood from. All loaded and ready to shoot. As many as he put out, however, it didn't help. He still wasn't secure. There was something happening out there. Something sinister. Brewing.

A presence in the forest.

All winter, there had been aircraft in the air. As many as one a week sometimes. Spraying poisons? Dropping off and picking up torture-druggers and sneak-arounds?

Certainly the sneak-arounds were out there. He had heard their voices several times. And although he hadn't yet found their tracks this winter, that didn't surprise him much. Of course, they were speaking through loudspeakers. Wireless radio receivers with amplifiers that could broadcast messages beamed to them from miles away. He had spent many days searching for the transmitters but they were planted up high in the trees and were probably too small to find easily. Indeed, he could well imagine they were very small because the messages they broadcast were usually so garbled.

Strange sounds. Twisted. And tortured.

But even in absolute silence, he knew they were around. He could feel them out there watching him. It was a feeling he knew well—the creepy-crawly feeling that he wasn't alone.

So far this winter, he had spent a lot of time hunting them. More time than he spent doing anything else. Over the past three months, he never went out without spending at least some part of each day searching for them. Even when the meat situation was at its worst and he was on the trail after moose, he always managed to swing around the cabin for a few miles to study the snow for any signs of them. And now that the food situation was stable again for awhile, he had gone back to concentrating most of his energy on hunting them. With the doggedness of a starving wolf hunting for prey, he had even developed a routine reconnaissance patrol that took him out every few days on a wide sweep through the bush. So far, he hadn't found them. But he would. They couldn't hide forever. Sooner or later, he'd run into them. And when he did, he'd kill them.

Still in bed, he decided that if it was snowing or blowing up a storm outside, he'd stay home and work on the stitching. But the quick peek he'd taken outside when he'd let the dogs out showed a sky that was clear and stuffed with thousands of stars. A perfect day for hunting sneak-arounds.

When the light was just bright enough to see outside, Oros left the cabin. A thick hoarfrost had settled in overnight, covering the older snow and now in the light of dawn, the trees looked like perfectly sculpted crystalline glass towers with delicate spires and flying arches that fell crunching and snapping when stepped on. But Oros wasn't paying attention to the beauty of the morning. He had other things on his mind.

Pulling the long snowshoes out of the snow where he had stuck them, he stepped into the harnesses and strapped them on. He had never seen snowshoes this big, although he had read once that the Tahltans made snowshoes bigger than their own bodies. They couldn't turn quickly and they weren't much good at going through any kind of thick brush but out in the open, in a straight line, nothing could beat them.

Swathed in layers of clothing, a light pack on his back, and a spare, smaller set of snowshoes strapped to that, together with his favorite rifle, the .303 British, on a sling over his shoulder, and his hands swinging freely inside large mitts, he stepped out from the cabin. Before he took ten steps, he stopped. Beside him and all around the moose quarter that was lying there were wolf tracks. Right outside the cabin.

Testy bastards, he thought. He had already trapped one of them near here and had followed the animal for three days as it fled with the pack, dragging a broken leg still in his steel trap. He never caught up to it but the shock it must have had on the rest of the pack had kept them away for awhile. He had thought they'd stay away for the rest of the winter.

"Well," he said to himself, "if they're going to come right in under our noses like this and eat us out of house and home, we'll have to teach the stupid bastards another lesson, won't we? Amazing the dogs didn't smell them or hear them outside. Just like sneak-arounds!"

Then without wasting any more time, he walked off. Lifting his foot, the front of the snowshoe rose with it and slid the tail along behind. With all his weight on top of the snowshoe, sinking hardly at all in the snow, he lifted the other foot and took his next step. Walking almost as fast as he would in summer, he put his back to the lake and marched off along a trail that wound through the bush. Without snowshoes, if he stood on the snow now, he'd sink right down to his waist; he'd flounder hopelessly. Without snowshoes, a person simply couldn't move. As he traveled through the forest, he wondered why the wolves had dared to return. With snow conditions like these, killing moose was as easy as running one down that had broken legs. It didn't make any sense they should be risking their lives to steal his meat when they could get their own just as easily. It probably meant something. Everything out of place always did. Still, he couldn't figure out exactly how it was connected to the sneak-arounds. But he knew there was a connection.

He walked about four miles out from the cabin in a northwesterly direction before cutting across the country toward the Teslin River at a point due north of the cabin. He figured this was the most effective way to search the area—if THEY were camped farther out, five or ten miles from his cabin, but walked in closer to it, even if they snuck up to a point only two or three miles away from the cabin, then he should cross their tracks.

Oros thought constantly of that day. If only they had left him alone. Everything could have and would have worked out the way it was supposed to, he knew. The way he had wanted it to, years ago. He was the first of the new pioneers and the rest were to follow. He had started the flow but THEY had stopped it. THEY spread their lies about him across the country to keep people away from him. THEY isolated him even as THEY tried to kill him. He was sick of being hunted like an animal. Baited and poisoned. He was tired of running. And hiding. There was no choice now but to fight back. To kill THEM.

It was still bitterly cold. Not as sharp as at dawn but harsh enough that he was having trouble breathing. He had to draw his air in slowly through his mouth. Every time he inhaled through his nose, the air passing through his nostrils froze them tight. It was an intense, dry cold that crept through his clothes, every single layer of them, to touch his skin in a powdery and numbing embrace. It was the kind of cold that calmed even the air molecules, slowing everything until a dead quiet prevailed.

Hearing nothing, smelling nothing, feeling only the frosty air moving through his lips, its stinging bite on his exposed cheeks and eyes, Oros listened to the expulsion of his own breath, which crystallized cloud-like in the air in front of his mouth. The moist air collected on the hairs of his moustache and beard, frosting them white. Squinting against the dazzling sunlight that reflected off innumerable ice surfaces, his hazel-gray eyes darted constantly back and forth across the earth, tirelessly, almost automatically searching everything for any sign of THEM. For anything they might have been careless enough to leave behind—a footstep, perhaps, or a ski track. It was quiet so far today. A few moose tracks plowing along heavily through the snow and a wolf pack on the run were the largest animals that had left any signs. Nothing with any human intelligence. But everywhere, there were lots of small prints, little fur coats running around on rat carcasses.

Around noon, he stopped for a quick lunch of cold jellied porridge and a couple of strips of stove-smoked but mostly raw moose meat, which he washed down with tea from a small plastic canteen he had tucked into his shirt to keep from freezing. As he ate, standing straight up with his feet apart in the long snowshoes, he studied the surface around him. It was so deep it had covered all the low ground, leaving only the mature, well-spaced trunks of trees to walk through.

It was easy going; but he hadn't come out for a walk.

Oros cursed, trying to control his anger. Every time he went out looking for them and didn't find anything, he always left behind his own tracks. Tracks THEY could follow. Try as he would, he couldn't convince himself that the snow was an ally. If THEY couldn't move in it without leaving tracks, neither could he.

Behind him, stretching all the way back to the cabin, was a trail his snowshoes had carved through the snow. The sight disgusted him. Obvious even to an aircraft flying at 1,000 feet. But there was no getting around it.

In fact, the snow didn't so much benefit either side as it changed the whole picture. In the summer he had the choice of hunting them or hiding, and his was the clear advantage; but now, in the dead of winter, he couldn't hide at all. Anywhere he went, they could follow him. All he could do was hunt them—searching for their tracks in the deep snow—while leaving his own behind as obvious as skywriting. To see if they were following, he had to constantly circle back around to his own trail. He cautioned himself that if ever he found their tracks, he'd have to be careful to be sure that they too weren't circling around on their own tracks. Circling around each other in the endless hunt and be hunted merry-go-round. If it ever came down to a face-to-face winter confrontation, he knew he'd have to act fast. And there'd be no running away.

An hour later, the sweat building under his clothing, the distant sound of an aircraft stopped him cold. Standing absolutely still, he listened intently to the faint noise of its engine, trying to determine from the sound alone which aircraft it was. It was a single engine. Or sounded like one. And it was heading from the west to the northeast. Probably from Atlin to Watson Lake. It was probably the blue one. It sounded like the blue one. And it sounded high. Probably to get a better look at the country below it. Plotting something evil. At least it wasn't close enough this time to be dropping off sneak-arounds!

He had kept track of all aircraft movements over the winter. Every flight he saw and heard was noted in the log; where it was heading, where it was coming from, identifying marks if it could be seen or the kind of sounds it made if it couldn't, and, finally, what it was probably doing. Oros treated every human contact like enemy troop movements, with a critical urgency, the minutia of each sighting occupying his mind for hours afterward. It was all part of the great puzzle. He was only one man and they were so many, so complex in their organizations and movements that it was sometimes overwhelming to him to have been burdened with the task of unraveling it all by himself. And of fighting them all alone. Such a heavy burden.

As he silently hunted through the forest, he was anxious for a living contact he could physically deal with.

Every twenty minutes, he stopped to quiet the stream of conversation that roared through his mind, and forced himself to listen instead to the sounds of the winter forest. There was so little to hear. Only a bird now and then, the occasional shrill chatter of a squirrel, the feathery rustle of snow filtering down to the ground through the needles of a spruce tree and the settling of the snow under his snowshoes. The crispy, crunching sound of compacting snow crystals. All natural sounds. The rifle which he unslung whenever he stopped was returned to his shoulder and he went on again. Stop, listen, and go. His mind once more released to be filled with a dozen roaring dialogues of his imagination.

At the frozen shore of Teslin River, having found nothing alarming, he turned to the south, ready to head home. But first, he paused at the edge of the forest. After scanning the snow-covered river for any sign of recent activity, he squinted up at the sky. The days were so terribly short. Judging from the position of the sun brushing the tops of some spindly spruce forty feet away, he figured there'd be just enough light left to get home in time to start a supper in the dark. Well, he thought, it didn't matter. It had to be done. He had to get out and check the trails. The day he let down his vigilance would be the day he'd regret. And since he hadn't found anything this time, he could at least sleep securely one more night. That was worthwhile. A little peace was such a hard thing to come by.

There were other reasons to feel good. Now with the beginning of March, the hardest month was past. February was over. January was the darkest, but it was always February that hit hardest. March was sometimes no better but the days were at least lengthening. Every day, a few more minutes were added before sunset, and that did wonderful things to the spirit. However hard it stormed now, there was no question but that he'd done it again. He'd survived another winter. The worst was over. Now, he hoped, if the gods were willing, spring break-up might start as early as late April—only a couple more months away. But if the God of Vengeance wished, the lakes might be kept icebound until June. Compared to Telegraph Creek, which was almost tropical in its own northern way, Hutsigola was akin to Fairbanks. It was a strange irony that he had left Alaska to escape the isolation and the winter and had ended up alone in a wilderness so remote it could have been its own undiscovered country with a winter nearly identical to Fairbanks'. It wasn't something Oros ever felt like passing judgment on. Life was full of strange surprises. Whatever had happened had happened. Life had its own mystic reasons for everything. It was all part of the cosmic flow. As unfeeling and as unfair as it might seem, it was useless to try to resist it.

As he walked the river home in the fading light, his shoulders hunched against the bitter cold, he thought wistfully about summers, until he reminded himself not to hope for much. It was so easy to forget the bad things about summer when one wanted only the good things it offered. Winter, summer, winter, summer. Winter was just the back side of summer. Easier to say now that it was ending. Finally.

Oros paused to contemplate that for a moment. There had been so many winters. All spent here—alone in the forest. So many that they stretched off in memory toward a dimming picture of another world he once lived in. In another life. Back then, the walk he was just now finishing might have taken him two days. The visions and dreams he had were so different then, before they all died off, snuffed out like candles, winter after winter. That first year, when he'd stepped out of the world and into the country at Telegraph Creek to be on his own for the first time, the land had been a haven, the wilderness a wonderful retreat, a safe sanctuary, an alternative to the insanity of commercial gods that ruled outside. Some things hadn't changed. He had left the bush a few times over the years to make quick trips down the west coast to California, and the reality he encountered on those occasions was even worse than he remembered. The forest was still a haven but after more years in it than he knew automatically, he couldn't help but wonder whether he'd ever get out. Living alone had never been part of the plan but he couldn't go back now. The past was clear.

He had, after all, recorded all the significant events and then read and reread his own history. Some of it, years old, written in distant places, motivated by moods he hadn't felt for ages, gave him a strange perspective. The pen was his and the words were his but the reality was so different now. There had been so many realities, all captured and frozen in time. Reading the old words, seeing the old visions through them, freaked him out. A voice from the past speaking to its future—his present. His own voice, talking to him.

Oros had spent many nights absorbed by the old words. The stories evoked memories, thousands of memories, some forgotten for years. Bringing them alive. Until time stood still, the years blurred and 1968 was all yesterday.

It was the future that was uncertain. A great black hole. An impenetrable wall of nothingness that began with tomorrow.

It was the loss of his diaries that he suffered the most. Hidden in several caches near Hutsigola, they weren't hidden far enough. The caches had been found, their contents searched and the diaries taken! And now that they were gone, there was little left to live for.

They had done more than keep the past alive. They were his salvation. They gave him purpose. More important than his own life, their publication, even at the cost of his own death, was worth the price. Now, only half consciously, he felt himself drifting in and out of purposes—the only constant left in his life, the last force remaining, being the matter of his own survival. But even that, he mused as he neared the cabin, the break in the trees on the skyline up ahead revealing the presence of the top end of Hutsigola, was as natural to him now as the instinct to breathe.

"Eat, shit, and sleep. Eat, shit, sleep, kill, and be killed. That's all that's left."

The ice heaved on the lake, sending a low rumbling murmur reverberating through the cabin as Oros ate his supper in the dark. The noise brought back vague memories of fighter aircraft experimenting with speeds faster than sound back home when he was a child. If they ever brought those down to use against him, he thought, only slightly concerned, then his little .303 wouldn't do much good.

Smoky wouldn't stop whining at the door and Oros got up at last. Sliding the safety back on the rifle, he cracked open the door and peeked out. If it was the wolves Smoky was whining about, he might be able to snap off a shot at them before they got away. But he didn't see anything. Against the bright white of the snow, even the darkest nights couldn't hide everything. That was one advantage of having the snow. There were so precious few. Smoky was trying to worm his way out between the door and Oros' feet and Oros finally let him escape, closing the door behind him. If Smoky wanted to risk the wolves, that was his business. If Smoky were a bitch, the wolves would rape her; but males, they killed.

It wasn't ten minutes later that the dog was back, crashing up against the door. Oros grabbed his rifle and rushed to the door. Smoky sounded scared. Flinging it open, he leaped out into the night ready to shoot. But again there was nothing to be seen except the thousands of stars that twinkled against a jet black background from horizon to horizon. Quickly, he examined the moose quarter that remained outside; it hadn't been disturbed. He immediately wondered whether Smoky had been frightened by sneak-arounds but decided as he studied the dog that all Smoky wanted was to come back inside. Fairly certain there was nothing threatening lurking nearby, Oros leaned the rifle up against the door frame outside and hurried around the corner of the cabin. Squatting, he emptied his bowels as rapidly as he could. The frigidly cold air surrounded him instantly, numbing his nerves and sending shock messages to his brain to cover his flesh. He ignored them. Squatting quietly with his pants around his knees wasn't life threatening with the door only a few feet away.

It was very quiet. There was a calm the winter brought to the north that no other place on earth ever experienced. As though all life was stilled. The kind of quiet one would expect in the depths of space. It was the cold that did it. A cold that froze the moisture left in the trees until even the wood fiber split open, bursting the tree trunks. A cold that froze the earth, stilled the swamps, and sealed the lakes under thick sheets of ice. Without the high-pitched whispering of the winter wind through the stiffened needles of the spruce trees around the cabin, it was so quiet he could hear the blood pulsating through his ears and the creaking of his own joints and muscles as they balanced his body. In the absolute silence that reigned over the night, while the earth was black and a million stars exploded the moonless sky, it was easy to feel he was the only man left alive. That in all this vast, vast space, life was the most fragile of all creation. It was a wonderful feeling. To be at the center of it all. To have the stars out there for his eyes only. To know that when he died, everything would die with him. There would be nobody else to take his place. To stand in wonder beneath the diamond sky. It was only in his memory that other people existed in other places far away doing other things. That somewhere, it was daylight and the wind was blowing warm over the land. He knew all these things but they didn't make any real sense to him. Telegraph Creek was real. He could picture the winter there. But California was light-years away. Literally another world. And they were as oblivious to the existence of his world as he was now to theirs.

Oros paused at the door for one last look at the night before going in. He would like to have stayed outside. He always felt better outside. But it was too cold. When he was outside, the sheer magnitude of the space, its greatness, filled him with awe and that, in turn, gave him a sense of well-being. Inside, the simple squalor of the frozen hut with its low, sagging roof and rotten, earthy smells produced very different effects. Outside, life had the quality of being rare and precious, the earth a single light burning all alone in the infinite darkness. But in the dank, squalid interior, the mood of the space was of quiet desperation, a feeling of such isolation and poverty that it often produced dark and terrible depressions. Most times, the dogs helped, but they were hardly the society of his choice. The books helped, too, to keep him in touch, and he still read voraciously for the communication they offered; but their pages weren't warm, living flesh. Tonight, though, he wasn't feeling the pain of loneliness. The crispness of the air had cleansed his mind. Tonight, there was a sharp clarity to his thoughts, a union in purpose with a greater reality that lay beyond the walls of his cabin, that made the mere fact of his physical existence a marvelous sensation. To be alive! He couldn't explain it but there was a meaning in it all that touched him deeply and left him feeling full of strength. He had felt it before, the experience of belonging, but only in the dead of winter. And only here, in the emptiness of the northern nights.

Oros crossed the room to his bed to get his coat, to wrap over his shoulders, but picked up the marten robe instead, deciding he might as well get all the use he could out of it. Wrapping it around himself with the fur inside, he looked like one of the buffalo hunters of the last century. With long, wild hair and a thick moustache and beard, and with gut-stitched, homemade skins and boots covering his body, he bore little resemblance to that younger man of his past.

His rough fingers searched gingerly across the top of a split log shelf over the end of his bed and, finding the matches, lit one. It cracked the darkness with its feeble light. Touching the flame to the stump of a thick candle, he flicked the match out and tossed it away into the dark. Moving the light to the stove, he broke some branches he had dragged in earlier and, stuffing them into the stove, built up a fire that cast its light and heat out through the open door of the firebox. He had grown used to being cold over the winter; he was cold so much that he hardly noticed the temperature inside the cabin. His moustache hadn't thawed all day, still hard and crusty with the moisture from his own breath which had crystallized thickly over it. As he fingered it and huddled around the darting light that escaped the cast-iron stove, he laughed, remembering a terrible fright he had had this winter when his moustache had frozen up so solidly in the night that when he awoke from a desperate dream, it felt as though someone had clamped his steel hand down over his mouth to stifle his screams as he prepared to slit his throat. The shriek that rose up within him, roaring in his brain, couldn't leave his mouth. He was being choked. He tried to open his mouth but couldn't. Flailing his arms in front of his face to grab the attacker met only empty air while the fist at his face kept its iron grip on him. Finally, when he felt his mouth, the hand that touched it struck a mask of ice that spread all the way from the base of his flaring nostrils, down, over and around his mouth tightly into his beard. The moisture from his breath had frozen his mouth absolutely solid, leaving only a small breathing hole in the center. Oros laughed at the memory. That was certainly a cold night.

Oros awoke in the morning feeling refreshed and lighthearted.

Slipping on his snowshoes, he walked over to a tree not forty feet from the cabin. There, in what had become a morning ritual, he lifted the rifle which he kept suspended from a branch on two wire hooks and quickly checked the action. Satisfied it remained ready to fire and hadn't frozen up, he hung it back on the hooks, crouched down beside the tree, emptied his bowels, and hurried back to the cabin. Just inside the door, leaning against the frame, was another rifle, loaded and ready to shoot. Beside the stove was the shotgun, more lethal than any of the rifles at the distance he expected he'd use it—from the stove to the door. His defenses ready and his morning ablutions over, he turned his thoughts to breakfast.

Dawn was breaking outside and the first pink light of a promising day was rapidly taking over from the open fire door as the principle source of illumination inside.

Oros put down his pencil, ending the day's first entry into his journal, took a sip of coffee from his mug, and then left the cabin again to study the sky.

The day outside would be a good one for hunting sneak-arounds.

If the clouds didn't move in. He didn't want to be caught out in a storm. There was no sign of that happening though. Blue and clear everywhere he could see. And still cold.

Cool, he reminded himself. Very cool. He studied his breakfast situation. There wasn't much choice. He was tired of eating porridge. The powdered eggs, he was saving for emergency situations; the few raisins and dried dates he had left were for the trail—they almost always went into the bannock; and the macaroni was for lunch.

"Well fellas, what do you say about tortillas for breakfast?"

The dogs ate anything he could feed them and whined expectantly when Oros talked to them, but he ignored them. Pouring some hot water from the stove into a bowl, crusty with the remains of other meals, he mixed in a fistful of cornmeal, added a pinch of salt, and stirred it together with the same old pewter spoon he'd had for years, until the cornmeal firmed up. From a jar of rose hips on his shelf, he picked out several and dropped them into his pot for tea. Already in front of him was a plate of meat he had cut up yesterday into manageable hunks. Prying one frozen piece away from the rest with his knife blade, he laid it in the skillet at the edge of the heat. It'd have to thaw a little before he'd fry it up with the cornmeal.

Not a bad breakfast, he thought. Moose, tortillas, and tea. It would be nice to have a little marmalade for the tortillas. Or blueberry jam.

The thought that he didn't have any blueberry jam angered him. He should have made some. And he would have if it hadn't been for THEM! There were plenty of berries in the fall. He could have had buckets of them. And saskatoon berries. Only THEY didn't allow him the time. He couldn't even hang his meat properly. THEY kept sneaking around drugging him, poisoning his food, and tormenting him with loudspeakers at night so that he had to spend so much time hunting that he couldn't even live like a man.

Oros had finished breakfast and was sitting with his socks up on the door of the stove, toasting his feet and sipping his rose hip tea, when the roar of a machine washed over the cabin. So sudden and unexpected was it that he didn't know how to react.

Low and screaming through the air just over the cabin was a helicopter. Out of nowhere.

Oros jerked on his boots and stood by the closed door, listening. Beside him, the rifle stood ready against the doorjamb. The sound of the powerful blade cutting through the air just outside sent his nervous system into an intense and uncontrolled frenzy.

In shock, his thoughts were a scrambled mess. His muscles went into uncontrollable spasms. Mindlessly, he stood there behind the closed door, paralyzed, as the helicopter began to settle down into the snow on the lake in a blizzard of its own making. Still he hadn't regained control of his reeling senses. Fighting an incredible inertia, he first commanded his hand to open the door, then for his feet to step outside and for his eyes to look. The sight he saw almost stopped his heart. The chopper had landed on the lake.

After all these years, there they were. They were sneaking up on him right now. In the open. The sneak-arounds. Two men were approaching. Moving away from each other. One on the right was already in the trees and the other one was walking right up the hill from the lake toward him. Straight for him! Walking. Yelling. He could hear someone yelling. The man coming up the trail from the lake was talking. Constantly. Yelling. Oros couldn't think. The man was yelling. Surveyors. A mining survey? Oros couldn't see the other men. There was a man in the pilot's seat but the door was open and there was a head crouching behind it. The man on the path was getting too close. Yelling something. Over and over and Oros couldn't think. All he could hear was the yelling. Grinning. Good morning. Surveying minerals. It didn't make any sense. The man in the trees was coming toward him from the side, smiling idiotically. The other was still talking, talking as he came closer. Asking questions. Over and over again. Questions, one after another, hundreds of questions. Behind the helicopter's door there was a face, peering over the metal frame.

Unconsciously, Oros had come out farther away from the cabin to get a better look. To see the helicopter. The man crouching behind the door by the pilot was looking at him. They were all looking at him. Voices were speaking all at once, talking to him, asking him questions, telling him things from grinning, friendly faces. They were in snowshoes, stepping carefully through the deep snow toward him. Strange men. There was a gun barrel pointing up beside the face behind the helicopter's open door. The pilot was sitting there motionless, a black, faceless visor pulled down over his head inside the plastic domed bubble.

It was so incredible it was unbelievable. Too much was happening at once, too quickly for him to comprehend. He couldn't think. The blade was still turning, around and around, sending streams of powdery snow into the air around it, obscuring it with whirlwinds. So dreamlike and misty. Foggy and unreal. The noise from the rotating blade spinning around, CHOP, CHOP, CHOP, CHOP, muffling their voices. Calling his name. Oros. Oros. They knew his name, these surveyors. Mike. Mike Oros. Nobody had called him Mike for years. He was Sheslay. Sheslay Free Mike! He tried to focus his brain. He had to know what was happening before it was too late. Things were happening too quickly, changing right in front of his eyes.

As though waking from a dream, things started to become clear. They weren't surveyors. They were sneak-arounds pretending to be friendly. The gun barrel poking up from behind the door of the helicopter was for him. To shoot him with. This was it! They were attacking him! He never expected this to happen—not this way. He had expected people running, screaming, guns firing, blazing away—but not this, people walking calmly toward him, lying, circling around him. Of course they had fooled him, they were the sneak-arounds. And they had drugged him to make him stupid, to catch him off-guard, to trick him.

His mind suddenly freed itself from its paralysis and the realization, burning with a white frenzy, flooded in—this was it! They had come to get him. Act! Act! React! His body finally under control again, he spun around as he jumped for the door. His closest rifle was there. Just inside the door. Ready to shoot.

Too late, he realized he had come ten feet from the cabin. The door, safety, his gun, were that far away.

To get a better view of the helicopter, which was obscured partially by the trees, he had stepped right into the deep snow beside the cabin.

Silently screaming in an agonized and fearful rage, he lunged through the snow, swimming in it, driving himself forward. If he could only get to the door. If he could just get a hand inside and grab the rifle before they killed him, he might kill at least one of them.

He strained his muscles—the door was right in front of him. But THEY were behind him! So close! Tearing at his heels like wolves trying to bring him down.

He was almost there—almost at the door. Less than five more feet and he'd have his weapon. They were right on top of his back now, the weight of their bodies dragging him down into the ground. Desperately he fought them off, lurching ahead, still clawing at the air for support, stretching himself as far as he could toward the sanctuary of his open doorway.

There were hands at his waist now, sliding down to close in around his knees, clamping his legs together so he couldn't move.

He fell heavily, crashing forward into the snow right in front of the door. They were pressing down on his back, tearing at his shoulders, wrenching his arms backward behind him as he screamed. The bastards! And then he felt the terrible bite of cold steel closing in around his wrists.

Oros lost control and screamed again.

Like a pack of wolves, they had him!

It was all over!

Chapter Fifteen

March 4, 1982. Atlin: Staff Sergeant Bomba was doing his best but Oros wasn't talking. At least not about anything significant—like what happened to Gunter Lishy. What Oros didn't mind talking about, indeed what he enjoyed talking about, was the conspiracy to poison him with drugs and drive him out of the wilderness, dead or alive. In that respect, Oros was even excited by the fact he was now in police custody. After ten years of living in the dark and fighting shadows, he was finally face-to-face with his enemies. And he, too, was looking for answers.

Bomba and Bird were still letting him talk but their hopes that he'd slip and hang himself were fading fast. All they needed was one break. One inadvertent reference to Lishy, the body, or its location. An opening. Anything. Trying not to crowd Oros, Corporal Peter Bird sat back in his chair acting relaxed and friendly as he listened with apparent interest to the man seated across from him while Bomba was asking questions.

Oros hadn't changed much since that day years ago when Lishy had taken his photograph on the Telegraph Trail.

In the unaccustomed heat of the detachment office, Oros had stripped off some of the clothing he had on when he was arrested but had politely declined an offer of a change of clothing or a bath, explaining candidly that he wasn't going to give them a chance to poison him with drugged water or clothing. Oros' hands were deeply lined with years of weathering and darkened with the smoke and ash of a thousand fires. As he talked and shook his head in answer to some of Bomba's questions, his long hair brushed back and forth over his shoulders. Hanging straight down, it was thinner and dirtier than it looked in the picture and his face was a little more lined with weathering, but otherwise he appeared the same.

The detachment office was small. A short counter separated a public area, which could accommodate no more than eight or nine standing people. Behind the counter, the working area was only ten feet by twelve. Two desks, some filing cabinets, a portable copy machine, and a computer terminal linking into CPIC, the Canadian police intelligence computer in Ottawa, filled the space. A door opposite the entrance led into a steel and cement cellblock with two steel-framed bunks for prisoners. Another door behind Bird led into his private quarters which were attached to the office. Bird had closed and locked all the doors for the privacy the interview required and, as a result, the smell of Oros' body permeated the air. If it were summertime, the windows would be wide open and the dry dusty breeze would blow in through the heavy screens, but they, too, were shut tight against the wintery air outside. It would be months yet before the sweet smells of summer grasses and the sound of the lake pounding against the shore 100 yards away would break the stale sterility of winter. In the closeness of the small space, the air was oppressive.

When Bird and Bomba had sat down earlier in the morning to question Oros, there was one fundamental truth both officers were acutely aware of. Only Oros knew what had really happened. And if they were ever to get a murder case against him, they would only get it through him. One way or another, Oros had to talk!

Bird concentrated again on their conversation as Bomba asked Oros about all the loaded weapons they had found yesterday around Oros' cabin.

"I need the guns," Oros replied.

"All of them?" Bomba asked.

"I never know when I'll be attacked. Or from where. Or by how many," Oros explained, convinced he wasn't giving anything away.

"Why didn't you use them against us?" Bomba asked.

Oros smiled slyly at Bomba as though they shared a secret Bomba wasn't admitting that Oros knew about. "You drugged me first," he said. "I wanted to fight you.... I was going to fight you but my mind and my muscles were numbed from your drugs. I couldn't think. I couldn't get back to the cabin to get them." Oros waited for confirmation of the truth of his statement.

Bomba didn't give him the satisfaction of an answer and asked instead, "Before you came out, you got a rifle ready to shoot, didn't you? And put it against the door frame inside, cocked and ready to fire?"

"I don't remember," Oros answered as though he didn't.

"But you remember the gun was there and you tried to get to it when you were arrested?"

"Yeah," Oros agreed, believing that whatever hadn't happened didn't have to be concealed from anyone. There were no thought crimes. Besides, they'd seen what he had done.

"And you wanted to use it against us? To shoot us with it?"

"Yeah," Oros agreed again, wondering where it was leading to.

"When did you know we were the police?" Bomba asked, getting to the point as obliquely as he could to prevent Oros second guessing him.

"As soon as I saw you."

Bomba knew that was a lie but didn't know why Oros thought it important enough to lie about. "You mean when you saw the helicopter?" Bomba asked.

"Yeah."

"Why didn't you shoot at that time?"

"I considered it," Oros said thoughtfully after a short pause. "I thought I could shoot at the helicopter's gas tank.... I knew you had no right at all being there so I knew it had to be you."

Bird was still feeling the terrible tension of yesterday's operation and although he hid his feelings from Oros better than most could, he was feeling anything but friendly toward him. There had been some bad moments yesterday that he never wanted to relive, if he could help it, and listening to Oros talking calmly about how he'd wanted to kill them, and had tried, made the matter of Oros' punishment for Lishy's death even more personal than it had been before.

Bird had gone in with the first helicopter. It had been a dangerous thing to do, with truly terrifying risks, but given the unusual circumstances of Oros' lifestyle, it was the only feasible way to arrest him. With a second helicopter carrying the backup team hovering a few miles away, ready to swoop in and drop behind Oros if he started shooting, the first helicopter had set down as close to the cabin as they dared without provoking a fusillade of bullets.

Bird would never forget the actual ground approach. While two of them in civilian dress climbed out of the helicopter and strapped on small, bearpaw snowshoes, the third officer stayed behind with the pilot, who was radioing every detail to the men listening in the backup helicopter.

Under the layers of clothing and body armor that he wore, the sweat had run freely down Bird's chest as he and his partner slowly approached the dark cabin in which they knew Oros was hiding. His hand inside his pocket, his fingers tightly squeezed around the pistol grip of his handgun, he swung his other hand freely, trying to show Oros, if he was somehow watching, that he wasn't armed. Past the wash of the prop, the two men had separated, spreading out as they walked toward the shoreline trying to decrease the target they made for Oros although, out on the lake with no cover at all, they were sitting ducks no matter what they did.

Their own lives had depended almost totally on their ability to keep Oros off guard until they got close enough to arrest him.

The third man in the helicopter behind them was armed with a rifle and scope. It was his role, if Oros started to shoot, to kill Oros before Oros killed them.

As Bird approached the cabin, a thick column of creamy white smoke rose straight up into the calm morning air from a stovepipe sticking out of the snow on the roof.

The approach had been excruciatingly slow. The temptation to run at full speed to the bush, to get off the open lake and behind some cover, was unbearable. But both men knew that that kind of action would probably precipitate Oros into firing.

Anywhere else, walking up to the home of an unsuspecting occupant would be a normal thing to do but here, nothing could be more alien and unusual than what they were doing. Approaching Oros' cabin was more dangerous than walking up to the home of an urban terrorist. Even with civilian disguises, Oros was crazy enough to try to kill them just for being in his space.

They were still out in the open when the cabin door opened suddenly and Oros stepped out. Although their hearts stopped, they forced control over their legs, moved steadily forward, and waved. Pretending cheerfulness, they hollered out their friendliest "Good morning!" over the background wash of the helicopter's engine.

Bird had hoped they'd look the part they were playing, a couple of private geologists collecting data in the winter. With their jeans, lumberman jackets, and heavy French toques, they were dressed differently from each other and as differently from any uniform as their own wardrobes allowed. But it didn't really matter who Oros thought they were so long as he didn't think they were the long arm of the law out to finally drag him in out of the bush. To snuff him out!

Without opening his mouth, without waving back, Oros had stood in the frame of the open door with his feet apart, staring at them. Their tension soared. Nerves screaming. Struggling toward him in the deep snow, they were as exposed as penny arcade targets. His hands were empty. It was a break. It would only take seconds for him to get a weapon; but the fact he wasn't carrying one right now was as encouraging as the situation could get. Forcing grins, they yelled out another "Hello!"

Standing silent sentry duty by his door, Oros didn't respond. Absolutely still, he watched them as they approached, wading through the deep snow.

Putting on the best show they could muster, they waved again and cursed the weather in loud friendly terms as though he were an old friend.

As they got closer, they kept up a constant stream of one-sided conversation, yelling things above the noise of the helicopter about surveys, rock readings, and electromagnetic fields. Mostly it was meaningless gibberish but only a few words got through against the background noise of the helicopter.

Nearer and nearer. Suspicious but confused, Oros remained motionless, his face expressing all the doubts he was feeling. Finally, too close, he opened his mouth and shouted at them.

"What do you want?"

They yelled back, their voices stumbling over their words—the exertion of the walk providing that excuse—a barrage of information in broken bits and pieces. The sentences deliberately chopped and breathless so Oros couldn't understand them.

"Mining geologists...northern surveys...plotting mineralization curves..." and then, something they were sure Oros would relate to. "Gotta shit real bad. Christ! You ever see the inside of one of those bastards?" Bird's partner threw his thumb casually over his shoulder at the helicopter. "Fuck, if I don't make it to a shitter real quick, I'm going to ruin my fuckin' pants!" He grinned heartily as he spoke.

Oros wasn't amused. In fact, he hadn't seemed to have heard them at all. Yet, their approach was working. Step by step, they were closing the distance.

Oros was obviously agitated. Deeply disturbed. But now, instead of retreating into his cabin, he started coming toward them. Like a wild creature, curiously unsettled by the unfamiliar sight of men, his normal reactions were suspended. Mesmerized by the strange visions before him, he had come right off the porch. Standing on the trail to the lake without snowshoes on, Oros was sinking to his knees and holding up his body with his hands. With his head high, his chin raised to get a better view of them over the snow, or perhaps to scent them through his flaring nostrils, he continued to wade through the snow toward them, each step taking him farther from the open door behind him and the weapons he had left inside.

Encouraged, they continued their bursts of information, speaking in friendly sounding tones. The distance between them was closing quickly now. Muffling their voices so Oros couldn't make out much of what they were telling him, they were rewarded by the sight of Oros taking a few more steps through the snow toward them.

They were close enough now to read the emotions raging across Oros' face. He was as wired as a nervous stallion vibrating on its legs. He stood there swaying, first backward and then forward, toward them as if to better understand them, then away from them as though to escape or to arm himself for a fight. Rocking back and forth. Intensely disturbed. The closer they got, the more frantic he became.

Almost as anxious but under tighter control, Bird and his partner pretended breathless exhaustion, promising answers when they got there. Promising he'd understand everything in a moment.

There was no going back now.

They were so close to Oros that if he grabbed a gun from inside the cabin, there was no cover for them to run to. Having come out past the bush that grew between the lake and the cabin, they were in the narrow band of clearing that circled the cabin.

Behind Oros, his dogs suddenly bolted out from the cabin and startled them all. Running to stand by Oros, they began barking furiously. As the two men approached closer, the dogs spread out, moving away from Oros, leaving him to face the threat alone.

Bird was grateful to see them. The dogs were a diversion and added another level to the state of confusion surrounding Oros.

"Your dogs won't bite, will they?" Bird tried to sound natural but didn't slow his advance. It was the kind of disarming question strangers have to ask. Men who are armed, men who are attackers, men who aren't afraid, wouldn't show the concern they were showing.

"Must be hard to keep your dogs fed out here?... You must know this country pretty good?... I'd like to come out here one day and try my luck at hunting.... Pretty nice country here.... God, I gotta shit bad!... Sure hope your dogs are okay...."

Bird could see Oros' narrowed eyes dart past them to the waiting helicopter and then back to them again.

"We just need a moment of your time and then we'll be on our way again," Bird yelled out. He hoped the men in the helicopter were staying low and didn't accidently show a gun barrel.

Oros' eyes continued to flicker back and forth between the two men on the ground and from them to the helicopter but if he had any understanding of the situation, his eyes still weren't showing it.

Bird had studied Oros' diaries over the past few months and knew that Oros' contacts with the outside world were few, often no more than the occasional distant sighting of an aircraft in the sky. As Bird had expected and planned for, what was now happening to Oros was too much for him to react to. He was being overloaded. Their sudden presence, the noise, and their words were overwhelming him. He was disoriented, disarmed with friendly words and smiles. The advantage they had was surprise. But Bird had never expected it to last long.

They were only ten feet away from each other when Oros' eyes locked on Bird's. In an instant, the mask of confusion which had covered Oros' face broke. Whatever it was that had given them away, the look of uncertainty dissolved into pure rage. There was no mistaking his reaction now. As though all of Oros' nerves were shocked electrically, his body convulsed. Spinning around, away from them, he started a mad dash for the open doorway behind him. He was off to arm himself. The battle had begun.

The same instant the bewildered gaze left Oros' eyes, Bird dropped his friendly facade. As Oros was turning away from them, Bird was already lunging for Oros at full speed. It was a race against death.

With Oros handicapped, floundering in the deep snow toward the open cabin, they closed the distance on him. They tackled him. Before he could lift his face out of the snow, his hands were handcuffed behind his back and he was their prisoner.

Bird would never forget that moment. Flushed with the sudden release of tension. They had him! Six months of planning had finally paid off. The good word was passed from the pilot of their helicopter to the second team, which was still airborne, and from them to Atlin, where it was relayed on down the coast to RCMP subdivision headquarters at Prince Rupert. Before the day was over, every radio station on the west coast from Whitehorse to Vancouver was broadcasting the news: Sheslay Free Mike had been captured. Alive.

Bird's mood soared immediately. But that was yesterday.

Oros was talking to Bomba about the CIA and the police waging chemical warfare against him by spraying him from aircraft with mind-altering drugs when Bomba interrupted him again, still trying to lead Oros into areas they wanted answers for.

"You said you'd shoot anybody who tried to get you, or tried to spray you from aircraft?" Bomba asked. "How do you plan on protecting yourself from that?"

"I told you," Oros answered, not at all impatiently. "I'm going to build a tower beside the cabin. I want it higher than the trees so I can see over top them and watch you guys fucking around with your planes...and if you come at me, I'm gonna shoot."

"How do you know if planes are coming at you or just flying by?"

"Oh, you can't fool me. Who else's flying around past the cabin there? I know what you're up to."

"Well," Bomba asked, baiting him expertly, "who's flying up there now?"

"We both know that, don't we?"

"Well, you haven't shot at them either, have you?" It was the question Bomba had been working around to ask, hoping Oros could be tricked by pride or led by logic into admitting that he'd been shooting at planes all along, which both Bomba and Bird believed. But Oros wasn't falling for it.

"I'm sorry but I've got to talk to a lawyer before I answer any questions like that," Oros said, pretending to cooperate for the benefit of the small Uher tape recorder sitting on the table between them silently recording every word, but consistently refusing to discuss anything that might remotely incriminate him in Lishy's disappearance.

There were reports on file in the cabinets behind Bird that went back for several years about somebody on the ground shooting at aircraft flying over the Teslin River system. Although nobody could prove it was Oros, it had to be him. Oros was the only one in the country there. For years now, the local pilots had been flying high and wide around any area they thought he might be in. As far as they were concerned, Oros was a navigational hazard and they weren't going to give him an opportunity to prove their fears. Listening to Oros talking, their fears were well grounded. Nobody was safe if they came within sight of him and—although Oros freely admitted, in no uncertain terms, that he'd try to shoot down any plane or person he found spying on him or trying to poison him—he restricted his comments to future events and refused, except in very general terms, to speak of the past. Thought crimes.

As Bomba continued the questioning, Bird mentally reviewed the details of the investigation he knew by heart, searching his memory for something to use against Oros. Something to break Oros' silence and tie him to Lishy's disappearance.

On July 30th, the day before Lishy left Atlin for Hutsigola, his closest friend, Dan Peacock, had inspected Lishy's supplies to ensure Lishy hadn't forgotten anything. Having Peacock as a witness was a lucky break for Bird. Peacock knew Lishy's habits well. How he set up a camp, swung an ax, joined wood, and tied knots. He had worked with Lishy's tools, could identify his supplies, and would swear to certain facts about Lishy.

One fact was that there were three things Lishy never went anywhere without: his lightweight, down sleeping bag, his small rucksack with the necessary tools to set up an emergency camp if he had to, and his .44 handgun. The .44 was his protection against bears and he always carried it with him. Always.

When Bird organized the searches in Hutsigola in September, there remained the possibility that Lishy had gone off along one of the trails and died from a heart attack, or from injuries. Among the most important items on the list to be searched for were Lishy's sleeping bag, his rucksack, and the .44. If they were missing, then Lishy might be somewhere out in the bush with them. But if they were found, if Lishy didn't have them, then they had been taken from him and something else had happened to Gunter Lishy. Something sinister.

Peacock had flown in with the search parties and had meticulously reconstructed all Lishy's movements from the time he was dropped off by the pilot Wiebe. He found the holes where Lishy's tent pegs had been and the remains of his cooking fire and his toilet pit. Ominously, there had been a crude attempt to conceal the latter two pieces of evidence. He carefully examined the trees Lishy had felled with his chain saw, the boards he'd cut up, the area he had cleared, and the police had recorded it all. Curiously, the logs which Lishy had cut and peeled had been moved from their original location and repositioned nearer Oros' cabin. There, they had been relaid into an octagonal pattern on the ground—by someone other than Lishy. Peacock was adamant Lishy would never have built a cabin in that design. It was simply too difficult, too slow, and too impractical.

On examination of the country around the lake, Peacock also recognized Lishy's work on a trail that ran from Hutsigola Lake to Zancudo Lake. Because Lishy often worked with skidoos, his trails had to be open enough to run a skidoo along, so he had widened an overgrown footpath that connected Zancudo with Hutsigola.

Like pieces of a time puzzle, Peacock had put it all together. And, in the end, he calculated Lishy's work as three days for the Zancudo trail plus seventeen days for the campsite. And one day of rest.

Twenty-one days from the day Wiebe dropped him off put Lishy at Hutsigola until at least the 21st of August. It was an interesting calculation at the time but it's true significance wasn't immediately apparent. Still, even what it said at the time was important enough. Lishy had spent three weeks working and had half finished his work. With three more weeks to go before the September 10th rendezvous with Wiebe, Lishy had suddenly stopped working. And disappeared.

The big question was why.

The search Bird organized in September had been as exhaustive as his budget allowed. Following a tight grid pattern through an area in a radius of only three miles from the cabin meant a search of almost thirty-six square miles. Increasing the radius by only one mile increased the area to be searched to sixty-four square miles. Even with two tracking dogs and all the men they had searching, there was simply too much country to find things. All Oros had to do was carry Lishy's body off for six miles into the bush and they'd never find it. Animals and weather would destroy all traces of it quickly enough, even if it were left sitting exposed on the surface although Bird doubted Oros would do that. Oros was so careful to conceal everything else that Bird was confident he would have buried the body or, would have eliminated it: sunk it into the lake maybe, or cut it into pieces and scattered it through the bush for the animals, burned it, or even fed it to his dogs. With Oros, anything seemed possible.

However, with the notable exception of Lishy's body, the search had turned up a lot of evidence and potential evidence. The canoe which had been reported stolen a couple of years earlier had been found only a couple of hundred yards west of the cabin, concealed in thick brush. A couple of axes had been found near the cabin, leaning against trees in the bush, and both were seized. Both had blood stains, hair fibers, and some kind of fleshy tissue stuck on their steel heads, and they were carefully packaged and sent to the crime lab in Vancouver. Forensic analysis could determine if the blood and hair was human. It wasn't. They had only been used for chopping up moose. The ash from the stove inside the cabin was screened and bone fragments found in it were picked out and saved. Analyzed later, they were parts of a bear's skull. Even the undigested bone fragments found in the dogs' droppings were also examined. Again, they were all animal in origin. Inside Oros' cabin, Peacock identified a recent issue of the magazine *Psychology Today* as well as several paperbacks stamped on their covers "Book Nook Whs YT" as, probably, having been Lishy's. Lishy bought all his books at the Book Nook in Whitehorse. There was also a new stove and a bundle of new stovepipes stored in the cabin which were identical to the ones Peacock had seen in Lishy's supplies. A washbasin on Oros' table was likewise identical to one that Lishy had brought into the bush with him. So, too, was a swede saw, cooking utensils, and the packaging of most of the food found inside the cabin.

As they searched for answers to Lishy's disappearance, they unearthed more and more of the secrets of Oros' life.

One of the first significant finds was the discovery by Bird and Peacock of one of Oros' hidden caches. The one across the lake. Bird well remembered the mixed feelings of trepidation and hopeful anticipation as they broke into it, half expecting to have Lishy's body tumble out. It was an older cache, with a design that Lishy didn't use. And cruder workmanship. Yet it was filled with Lishy's building materials. More significant for the investigation was the discovery there of Lishy's lightweight sleeping bag. It was the expensive down bag Lishy had bought in Whitehorse—one of the three things Peacock swore Lishy never went without. It was a bad sign.

But Lishy's rucksack and Lishy's powerful handgun weren't among the things in the cache. Instead, buried under Lishy's belongings, were sheafs of old notes. Writings scribbled on all manner of paper, bound and unbound, water stained and bug squashed. Some of them were faded and barely legible. The dates written on them went back to 1971. That they were among Lishy's belongings spoke of Oros' involvement in Lishy's disappearance.

The papers were Bird's first really close look at the personality of the man they were hunting. Sorting through them with Peacock, Bird found some that had been written more recently. Within the last few years. And reading them sent goose bumps up their arms. In them, Oros had recorded the details of an ongoing war involving people Oros described as terrorists and sneak-arounds. Of gun battles in the night. Of voices mocking him, of physical sensations and unbearable pains, the symptoms of a slow poisoning by the torture-druggers, blurred vision, aching joints, weak muscles, and a collapsing memory. There were planes that hunted him with infra-red and satellites that tracked his movements by the smoke from his campfires. The writing revealed the world of a madman.

The vivid descriptions Oros had written of elite paratrooper teams armed with automatic weapons being dropped off at different locations in the forest to hunt him down and kill him caused Bird and Peacock to look up nervously from the notes and repeatedly scan the bush with a creepy sense that Oros might be nearby and watching. Or stalking them. The description of his imaginary attackers was uncomfortably close to the very teams Bird had searching the area.

What the cache didn't contain, among Oros' records, was his current journal. The diary notes for August. That was something Bird wanted to get his hands on. Oros' journal entry for August 21st.

The next significant find was made a few days later. And again, it was Peacock, roaming at will around the bush while the police searched methodically in grid patterns, who found it. A second secret cache. Like the first, it was a high cache, built like a small cabin, on four corner posts ten feet off the ground. But unlike the first one, this was filled mostly with Oros' things: mouldy clothing in odd pieces and sizes, glass bottles and rusted cans he'd collected, dried-out animal hides that were so old the hair was falling out of them, and an assortment of other things, natural and man-made, that Oros had made or found and saved over the years. Sealed inside some of the jars, carefully wrapped up in waxy paper and tied with string into small packets, were locks of hair. Whether they were clumps of Oros' own hair that he had cut off but couldn't part with or souvenirs of battle, the hair from people he might have killed—like Lishy—and saved as trophies, or whether they came from other more obscure sources, they were carefully packaged and flown out to Vancouver for forensic examination. Also stored inside this second cache were some early science fiction stories Oros had started writing and more diary notes, in pencil which, like the first, were so worn, water-stained, and faded as to be mostly unreadable. Overtop Oros' things were still more of Lishy's building materials:

another roll of tar paper, his tools, his chain saw, his gas can, and several bags of assorted nails.

But the most significant item of all was one of the last to come out. Stuck inside the cache, buried under the rest of the things as though Oros himself knew how important it was, was Lishy's packsack. Peacock recognized it immediately.

As soon as he threw it to the ground, Peacock unzipped the pockets, lifted the flaps, and examined their undersides. Peacock knew that inside one of the flaps Lishy had sewn on a small name tag. There was no reason to do it except Lishy liked to personalize the things he considered important. Just one of those odd-ball things Lishy used to do, Peacock said. But when they searched for it, all they found were the tiny holes in the canvas where the thick thread had been.

Oros, too, had apparently carefully examined the pack. And presumably having found the tag, he'd cut it off.

With his concealment of Lishy's things and his extraordinary careful cover-ups of Lishy's presence at Hutsigola, Oros' attempts to erase any link between himself and the missing German aristocrat-trapper spoke loudly to Bird of the opposite conclusion. With all that evidence of concealment and with Lishy's sleeping bag and rucksack both having been found in Oros' hidden caches, there was no longer any real possibility that Lishy had abandoned his plans for a Hutsigola cabin and left. Or that he had gone off into the bush and died of natural causes somewhere.

It only remained to find Lishy's .44 magnum. It would be the final proof that Lishy hadn't left the camp alive.

And that, they'd found yesterday. After Oros had been arrested, the cabin was searched again. Stuck into a box with the handle up, loaded and ready for quick use, was Lishy's .44. Right beside Oros' bed.

And there was more. Sitting on the table, spread open where he had left it, was Oros' diary. He had been entering his morning plans in it when the helicopter landed outside the cabin.

In it, Oros had chronicled his life and his secret thoughts for the past year. Hopes soared. No evidence could be better than to have a complete description of the killing in Oros' own pen. A confession in his own diary.

So compelling was Oros' urge to communicate and to keep records, and so total was his delusional system, that Bird thought it likely that Oros wouldn't be able to resist writing down the minute details of his encounter with Lishy. Certainly, the killing of another human being would be a powerful experience that Oros would find hard to contain and impossible not to analyze over and over again, the way he did mere sightings of aircraft.

But Oros had anticipated the diary falling into their hands. Just as he knew they had seized the other records in the fall, those which he had hidden in his caches, he knew that this one too might be used against him. Crudely, it had been edited. Whole pages had been ripped out. Still, it answered important questions.

With daily entries faithfully recorded, the diary not only revealed Oros' movements up to the time of Lishy's disappearance, but it also revealed his mind-set. In it was an explanation of sorts for a killing. Almost a motive.

When Lishy was flown into Hutsigola at the end of July, Oros was far away to the south, moving around through the forest near Sheslay. Over the next twenty-one days, while Lishy cleared the bush beside Oros' cabin, limbing the lower branches off the trees, sawing logs, peeling them and cutting them up into lumber, Oros was slowly working his way back to Hutsigola along the old trail.

For the most part, he was calm. Ever vigilant, his diary described no disturbances. Spending time setting up camps, he moved every few days, scouting the country. Hunting. The activity was all nonthreatening. Until he neared home. Then, just six days before his arrival at Hutsigola with its inevitable confrontation with Lishy, everything changed. From that point on, Bird thought, his diary read like a countdown to murder.

Six days from Hutsigola, the relative peace was shattered by a small floatplane which landed on a lake Oros had been camped near. On his belly in the weeds watching the two men who stood on the pontoons, Oros focused his gunsights on them and contemplated killing them.

Reading the detailed notes, Bird guessed the intruders were probably retired fishermen or perhaps Americans exploring the country. They frequently made illegal crossings over the wild international border along the Alaskan panhandle to hunt and fish in Canada. There was virtually nobody to stop them. Except Oros.

But to Oros, they were torture-druggers, landing to reconnoiter before continuing with their aerial poisoning of the wilderness. Knowing the plane would be impossible to hide, he decided against killing them and fled instead. For his life.

Five days from Hutsigola, he had returned, back to the same lake, to recover a knife he'd lost there. In an increasing state of fear and tension, absolutely convinced the forest was now saturated with torture-drugs, he fled again. Crossing a river, he severely beat one of his dogs for some perceived disobedience. Crippling her.

Four days from Hutsigola, exhausted and dizzy, recording his physical sensations as proof of drug-poisoning by sneak-arounds, he'd continued his desperate flight. In anguished detail, Oros described the injured dog, a puppy, crying in his ear as he carried her on his back the entire day. In the evening, they reached Disella Lake and Oros discovered the dog, which had by then fallen silent, had died. The puppy's death worked a complete transformation of Oros' feelings.

The fear of sneak-arounds, which had been driving him, evaporated. He set up a camp and buried the dog under a rock pile near the shore. And then, in pages and pages of his diary, he poured out his grief.

He had sat up the entire night in a kind of funeral vigil and, by morning, his tortured mind had worked out a twisted logic that transferred his own guilt at killing her to a hatred for the sneak-arounds that had made him do it. They had drugged him, making an instrument out of him.

He loved her and they killed her. The way they killed everything beautiful. And everything he loved.

Three days from Hutsigola and the handwriting in the diary had become unrecognizable. Violent and insane. In large, bold but trembling print, the rage he felt apparent in the force pressing down on his pencil, Oros had written one word:

KILL.

The next page in the diary had the same one-word message.

KILL.

And the next, and the next.

KILL. KILL. KILL. KILL.

Oros filled pages with it.

Two days from Hutsigola, Oros was sleeping on the trail coming home. Getting closer.

One day from Hutsigola and Oros arrived at Zancudo Lake in the evening, only a half-day's hike from Hutsigola.

The last entry, written at Zancudo in the evening as he was settling down for the night, was a short one.

"Zancudo Lake and home cabin tomorrow!"

That diary entry was dated August 20th.

The significance of Peacock's calculations, made in September, was loud and clear.

Peacock calculated Lishy had stopped work on August 21st, the day Oros arrived back at Hutsigola.

Now, too, another of Peacock's September discoveries assumed greater significance. Lishy had widened the trail from Zancudo to Hutsigola. As Bird read Oros' diary, he realized that this was the very same path Oros would have used on his way home.

Like a neon highway, the path would have shouted out Lishy's presence to Oros—and his designs on the area! Following it straight to Lishy, Oros would have seen him there, right beside his own cabin, clearing the bush and moving in. Taking over.

"Home cabin tomorrow."

Bird guessed that Oros had probably killed Lishy the very first chance he'd got. As soon as he'd seen him.

And there was no question he had recorded the event. In detail.

He had filled pages after August 20th with his private world. Pages and pages.

But they were all gone. Every page which recorded any contact with Lishy and the aftermath was gone. The memories and the records had been violently excised from the diary. Ripped out. The page stubs left in the binding created a gap so large the book automatically fell open to it, almost as a message itself that here, in this empty space, had been something different from all the rest. Something more terrible and more horrible than everything else. Something real. Bird had no doubt what that had been.

The next diary entry left intact after the gap was as false and contrived as the earlier rage had been real and genuine.

It was dated September 11th, the day after Wiebe had returned to Hutsigola to pick up Lishy.

"A pilot landed on the lake yesterday. Said he was supposed to meet someone here. I believe he got his lakes mixed up. Nobody around here except me and the dogs. Widened trail all day to Zancudo and camped there."

Bird could well imagine Oros writing out the entry with an Orwellian awareness in case the diary ever fell into police hands. Knowing that the police would read what he'd written, he could create his own truth, saying enough to satisfy them and yet protect himself. Oros would have known the pilot would report on what had been said on the lake, so he had repeated the same things in his diary for consistency, as though the telling of it would make it so.

The reference to cutting the trail was clever. Lishy had cut the trail from Hutsigola to Zancudo. But that, like everything else Lishy had done, was appropriated by Oros as his own work.

There was another written record Oros had left behind that also made more sense to Bird now. He remembered the note Oros had left on his cabin door for the police to find.

It had warned of mind-altering drugs and blamed the CIA and other agencies for spraying them. Was his statement that people under the effects of these drugs were not responsible for their actions an excuse for killing Lishy? The way Oros transferred his guilt for killing his dog, Lola, to the sneak-arounds, was he blaming the CIA and the RCMP for his actions? For killing Lishy? It certainly seemed that way.

In fact, everything fit together so perfectly that Bird didn't want to believe they didn't have a case yet. Even without a confession, or the body, everything pointed so clearly to Oros coming out of the bush in an insane and murderous mood, finding and killing Lishy, destroying his body and taking his things, that if it were up to Bird, Oros would already be doing life for murder.

Only it wasn't up to Bird. And he knew it wasn't enough.

In fact, until yesterday when they got him with Lishy's handgun, the only charge they had against him, and the entire legal basis for their arrest, was still the old theft charge. It had been on file for almost two years already but it was for the same canoe they had recovered in September. Oros had stolen it from an Alaska State Fisheries officer on holiday on Teslin Lake. It wasn't much of a charge. They weren't even sure the canoe's former owner was still in Alaska or whether he cared enough anymore to want to come to court.

To do any better than that, Oros would have to open up and start talking; but Bomba wasn't scoring any points there at all.

"I can't answer that one either until I talk to my lawyer," Oros replied again to one of Bomba's questions. The dry, dirt-cracked edges of his mouth pulled back momentarily in a just-perceptible smile. It was his look of smug superiority that both officers found hard to ignore. Oros thought he was smarter than they were, that he was beating them at their own game. All of his fear had apparently vanished. He was absurdly confident that the police, although a part of the conspiracy organized to kill him, couldn't and wouldn't mistreat him now that they had him in their control. He was now playing games, trying to bait them into admitting they were part of the whole torture-drugger, sneak-around conspiracy. He had no fear of them at all.

Listening to Oros made Bird mad. Oros was enjoying himself and was loudly saying next time he'd shoot to kill. They'd never arrest him a second time. For anything.

Bird wanted to tell Oros that he had to explain his actions. He wanted to demand answers. But he knew he couldn't, that every time Oros said, "I won't tell you that," that Oros' right to silence, his right not to have to explain himself or to cooperate, was protected and guaranteed by law. The human desire was to get at the truth but the rules that governed the moves prevented that, turning the matter of criminal investigations into a game that favored criminals. It seemed like such a small price for society to pay—requiring Oros to explain his actions.

But Oros had no responsibility at all to account for having Lishy's property in his caches. He didn't have to answer for anything. Not even how or why he had Lishy's .44 magnum. Bird didn't like it. It meant the worst criminals, the most dangerous, the most professional, the most experienced were always the hardest to convict. If they were smart enough to leave no evidence, they couldn't be caught. And if they didn't suffer enough guilt to want to confess on their own, the law protected their right to silence. Bird didn't think that was fair. The system wouldn't suffer if Oros had to talk. And the alternative was so much more severe. More missing persons. More innocent victims. More murders. Bird was sure of that.

It was useless to get mad. He didn't have to like it but it was the way it had to be played.

"Well, you tell me, then. How do you explain all of Lishy's things in your possession?" Bomba was asking Oros. Resisting their natural impulses, both officers had been scrupulously polite all morning, even acting friendly and trying to joke with Oros in an attempt to relax him enough to let his guard down.

"I can't answer that without my counsel's consent," Oros replied.

"You can call a lawyer anytime you want to, you know that."

"Yes. But I don't have a lawyer."

"You can call any lawyer you want. I can even give you a list of lawyers if you like and you can call one of those."

Oros smiled. "No thanks."

"You think I'm trying to trick you?" Bomba asked, aware that Oros was paranoid enough to think that a long list of lawyers' names the police had would all be police agents.

"No," Oros answered, not convincingly, and still smiling as though he wasn't going to be fooled.

"You know I can give you a Vancouver telephone directory which has all the Vancouver lawyers listed in it and you can call any one you want...you pick your own lawyer."

"I don't want a lawyer right now."

"Alright. I'm not saying you have to have one, only that you're entitled to one if you want one."

"I know that."

"Well what do you think your lawyer would tell you to do?"

"I don't know." Oros wasn't being honest.

"Why do you need your lawyer's permission to answer these questions, then?"

"My lawyer will have to answer that."

"Well you don't have a lawyer."

"No."

"And you don't want a lawyer?"

"No."

"So how is he going to answer that?" Bomba asked—trying to keep his voice pleasant sounding.

"You'll have to ask him!"

"Look!" Bomba said. "You and I both know how Lishy's stuff got into your caches—you put it there!"

When Oros didn't reply, he added, "I understand how you feel.... Lishy deserved what he got. I mean, I'm with you on that...you'd been away for a few weeks and then come home and find this guy right in your camp. I mean the guy's trying to move right in on you. I think that would just about put anybody off. Certainly would piss me right off.

Cutting down the trees around my place—just like a goddamned bomb crater, wasn't it? Shit!"

Bomba talked as though they were of one mind, close friends who shared a secret, who were discussing something they both agreed on. It was to form a bond with Oros, a link in sympathy, that Bomba was using words and ideas that Oros himself might use.

"He and his goddamned tent set up there, shit holes dug all around it, a pile of lumber from all the trees he chopped down...he was really fucking the place up! What the hell was he doing out there anyway?"

Oros didn't fall for it, although he listened carefully. And he even seemed to like what he was hearing. Now that a question was put to him, he paused, collecting his thoughts before he spoke, and replied in the usual way. "I can't answer that without my counsel's consent."

Bomba continued on as though he hadn't heard, criticizing Lishy, justifying his killing, describing what they knew and letting questions drift out like tiny hooks into a fast trout stream. Trying to get Oros to rise to the bait. Looking for a wedge in the door. Something to work on.

Oros wanted to listen. And he did. But he was controlling his need to talk. Alert to every subtlety, he was also consistent in all his answers—even with the lie he had told Wiebe on September 10th, that he'd returned to Hutsigola in early August and had been there all month and hadn't seen Lishy. Even in the face of the contrary evidence in the last diary they'd seized. Not offering any explanations for any inconsistencies, he refused to allow himself to be trapped by talking about anything he felt was important to them.

As Oros and Bomba returned to the topic of Oros' choice—the black-hooded assassins who stalk the bush around Oros' camps and cabins—Bird wondered about his sanity. Over the winter, he had read and reread the diaries which had been seized in September. It was an odd experience. Studying the private journals had put him inside Oros' head. It wasn't so much what Oros saw that made him crazy but rather what he thought. The interpretation he gave to his visions. He had crazy ideas, the way a man living alone in the bush for too long was apt to get bush crazy. Oros saw himself as a Jesus figure, a savior with an important message for humanity. It was the main theme of his life. The subject of his creative energies for years. Turning it over and over and over in his mind, almost half of all his writing was devoted to it. And yet, in the final analysis, when it was all distilled to its essential elements, there was only one message that Oros had to deliver. And that was that THEY—whoever they were—were trying to kill him. They wanted to kill him because he was dangerous to them. And because they wanted to kill him, he was important. A savior with a message for the world. Because he had this message, those who wanted to enslave people wanted to kill him.

There was nothing else. His whole philosophy was totally empty. Going around and around like the wheel in a rat's cage.

While they talked in the detachment office, Bird watched the time. The men would be back in Hutsigola by now screening everything once more for clues. Before they had flown out with Oros, there had been some discussion out of Oros' hearing with the Regional Game Warden in Cassiar about Oros' dogs. The question was what to do with them. Would he come in and capture them? Or should they kill them? Short of tranquilizing them, there wasn't much chance of catching them and the expense and effort involved in doing that wasn't justified. Snarling, spitting, and barking, they had had so little contact with other humans they were reacting the same way they would upon being confronted by bears. But they couldn't just leave the dogs behind in the bush, either. The law required that dogs running at large in the bush had to be killed. Domestic dogs either died slow, miserable deaths of starvation or, amateur hunters, they mauled the wild game in the country and caused unnecessary suffering. The men who had gone into Hutsigola this morning to finish the search were going to make one more attempt to catch them and, failing that, had instructions to shoot them.

Bird watched Oros and wondered what effect it would have on him if he were told his dogs were being killed. Would he trade information for their lives? It was an interesting question but an impossible one to put. The dogs had to be destroyed, as unfortunate as that might be, and Oros had to be questioned, but the two events were, in the present circumstances, unrelated and had to remain that way. Although Oros had been asking about his dogs this morning, neither Bird nor Bomba told him anything.

Bird's attention was drawn away from Oros and out through the sealed window beside him by the metal shriek of a racing engine and he watched as a skidoo roared past the small detachment office. The boy operating it stopped at the edge of the road and then shot across it and off down the slope on the far side to the lakeshore where he ran the machine out over the ice at full speed down Atlin Lake. Swathed from head to toe in a black one-piece snowsuit with a black helmet, mitts, and boots, Bird didn't recognize the boy but he knew the machine and could make a pretty accurate guess about the operator. He'd have to remember to go out and talk to the boy. It was obvious the machine wasn't licensed and it was an offense to drive it over a public road without insurance. Not that it really mattered much in Atlin but still it was against the law and the boy should learn what was right and wrong. He'd have to talk to the boy's parents too. Explain the rules to them. From skidoos to murder.

Oros' body was rank with his stale odors. His suspicious eyes squinted piglike at them in the light, hostile and yet confident in the security of his position. Their mandated politeness wasn't lost on him. Indeed, it seemed to buoy him even more until his confidence broke into an openly contemptuous attitude. Oros was telling Bomba how THEY were organized.

THEY use children, he said, because the kids are quick, slip easily into the bush, and are hard to spot. Hiding in trees, wearing black balaclavas and black clothes, they follow him through the forest, from camp to camp. Waiting until he falls asleep, they sneak in at night to steal his things and spray his clothes and food with their poison drugs. He had seen them, he said, more than once, when he had stayed up watching for them or had woken up in the middle of the night to find them moving in the dark shadows through the trees around the camp. Drifting in and out of vision like vaporous beings, they were barely visible and impossible to shoot.

Oros turned his head at the sound of the skidoo making a run back up the lake, and jerked his chin up to indicate the boy on it.

"He could be one," Oros said softly.

They knew he meant a sneak-around.

"Why?" Bird asked, breaking his own long silence.

"He looks like one," Oros replied simply.

"And you'd kill him for that?"

"If he was a sneak-around!" Oros answered directly.

Bird turned back to the window again, barely controlling the hot surge of anger that welled up within him at the revelation that Oros suspected children too, of being part of the conspiracy against him. The fact that Oros could kill a child as easily as he could kill an adult, a child like the one on the snowmobile made Bird sick. Behind him, the door that closed off his private living quarters from the business part of the detachment wasn't soundproofed enough to stop the noise his own small children were making as they ran around the house chasing each other. Their mother's voice, too, came to Bird, clearly telling them, sternly, to be quiet when "daddy is working," which only made them want to run into the office through the door to see him. The crashing boom of their small hands hitting the office door before their mother could carry them back into the living room was loud enough to register on the tape recorder which sat on the desk between the men recording continuously ever since Oros had been brought out of the cell. It was the kind of noise that, when played back later, would inspire office jokes, the background screams and thumping noises being the kind of "informal persuasion" people believed the police resorted to for confessions. In this case, even as a joke, Bird knew he wouldn't find it funny. Not unless Oros was locked away some place far from Atlin.

It was too soon into the investigation to feel pessimistic—there was still much that might happen to change the whole picture—but Bird couldn't help but feel frustrated. Almost defeated. As surely as Oros had killed Lishy, just as surely he wasn't going to confess to any crime. Oros wasn't opening up at all. Once more the thought of Oros being released for lack of evidence and walking away free, more dangerous than ever, made Bird want to grab him and demand answers. But he was too professional to lose control like that. And Bird respected the law. That was the main reason he had joined the police force. But the situation he was now in was gut-wrenching. More than anything else, Bird wanted to do his job. But he was fighting a growing knot in his stomach with the suspicion that it was impossible.

Bird wouldn't admit defeat. There had to be something more he could do. What if Oros killed somebody else? Whose responsibility would that be? On whose shoulders would the guilt rest? And if the next victim was a child? Could he do nothing? Just wait and hope that next time Oros made bigger mistakes? Mistakes big enough to convict him. Or would Oros learn from this encounter and become even craftier. The way most criminals learned. To be released again. To kill again. And again. They were terrible thoughts and Bird tried to tell himself that he was doing his job, that there was nothing more he could do. But he wasn't consoled. The fact people would hold the police responsible, would blame him if, instead of being brought to justice,

Oros was allowed to kill again, bothered him. The same people who favored the laws which made truth a game, hamstringing the police and safeguarding the criminals, were always the first ones to feel the police failed them.

The best solution of all would have been to find Lishy's body with a bullet in the back and a forensic matching of the bullet with Oros' gun. Or a full confession. From out of Oros' mouth or in his diary. But that was all wishful thinking now.

Earlier in the investigation, Bird had investigated the possibility of having Oros deported. But Oros had covered his bases there, too. Much to Bird's surprise, Canada Immigration had a file on Oros. When Oros was still a relative newcomer to the country, he left the bush, hitchhiked to Winnipeg 2,000 miles away, and signed up under an amnesty program for illegal aliens. With landed immigrant status, Oros had the right to live in Canada for as long as he wanted to. Bird was stuck with him.

However, there was still a solution of last resort. Early into the investigation, Bird had been in contact with a psychiatrist from the Vancouver Forensic Psychiatric Center for a medical perspective on Oros' character. After reading Oros' diaries, Bird had wanted to know everything he could about Oros before they went in to arrest him.

Based primarily on Oros' own diaries, the psychiatrist's tentative diagnosis was paranoid schizophrenia.

"What you commonly see with schizophrenics are major disturbances in the content of their thought, usually involving delusions that are patently absurd, with no basis in fact. In Oros' case, his delusions of a grandiose savior role is probably an example of the kind of markedly illogical thinking I'm talking about."

"And he wouldn't be aware he was wrong?" Bird had asked. It seemed impossible.

"Would he know he's crazy?" The doctor had rephrased the question before answering. "Not necessarily. As a paranoic, he could even have a permanent and unshakable delusional system and yet manifest clear and orderly thinking. He might even know that others don't share his beliefs and hide them—but they're still unshakable. Paranoid schizophrenics are the most dangerous of all because they have the complete backing of their whole moral character to do the things they are convinced are necessary to be done."

"Without any guilt?" Bird had asked, more to confirm his own understanding.

"You have to remember that his own experience is as real to him as the vision produced by our own eyes and our own experience is real to us. In his world, he's right. There are things haunting him. There are people after him trying to kill him. And its not the kind of illness that allows for rational communication. If he has to be approached, then the people who are doing it would have to know the kind of reality that Oros sees himself living in and then plug themselves into that. And if Oros saw them as enemies, nothing they could say or do would change his mind. I think, given the situation of Oros armed and out in the bush, that he has the potential for being very dangerous indeed. You'll have to be extremely careful how you approach him."

Now that Oros was safely in their custody, Bird recalled those earlier conversations and was reassured by them. If all else failed, they could have him locked up as a mental patient. All they had to do was establish that Oros was insane. And potentially dangerous.

If he couldn't see Oros convicted, Bird could at least ensure that Oros was neutralized. Forced into confinement in a mental hospital. And whether Oros wanted treatment or not, the doctors couldn't let him go until it was safe to do so. In fact, there was no cure. That result would at least keep Oros out of the bush and away from guns. It didn't really matter how it was done as long as the threat was removed. That was his first duty—to protect his community. And as Bird sat back in his chair watching Oros, his desire to see Oros safely locked away was, at the moment, the only thing on his mind.

Oros' eyes turned slowly away from Bomba and fixed themselves on Bird's, almost as though he read Bird's mind. For a moment, which stretched on, longer and longer, the two men stared at each other. Locked in a personal battle of wills. Almost imperceptibly, the muscles of Oros' face shifted, revealing another face that lay concealed beneath the false mask of friendly civility he was wearing. It was a chilling vision. For Oros, there were no rules. No controls. And the feelings he displayed through his eyes were as pure as any Bird had ever seen. A loathing. It was a vision of murder, the same look in Oros' eyes that he saw yesterday. When Oros had gone for his gun. Oros wanted to kill him. And Bird had no doubt he'd try, if Oros was ever given the chance.

Early the following morning, on March 5th, Oros was flown south in an RCMP aircraft to Terrace. There, in the police station, he was again locked into a cell. Unlike Atlin, Terrace was a busy place. Oros even had a cellmate. The two men eyed each other suspiciously for a few minutes until Dr. Arturo Aranus arrived. Let into the cell by the guard to talk to Oros, Dr. Aranus introduced himself and sat down beside Oros on the edge of his bunk.

Pleased with the company, Oros was happy to talk to him—but only about one thing: the conspiracy he'd been fighting all these years. In fact, ever since his arrest, he'd been trying to tell anyone who cared to listen all the graphic details of his own dirty war. As long as they didn't ask any police questions, like 'what happened to Gunter Lishy?' then he was more than willing to talk about his private life. But everybody who had talked to him so far seemed only to care about Lishy. Until Aranus. This doctor was different. He didn't care about Lishy at all. Instead, he wanted to hear everything Oros had to say about the nightmares he'd been fighting alone these past ten years.

Oros talked freely.

By the time Aranus left, Oros was feeling so much better than he had since he was arrested that he even wanted to talk to his cellmate. Posing as a convict awaiting transfer to a Vancouver jail, Corporal Henderson started working on Oros. Dropping details here and there about the robbery he'd pulled, details, he said, that he'd told nobody else, he tried to draw Oros into a confidence. There was a natural camaraderie to build on—they were both behind bars, both were fighting the system, they were both alone, they both hated the police, they both had terrible secrets that had to be told to people they could trust. Or at least those were the premises Henderson was working on.

Henderson backed away from Oros in the close space of the cell, examining him critically for a moment, and then laughed derisively. "Shit man, you look like you never been in trouble with the law before in your life." Henderson tried to project himself as a hardened con, a killer. Suddenly his eyes narrowed and his expression darkened. "I'd tell you my secrets friend...unless you're a fink.... Now that I think of it, you look like one of them! A fuckin' cop! Or a stooge! Are you?"

Oros, having his own deep suspicions, looked at him for a long, hard moment, and then said he wasn't.

Henderson, the confessed robber who bragged of using a .44 on all his jobs, suddenly relaxed, laughing hard and long as though there was never really any question at all in his mind about it.

"Shit, man," he said, still laughing, "if I can't trust you, who the fuck can I trust?"

Oros laughed too.

A line of communication had been established; but Henderson was careful not to ask questions prematurely. He had spent the past two days preparing for the role and had all night to talk to Oros if he wanted to. It wasn't an easy task. Even with the sane criminals, there was always the fear of informers or bugs. And with Oros, it was far more difficult. His paranoia was almost a tangible thing. Henderson worked on him slowly. Asking no questions, he filled the space with his own confessions instead, talking constantly if Oros seemed interested, dropping into private silences of his own the moment Oros wandered. Revealing bits of himself. Cursing the cops. Building common ground, talking about the cities he hated, the concrete-and-steel canyons, the social isolation, the terrible smogs and polluted ways of living they offered. And then, in contrast, about the bush he loved, the givingness of wilderness spaces, anything he could think of that Oros might relate to.

Oros started to respond but, still guarded, was careful not to reveal anything that might be useful to the police. They were talking about survival in the bush when Henderson asked Oros how he'd get rid of a body, as though that were something Henderson might have to do some day and he was deferring to the expert on matters of wilderness living. Oros thought for a long time and then asked, seriously, "Hypothetically?"

Henderson smiled disarmingly and assured him it was only a hypothetical problem.

Oros smiled back. "Hypothetically," he said, giving Henderson a look he took as being full of contrary meaning, "you can bury a body anywhere. You could just roll up the moss, wrap up the body in a tarp and then roll the moss back down over it... or," and he paused as he considered another option, "if you wanted to really dispose of it, you could cut it up into little pieces and scatter them through the forest for the animals."

They both laughed.

It took a while for Henderson to turn the conversation back to the topic of Lishy. Oros had already told him the details of the police interrogation in Atlin and of the fact that he was suspected of killing Lishy. Until now, however, he hadn't volunteered anything from his side of the story, sticking only to what the police had been doing and what they had said. But now, out of the blue, Oros suddenly let slip that Lishy had two inflatable raft seats adrift on Hutsigola Lake in August.

That was it! Click. The door had just opened.

Oros had finally admitted that Lishy was there. Henderson fought to stay calm.

"What the fuck was he doing with inflatable raft seats?" he asked casually and quite naturally.

But Oros realized immediately what he'd just done and dropped the subject. Henderson tried to open it up again but Oros clammed up completely, withdrawing into himself tighter than ever before, closing off all conversation.

Henderson never got any farther.

It was almost noon when Oros was finally removed from the cell for his first court appearance before Provincial Court Judge Don Waurynchuk. He was arraigned on three recently drafted charges: possession of a stolen canoe, possession of property stolen from Gunter Lishy, and possession of a restricted weapon without a permit, namely Lishy's .44 magnum.

Oros wasn't concerned about the charges. Legal Aid had authorized a lawyer to act for him and Oros was pretty confident that Dave Warner could get him off. And even if he couldn't, he knew, it wouldn't matter that much. The charges weren't serious and the court probably wasn't going to send him to jail for them even if he was convicted. Everybody knew that what the police really wanted was to charge him for the murder of Gunter Lishy. But they didn't have a case yet. And wouldn't. Unless he gave it to them. And there was no way he was going to do that. He spent a few minutes with his lawyer in a special interview room at the courthouse before his appearance. Oros understood the whole situation quite clearly. If he kept his mouth shut, he'd be released on bail within the hour.

The court appearance itself was very brief. The prosecutor surprised him by asking the judge to adjourn the bail hearing for three more days to allow the police to better prepare their case. Over the objections of his lawyer, the judge granted the order. Oros was returned to cells. For three more days.

For the rest of the night, Oros was in a foul mood. Caged and intensely paranoid, he paced most of the night, deep in his own thoughts.

In the morning, Corporal Harold Schoonmaker located Margaret Oros and telephoned her in the United Stated to solicit her support. Maybe she could find the answers they wanted.

There was little she could offer. Not having seen or spoken to her son in over ten years, it was doubtful he would open up even to her. She confirmed some facts: that she had divorced Oros' father soon after his birth and had had no contact with him afterward, that Oros had rebelled against the Vietnam war and that she had last seen him when he was living on a commune in New Mexico. But if she was aware that Oros was haunted by the ghost of his father, she kept that, and any other dark secrets she may have had, to herself.

Instead, she described him as a normal boy who used to enjoy playing the trombone with a school chum who played the piano. Before she hung up, she thanked him for the call and told him she was on her way to Canada to see her son.

Schoonmaker brought Oros the news but he took it coldly. Then for the next few hours, he and Bomba took turns interviewing Oros continuously while the hope of solving the case by cracking Oros was dying fast. After four hours, they gave up.

There were no breakthroughs.

Alone in his cell, the guards kept a close watch on him. His mood swings were extreme. Manic, he'd laugh uncontrollably one moment and then burst into a torrent of rage, violently shaking himself from the bars while screaming obscenities down the cellblock. Convinced the food they were giving him to eat was drugged, he refused to touch it.

In the guardroom, a sign was taped to the wall underneath Oros' cell number.

WARNING: THIS PRISONER IS MENTALLY UNSTABLE AND POTENTIALLY EXPLOSIVE. EXERCISE UTMOST CAUTION.

On the morning of the eighth, at the end of the three-day remand, Oros was once again removed from the cell and transported in the police wagon to court for the bail hearing. Although he was handcuffed, it wasn't necessary. In the daylight, Oros was happy. His spirits were high and his mood, partly from hunger, was lightheaded. He had weathered the last three days without giving anything away, and he was finally going to have his freedom. Now it was up to the prosecutor to prove to the judge why he should be denied bail and, he was convinced, that was an impossible task. The charges were minor. His record was almost nonexistent. There was no reason to keep him in jail. The prosecution didn't stand a chance of getting its way. He'd be released. Oros was confident about that.

He wasn't at all prepared for what happened next. Instead of proceeding on the bail hearing, the prosecutor announced he had a preliminary motion. Then, as Oros listened carefully, the color emptying from his face and his eyes staring wildly, malevolently, at the prosecutor, the state's lawyer outlined for the court all the information they had learned about Oros' background. Things Oros himself had forgotten. His youth, hospitalization, his antisocial lifestyle, his severe and prolonged isolation in the wilderness. And then the diaries. At the mention of them, Oros stiffened. His precious diaries. The ones that had been stolen from him by the police in Hutsigola in September. The prosecutor had them. And was reading them aloud, in selected passages, to the judge. And not as proof of the conspiracy but as evidence of insanity. Insanity! At every mention of the word, Oros' body convulsed.

Oros' expression grew even darker when Dr. Aranus entered the courtroom to take the stand for the prosecution, repeating to everyone their conversations in the cell. About the drugging and the torture in the bush. About the sneak-arounds and the attempts on his life. About the conspiracy to subvert all free men.

He wasn't a psychiatrist, Aranus said, and the information he had wasn't sufficient to make a clinical diagnosis; however, he testified, it was nevertheless evident to him that Oros was demonstrating delusional thinking of a paranoid nature and was probably suffering from a major psychotic illness.

Now, with the issue of Oros' sanity clearly put into question, the judge was required to postpone the bail hearing once more. Before it could do anything else, the court had to know whether Oros was even fit to stand trial. Or whether he was mentally ill.

Once more, Judge Waurynchuk ordered Oros to remain in custody. This time for thirty days. And to be sent to the Vancouver Forensic Psychiatric Hospital at Essondale for a complete assessment.

Oros was devastated. Thirty more days behind bars. The first thing that came to his mind were his dogs. He'd been concerned about them ever since he'd been arrested in Hutsigola. For the past three or four days they would have found enough to eat around the cabin. They could chew at the moose quarter if they needed to. Or, like himself, they could go hungry for a few days, the way they had all done so often before. A few days wouldn't hurt them. But they could never last a whole month. He knew if he didn't get back to them before that, they'd starve. Or the wolves would come in and kill them. Either way, they'd be dead in a month.

"What about my dogs?" Oros yelled to the judge as he rose to his feet in the prisoner's dock. His lawyer rushed to his side and after a quick exchange with Oros relayed Oros' concerns to the judge.

In reply, the judge looked at the prosecutor and raised his eyebrows to punctuate the obvious question.

Promising to find out and have Oros advised, the prosecutor called the next case on the docket and Oros was led out of the courtroom by a sheriff through a heavy steel door in the wall of the prisoner's dock.

Oros was once again behind bars, too numbed by the decision to be immediately angry. His expectation had been to be free but, here he was a prisoner. Last time it was for three days. This time it was for thirty. Would it be 300 next time? Delusions of persecution? Hallucinations? A secret war? The prosecutor had said it all. If he was wrong, why were they locking him up? Were they all part of the conspiracy as well? Oros had only to listen to know what the state—the lawyers, the judge, the doctors—considered to be madness on his part. And if they believed him mad, they'd never let him go.

A meeting with his lawyer after court confirmed his fears. He was being sent to a psychiatric facility to give the doctors there an opportunity to examine him for mental illness. And if they found him mentally ill, they could lock him up.

Oros had never anticipated this. To be labeled insane! He well remembered listening to a CBC radio call-in show when he was at Hutsigola. The program was about criminals getting off their charges because they pretended to be insane. He had always thought that if they ever caught him for killing somebody, they'd try to change the law to deprive him of that defense and then, afterward, change it back again. But this was different. Here they hadn't charged him with murder and they were using the insanity laws against him. If anything was insane, it was what they were now doing to him.

He had felt safe revealing the details of the conspiracy against him to anyone who wanted to listen; but he wouldn't anymore. He had talked openly about it but now he quickly resolved never to speak of it again. He had written down the events outlining their operations against him, but now knew that he could never write about it again. And worse. Most painful of all, he would have to disclaim ownership of his own diaries, of all the writings the police had robbed from him. If they could use the diaries against him, to lock him away—if, instead of proving his salvation, they were the source of his imprisonment—he would have to deny he ever wrote them. It was supreme madness. To be forced to deny his own life. To cut out his own soul. But he had no choice.

As always, they made him do terrible things.

The decision to denounce his own journals, to deny their authorship and never to write of these things again caused him deep anguish. The writing had been his only release for years. And now it, too, was gone. When Oros resolved to withdraw this last major step, he surrendered whatever chance he had of returning to society. There was nothing left now that Oros could trust anyone with.

"Do I have to cooperate?" he asked his lawyer about the transfer to the psychiatric facility.

"Only if you want to," his lawyer answered honestly.

On his way back to the police cells from the courthouse, Oros was fitfully pensive. There were two things he was trying to fix firmly in his mind. One, that anything he told the psychiatrists about any crimes he may have committed could be used against him in the same way a confession straight to the police could. And secondly, if he repeated to them the events he had written about—the things the prosecutor told the judge were his symptoms of madness—they might just think he was insane. He had to remember that whatever the prosecutor wanted to prove, he had to deny. The safest course of all was to say nothing.

By the time he was locked back into his now familiar cell at the police station, he was in a black state.

Glen Carson's guard duties were simple. Every twenty minutes, he had to walk the twenty-three feet from the guardroom to the cellblock and inspect each prisoner through the bars to ensure they were all right. Apart from Oros, there were only two other prisoners in the cellblock when he came on shift. Both drunks, they were sleeping peacefully and, if he was lucky, would continue to sleep until his shift ended at seven in the morning. He read the caution sign attached to the notice board for Oros' cell but Oros hadn't been any trouble all evening. Lying in his cell staring wide-eyed at the ceiling, he was lost in his own headspace. At eleven o'clock, Carson went on his rounds into the cell block, his own footsteps on the hard concrete floor and the rough snoring of the drunks the only sounds. As he approached cell number eight at the end of the block, he had to stand close to the bars to peer into the dim cell, half-lit for nighttime. As he placed his hands on the bars and his face close to the steel, a figure rushed at him from the other side, spit full into his face, and screamed wildly. Carson pushed himself backward, away from the bars, just as Oros jumped up against them to cling suspended from the bars like a fly, spitting as hard as he was able through the bars at the jailor.

"What's your problem asshole?" Carson responded, wiping Oros' saliva from his face.

"Fucking son of pig shit!" Oros screamed.

Carson hurriedly left and returned to the guardroom where he noted the time of his check, that all three prisoners were alive and well, two of them asleep and prisoner number eight "starting to act up." He wrote down a couple of the things Oros had yelled and then returned to the cellblock to tell him to shut up. He didn't want the other men to wake up and join in the chorus.

"Pig bastard!" Oros was livid. Spewing out a continuous stream of obscenities at the guard, Oros had worked himself up into a state of uncontrolled rage.

Carson returned to his own station and tried to let the night take its own course. Forty-five minutes later, Oros still hadn't shown any signs of quieting down on his own and Carson again tried to reason with him, but as he approached the cell and came within sight of Oros, still gripping the bars, Oros spat at him again through the bars and screamed with renewed frenzy.

"Pig fucker! Slut! Whore!"

Oros had passed the point of rational control. Curious, Carson stood there watching as Oros moved about inside his cell like a wild thing. Bending over the heavy, industrial toilet bowl that was bolted securely to the floor, Oros wrapped his arms around it and, with a mighty heave, lifted it straight up, ripping it right off its mounts. Breaking the porcelain away from the steel bolts that held it to the concrete, he screamed a challenge into the air.

"I'm here piggies! I'm waiting for you piggies! Come and get me!"

Raising the toilet bowl over his head, he heaved it against the bars and, as Carson leaped away, it smashed into a hundred knife-like shards, which scattered across the floor. Oros lifted a large jagged-edged chunk and waved it in front of him in broad cutting actions. With the strength of a madman and the will to kill, Oros, completely out of control, was now armed!

Carson ran for help.

Constable Yeomans, who arrived first, watched the sink follow the toilet. It, too, disappeared into a thousand pieces against the steel bars of the cell. Some of the larger chunks skidded noisily along the polished floor of the corridor and into the opposite cells.

"There goes your fuckin' sink piggies!... C'mon piggies! I'm waiting for you!"

Oros grabbed onto the bars and swung out from them on his elbows then straightened out his arms. All the weight of his body was being carried on his wrists. It was an impressive display of strength. Without thinking, another of the officers who had answered Carson's call for help stepped up too close to the bars—and took a mouthful of spittle full in the face.

"Here I am piggies! Come and get me!"

The corridor outside cell number eight now held most of the RCMP members from the night shift, watching, but numbers alone didn't change the situation. Nobody wanted to go into the cell with him, not even in a group. As Oros started piling the larger pieces of jagged porcelain on his bed, the men moved farther away from the cell.

"C'mon piggies! I'm waiting for you! Come and get me!" Oros was yelling maniacally.

"Hey, he wants you!" one of the junior officers joked to another.

"Fuck you! I ain't going near that crazy cocksucker," he replied. "Guy's a fucking gorilla! Only way I'm gonna go in there is after he's dead."

"Hey, Sarge," another one called, pretending to be concerned but enjoying the diversion Oros was giving them from the usual routine. "Permission to kill him, sir?"

"Cool it!" Snapped the man whose job it was to keep things under control on the night shift. The situation was out of hand. At least they had control over the water to the cells. Even with the fixtures ripped off the pipes, there was no water anywhere. With Oros in the cell, everybody was safe; but he couldn't leave it like that. Oros was his responsibility as well. He couldn't leave him in the cell littered with glass fragments. If Oros cut himself, or killed himself, the responsibility would fall on his shoulders. Then, too, Oros was going out on the morning plane to the Vancouver psychiatric center. They had to get him secured for the trip—which meant going into the cell, sooner or later.

"What about a tranquilizer dart, Sarge? Get him right through the bars."

For a moment, he thought about it. The game wardens must use them locally for bear. But then another officer killed the idea. "No, those things are for animals," he said. "And they're dangerous. Besides, it sounds pretty stupid, shooting someone in our own cells with a tranquilizer dart!"

"So you want to go in there buddy?" argued the officer whose idea it was.

"No way! Just saying the dart's a bad idea, that's all."

"Not if we can add some sodium pentothal to it."

"Dream on."

Not ten feet away from the men who were talking, Oros continued to jump up onto the bars, swing himself around from them, and drop to the floor. Outside the cell, the highly polished surface was pitted with wet spots as Oros spat out at them with as much force as he could while he continued to scream abuse and challenges. Although he wasn't built for strength, the power Oros was demonstrating with his acrobatics belied his medium frame. There was no man among them who felt confident in matching Oros' strength. And none of them were about to give Oros the opportunity of proving it. Especially with Oros armed. The broken pieces of porcelain he had were as deadly as knives.

"I know!" one of the men shouted suddenly, sounding so inspired the others turned to him. Over the deafening racket Oros was making, they had to shout and stand close to each other to be heard.

"Bude!" he yelled. He said it as though the name itself explained everything.

"Bude?" the sergeant asked, repeating the name to himself as he thought it over. He knew the officer meant Mike Buday. But even if Mike were around, he didn't know if Mike would do it for them. Constable Mike Buday was on a different shift and had no responsibility at all for the situation they were now in.

"Yeah," the first officer added, thinking aloud about his own solution, "Bude ain't afraid of nothing. Fuck, he could take this animal!" There was a rising excitement in his voice, as though having named his own champion he was anxious to see the fight. His enthusiasm to see someone else get involved wasn't missed.

"You afraid of this guy?" another asked him, jerking his head toward the bars which held Oros back.

"Fuckin' right I am! And don't give me that hero bullshit; so are you!"

"Well," said the sergeant, finally interrupting them, "we can't stand here all night scratching our asses and listening to this animal calling us names. We can all go in together—rush him—and try to put the straitjacket on him...or we can call Buday."

They called Buday.

A mile away from the station, Buday was settling in for a few drinks at the Skeena Hotel with his partner and closest friend, Garry Rodgers, when the police dispatcher found him. As soon as he heard they needed him, he was on his way. Although, once he got to the station a couple of minutes later, he cursed them all good-naturedly for the woman he'd been forced to leave at the bar.

Born on a farm outside Brooks, Alberta, Mike Buday had only been in the RCMP for four and a half years, but had already earned himself a reputation as perhaps the strongest man on the force. Entirely comfortable with himself and his own capabilities, he was seen as a bit of a radical who was not the least bit intimidated by authority. Inclined to speak his own mind and with no need to prove anything to anyone, Buday had more than once gotten himself into trouble in the force for refusing to observe the hierarchical rules of rank. Instead, he treated everyone with the same even-handed approach, from the lofty position of RCMP superintendent to the street drunk. He was a hero of the rank and file.

Buday stripped off the lightweight winter parka and his sweater until he had on only a tight-fitting T-shirt, his jeans, and his running shoes. Massively muscled, his dedication to long runs in the drizzly Terrace dawns toned his body. He was also thick in the shoulders and arms from hours in the gym. But it wasn't his physique that was most striking. Entering the cellblock area to look at Oros, Buday exuded a mood of calmness, of quiet strength. It was something entirely apart from his physical prowess, something he had absorbed from the open prairie, or had learned on the farm. But wherever it came from, it gave him that rare ability to defuse tension. With junkyard dogs or brawling drunks, he could work miracles.

But now, neither his ability with animals nor his powerful build had any effect on Oros, who was still screaming to fight.

With no hesitation, Buday unlocked the door, opened it, and stepped quickly into the cell. Screaming insanely, Oros flew at him. The two of them went down heavily, with Oros flailing his arms and legs and trying to gouge Buday's face with a knife-like piece of porcelain. As Buday used wrestling holds, trying to pin him down so the others could grab an arm or leg, the two rolled around on the floor over the broken porcelain with such speed and violence that there was no opportunity for anyone else to help. Finally, Buday grabbed an arm that was thrust into his face, spun it around until he had Oros' back, and then put Oros into a hammerlock, cutting off his windpipe. When Oros still tried to gouge Buday's eyes with his fingers, Buday applied a little pressure to the carotid artery of Oros' neck and, immediately, Oros was out cold. The others quickly strapped Oros into a straitjacket and had him gagged and tied down to the hard frame of a stretcher on wheels before he recovered consciousness.

Packaged and ready for shipment on the plane in the morning, Oros was left behind in the cellblock as the assembled group, still in a high state of excitement, moved en masse to the main detachment area.

Once there, the men wanted to discuss what had just happened, one of them describing Buday almost reverently as a "fucking machine!"

Buday laughed at the words, thinking of their double meaning.

The sergeant, not wanting to make a big thing of it now that it was over, asked, "Why don't you stick around for a while? Have a coffee."

Buday grinned and looked him slowly up and down. "Hey, you're cute but you're not my type! Besides, me and Garry have company at the Skeena."

"I'll even buy!" the sergeant said, still talking about the coffee. "You deserve that at least!"

Buday laughed aloud. "Hey! You owe me at least a beer."

The sergeant grinned back at him. "Look, if she loves you, she'll be waiting for you."

Buday shook his head good-naturedly. "You must be getting senile, I'm not talking about love!"

Buday turned to the chair where his clothes were and picked them up without putting them on. His body still had a thin film of sweat over it and his T-shirt was damp. The sergeant leaned close to him so that the other men wouldn't hear and said quietly, "I'll be giving the old man a report on this Mike and I'll be sure he hears a good word about you."

"Don't waste the paper Sarge. I didn't do this for him. Just buy me a beer some time."

The older man looked at him warmly. "I'll buy you two," he said. And then almost under his breath added, "and...thanks, Bude."

With a quiet seriousness that also revealed the true depth of his concern—a message that he'd always be there, whenever he was needed—Buday replied simply, "No problem." And then left.

The next morning, in the winter's late dawn light, Staff Sergeant Bomba stood on the asphalt tarmac at the Terrace airport watching the passengers load into the 737. A coastal storm was blowing gently off the Pacific, less than forty miles away at Kitimat, and cold, misty rains were falling from low, gray clouds which were hugging the earth in their clammy embrace. Until its wheels touched the ground, it was a question whether the plane would risk a landing or fly on to Vancouver without stopping. Bomba was glad it had come in. There was a certain relief in getting Oros shipped off. Bomba had received the report of Oros' behavior in the cells last night and noted with some satisfaction that Oros was digging his own grave deeper. The violent outburst was but one more example of Oros' volatile and unstable character, which the psychiatrists would look at with everything else. Ironically, the charges that were being prepared against Oros for the destruction of cell number eight, were the best charges they had against Oros so far.

With his collar up against the freezing rain, Bomba saw two heavily built men wearing the brown uniforms of the sheriff's office wheel a stretcher away from the terminal building and through the rain toward the waiting plane. Encased in a straitjacket, strapped down into the stretcher, gagged and tranquilized, Oros was on his way to the Forensic Psychiatric Center at Essondale. At the bottom of the steps to the plane, the guards kicked the stretcher's legs, which folded up under the bed, and lifted the stretcher up the steps and into the aircraft. Bomba waited until the engines were started and the plane had swung away from the building and off toward the runway, spraying clouds of water vapor into the air, before he turned his back to it. Together with Peter Bird, they had done everything they could do. Now it was the doctors' turn. Bomba was feeling pretty confident about the next step. The doctors had a different focus than the police had. An easier one. All they had to do was to determine whether or not Oros was insane. Bomba was sure that Essondale would want to hold him. They couldn't let a man like Oros go free. He was much too crazy. And dangerous.

Chapter Sixteen

August 24, 1982. Terrace: The men who followed the prosecutor from the courtroom to his office were feeling stunned and angry.

"Fuck!" one of the policemen said as soon as the door was closed to the outer office. "You see his face when the judge said, 'You are entitled to be acquitted, sir!' SIR?... He even called him, Sir! After the animal show Oros put on in the cells jumping around and hanging from the bars just like a fucking monkey screaming, 'C'mon and get me, Piggies! Piggies! Where are you piggies?... C'mon and get me fuckin' piggies!'"

The police officer's voice rose in pitch as he mimicked Oros. His voice, almost screaming, carried easily through the hollow, plastered walls that separated the offices in the courthouse and filled the floor the way Oros' had filled the cellblock when he'd gone on his rampage. As the young man ranted, the prosecutor and the rest of the men in the cramped office watched him absently, letting him vent his feelings without interruption.

"You see the look on Oros' face!?... He smiled!... He turned to us and smiled in the courtroom! As though he was right. As though he won.... Fuck! The guy's a puke. He goes crazy in the cells, destroying property, calling us every filthy name he can think of, and the judge is apologetic to him! Shit I can't believe it!"

As he talked, he unconsciously straightened his uniform jacket with nervous tugs from his otherwise idle hands. The hostility toward the uniform was something the young man didn't understand. Even worse, the court's gentle treatment of Oros felt like a betrayal.

"I thought we were all on the same side. Where did we fuck up?"

As Bird knew all too well, it was much worse than the constable realized. For Bird, "free to go" meant a lot more than the simple acquittal on the mischief charge. It was the final slap in the face that closed the year-long, international police investigation. They had done everything they could possibly do. And failed! Oros was free again and the gift of unhindered freedom was a death warrant in blank.

There weren't enough seats in the small office for the men who now filled it, so most of them stood or, agitated, paced the open spaces, pausing to examine everything around them in critical detail. Others were leaning back against two long credenzas that lined one wall. Above the credenzas, the wall was covered to the ceiling with large poster calendars with courtroom assignments and major trials noted six months in advance. Another wall was taken up from floor to ceiling with bookshelves. Pete Bird stood in front of the books with his back to the room speaking to nobody. His face lined and his eyes intense, he frowned as he scanned the same book titles over and over again without seeing them. Against a third wall was a chesterfield with half its seating taken up by open trial files. Beside the files, squeezed between them and a bank of steel gray filing cabins that were pushed up against the wall from the edge of the sofa to the corner, sat Corporal Murray Dreilich staring at the other men in the room. Above and behind him, hanging from the wall, was a huge canvas; white and gray, the storm clouds that were painted on it seemed quite appropriate for the occasion.

Sitting in front of the storm, Dreilich, like Bird, also had a disturbed expression on his face. He, too, had been one of the men who had gone in to arrest Oros in Hutsigola in March and, like Bird, had been privy to all the information the force had gathered on Oros. With nearly fifteen years in plain-clothes duty and now head of the G.I. section of the RCMP office in Smithers, Dreilich had a good sense of people. And trouble. He knew Oros almost as well as Bird did, and was responsible for half the file. The investigation that involved Lishy remained under Bird's care in Atlin but the investigation into other possible homicides, committed during those rare occasions when Oros had come out of the bush and hitchhiked around the country or down into the U.S., had been transferred to Dreilich.

Like Bird, Dreilich wasn't directly involved in the day's court proceedings upstairs but had come to watch.

It was an unfortunate end to all their efforts—to see Oros turned loose, untreated, unrepentant, and insanely hostile. It wasn't every day that they watched a killer walk out of a courtroom returning their stares with a knowing smile.

"Next time!"

There was no sense reacting to any of it. The question now was only whether there was anything else they could do to prevent Oros from killing again.

"You gonna appeal?" asked the first officer suddenly.

The prosecutor looked at him over a high bank of thick crime files that were stacked along the front of his desk and asked, "What for?"

The prosecutor had his chair pushed back from his desk and was resting the back of his head against the room's fourth wall. Lining the wall over his head and scattered around the room covering empty wall space were various professional certificates and memberships. Framed photographs competed with the official documents for available space —images of other times and distant places.

"Do you think he was right?" the young policeman asked, as though that was the only criterion for action.

"No," the prosecutor agreed. In fact the case seemed so open and shut that the judge's decision to acquit Oros had surprised them all.

Oros had been charged for damaging public as opposed to private property and because everything over which the RCMP exercised control was, by law, government-owned and therefore public, and because there could be no question that they exercised control over their own cells, there shouldn't have been any issue at all about the point. The judge, however, saw it differently, reasoning out loud that "it could be possible that the property is only leased by the government from a private person." Therefore, concluding that he had a reasonable doubt as to the matter of whether or not the police cells were public property—believing, as he said, that they might be private property—he dismissed the charge against Oros.

"Why'd he let him go?" asked the second officer who had spoken. Nobody really believed the reasons the court had given.

"Who knows?" said the prosecutor. "Maybe he felt sorry for him. His lawyer did score a point on the dogs. Maybe the judge wanted to let him go as a kind of *quid pro quo* for his dogs you guys shot. The idea being that he'd already been punished."

Dreilich looked up with his sad, serious eyes and said plainly, "We had no choice but to kill his dogs."

"I know," the prosecutor said. "It's no big deal."

"Was to the dogs," Dreilich added with a cynical smile.

"Fucking lawyers!" the first officer complained and then, looking at the prosecutor, quickly added, "I don't mean you, man. I mean defense lawyers. How can they defend an asshole like that?"

"No," the prosecutor shook his head, disagreeing. "He's only doing his job. Keeping the rest of us honest. That's all they do."

"Actually," Dreilich said, cutting in with a more genuine smile, "the more I think about it, the more I think we should be commended for killing those dogs. That's probably the only good thing that's come out of this whole thing.... We saved the poor bastards the misery of having Oros as a master."

"How the hell could anybody sympathize with a loser like Oros?" the first officer demanded, ignoring Dreilich's comment.

"Oh, there's a certain kind of sixties appeal to the guy that a kid like you wouldn't know about," Dreilich said from his couch, playing the devil's advocate and trying to lighten the mood.

Bird continued to stare into the books with his back to the room and the people in it. There was a short silence then before the prosecutor picked up Dreilich's thread and continued.

"Murray's right," he added, looking at Murray Dreilich. "Other than his paranoia and obsession with murderous conspiracies, he could have stepped right out of a sixties *Whole Earth Catalogue* or, going even farther back, from some buffalo hunter's camp in the early 1800s. He typifies the free spirit generations."

The young officer looked more critically suspicious than skeptical. "You think he should've been let out?" The question was directed at the prosecutor.

"No," he answered. "In fact, I think he should be doing twenty-five without parole for first degree, but he wasn't charged with murder and I'm just telling you why others might want to defend him. Why the judge may have decided to let him go."

"So, do you let a drug dealer go because his business epitomizes the spirit of free enterprise and the dream behind the Boston Tea Party?" Still too upset to relax, the first officer needed answers before he'd calm down.

The prosecutor turned to Dreilich, who had an almost genuine smile on his face now, and asked, "Now that the policy is to hire university graduates only, how do you keep guys like this in line?"

Dreilich raised his eyebrows but didn't say anything. Another man who hadn't spoken until now seized the opportunity to add his own point of view.

"You know, I agree there are people who'd sympathize with Oros. You gotta admire a guy who can live for ten years all alone in that kind of wilderness. That's pretty incredible. I can't imagine doing it."

"That's because you're not nuts!"

"What comes first, the madness or the bush?" Dreilich asked, looking about the room; but nobody answered him.

"So what about the appeal?" the first officer asked stubbornly.

"Jesus, you got a one-track mind," another said.

"I'm not getting any answers," he insisted, getting angry. Nobody seemed to be taking the acquittal seriously enough.

"Look," the prosecutor said. "Oros is history. If we want to appeal, we've got to find him and serve him with appeal papers in a couple of weeks." Turning to Dreilich, he asked, "Murray, how would you like to take a helicopter into Hutsigola in a few weeks and serve Oros with a notice of appeal on a mischief charge?"

Dreilich shook his head. "It's not worth risking my life for."

"Pete?" The prosecutor was looking at Peter Bird's back.

Without turning around, Peter replied, "The next guy that goes in there after him is getting killed." There was no humor at all in his voice.

"It isn't right he gets off! It just isn't fair!"

"Stick around," one of the older men said. "You ain't seen nothin' yet!"

"Yeah, life's tough," another cop said. "As my old man used to say, 'you don't leave this life alive!' "

"Look," the prosecutor strained to be patient. "Even if we serve him and even if he comes back for the appeal, and even if we win the right to have a new trial, and even if he's convicted after a new trial or on the appeal itself, so what? I mean what's it going to prove? Remember, if the court has to make up reasons to acquit him, you can bet he'll get a light sentence after a conviction. There's almost no chance at all any judge would give him jail for it. And if they did, say he got sixty days, is there anybody here that's going to feel that we scored any kind of victory? I mean, let's face it—the mischief charge is chicken shit! What we really want is a murder charge but all we got was mischief. And you can't blame the court when it won't pretend that a toilet bowl is as important as a man's life. Or his freedom. We're looking at different pictures here. If it was up to us, sitting here in this room, we'd convict Oros now of murder because we all know he did it. But those aren't the rules. We gotta do better than that! We have to prove he killed Lishy. With no questions left unanswered. And we gotta do it by all the rules while Oros gives us the finger, spits at us, and not only insists on HIS rights but has the sympathy of the court. We've lost, boys. We can't prove he killed Lishy and that's what hurts."

"Somebody ought to waste the asshole!" one of the men suggested.

"Hopefully somebody will," another added.

"I'd do it," said a third, quietly.

"Oh, go ahead!" joked the second. "Why don't you go up there this summer for holidays and hunt him down. Should be pretty wild sport. No rules and no questions ever asked."

"Fuck, what an idea! Who'd be the hunter?"

"You need a drink, buddy," another said in an attempt to lighten the mood, which had grown heavy again.

"We all need a drink," the prosecutor said.

"You don't have to convince me," Dreilich said. He seemed ready to go right now but he remained seated.

"Some of us gotta work," one of the uniformed men said.

"Yeah, tell me about it," Dreilich said. "You're getting paid double time just for sitting here and bullshitting."

"And it's not enough to listen to all this crap."

"You could always go out into the bush and try living like Oros if you need a change," Dreilich grinned.

"So you bastards can screw me around with your aircraft! Hunt me down for sport and poison everything I touch! Fuck you! Oros told me you guys did a number on his balls so bad with your drugs one was the size of a basketball and the other was a great big fucker!"

Everybody laughed. Resuming a more natural tone, he expressed an idea that had just occurred to him.

"Unless he's fucking his dogs, he's probably building up a lot of back pressure in his balls...if he hasn't gotten it in ten years, the asshole's probably always getting lover's nuts and he's figuring it's poisoning."

There was a simple logic and justness to the idea that the men laughed again, agreeing that that was probably the most likely explanation for Oros' frequent complaint of swollen testicles. And, with that, one of the men opened the door, said good-bye, and left. The others soon filed out after him to return to work, leaving only Dreilich, Bird, and one of the more senior officers and the prosecutor for the final postmortem.

It was only after everyone else had left that Bird came to life. He closed the door and sat down in front of the prosecutor's desk on a recently vacated seat. All business.

"What about an inquest?" he asked earnestly.

"You mean to force Oros to testify?" the prosecutor asked.

Bird nodded.

"I thought of it," the prosecutor said. "If we could get Oros served with a subpoena to testify and then get him to the inquest, you think he'd answer the questions? And even if he did, do you think he'd tell the truth?"

"It's worth a try." Bird shrugged as he spoke, still ready to try anything.

"Well, it might be, if we could do it. But we can't. I already ran it past my boss. In the circumstances, the only reason to hold one would be to try to make Oros talk. And he said that we couldn't do it. The attorney general wouldn't go for it. We can't have an inquest unless we can prove Lishy is dead."

"Just an idea," Bird said.

"I thought it was a good one," the prosecutor said. He, too, had already tried everything open to him.

"What happened at Essondale?" Dreilich asked. "After I left Atlin, all I heard was that the shrink who peeked into Oros' skull didn't find anything, so they sent him back."

"Oh, that's a whole story in itself," Bird said. "You know we had to drug him and fly him down in a straitjacket, eh?"

"How'd he take the drugs?" the prosecutor interrupted.

"If he could have killed us all, he would have," Bird answered. "One of the doctors from the local psych ward gave him a shot while he was tied up. C.P. Air wouldn't take him otherwise. Bad for business to have screamers aboard!"

"Jeez, I can't understand why?" Dreilich laughed.

"Yeah, well anyway, once we got him to Essondale, he stopped talking. He followed the same kind of line he used when Bomba and I interviewed him in Atlin. Said he wouldn't answer any questions without his lawyer being present. Dr. Phillip Adilman saw him but didn't make any observations that would allow him to certify Oros.... One thing that did happen was pretty interesting, though. When Oros was there, his mother went to see him. Lady hadn't seen her son since 1968 apparently. So she flies up from the States to Vancouver to meet him at the psychiatric hospital. After they talk for a few minutes, he decides he doesn't want to see her any more, so he calls it quits and she leaves. Flies back down to the States. And you know why he didn't want to see her?"

Dreilich shook his head without speaking.

"Because Oros figured she was a fake! A plant!"

"No kidding!" Dreilich said.

"Yeah. Whatever she hoped to find, I think she left sadly disappointed.... Oros took one look at her and clammed right up. Said he remembered his mother. The guy's got quite a memory for faces, it seems, and he could describe her down to the last hair. Only the face he remembered was a face he last saw twelve or thirteen years ago. Anyhow, he remembered their last words, the look in her eyes the last time he saw her, every line on her face, every wrinkle and every chip on her teeth. Right? The teeth were really important to him. Said the woman who was masquerading as his mother had a false tooth. And his mother didn't. And the woman had lots more gray hair than his mother had. More lines, more wrinkles, and she was older. Can you imagine that?" Bird asked. "Thought she was lying when she called him son."

"Oros doesn't know the facts of life," Dreilich said.

"Apparently not," Bird continued. "Oros said she was close but not close enough to fool him. She was a plant, so he wouldn't talk to her. Jesus! You'd think there'd be some kind of presumption against sanity in a case like that but there obviously isn't. Adilman didn't have any more luck than she did in trying to talk to him. In fact, they couldn't even do a routine examination on him because he refused to take off his clothes all the time he was there. Wouldn't let anyone touch him. Wouldn't even wash. You know, he even saved his own hair. We found packets of it in jars stashed in caches around his place up north. Figured maybe he was taking souvenirs off bodies. But it was all his own hair. He saved everything. We had an order from the court for a thirty-day psychiatric remand but Adilman called us after only two weeks to get him out of there. Two weeks early."

"And he didn't think Oros was nuts?" Dreilich was surprised.

"Oh, he knew Oros was crazy. He even diagnosed him as paranoid and believed Oros was dangerous. But he wasn't certifiable. The only two questions Adilman was supposed to answer were whether he was certifiable under the Mental Health Act and whether he was mentally fit to stand trial. Oros is no dummy. If a guy knows what he's charged with, understands the role of the judge and the lawyer and is able to instruct his counsel, he's fit. And there's no question Oros knew what we were after. Twenty minutes alone with him tells you that."

"And they wouldn't keep him under the Mental Health Act?" Dreilich asked.

"No. I thought they could take anybody who was mentally ill but there's more to it than that. It's a question of degree. When Oros wants to, he can present himself fairly well. He's nuts but he's not completely out of touch. Anyway, they did the best they could, I guess. I was sure hoping they'd do more but without Oros opening up, then I guess nobody can do much."

When Bird fell silent thinking about something he didn't share, Dreilich had to prompt him to continue. "And then?"

"And then, when he got back from Essondale around the end of March, we had the bail hearing and he was released. He's stuck around town for the last five months waiting to clear up the charges before he takes off. But really it was all over then. Before he even went to court."

"What happened to the other charges?" Dreilich asked.

"He was acquitted on those as well," Bird replied.

"I know that," Dreilich said. "I mean why? What happened?"

Bird looked at the prosecutor who answered for him. "The witness we needed to prove the theft of the boat was an American and he disappeared. We had no evidence left so we had to drop that charge. Then we sat down and rethought the case against Oros for possession of Lishy's property but we couldn't prove Oros stole any of it. We just don't know how or why the stuff got into Oros' possession. Maybe Lishy gave it to him. Anyhow, we couldn't prove Lishy didn't give it to him. Or maybe Oros found it. Or maybe Lishy himself put it up into Oros' caches. Who knows. Maybe they were partners. We just didn't have the answers so we pulled the charge before it was thrown out of court.

"The only one we took to trial was the charge that he was in possession of the handgun. Even if Lishy gave it to Oros and they were best of friends, he still wasn't allowed to have it without a permit. And we figured it was pretty obvious Oros had the gun with him for six months before he was finally arrested. Not the best case but we were still hoping there was enough there. Hardly got off the ground. His lawyer argued that the fact it was found beside Oros' bed doesn't necessarily lead to the conclusion that Oros put it there. What if Lishy put it there? We couldn't prove Lishy didn't. And just because the police didn't find it in September doesn't mean that Oros had it since then either, he said. And he was right.

"Or, another argument he used, what if Oros found the gun inside the cabin? Or lying on a trail in the bush? What if a grizzly or black bear killed Lishy, dragged off the body and left his packsack behind with the gun in it? Finding it isn't a crime.

"Anyhow, the judge said the whole case was very suspicious but he wasn't satisfied that we proved Oros had acted criminally so he had to acquit him. No complaint about that logic."

"What did Oros say about it?" Dreilich asked.

"Nothing. Never took the stand. Just sat there and stared quietly. Hardly even moved his eyeballs."

"So where do we go from here?" Dreilich asked.

"Unless you guys can dig up something else, we wait for another killing," the prosecutor said.

The men were still talking when a call came through for the prosecutor that his secretary said he'd probably want to take. She was right. It was Oros.

"Are you the crown counsel?" Oros asked. His voice was soft and quiet as though he was holding the phone away from his mouth and speaking in a whisper.

"Yeah."

"My lawyer suggested I call you," he explained and then, in a firmer tone, said, "I want my property back."

"So?" the prosecutor asked, "What am I supposed to do?"

"Well, my lawyer said you could help me."

"Why should I help you?" the prosecutor asked.

"That's your job. You have to!" Oros demanded.

"I don't have to help you do anything."

"What about my property? What am I supposed to do to get it back?"

"What property are you talking about?"

"Everything that was taken from me," Oros said.

"The police didn't take anything from you," the prosecutor said.

"They took out planeloads of things," Oros insisted. The prosecutor was surprised. It was a brazen attempt by Oros to get back Lishy's property. "They didn't take anything that you owned."

"They took it all from me," Oros said, careful to make the distinction.

"So you figure you should get it all back, do you?"

"You took it from me, you have to give it back," he said.

"Is that what your lawyer told you?" He doubted it. More likely Dave Warner aimed Oros in his direction to get him out of Warner's office.

"If it's in my possession, you can't take it away from me."

"Are you talking about the gun, too?" the prosecutor asked wondering how far the acquittal had emboldened him.

"Everything you took," Oros said.

"Including the gun?"

"Everything."

"Are you saying the gun was in your possession?"

Oros thought for a moment and then answered, "You'll have to ask my lawyer that."

"I don't have to ask your lawyer anything," the prosecutor replied, ready to hang up. There was little point in continuing the conversation.

"If the police don't bring it all back then I'll have to sue them."

"I'm sure that idea's going to worry them," the prosecutor said.

"I've suffered a lot of damages," Oros said, almost defensively.

"Like the loss of Lishy's gun?" the prosecutor asked sarcastically.

"The judge said I'm innocent. It was taken from the cabin and so you have to put it back."

"I don't think anybody would ever say you're innocent."

"The judge said Lishy gave it to me."

"Did he?" the prosecutor asked, meaning Lishy.

"I'm sorry you'll have to ask my lawyer that question."

"Look," the prosecutor said, growing tired of the conversation as well as angry, "I'm too busy to waste time on your bullshit." He was going to hang up but Oros asked quickly.

"What about my stuff?"

"It has nothing to do with me," the prosecutor answered honestly. "Call the police and ask them. But I don't think they'll give you anything. It's almost all Lishy's stuff, isn't it? All things you stole?"

"My lawyer said you can tell them what to do," Oros insisted, ignoring the questions.

"Not about this."

"You can't help me?" Oros asked to confirm his understanding.

"Not even if I wanted to," the prosecutor said.

"You ruined my year," Oros said, changing his tone with the subject, as though he wanted to be part of their postmortem. Feeling empty, like the rest of them, and unsatisfied by it all, he wasn't ready yet to cut the ties that held the case together. Only his point of view was different. He was being misunderstood, and didn't want that to happen.

But the prosecutor wasn't sympathetic. "Tell it to your friend Lishy," he said.

"You have no idea what I have to do to live," Oros said. He still didn't want to end the conversation. His voice had dropped to a whisper, with a hint of desperation in it.

"Oh, I think I have a pretty good idea what you've done," the prosecutor said.

"It's August 24th already. The summer's already over up there," Oros said. "I haven't done anything to get ready for winter yet.... I had to stay here all summer to wait for the trials...now I'm not ready for anything." His voice was pleading for sympathy. But he wasn't getting it.

"You want my advice?" the prosecutor asked. The change in Oros' tone was dramatic. He had suddenly opened up.

"What's that?" Oros asked.

"Don't go back into the bush. Stay here for the winter. I'll help you get set up with a counselor to talk to..."

Oros didn't wait for the prosecutor to finish. The angry tone in his voice was back and he said simply, "It's where I live." And then he hung up.

The investigation, essentially spent and exhausted, had pretty well ground to a halt over the summer. The focus of attention had shifted fruitlessly on the ponderously slow machinery of the criminal courts, and now that it too had finally run its course, all that remained was the hollow feeling of emptiness.

"What's the next step?" Dreilich asked Bird.

"There isn't one," Bird said.

"Well, let's hope we get him the second time around," the prosecutor said, getting up to open the door. There was nothing left to be said.

"Yeah, let's hope so," Bird agreed.

He rose slowly out of his seat, reluctantly, as though leaving was the final act of defeat.

It was a depressing end. However they looked at it, the feeling lingered that somehow they had failed. Almost an entire year had passed since Lishy's disappearance and on this, the first anniversary of Lishy's murder, Oros was now on his way back to Hutsigola.

His freedom was a defeat felt personally by everyone involved in the investigation and whatever happened next, whatever Oros did now, they'd always feel responsible for it.

Chapter Seventeen

February, 1985: He was sure the dreams were getting easier. It was a good sign that the drugs were wearing off. The secret lay in washing his clothes in running water. Hard to do under three feet of ice but a bucket didn't help at all, the water had to flow to dilute the poisons and carry them away instead of simply stirring them around in the same pot with the poisoned water. Ever since he had changed the way he washed, his dreams had gotten better. He was glad for that. They had been so terrible for most of the winter that he had welcomed each dawn which brought salvation from the nightmares that held him captive every night.

Now he was even finding some of the dreams prophetic. Even better than the Tarot which had served him so well for years. If only he could remember more of the details after he woke up, the dreams would tell him much more, he was sure. But in the morning, only bits and pieces remained, fragments of visions like pieces of a jigsaw, too hard to fit together. Still, he had been recording faithfully all the details he could remember for some time now and patterns were starting to emerge that he found meaningful, as well as recurring themes—confrontations, urban collapse, police chases, shoot-outs, naked boys and aging women wanting him for sex, chasing him through the streets with machine guns. Battles and bodies. Blood that glistened in crimson pools and ran thickly over the concrete curbs. The civil war that had finally been taken to the cities raged almost nightly.

Last night, he dreamed of Los Angeles and, upon waking, he immediately set it down on paper. It was a different kind of dream from the rest. From a time before the war. He knew it was more prophetic than usual, although he hadn't figured it out yet. The clarity of detail that remained in his mind was among the most vivid he had ever experienced. And there was something else to it. Something familiar but undefinable. The way a smell stirs distant and forgotten memories, there was a quality to it that was somewhat reminiscent, almost nostalgic, as though it were more a memory than a dream. A real journey he had experienced. As he recounted it again, it gave him a sad pleasure. In it, he felt younger, a boy himself with smooth white skin and soft, feminine hands. His mood, too, was childlike, absolutely carefree. He was sitting in the back seat of a car and they were heading out into the countryside away from the city for a picnic. He loved country picnics. He wasn't sure who he was with although it felt like he belonged. They started the trip in a mood of wild exuberance. Then, as though in a rocket ship hurtling through space, they were clearing the city limits at light speeds, their anticipation boundless. It felt so good. To be free of the city. But there were hazards. Surrounding the city was a gray, featureless netherworld. And as they penetrated into its nothingness, a cloud chilled them, dulling their joy. There was a moment of anxiety, not strong enough to be fear, when he thought that there might not be any country at all—only the endless, gray barrens that stretched off like a lead sea in all directions as far as the eye could travel. However, almost magically, like doubt itself driven away by faith, it passed. And then, instantly they were out of it.

There was something else that was odd, too. The car was a gleaming aluminum cylinder. A rocket ship. Behind the wheel, when the driver touched the gas, they moved, not in linear lines across the ground but from space to space without transition, without time to prepare, to adjust. From concrete to cold mists to the ultimate country, the destination was achieved with the speed of thought.

From thought to action, without having left the car, he found himself on his feet, transported instantly into the heart of the forest. And the country. Real country. Even afterward, Oros couldn't shake the visions of it from his mind. It was a landscape he had never before experienced. More magnificent than anything he had ever imagined. With wild, unlimited expression, the growth was overwhelming. Psychedelic ferns and emerald mosses were growing thirty feet high. With impossible colors, brighter than neon but metallic, gleaming in the sunshine, the light fractured into dozens of colors and thousands of shades which filled the wild spaces towering around him. An utterly exuberant expression of form, color, and light.

Enthralled by the wonderland that surrounded him, he stood still, breathlessly awed. Until, like poison gas seeping into a closed room, a new realization slowly dawned. It was too incredible.

The problem was at first unarticulated, the flaw being felt instead. Of course it seemed unreal. It was! The colors were unnatural. As though awakening to a horror he couldn't escape from, he remembered that a real forest would be green. Living green. While, instead everything around him was permanently embalmed. A fantastic tropical plant collection sprayed with liquid nitrogen, thawed, and then, limp, quick-frozen again into crystal formations that shot off in all directions like fireworks displays molded into solid forms. But it was all dead! Worse, as he reached out to touch a gracefully curving arch of glassy growth near him, was the discovery that the crystal forest which surrounded him now as he stood all alone within it, would shatter into a million deadly shards if touched, exploding like another dream—another memory sparked and then lost—to bury him under a matchstick pile of broken crystal with razor edges. Trapped forever into stillness by the towers of death that needed only movement to bring them down. And there was no way out!

The crystal forest was a trap and he was caught—immobilized.

A strange and terrible dream.

Instead of releasing him from the feelings it caused, writing out its details exhausted him to the point where he began feeling sick. His physical reaction was so real to him that he thought that his enemies, the sneak-arounds, might have been in during the night spraying everything while he slept. The dream was so unusual it could have been drug-inspired. That thought angered him and he rose from the table, lifting up the .303 rifle that was laying beside his notebook and walked to the window with it. As soon as he felt up to it, he'd go hunting them again, he thought. There were a couple of places he suspected they might be camping out that he could check. But not today. Not with the poisons exhausting and draining his energy. Even his joints were aching again. As he stood looking out the window, he slipped the safety off the rifle and lightly fingered the trigger.

He could tell from the sway of the trees that a light wind was blowing from the north. Outside, on the snow, his one dog, named Dog, was lying stretched out pretending nonchalance at the presence of a large raven flopping around over the snow only a short distance away. The bird was playing its game of tease. Watching the dog keenly, the raven would flap-hop over the snow toward the dog and then stop. It came closer and closer, trying to antagonize the dog into action. Oros could see that Dog was playing her own game, pretending to ignore the large bird as it came closer and closer. Dog's nerves cracked first. When the raven was no more than eight feet away, she sprang up and lunged clumsily at the bird, but it was already in the air and safely out of reach. Croaking loudly as if laughing, the raven swooped low over the dog as she raised her head up and snapped her jaws at it. Not the least bit afraid, the bird finished its swoop and landed gracefully behind the dog. Obligingly, Dog lay down again pretending to ignore the bird as the raven once more began creeping up on her from behind. Once again, Dog's breath, freezing in rapid puffs, betrayed her keyed up condition.

With his face pressed up close to the smoke-greased and dusty windowpanes, Oros judged from the temperature of the glass that it was close to twenty-five below outside. He then looked at the outside thermometer, which was registering the temperature at twenty-eight degrees below zero, and was pleased to see he was so close. Not too cold, he thought. It was a lot warmer than that in the cabin. Opening the door of the stove, he probed the ashes, looking for live coals, but everything had burned out during the night. Still, it was so warm he couldn't even see his breath. Oros had a day's supply of wood stacked up beside the stove; he selected one piece with even splitting grain and he started to chop it up into kindling on the floor. Before he had finished cutting enough to start a fire, he felt so exhausted by the effort that he had to sit down and rest. Examining the chair he was sitting in, he contemplated breaking it up instead. Its wooden spokes were perfect sizes and it'd be easier to kick it apart than to swing the ax a few more times. Not for the first time, and with some effort, he resisted the temptation. As necessary as it was to have a fire, each one, like a thousand unmemorable days he had spent over the past few years, would burn itself out without a trace left in time, whereas he knew with a certainty that he'd want the chair tomorrow to sit on.

As the fire's heat spread through the stove, the translucent moose grease coating the pans on top clarified and started to sputter; he got up and slid them away from the heat, over to a cooler corner of the stovetop. He next began pouring some water from a plastic bucket into an aluminum pot on the stove for tea when he suddenly froze in midaction. Cursing, he stepped to the door, roughly kicked it open, and hurled the water away from the cabin with a violent force. If, as he now suspected, the sneak-arounds were about last night, then the water, too, was probably poisoned. And he had almost used it for tea!

Oros sat down heavily and pulled his boots on over his socks. They were from different pairs and didn't match, both boots being for the right foot, but the felt liners were still reasonably thick and the rubberized soles and leather uppers were still in good repair. Oros liked them. With two sets of socks, they were as warm and comfortable as any pair he'd ever owned.

With the boots on, he sat there wondering what it was he was supposed to do. It was the drugs. His memory was slipping.

Oros looked around him at the inside of the cabin. He'd leave if he had a better place to stay. Not that the cabin wasn't comfortable or warm. Only that the sneak-arounds had torture-drugged it so badly since he had moved into it that he always started to feel sick if he stayed inside too long.

Oros had used this cabin on and off over the years many times, passing by on his way to or from Teslin with supplies, but this was the first winter he had stayed here. The past couple of winters he had spent holed up in Hutsigola but he had run out of supplies early this winter and had ended up moving in here for the convenience it offered in being closer to the caches he was raiding about Teslin Lake. He had no idea who owned the cabin but from the way it had been well-stocked and furnished and by its location a half mile in the bush across the lake from the mouth of the Jennings River, he figured it was a tourist's summer home.

It wasn't well-furnished anymore. Over the course of the winter, Oros had made several trips back to Hutsigola with his sled heavily laden with things he had stripped from it. There was more to move before it was emptied out completely, but he was confident he'd finish the work before spring.

Little had changed since he had left Terrace in the late summer of '82. The early euphoria of being vindicated by the court had worn off quickly, leaving a bitter taste of aluminum metals in his mouth and the thick feeling of drug-logged muscles. As he returned home from Terrace, all the way north, he felt as though he was being constantly followed and spied upon by the torture-druggers. In Dease Lake, he had spotted the RCMP members and watched them watching him. It was then that it became clear to him that it was the police who were torture-drugging him. They might still be doing it for the CIA, which was controlled by the big corporations, but he was more sure than ever that they were all in it together. What surprised him was the size of the organization. They were bigger than he had ever imagined. That the RCMP wanted to kill him was never more obvious than when he walked through Dease Lake. He could feel their eyes on him. And sense their thoughts. Truly evil thoughts. After only a couple of hours in Dease Lake, he retreated to Hutsigola.

All that first winter, he raged, writing justifications for breaking the law. As he saw it, everything now was a matter of survival. THEY had denied him the right to live and prosper, so he had to live by the other set of rights. The right to roam free, to rob, and to kill. There was no other way. To give in to THEM, to obey their laws, would mean THEY had won. And they wouldn't, he promised himself. He'd never surrender. EVER!

It was winter again. Another winter. Almost three years since he'd been caught at Hutsigola. As always, he remained more than willing to defend himself but, gradually, he had been changing his own tactics. Ever since he had been acquitted and released, he had become more confident. And more aggressive. He had stolen, and stolen frequently, but he hadn't killed yet. Not that he didn't want to. This past winter, he had gone out frequently, sometimes day after day for weeks. Routinely, he tracked for miles through the bush, taking long sweeps around the cabin, hunting for their tracks the way he hunted for moose. He had found a lot of moose this winter. And killed plenty of them. But he hadn't yet seen any people. Not that they weren't out there, be believed, just that they were so careful in covering their tracks. Still, it felt good to hunt them. And his nightly dreams of open warfare with visible enemies lifted his spirits by day. He always won in the dreams. It was a good feeling but they were only dreams. Sooner or later, he'd really find them and, this time, as soon as he saw them, he'd shoot them on sight. First chance he got.

After all these years, the only philosophy left was kill and be killed. The ultimate knowledge was that the battle was already lost and darkness was descending with the speed of a snowflake from the sky, floating gently but relentlessly downward. Soon, he knew, it would happen. The final battle was coming. He could feel it. And he wrote about it often. It was only a matter of time before it would all be over.

Remembering finally that he hadn't had breakfast yet and that he needed water for tea—fresh water which wasn't drugged—he got up again and, feeling a little stronger, pulled on his coat, tossed a tin cup into the bucket to fill it with, threw in the ax and, picking up his rifle with one hand and the bucket with the other, went outside. He stood for a moment by the open doorway breathing deeply of the air, fresh with the faint smell of pine, while his dog jumped up at him in friendly excitement. Stepping carefully through the area he used for his toilet, he started off along the path that led down toward the lake without bothering to strap on his snowshoes. It was a mistake. Even here on the path, as wide as two snowshoes laid side by side and beaten down by his almost daily traffic to the watering hole, the powdery snow wouldn't hold up his weight and he sank down into it with every step.

Plowing ahead, he forced his way through it by brute strength. Off the path, walking through the virgin snow, was much more difficult. Almost impossible. Even the moose couldn't do much better. Over the past several weeks, he'd run into moose every few days bogged right down and floundering desperately in the deep snow. Running into ravines where the snow was deeper than their legs, they'd get hung up altogether and he could have easily killed the ones he found with an ax, the way the Indians did, if he had wanted to. It was the only time of year when a man on snowshoes could ever hope to run down a moose and kill it with his hands. This was the season for wolves. The bitches were already growing fat on meat and litters.

Angrily, Oros cursed every step of the way to the lake, but refused to go back and get his snowshoes. At first, he simply didn't want to give in to the snow, but then he started to enjoy the effort, which caused his body to heat up and the ache in his joints to subside. Behind him, the dog struggled along, eagerly trying to keep up by sticking to Oros' tracks.

At the edge of the forest, he stopped before stepping away from the safety of the trees and exposing himself to view on the open ice. Squinting against the brilliant sunshine, he studied the frozen expanse of Teslin Lake. The lake, a long and narrow body of water, disappeared into the distant horizon to the north; there was nothing out on it that he could see. Over the ice by snowmobile, it could take less than an hour to ride to the town of Teslin but the locals who lived there preferred the trails that didn't lead down to the bottom of Teslin Lake. Oros had worried about snowmobiles earlier in the winter when the snow cover was lighter, but now that it was so deep, the heavy machines couldn't run through it without sinking out of sight, so nobody was likely to use them in the area for what remained of the winter. A man could go a lot farther and faster on foot. But nobody from Teslin had any business being down the lake this time of year on foot either.

Here and there, crossing the lake from shore to shore or running along the shorelines close to the trees, were ruts dug through the snow by wandering moose but, otherwise, the snowbound ice surface was slick and unbroken.

Except for his own noise, the air was dead calm. In the distance, he could hear the calls of ravens. Their guttural croak carried through the still, cold air for long distances.

Leaving the bush, he walked directly to the closest hole and examined it for signs that it had been tampered with since yesterday. It appeared to be undisturbed. From there, he checked the next hole, and then the next, until he had examined them all and found them safe. Or as safe as he'd ever believe they could be. He had cut most of them to fish through but he also used the holes to draw his water from, rotating his source just in case THEY had drugged one of them. Chopping away the ice that had formed over the top of the one he picked, he scooped the pieces of ice out and then raised a cupful of water up close to his face to study it. It looked alright. But then it always did. The problem with the drugs was that they were tasteless and odorless. It was only afterward, after they were inside him and their hideous nature started to unfold, that he could tell he had ingested them. Still, he had no choice, he reminded himself, and filled the bucket with water.

The heat that had rushed through his body with the physical exertion warmed him and he noticed that the soreness he had felt earlier was all but gone now. Already after being outside for only a few minutes, he was thinking clearer and feeling better than he had when he was inside the cabin. Right then, he resolved to stay outside all day. It was a perfect day for hunting the torture-druggers.

As soon as he finished his first cup of tea, his resolve began to slide. Sitting warmly in front of the stove with the fire door open, watching the wood burning, a laziness overcame him. Giving in to it, he crawled back into his sleeping bag with all his clothes on. There was nothing urgent to do, anyway. He had enough meat left at the cabin to last a few more days and the rest of the moose, over half the carcass, was less than three miles away. The most pressing problem was stopping the torture-druggers but that was a problem that had already lasted twelve years. It could wait one more day.

Gradually, sleep transported Oros from the deep stillness of the late winter to the warm, humid air of summertime. He dreamed he was in a beautifully soft river valley, fleecily lined, with blooming deciduous trees. On the edge of a river, two moose were asleep in the sunshine and with one, well-placed shot that went through them both, he killed them and was happy. For a moment, it was Glenora on the Stikine River. Until the river traffic came by. Stern to bow. Boats crowded with city folk dressed in rags. White boat people selling rats in cages along the docks. Cat food. He was holding the cat wrapped up tightly in a blanket, away from himself and over the edge of the balcony, and then let it go to watch how it fell. Falling. Hitting the rooftops way down below, it smashed holes through them and people flooded out of the damaged buildings looking up as they ran after him. Screaming. Chasing him through the streets—and he'd forgotten his gun somewhere. It was impossible. He never left his gun behind, anywhere. The bullets were flying close but then he remembered that he was immune to them and he stopped running when he got to the German's house on the river beside huge fields of wild marijuana, and he knew he was safe again in the country. Walking along the river, he was talking to a fantasy book that spoke to him with several different voices, mostly of children. They talked about sex. The book had its own sound effects, which it made as they walked along chatting in the sunshine. The last thought he had before waking was he hadn't been so happy since...since he couldn't remember when.

With his eyes awake but his mind still rooted in his dreams, he grew angry at the idea that here was another secret the corporations had kept from the people—talking books. Well, now that he had discovered they existed, he'd make a fortune off them. And it was all so incredibly simple. There was nothing anyone had to learn to do; all they had to do was open the books and the books would do the rest.

Absorbed by the greatness of his discovery, Oros lay in his sleeping bag, his eyes wide open, seeing only the images of psychedelic skies and quicksilver lakes and naked, bronzed children as innocent as birds that the book had described to him. The contrast of that fanciful world with the realities of the cold cabin, when his senses finally returned to him, changed the dreamy euphoria he had been feeling into a heavy-hearted bitterness.

THEY had taken everything from him. Spreading rumors about him to keep away the girls, he had been turned into a pariah. Even the homosexuals were afraid of him.

All those years. Destroyed. And now this—lying in bed at midday.

He remembered that his urine was as clear as water this morning and made a mental note to record that fact, although all that really mattered anymore was the battle.

Once—a long time ago now, it seemed—he had hoped to survive it but now death didn't scare him the way it used to. In fact, with the fear gone, he was looking forward to the fight.

The end was soon, he knew, although he wasn't sure when. Not exactly. But sometime this summer. Within the next year, at any rate. He had already started last winter to make predictions about when the big shoot-out, as he called it, would happen. Back then, he wasn't sure when it would happen but now, now that he was committed to hunting them down, he knew it was only a matter of time before he found them. And when he did, it would be over. All he could hope to do was kill as many of them as he could before they killed him.

Oros wanted to go out and hunt torture-druggers but he still didn't feel up to the effort. And it was late. Already the light was fading outside. The day was over.

For the rest of the month and into the first few days of March, with temperatures still reaching thirty-five below and gale force winds blowing snowstorms across the land, Oros spent most of his time inside. He saw everything now as part of the great conspiracy. The contrails of jets were noted as evidence of spying and CBC radio was an elaborate system for creating disinformation. Lower-flying aircraft, especially the ones he could hear, would send him into a state of extreme agitation. He listened to the radio daily, interpreting every news item as an event demonstrating either the strength of the enemy or resistance to THEM.

Occasionally he made a reference to Lishy in his journals; although the radio hadn't mentioned Lishy's name in years, Oros hadn't forgotten it. Oros now openly described Lishy's disappearance as a killing, as though it was a known fact, but he was always careful to blame others for it—that Lishy had been killed with the torture-drugs. His comments suggested that the person who had in fact done it was only an instrument of others.

By early March, the weather began to turn and daytime temperatures started melting snow. The warmer weather was a mixed blessing. Although it released him from the confines of the cabin for longer periods each day, it also meant the sneak-arounds would become more active too.

March 3.
    S. Wind.
    Cold.
    The wind is raising powdery snow-devils outside. Dreamed of killing three sneak-arounds that rode into sight. Shot them right out of their saddles. Neurasthenia—this is the dictionary word for what the torture-druggers have done to me.
    Canadian Propaganda Radio said today the co-inventor of the birth control pill has a new drug to stop cockroaches from breeding. These are the people from San Jose and Palo Alto who have been using their torture-drugs on me. They also make us act homosexually. Hunted for sneak-arounds to kill today. Climbed a mountain searching for their tracks.
    Nothing. So far.
    Hauled back some moose meat. Load too heavy and broke toboggan.
    The Tarot speaks of caution and during the night, I heard the sound of a strange dog barking. Spies are around. Watching us. If I leave the house for long they will radio in their planes or a helicopter.

His belief that sneak-arounds or torture-druggers would soon be at the cabin tracking him through the snow had already prepared him for the encounter he would soon have when Frank and Eileen Hase arrived, as they would, on March 16th.

That was to become the trigger setting off a chain reaction and lead to the final confrontation that Oros had been waiting for.

Until then, he continued to plan, to hunt for his enemies, and to dream.

March 11.
    Two of the sneak-arounds were hiding behind parked cars waiting for me to walk down the street. Instead I shot them both and skinny dogs came to feed on the blood that drained into the gutter. A woman sat crying for her baby. A bus driver recognized me and stopped the bus to give me a ride and inside was a beautiful 11 year old girl waiting for me. Naked. Then the sky exploded with lights which was a sign that everything was alright.

The next day—the twelfth—he moved more stuff into his emergency cache, hoping to keep it safely hidden from the sneak-arounds, and noted a plane flying over, three miles to the south.

His entry on Wednesday morning, March 13th, was brief:

No political statements.

The rest of the day and into the next, Oros was on the trail. Expecting trouble, he had started to move his cached supplies out of the area. Dragging them on his sled, he was hauling them south to safety, at Hutsigola.

By Friday, March 15th, he was back in the cabin at Teslin Lake. The daytime temperatures were once again climbing above freezing, making travel over the snow, pulling a toboggan, nearly impossible.

When Oros sat down to log the night's dreams and the day's events in his journal, he had no idea this entry would be the last he would ever write.

Friday, March 15.
+36
Too warm for snowshoes.
Was at Home Cabin moving in new supplies. Just as I got there an airplane flew over the cabin heading S.E. They're up to something for sure.
Scientists from San Jose and Palo Alto are running camps for horny preteens who want to get fucked but don't know how. Experimenting on them with new drugs. Like the torture-drugs they use on me.
Dreamed of a long beach and big surf, scoring dope with my pockets full of money and an old lady who stopped me to try to figure me out.
But couldn't.

Chapter Eighteen

Saturday, March 16, 1985: Frank Hase wasn't expecting trouble when he and his wife unloaded their skidoos at a lake landing in Teslin. They hadn't been down to their cabin at The Narrows since Labor Day weekend in September but, in all the years they'd owned the cabin, nothing really serious had ever happened.

That was one of the advantages of being way out in the country, far from the urban areas. Country folk were better neighbors.

Before they left Teslin, Frank Hase shared a coffee with a couple of the pilots in the Yukon Hotel who told him about seeing some activity down on his part of the lake. Nothing definite. Just some smoke a few times and a snowshoe trail along the edge of the ice, hugging the trees. Hase wasn't worried. Most probably it was only Indians from Teslin working a trapline on foot or somebody winter hunting for moose. The moose season was over but everybody poached around here. Moose were more plentiful than beef in the Yukon. And cheaper.

It was a warm day when they set out, heading south across the frozen lake. There had been some winter skidoo traffic down the lake for the first few miles, which had packed the snow and they rode on the trail for as long as it lasted. Once they neared the northern border of British Columbia, crossing out of the Yukon, the trail they were on swung around and returned back up the lake to Teslin, seventeen miles behind them. In front of them, unbroken for miles by any trail, lay the snowbound surface of Teslin Lake. Twenty-five more miles south of the border lay their own cabin. Across the lake from the abandoned gold-rush community of Johnsontown was a small creek which emptied into Teslin Lake. Approximately half a mile back into the bush, hidden from sight, along the creek, Hase had built their summer house.

Originally, they had planned to homestead it but the isolation soon changed that and they moved to Whitehorse. Now it was their private retreat and they were both looking forward to spending some time there after a long absence.

It wasn't an easy trip. The snow was three feet deep and had drifted to twice that in places. Without a trail to follow, the heavy machines kept floundering on their sides and sinking beneath the surface. Worse, with the warm temperature, the snow was melting. Thick and sticky, it kept jamming up the tracks and, just to keep them running, Frank and Eileen had to push their machines over every couple of miles to chop the ice out of them. It was an exhausting effort but the glory of the day wasn't lost on them either.

The morning's pink dawn shone through a haze that blurred the clarity of the light washing sharp definitions into a creamy rinse of pastel colors. As the sun rose higher in the sky, its rays covered the fields of unbroken snow that blanketed the rounded mountains south of Teslin, reflecting a silvery light into the clear blue sky. They were in good spirits. A grand day was unfolding.

They were nearing the mouth of their own creek only a half mile away when they had the first sign of trouble.

Even from that distance, they could see that the cuts in the snow around the mouth of their creek were regular and ordered. These weren't wandering animal tracks.

Closer still, Hase saw the holes in the ice. There were ice holes all over the place. Someone was fishing here. And had been for a long time. There were trails connecting the holes. From hole to hole, the snow was beaten down from regular use. There were other trails, too. Leading off down the lake, hugging the shoreline, a fresh trail disappeared in the distance in the direction of Hutsigola to the south.

At the mouth of the creek, the trail from the south merged with the other trails from the lake into one, deep, wide, and well-traveled path that moved off the ice and disappeared into the bush, following the creek that lay buried there under the snow.

Hase knew exactly what it meant. The main trail led straight to their cabin. Someone was living there.

A short distance from the ice holes, they cautiously turned their snowmobiles around on their own trail. Ready for a quick escape back to Teslin, they shut them off and listened. The air was dead calm.

Hase hoped the sound of their machines hadn't carried to the cabin. He had deliberately built the cabin back far enough into the bush that nobody passing by on the lake would ever know it was there.

Hase wasn't sure what to do next. He wasn't armed. Although there had never seemed any reason to carry a gun in winter, he now wished he did. Still, they couldn't very well leave without at least seeing the cabin.

After a hurried conference with his wife, they decided that they should sneak through the bush to get within sight of the cabin. They could decide then if it was being occupied or not. And by whom.

They made a careful approach. Creeping slowly through the forest on snowshoes, they followed the stranger's trail toward their cabin, stopping every few feet to listen and study the ground around them. The tracks told Hase a lot.

The trails were made by toboggans. Two of them. One was small, a sled with runners, about the size of the one he kept at the cabin for hauling firewood. The other was larger. And it left a trail unlike any he'd ever seen before. Rougher. Crude. And a machine had not been used to pull these sleds. As clear as the dog tracks left in the snow were the pad prints of huge snowshoes. The tracks were evidence of a primitive existence. A man with a dog was hauling these sleds with brute strength.

There was only one man who lived like that. Sheslay Free Mike. The man the newspapers called Oros.

Hase unslung his binoculars again and scanned the bush ahead of them before moving forward. One step at a time.

At the edge of the clearing, they stopped, still under cover of the trees, and studied their home. Their distress at being violated tempered by fear, they examined the cabin with the binoculars. Silent and smokeless, it remained darkly secretive.

But the sight of the ground around it spoke of long use. Strewn about the clearing were bits of bone and clumps of hair-tangled hide. The remains of at least one moose. Smears of blood near the door were freshly frozen into the hard-packed snow. Running through it, a well-beaten trail led right around the cabin and, at one corner, near the door, some distance from the outhouse, was the toilet. Small mounds of feces, some only darker shadows under a layer of fresher snow, bore mute testimony to the permanent habitation of their cabin. Fanning out around the entrance, just outside the door, urine stains spotted the ground.

A huge pile of firewood, almost two months' supply that Hase had cut in the summer and left piled against the cabin, was gone. And from the surrounding bush, Hase could see where the nearest trees had been chopped down and dragged to the cabin.

Still, it seemed deserted. There was no fire burning and no sign of the dog. From the edge of the clearing, Hase hollered out their presence. And waited. In silence.

Nothing happened.

Carefully, slowly, they approached the cabin and swung open the door. To their immense relief, it was empty. But it was a short-lived feeling.

Stepping through the door, they gasped at the sight. It was a horror. Their home had been stripped and turned into a slaughterhouse! Everything of value was gone. Pools of dried blood and caked hair covered the floor around the entrance and kitchen area. Hardened chunks of moosehide and chewed bone were scattered everywhere. Carcasses had been carved up inside. The force of the ax blows cutting through flesh had chopped and splintered the floor, driving hair and blood into the cuts.

And the stench. It was overpowering. Even in the near-freezing air, the cabin stank. Of rot and blood. Of green hides and urine. Of decay and death.

Depressed, they started to take an inventory of all the things that were missing: his rods, reels and tackle, his canoe, two expensive parkas, all his clothes, his woolen socks, his bush pants and shirts, even his underwear, two sleeping bags, two sets of snowshoes, his .303 British rifle and boxes of ammunition, cases filled with reloading equipment to make thousands of bullets, a pair of binoculars, all his tools, his chain saw, an Alaskan Saw Mill, a come-a-long, a block-and-tackle, all his books, all the food, cutlery and cookware, his toboggan, a portable sewing machine, a portable typewriter, the lighter furniture, and most of their personal things. Even his wedding ring. Exhausted, they gave up.

They had lost it all. And, without insurance, they'd never be able to replace it. Hase was angry—and of half a mind to try to get it back. It'd be easy to follow the trails. He knew now exactly who had made them.

Left behind by the thief was an old homemade dog pack. Frank and Eileen both recognized it, having been forced by a winter accident in 1979 to take shelter in the Colberg's cabin down near the southern end of Teslin Lake. The wild storm that blew outside had driven another man to the same shelter. It was their first and only encounter with Sheslay Mike but for three days, as Frank tended an injured leg and the storm raged unabated outside, they had been cabin-bound together. It had been a curious experience. Mike had kept his thoughts mostly to himself. And when he hadn't, he talked about conspiracies to poison the wilderness. But he hadn't seen the Hases as enemies and they hadn't felt threatened by him. Mike had spent a couple of hours each day they were together working on a pack for the dog he had with him, stitching it with a heavy awl.

There was no question about it. The pack left behind in their cabin was that same pack.

Sheslay Free Mike had taken over their cabin.

As angry as he was, Hase didn't want any confrontation with Mike. Although he hadn't run into him for six years now, he knew that after all those years alone in the bush, Mike had grown dangerous.

There had been hundreds of stories about Sheslay Mike since they had met, stories in the press and on the radio, in the bars and cafes, about the wild man who haunted the wilderness between Telegraph Creek and Teslin, wandering endlessly along the old Telegraph Line and gold-rush trails. Rumors were that he killed people, that he was a cannibal, that he had sex with his dogs, that he set deadly traps for people along the old trails. The rumors kept a lot of the locals who heard them out of the bush. The more superstitious Tlingit Indians wouldn't even go into the region for fear of running into him.

Until now, Hase had never seen himself as a possible victim. But now, far from Teslin, hours from help, alone and unarmed, they were full of fear. Too late to go back, they stayed in the cabin and passed a fitful night.

In the morning, feeling a little more confident, Hase found a pencil that Sheslay Mike hadn't stolen and wrote out a note for him in bold print in case he returned to the cabin.

MIKE,
   WELL, YOU REALLY DID IT THIS TIME! YOU PACKED OUT JUST ABOUT EVERYTHING WE OWN. WE HAD TO WORK FOR ABOUT 6 YEARS FOR OUR LIFE-STYLE OUT HERE AND YOU DESTROYED WHAT WE'VE WORKED FOR IN ABOUT 6 MONTHS OF LIVING LIKE A FUCKING BUM LEACH AND A FUCKING PIG! I DON'T SUPPOSE YOUR CONSCIENCE WILL EVER BOTHER YOU BUT YOU BETTER START CARRYING AROUND A HEALTHY DOSE OF FEAR. BECAUSE YOU WILL BE BROUGHT TO JUSTICE

FOR THESE HIDEOUS CRIMES. YOU WON'T LIVE TO BE OLD!
   KEEP WATCHING OVER YOUR SHOULDER—
   THE DAY WILL COME!
   I CAN GUARANTEE THAT YOUR ACTIONS HERE WILL BE AVENGED. IF I WERE YOU I WOULD HOPE THAT THE LAW CATCHES YOU BEFORE I DO!
   FRANK AND EILEEN HASE
   P.S. SLEEP WELL BUT KEEP ONE EYE OPEN.

Out in the open, vulnerable again, they hurried back to the lake where they had left their snowmobiles.

Passing out of the forest onto the frozen lake, Hase noticed a dark form, far away. Out on the ice to the south of them near The Narrows, it was stationary. Motionless.

Hase quickly unpacked his binoculars for a better look. And what he saw almost made him drop them. It was Oros, all right. But even as Hase studied him with binoculars, Oros was crouched down over his toboggan studying them with binoculars.

Watching each other.

It was an eerie, creepy feeling.

Oros was too far away to read any expression in his face, but there was no mistaking him. Or the parka he was wearing. It was the one Hase had kept in his cabin. And the toboggan Oros had behind him with his dog was also Hase's. Sticking up in the air beside the toboggan was the point of a rifle.

There was no question of confronting Oros now. Yelling to his wife to hurry, Hase rushed to the snowmobiles to escape.

Oros was returning.

Grateful for the powerful machines, they were soon out of harm's way and putting more miles between them as they raced back to Teslin.

Curiously, Frank Hase didn't make the complaint to the police until hours later. So late, in fact, that the day was already over and there was nothing the police could do. The delay had given Oros a whole day to prepare. And when Constable Jack Warner took Hase's call at nine o'clock that night, there was no mention of the note that had been left behind for Oros.

Warner knew Oros' reputation and was a little apprehensive about how to deal with the complaint. However, Oros had committed a serious crime and he had to act.

Together with his boss, Corporal John Grant, they decided that Warner would fly out in the morning to check the cabin by air.

At dawn, Warner was in a Maule aircraft chartered from Coyote Air in Teslin. The pilot, Denny Denison also knew Oros' reputation for shooting at aircraft and, to be safe, he decided to approach the Hase cabin from the bush side rather than over the more exposed lake side.

Flying around the western slopes of the Dawson Peaks and then southeasterly from there, they were soon approaching Hase Lake, the marshy lake that drains out into Teslin Lake past the Hase cabin. Two miles away from Hase Lake, Denison cut his altitude right down to 200 feet and held it steady at that height as they flew straight over the cabin.

Everything seemed quiet.

Denison banked the plane for a slow turn to check it again more closely. With the flaps extended like a goose fanning its wings for a landing, the Maule cruised slowly through the air at fifty miles an hour. Circling around to the north, Denison dropped right down to fifty feet. They were going in for a really close look.

The plane again swept over of the cabin, but there was absolutely no sign of Oros or his dog. Nothing was moving.

The trail Oros had made was clearly visible and they started to follow that.

A moment later and they were at the edge of Teslin Lake where Oros' trail broke off to the south hugging the bush.

Just beyond a point of land which jutted out over the frozen lake, Oros was waiting.

As soon as they sailed over the trees and broke out again above the ice, they spotted him.

Crouching beside a sled, he had his rifle up, aiming at them: not more than 100 feet away, and Oros was ready to fire.

"There he is!" yelled Warner and then added immediately, "Oh Shit! He's pointing a rifle at us!"

They were desperately close.

The broad wingspan of the aircraft shadowed the snow beneath them as they swooped over Oros.

Frantically, Denison banked the plane steeply to the right as he rammed up the power trying to push their craft behind the cover of the trees.

With the plane in a bank, their vision of Oros was suddenly cut off and they couldn't tell whether they were still in his gunsight, but they heard the shot clearly.

A sharp BANG.

And then they were over the trees. And out of sight.

"Christ! He shot at us!" Denison yelled.

"You all right?" asked Warner.

"Yeah. Shit! That was close! I never thought he'd really shoot at us."

"No," Warner agreed. In spite of all the rumors, he hadn't either. People like to exaggerate things. But now his opinion was changed. He was feeling lucky they were both alive and unharmed.

"You know, when that shot went off, I could almost feel the concussion," Denison said, his adrenaline still pumping. It had been much too close.

Corporal Grant was waiting for them at Teslin's airstrip when they landed.

Together, they inspected the aircraft but, surprisingly, the bullet hadn't struck the plane.

Grant immediately made contact with his boss at "M" Division headquarters in Whitehorse. Staff Sergeant Legassicke received the call and in turn broadcast the news through the office.

The senior staff remembered Oros. Three years ago to the month they had received a similar call requesting assistance in bringing in Oros. Officers from the Whitehorse office had even helped in the arrest of Oros. And afterward, they received copies of the file. In fact, all the detachments in the north had been sent copies of the file. Oros was now well-known everywhere.

But Whitehorse was in a bit of a quandary. Warner and the town of Teslin were under the jurisdiction of "M" Division. But "M" Division's jurisdiction was the Yukon.

Oros and the Hase cabin were in British Columbia.

There was yet another, even more serious, complication. As good as they were, the men policing the Yukon had been effectively banned from arresting Oros.

The old file on Oros was stamped EXTREMELY DANGEROUS. A decision had been made long ago, after Oros was last arrested at Hutsigola and the details analyzed, that if he were ever to be arrested again, the regular members of the RCMP were not to be involved. Only the specially trained members of the RCMP's elite ERT teams were to attempt it. Trained for antiterrorist operations, the Emergency Response Teams were considered to have the force's most capable members. Oros wasn't going to be treated lightly.

They would do what they could to help but when the commanding officer of "M" Division contacted the superintendent in charge of the Prince Rupert subdivision, who had jurisdiction over northwest British Columbia, it was to pass control of the entire operation to him.

The superintendent didn't waste any time.

Within minutes, the cryptic messages were out.

Assemble the ERT teams.

A little while later, at one o'clock in the afternoon on Monday, March 18, Constable Warner and Denny Denison were directed to return to the bottom of Teslin Lake. Their instructions were simple. Find and maintain surveillance over Oros.

Flying high and out of gun range, armed with powerful binoculars, they spotted Oros shortly after 2:00 P.M. Inexplicably, instead of retreating toward Hutsigola, Oros was moving closer to Teslin.

When they'd seen him last, when he had fired, he was traveling south from the mouth of Hase Creek but after that, he had changed direction. Now, traveling at no more than two miles an hour, he was moving north.

They watched him, dragging a heavily laden toboggan, fight his way with great difficulty over deep and unbroken snow. Behind him, following in his tracks, was a dog pulling its own smaller sled. It was difficult to judge what his ultimate destination was because, as Oros moved north, a long, narrow body of open water paralleling the shore forced him to move in a straight line even if, as they suspected, his real goal was to get across the lake to the abandoned town of Johnsontown.

It was too late and his load too heavy to go the distance and Oros made directly for Big Island, which jutted out of the ice in the middle of the lake.

At seven that evening, as darkness was forcing Denison to turn back to Teslin, they made their last flight over Big Island. Oros had made camp on the northern tip of the island. He now had a fire going and appeared to be bedding down for the night on a carpet of spruce boughs over the snow.

Oros had chosen his camp well. From there he had a broad, uninterrupted view across the frozen expanses of Teslin Lake to the north, where the police would have to come from. They wouldn't surprise him.

But it was also a good camp for the police. If Oros could watch them coming, so, too, could they watch him. He was trapped. He couldn't get off the island without exposing himself.

If they could only get the ERT teams in position before Oros crossed back over to the bush, they'd have him.

But they'd have to move fast.

Chapter Nineteen

Saturday, March 16, 1985. Terrace: "I'll bet you a forty pounder you'll be back there tonight," Garry Rodgers said, grinning at his best friend Mike Buday.

"Nope," Mike insisted, shaking his head seriously. "I've had it. It's over. Shit!... Everything I had at her place was outside. Just dumped in the fuckin' snow. Aw man, I don't need that bullshit! No sir, it's over. I'm never going back!"

Garry wasn't convinced. He knew his friend too well. "A forty pounder says you can't stay away tonight," he said and then, goading him, thrust out his hand to shake on the bet.

Mike grinned back. "You really want to bet on it?" he asked. Garry nodded his head and Mike continued. "Then make it two forty's." He thrust out his hand to shake but Garry quickly withdrew his.

"Oh no," Garry said. "You want to raise the ante, then make it a case."

Mike laughed. "Piss on that!" Then raising the bet astronomically, he shouted, "One year's bar bills!"

"You'll bankrupt us," a voice from the kitchen said sweetly. Garry's whispering voice of conscience. Married to him for a year and a half, Rita knew her husband could be as wild and reckless as his imagination would take him, but that was something she liked in him.

"Fuck, that much booze will kill me," Garry replied, ignoring her.

"You got to win it first."

Garry studied Mike's hand deliberately for a moment. Then, shook on the bet solemnly before laughing again. Mike's dog, Trooper, a large but still young German shepherd, had been watching the exchange so intently one could almost believe he understood it. He whined now at Mike and Garry. Garry, who knew the signal as well as Mike did, joked, "He's giving you shit for throwing away all the money you're ever going to make."

"You're going to drink those words buddy," Mike shouted back from the kitchen, where he had gone to let the dog out. Waiting until the dog was finished and had come back in, Mike returned to the living room and dropped himself down into his favorite chair while Trooper took up his usual position close by Mike's feet.

"All this talk about free liquor's got me thirsty."

Pressing his hands down on the armrests and using only the muscles in his arms, Mike sprang up lightly. Agile and powerful, his usual exuberance was tempered somewhat by last night's fight with his girlfriend.

"Anybody else for a beer?" he asked.

"Sure," Garry replied. Rita nodded.

As comfortable in the home as though it were his own, he came back from the kitchen and laid the beer down in front of them. Mike had been living with Garry and Rita for most of the past year, having moved in one night soon after they had bought the house.

When he had been accepted into dog service, Mike had sold his own house and then left on the long course expecting to be posted to another detachment afterward. When he'd finished the special training for police dog handlers, the opening he'd wanted hadn't come through yet and so he had returned to Terrace unexpectedly one night. Having consumed a considerable amount of alcohol beforehand, he'd appeared homeless at Garry's front door in the middle of the night. With only his truck, a suitcase of clothes, Trooper, and a chain saw, Mike Buday was traveling light. The chain saw was the key to successful gate crashing. Starting it up, he'd sliced into the cedar front door, carving a huge hole out of the center. Stepping through, into the dark interior, he'd frozen, blinking, when the light suddenly came on. Its intensity was blinding and, for a moment he'd wondered whether he'd had the wrong house. But then the haziness cleared and he'd recognized Garry and Rita standing there in housecoats, Garry's hand still on the light switch, both staring at him.

Buday warmed at the sight of his friends. Weaving in a small circle and still slightly unfocused, he'd kept blinking and then said, somewhat surprised but grinning from ear to ear, "Oh, you're up!"

It was a bizarre scene. Three-thirty in the morning—Mike in a happy stupor with the chain saw dangling from one arm—still running. Garry was controlling himself but Rita had lost it at the sight of their new, heavy wooden entrance door with a huge hole in it and Mike standing on the missing piece waving at them with the chain saw as though it was the most natural thing in the world. As cold as it was becoming without a front door, Rita had to sit down to control the pain in her stomach, she was laughing so hard.

"Jesus Christ, Mike! What did you do?" Garry had finally shouted.

Mike looked down at his feet and the door he was standing on as though he was given a puzzle to solve. A tough one. His mouth started to twitch.

"Your door was locked," he said at last.

"Why didn't you knock?" Garry demanded.

"I didn't want to wake you," Mike said with a tone that was so sincere, with a real concern expressed in it for Garry, that Garry had to shake his head to keep from laughing.

Focusing on Rita, Mike said in as friendly a manner as he could muster, "Hi, Rita. Sorry to wake you."

It was all she could do to wave back at him.

Mike's tone suddenly changed and he looked at Garry indignantly.

"Some fucking welcome! Here I am standing here in the fucking freezing cold and nobody's even offering me a goddamned beer."

Garry finally lost his grip and fell to the floor beside Rita.

Ignoring the fact they were both on the floor, Mike started examining things around the living room. "Hey, nice house, Rita... I think we'll be pretty comfortable here if you can ever get your old man off his ass and do a little repair work. Place is already starting to fall apart."

With tears running down his cheeks, Garry walked Mike into the guest room and shut him off. Mike Buday had moved in.

Mike had been waiting for the opening he wanted in Prince George. But until that happened, as a qualified dog master, he remained on duty in Terrace and a guest in the Rodgers' home.

As was so often the subject, they had been talking about Mike's future on and off all day.

"Hey Bude," Garry said, getting Mike's attention. In the lull in conversation, Mike had started to drift away into his own thoughts. Garry wanted to lighten things up. "If you won, your liver wouldn't thank you," he said.

"Hedging on your bet now?" Mike asked.

"No, just concerned about your welfare," Garry joked.

Mike smiled, "Well, I don't know about that," he said, answering Garry's first statement. "It's the best liver I've ever had."

"What do you really want to do when you get to Prince George, Mike?" Rita asked him, bringing back the whole question.

"Nothing I'm not already doing," he answered seriously. "I've always done what I want to do."

"I can think of at least two or three you wouldn't want to do that you did," Garry interjected quickly, talking about women.

"Yeah," Mike agreed, thinking about it and grinning at him. "Daylight sure gives you a different perspective, all right." Next to his work, women had always been a driving force in his life.

"Don't you think you've had enough women?" Rita said. Her own point of view was well-known.

"No!" Mike grinned, his response immediate. "I don't think any honest man can ever say he's had enough women." And then, looking over at Garry, he exaggerated a wink. "Except, of course, for your old man here, but then look what he's got to keep him happy."

"Oh, no! You leave me out of this," Garry objected. "You're on your own."

"Don't you want to settle down?" Rita pressed, ignoring the oblique compliment.

"No," Mike answered truthfully. "I could have stayed at home if I wanted to do that. Doesn't have any appeal to me to be tied down. I couldn't live with just one woman. It wouldn't work. And I don't want kids. I'm happy enough with this guy here." He inclined his head toward his dog. Trooper responded immediately by banging his tail on the floor.

The conversation had taken such a serious turn that Garry suddenly felt a wave of compassion for Mike. For his future. He couldn't go on forever the way he had been. Garry asked him seriously, "Bude, what's going to become of you?"

Mike Buday understood his meaning, thought about it for a moment, and then shrugged his shoulders and laughed. The future would have to take care of itself. If Mike had any real anxiety about it, his closest friend Garry couldn't tell.

"Oh, I don't know," Mike joked. "I'll probably die of alcohol poisoning in a few years."

For Garry, the moment had passed and he shook his head, disagreeing with him. "Naw, you're going to get killed in a car accident," he joked.

Rita didn't like to joke about death and Mike, responding to the expression in her eyes, said, "Rita, I know you want to see me married with a couple of kids but I couldn't be happier than I am. Honestly. I like everything just the way it is. I wouldn't change anything."

Later that evening, the two men left to go to their favorite bar and as they were enjoying the warm ambience of the Skeena Pub, crowded with friends, drinking, laughing, and telling stories, 400 miles to the north of them another, less pleasant scene was developing.

There, off the west side of Teslin Lake, Frank and Eileen Hase huddled together in the cold darkness waiting for the light of dawn to escape before the madman who had taken over their cabin, permeating it with foul smells, returned to find them.

In the Skeena Pub, as happened more often now that he was married, Garry left Mike to his own devices while he returned home to be with Rita. It wasn't until the following morning, when they were up having a late Sunday morning breakfast, that Mike finally came crashing in through the front door. He'd been out all night.

Looking thoroughly embarrassed, a self-conscious smile on his face, he wouldn't sit down at the table with them but went directly to his room without speaking. Returning with his checkbook, he wrote out, ALL THE LIQUOR IN THE WORLD, and dated it, Sunday, March 17, 1985, signed it, and handed the check to Garry, who laid it wreath-like and with great ceremony on top of the fridge.

Mike's face was gray.

"Jesus, you look sick!" Garry said.

"Oh fuck, I feel this one," Mike groaned. "Too much fucking liquor and no sleep!"

"Too much fucking, I'll bet," Garry said, curious to hear all the inevitable details. "So, she let you back in, did she?"

Mike nodded his head sickly.

"How'd you manage that?" Garry asked amused.

"I proposed."

Rita choked and started coughing. Mike was obviously reluctant to talk about it and she didn't want to make it any harder on him; but Garry wasn't so charitable.

"Proposed what?" he asked, pretending complete ignorance.

"Don't rub it in," Mike pleaded.

"I heard a rumor this morning on the phone before you came in that you also bought a pair of old sheep boots off some rubby in the bar after I left and drank beer out of them all night?"

Garry raised his eyebrows merrily to punctuate the question; but Mike wasn't in any mood to talk.

"I'll betcha you won that bet," Garry said.

"Oh, leave me alone! I feel like I've been run over by a sixteen-wheeler," Mike groaned.

"Taste of rubber still in your mouth?" Garry asked cheerfully. Mike turned toward his bedroom. "You've got my check. I'm bankrupt now."

"A fine husband you'd make," Garry laughed.

"Oh, I feel sick," Mike moaned. "If anybody calls for me, I'm out, okay?" And then he excused himself hurriedly to spend the rest of the day sleeping in his room with the shades drawn tight.

Sunday, March 17th was passed quietly.

Feeling completely refreshed and hungry, Mike was up well before dawn on Monday morning and anxious to burn off the energy that a day in bed had built up. Before Rita and Garry woke up, Mike took Trooper for a long, hard run in the predawn starlight through the deserted streets. It was a cold, frosty morning with snow patches filling deeper ditches but the sky was clear and the air had that musky smell of early spring. Sheltered from the weather in gardens pressed up tightly to their houses, the first of the crocuses were trying to sprout.

Before they left together for work, they sat at the kitchen table in front of the window watching the sunshine light up Sleeping Beauty Mountain to the west and Garry kidded Mike about some other, even wilder stories of Mike's behavior at the Skeena Bar that he'd heard yesterday from their mutual friends.

Mike was in good spirits and laughing now about the events of Saturday night. Mike enjoyed his reputation. On his own time, away from the strictures of work, Mike Buday lived life with a passion, putting out more than anybody else Garry had ever met. When he was out for fun, there was almost no boundary he wouldn't cross. Still a young man, Mike was already a character about whom people loved to tell stories. And everybody who met him had a story to tell. And while they laughed at his antics, they sought after his company and there were no critics among his peers. At work, he focused the same energy and commitment to every task he was handed. Absolutely trustworthy, his partners had nothing but confidence in his abilities as a policeman and risked their lives on his judgment. Mike considered his job a sacred trust and had never let them down.

Within the RCMP, he had two special roles: he was both dog master and ERT member. Each position alone put him at risk more often than any other general duty policeman and, combined, the two functions made his indisputably the single most dangerous job on the force. His was the role of point man, the first on the line in every dangerous situation, the most obvious, vulnerable, and frequent target in armed exchanges. Those who didn't know him believed his wild escapades were in reaction to the tensions of his work. But those who knew him, knew differently. He had sought out the role for exactly those reasons. It offered excitement and a chance to walk the brink from time to time.

Garry finished repeating the stories he'd heard to Mike, who sat grinning as Garry talked, pretending to have forgotten most of the night.

"Fuck, no wonder I had a hangover," Mike said.

"Jesus, I'm sorry I missed that one," Garry said. "If I knew you were in that kind of fine form, I'd have stayed."

"Oh, it was some crazy night, that's for sure," Mike agreed. There was no sign of Saturday's wear left on him at all.

They arrived early at the office before the morning changeover in the uniformed shift and went directly to the plainclothes G.I. office where they worked. Although Mike was in "dogs," he had no special office and, for convenience, his desk was located right next to Garry's in the special investigation section rather than in the general duty branch. They were expected to put in full days but they didn't have regularly assigned hours and, instead, worked as the job required, nights and weekends if necessary. And there was always more work to do than time to do it in.

The G.I. office was small, twelve feet by twenty, and located in the basement of the detachment with a bank of narrow windows along the top of the outside wall. Around them, the walls were plastered with bulletin boards covered with memos, photographs, and posters of wanted persons. The furnishings were all from the forties and fifties, well-worn oak desks with black metal tabletop trays and old wooden swivel chairs covered in thin foam cushions. Files, boxes, and papers were everywhere. Telephones, two to a desk, were constantly in use and a specially designed row of heavy-duty steel filing cabinets, secure against theft by locking bolts that were welded down their fronts, contained all the sensitive investigation files. Completing the room were a few expensive Uher tape recorders, various pieces of video equipment, and assorted paraphernalia including souvenirs from major investigations hanging on the walls like stuffed heads in a trophy room. The room was a mixture of old and new, of equipment and technology. In an adjoining locked room, padded and soundproofed, was the sophisticated listening and recording equipment used for electronic surveillance. There were no cases at present under investigation using it and the listening post was locked and unoccupied.

Hank Gerrits and Murray Dreilich were in the office when the two friends entered. Gerrits' chair was pulled back into the center of the room and his heavy cowboy boots were on top of one of the desks.

"Hi Bude, Garry." Gerrits' deep, gravelly voice was coarser than usual.

"Rough weekend?" Buday asked him sympathetically. They were all close friends.

"Fuck, you got no idea! I'm surprised I'm still alive."

Dreilich laughed at the idea. "Yeah, I've stayed up all night a few times to watch my breathing to make sure it didn't shut off on me when I wasn't paying attention."

"I think I need an iron lung," Gerrits said as he mashed out a cigarette into a stained ashtray which already had a few of his butts, and then immediately lit another one, which he drew heavily on.

"You guys hiding out or in on business?" Buday asked.

Dreilich was the corporal in charge of the G.I. section in Smithers, 120 miles east of Terrace, and Gerrits was a corporal in G.I. working with the brass in the subdivision headquarters in Prince Rupert, ninety miles to the west. Gerrits had recently been promoted to sergeant to run the G.I. section in Penticton in the Okanagan Valley but he wouldn't get the third stripe until his transfer was complete.

"Ah, we're workin' bye, sure as the Lard made crooks to keep us busy," Gerrits said, putting on a Cape Breton accent. "Remember that big Jesus theft ring me and Murray were undercover in? We got the prelim in town for one of their fences today."

"You're up early for court," Rodgers said. The courthouse didn't open until 8:30 and court never began before 9:30. It was just now turning seven.

"Fuck that!" Gerrits looked indignant. "Who's gone to bed!"

"Why don't you crash for a couple of hours?" Buday suggested.

"I don't think I'd ever be able to get up again."

"Just what I told you," Dreilich grinned.

"I'd get you up," Buday promised.

Gerrits laughed heartily. "I don't like the sound of that. Thanks, buddy, but I'll take my chances with falling asleep in court."

"You got a room in town?" Rodgers asked.

"No. Just got in a half hour ago. Came straight to the office," Gerrits answered.

"How's your case look?"

"Oh fuck," Dreilich said, chuckling and shaking his head. "We got those bastards cold! Jesus it was funny! Me and Hank were doing the negotiations with them to buy the property, eh? And one of their guys padded us down, checking for wires. Well, fuck, I almost shit. I was wearing a body pack and it was recording everything they were saying and he feels it through my pants, eh, and gets all hostile right away, saying, 'What the fuck's going on?' and I says to him, 'My bladder's fucked and it's my urine bag.' Jesus he took his hand off it so quickly he almost fell over. And then when we went to pick up all the stuff they were selling, we had that big truck with the roll-up back and we were standing behind it with them at their warehouse checking their stuff and paying them when one of their guys says, joking, eh—'I sure hope that truck ain't full of cops!'—and then we fired up the back and it was full of cops! Just like the Trojan Horse. Shit that was funny. You should have seen their faces. The whole thing was worth it just to see their reaction when they realized they were had."

Gerrits and Dreilich had spent so much time working crime over the years, from drugs to theft rings, that they were the favorites for all local operations. Gerrits was a big man with light hair, a broad face, and a weathered, rugged look, like an ex-junkie, bank robber, cowboy, and country singer rolled into one. His was the face of a man who had seen too much suffering to put it behind him but he was compassionate rather than hard and, in spirit, as wild as Buday. Where Gerrits was a big man, fair in appearance, expansive in mood, and country in style, Dreilich was thin, dark, intense, and urban. Also a heavy smoker, Dreilich could play the part of any number of urban hustler roles, from dealer to terrorist to pimp. Undercover work was the ultimate theater game, with serious and sometimes potentially deadly consequences if the play wasn't real enough, and they both loved it.

"We gonna have a few beer together after your case or do you guys have to split right away?" Buday asked.

"Sounds good," Gerrits said. "No, we're not leaving right away. Me and Murray got to work on another old file together. That's why we came in early. Ever read the Lishy file out of Atlin?"

"Yeah. With that crazy man, that American guy..." Rodgers struggled with the name.

"Oros," Dreilich said, supplying it for him.

"Yeah, I remember him," Rodgers said, his interest picking right up. "Why, what's happened?"

"Oh, fuck-all," Gerrits said quickly. "It's annual checkup time, that's all."

RCMP policy on unsolved murder files was to keep them open forever, reviewing them once yearly to see if any new information had surfaced. It was not uncommon for a witness, or even a suspect, twenty or thirty years after the commission of a major crime, to feel safe enough to leak their secret—and solve the case.

"And?" Rodgers asked. "Anything at all?"

"We're no farther ahead than we were three years ago," Dreilich answered. "Unless a miracle happens, from now on it's only paperwork."

"I wonder whatever happened to him," Rodgers mused aloud. "That guy was so fucking dangerous we'd have heard of him by now if he was still alive."

Ironically, even as they spoke, Oros was moving toward national attention. He had just shot at Denny Denison's aircraft with Constable Warner on board.

Buday, who was sitting backward in one of the chairs with his arms up over the top of the backrest, looked thoughtfully at Rodgers. He, too, remembered Oros.

"I betcha somebody did that prick in," he suggested, and then added, "And nobody's going to report him missing."

Rodgers laughed. "Well, he's been missing three years now. Any volunteers to go looking for him?"

"Fuck that!" Dreilich snorted. "I went in once to get him in '82 and that was enough. I don't ever want to see that son of a bitch again!"

"That was sure some brilliant plan," Buday said without any sincerity. "You guys are bloody lucky you weren't all killed."

"You're sure right about that one," Dreilich said. His face grew even darker with the memory. "It should have been an ERT operation."

"Why wasn't it?" Gerrits asked.

Buday answered him. "The old O.C. in Rupert vetoed the plan. Figured regular duty members were as capable as anybody else. He didn't like the idea of specialization at all. The old boy mentality. They didn't use an ERT team to get Albert Johnson so why use one now. It was his decision whether to use the ERT team or not and he wanted to prove he could bring Oros in without them. Just like the old days."

Dreilich was the only one of the present group who had been in on that arrest and Gerrits looked at him. Dreilich nodded his agreement with Buday's comments and Buday continued briefly. As he spoke, he became more and more critical. Completely confident, Buday challenged authority whenever he felt it was needed and although it sometimes put him into conflict with the brass, his integrity was unassailable and his judgment seldom flawed—especially when it involved his specialty.

"No ERT team would ever have agreed to do anything as stupid as that. Just a crazy risk. Imagine, landing a bunch of guys out in the open like that in full view of Oros and then walking up to him. You could have all been killed."

"You guys know something I don't?" Gerrits asked. Looking at all three of them before centering out Buday, he asked, "I'm not surprised Garry knows about the case—he's read every goddamned file in subdivision and memorized them all—but you're in dogs for Christ sake! How do you know more about it than I do?"

"Oh, I've got hands on knowledge," Buday said casually, and smiled knowingly at Rodgers. "I choked the cocksucker out in cells here in the spring of '82 when he went animal on us."

"Oh!" Gerrits exclaimed. "That was you! I read the file about the damage he did but all it said was that they had to go out and bring in a member to restrain him but it didn't give any names." He finished explaining and then asked, "Tough guy?"

Buday thought about it for a moment before answering. "Yeah, he was pretty healthy, all right."

"Don't wonder," Gerrits said. "The guy lived in the bush for over ten years. He'd have to be pretty tough to survive that long."

"Yeah, got to hand it to the guy, that's pretty impressive. There's got to be a lot of hard survival in those years," Buday suggested. Since he had joined "dogs section" he was also involved in search and rescue missions and had made a thorough study of bush survival. Like Rodgers, he too was a competent woodsman, but a decade alone in the wilderness in primitive conditions was mind boggling.

"Funny thing about that guy," Rodgers said, cutting into their thoughts. "You'd think the last place he'd want to be would be near the police, right? But that summer when he was hanging around town waiting for his trials, the guy used to sleep right here in the station. Can you believe it? You know that bench upstairs, just inside the public entrance, in the landing?"

Gerrits nodded and Rodgers continued. "Well, that was his home on bad nights. Whenever it was blowing or raining outside, he'd come in late at night, crawl up on the bench, and stay there till morning. It was kinda freaky, this guy lying there watching you as you went by. Really weird vibes. He'd talk in whispers all the time. Figured it was his right to sleep in any public place. Couple of the guys put the run on him, threw him out, but he'd come back in as soon as they were gone. Bude used to stand up for him, told the guys to leave him alone."

Gerrits looked surprised and Buday explained, "I kinda felt sorry for the prick."

Gerrits laughed, "You always did like animals, didn't you?"

Buday shrugged his shoulders. "Guy wasn't hurting anybody." And then he suddenly grinned and said, "Besides, I've had the same problem myself—three o'clock in the morning and no place to sleep."

They all laughed. "Ain't that the truth though?" Dreilich said. "And a park bench ain't far off the mark either."

"So you still didn't explain why you know so much about the arrest in Hutsigola," Gerrits said to Buday.

"Oh, we studied it," Buday answered. "Oros was arrested in March of '82 and a month later Garry and I joined the ERT team. When we flew to Ottawa for ERT training, we took the whole arrest scenario from the file with us to discuss it. Ron Flack came with us as well and he had been part of the arrest operation. And, fuck, was he ever hot about it! We had all the reports and Flack had all the details and we used it as a classroom scenario for analysis and general discussion. Since then, it's become a classic. Everybody studies it. Anyhow, you should have heard the comments. Everybody equated Oros with Albert Johnson and agreed it should never have been attempted the way it was. Bad decisions cost lives."

Dreilich didn't need any reminding of the risks they had taken.

When Buday finished, all he could do was shake his head at the memory. "Let's just hope that prick's dead," he said.

They all agreed with the sentiment.

Just before one o'clock, Gerrits returned to the office, his face white. Dreilich had finished court as well but he had gone back to Smithers. Buday and Rodgers were alone when he entered, his booming voice a little breathless.

"Speak of the devil! I just heard that they're having problems with that goddamned Oros up there. He just shot at an aircraft at Teslin Lake after ransacking some guy's cabin out in the boonies."

He looked at them hard and seriously for a moment before he told them the rest. "It looks like they have to go after him and they're thinking about calling out the ERT teams for it."

His expression was full of concern for them.

"Haugen know?" Buday asked. Constable Paul Haugen was the third member of the Terrace team in town. Corporal Harold Schoonmaker, head of the Terrace G.I. section and Garry Rodgers' boss, was also on the team but he was tied up in the middle of a three-week murder trial in Prince Rupert which had taken him a year to put together.

"Not yet," Gerrits answered. "I was just walking past the boss' office when he was getting off the phone with the message and he told me to tell you."

They were all silent then, remembering what they each knew about Oros. Rodgers spoke up first. Reacting to the heaviness of the moment, he tried to sound enthusiastic. "Oh, good!" he said. "I'd like to get some action... A trip to the Yukon will be a real break from the paperwork here!"

Rodgers didn't like to take the grim view of things, by inclination or by choice. Focusing in on fear only fed it, giving it the power to influence thought and action. In a situation where split-second thinking and a controlled, physical response would make the difference between life and death, there was no room for fear.

Buday was uncharacteristically serious. He looked at Rodgers steadily for a moment and then, responding to his friend's apparent cheerfulness, said slowly, "You know, that might sound like a lot of fun, flying up north and getting into the bush, but that asshole is really fuckin' dangerous." Buday's tone was flat, accentuating his concern. His own usual tendency to play down fears was conspicuously absent.

"It'll diffuse itself," Rodgers said quickly and then, looking at Gerrits, who was past the age of being a member of the ERT teams, explained, "Like most of these, eh? It'll pass. We haven't had a real call out for months."

But Buday didn't agree at all. "Not this one!" He whistled and then shook his head. "Fuck!... Of all the people! This guy!... And there's no surprise this time, either. If he's committed himself to shooting at an aircraft and he's on the loose in the bush, then he's going to be in there waiting for us.... Rotten cocksucker!"

"Maybe this is just a false alarm," Gerrits suggested hopefully, picking up on Rodgers line. But they all knew better.

Buday had been thinking about it since Gerrits brought them the news and he had his assessment ready.

"You know, you two guys are hunters. Here we are going after something with the intelligence of a human being and the cunning of an animal. Worse, it's on its own turf and it's armed with a rifle. Can you imagine a more dangerous hunt?

"And the cocksucker's expecting us."

Chapter Twenty

Monday, March 18, 1985: They started packing even before the decision was official. In close radio contact with the other ERT members stationed in Prince Rupert, the men in Terrace had followed the events in Teslin all day, the spotter plane flying surveillance over Oros broadcasting his every move to them.

When Oros started to make camp for the night on Big Island, they shifted into high gear. To take advantage of the situation, they had to get up to the Yukon—tonight. And if they could deploy before or at dawn at strategic locations around the lake, keeping Oros contained out on the open ice, they could force him to surrender.

But if they missed their chance to arrest him quickly, if Oros got off the ice and slipped away under cover, into the bush, then they'd be facing a long, grueling and dangerous hunt to catch up to him again. They hadn't worked out any details for that kind of operation yet, but they had to be prepared for it. If necessary, they'd chase him through the bush, on snowshoes, with sixty pound packs, in subzero weather. And with thousands of square miles of wilderness, Oros could lead them on a chase for days. Or weeks.

Although it was already turning into a wet, coastal spring in Terrace, the conditions 400 miles north weren't so benevolent. Teslin was still in the final throes of deep winter and there'd be blinding snowstorms and twenty below temperatures to face before it was over.

Contemplating the possibilities, each man wanted to pack everything he could possibly need.

The police force had supplied each ERT member with two pair of issue snowshoes as part of their general equipment. One pair was an aluminum-framed, oval-shaped, bearpaw snowshoe designed for traversing hard-packed avalanche areas. The brilliant orange nylon webbing of these bearpaws made them easy to see and locate on an otherwise colorless plane; but it was an obvious disadvantage if one wanted to remain unseen while wearing them. The other pair was a more traditional set. Rodgers had three of this own pair and in preference to the ERT issue snowshoes, he selected two pair of his own to take with him. Wooden-framed, gut-webbed Ojibwas, they both had long tails and provided good surface support for deep, soft snow.

When he saw Buday packing the bright orange bearpaws for himself, Rodgers was surprised. Below the white nylon shell covering they were all wearing for winter camouflage, the almost fluorescent orange would stand out like a neon light.

"Bude, what are you doing?" Rodgers asked.

The son of a trapper and mink rancher, Rodgers had grown up in the bush of the Whiteshell area on the Canadian Shield between Winnipeg and Kenora. From the time he was old enough to carry some weight, he worked the trapline on snowshoes and had gained considerable experience in winter conditions.

"I'm taking these," Buday replied, aware that Rodgers didn't approve. And why.

"Don't!" Rodgers insisted. "They're garbage!"

Buday continued packing them. "I like 'em," he said somewhat defensively but determined to have his own way. "I want to stay light and flexible and these are fast."

"Yeah," Rodgers agreed. "But only on hard snow. They're no good for the mush we'll be into. They won't hold you up. I got some better ones for you…"

But Buday interrupted him. "No! I'm happy with these, thanks. I don't want anything bulky."

"Bude, they're shit! They're too small and…fuck! Just look at them! They stand out like goddamned flares!"

It was no use arguing. Buday wasn't going to change his mind about something as important as this. In the choice of equipment, each member had virtually a free hand and each had to decide what his own most important considerations were. In Buday's case, it was simply the size of the snowshoes rather than the risk of being exposed or sinking in soft snow that he considered most critical. Flexibility over camouflage.

Equally convinced that Buday was wrong, Rodgers wouldn't give up completely.

"Well, look. We'll all be needing two pair anyway, in case we break one. So take the other pair with you too. Then you can decide what to wear when we get there."

Buday agreed and packed both pairs.

For clothing, they took articles they could add or strip off as required, as well as, ERT issue winter camouflage suits and their white arctic anoraks.

Weapons were next. Haugen was the team's marksman and he packed two of his favorite rifles. A .22-250, with a Startron scope, which fired a fast, light bullet that was straight shooting and ideal for the open conditions over the ice, and a .308. Unlike the .22-250 bullet, which deflected easily, even in strong winds, the much heavier .308 bullet would fire true through the bush if they were faced with those conditions.

Buday and Rodgers both chose modified M-16 carbines rather than the shorter-barreled, German Heckler and Koch M-P-5 assault rifles. Firing nine-millimeter bullets, the M-P-5 automatics were designed for short ranges which was reason enough to reject them in favor of the less reliable but more accurate M-16s. For import customs controls, the M-16s were factory modified in the U.S. for the RCMP and not converted to fully automatic. Still, they were fast to fire, surprisingly accurate, and, with their short barrels, good bush guns.

For backup, they each packed a handgun and one shotgun between them with a box of shells loaded with C.S. gas.

Next to clothing and weapons, communications were critical and the team members spent some time making sure their radio equipment was in good order. Each had his own miniaturized radio set, with a fitted earpiece for a receiver and a tiny microphone which, pinned to their collar, allowed them to speak normally to each other or to whisper without hands-on contact. With their sets and extra batteries packed, they examined the portable repeater. It was the centerpiece for their communications system. Without it, the effective range of their tiny headsets was only a few hundred meters. Without it picking up, amplifying, and rebroadcasting their own weak radio transmissions, they wouldn't be able to reach the other teams. Or to talk to their air support.

As they loaded the repeater, cradled in its own padded, aluminum carrying case, into their van, they had no idea they'd soon be forced to leave it behind. Without it, they'd be on their own.

Without radio communication, without their eyes in the sky, it'd be a far more dangerous thing they were about to do than any of them knew.

Rita was anxiously waiting for them outside when they drove up to say their good-byes. Like the men, she remembered Oros and the stories that had headlined the news about him a few years ago. She studied their faces for signs of things they knew but wouldn't tell her.

Garry's feelings were well under control but Rita didn't miss the heaviness behind Mike's smile. His face confirmed her worst fears.

Garry was noncommittal, trying to diffuse her fears, but she wasn't being misled.

"How long are you going for?" Rita asked again, not satisfied with Garry's earlier answer.

"I don't know," he replied honestly. "We might be back soon. Maybe only a few days, maybe longer."

"How much longer?"

Garry was uncomfortable with the questions. He didn't want her to worry. "I don't know...maybe a few weeks."

"Well, what do you have to do?" she asked, alarmed.

Garry laughed. "All we have to do is arrest that prick! Eh, Bude?"

Seated across the table from Garry and gulping down the dinner Rita had made for them, Mike looked up from his plate at Garry and nodded obligingly before Garry continued.

"The problem might be in finding him, that's all... if he takes off on us and hides, he's got a hell of a lot of country to do it in."

Rita turned in her chair to face Mike, looking straight into his eyes to put her question. "Mike, it is dangerous, isn't it?"

Mike looked quickly at Garry first and then at her before smiling and shrugging his shoulder. "Sure, it's all dangerous, though, isn't it?"

"Like this?" she persisted.

Mike didn't answer her with words but his silence spoke eloquently of the danger they were facing.

For Rita, the situation was awful. She knew they'd be risking their lives. And worse, she knew they didn't have to. Participation in every ERT operation was strictly voluntary. Like membership in ERT itself, each man was committed only by choice.

She wanted to plead with Garry not to go but that would be emotional blackmail and she knew Garry would never turn his back on any assignment. Not while he remained a member of the ERT team. Rita knew it was important to Garry but the price of his membership cost her too. He had faith in his own survivability, which kept the fear at bay, but then, on another level, the fear was itself a kind of motivation—an intensity of being, almost an exhilaration, of focused energy and purpose, something few other experiences could ever equal.

But for Rita waiting at home for the phone to ring, it was altogether a different experience.

It seemed like they had just come in the door and it was already time for them to leave. Her long wait was about to begin. And Garry had said it might take weeks.

As if the extraction of promises could change the equations reducing the risks, Rita pressed them for that small concession.

"You guys WILL be careful, won't you?"

"Of course," Garry replied, much too casually for Rita to believe him.

Rita looked at Mike. He hadn't answered her. "Mike?" she asked insisting on a commitment from them both. Mike was a part of their family and she cared for him deeply. Mike understood that.

"Yes," he replied.

"Promise?" she asked seriously.

"Promise," he replied seriously.

"Promise?" she asked Garry.

"Promise," he answered her, smiling.

It wasn't enough. They were already on their feet, standing, ready to leave.

Instead of being reassured, she was growing visibly more upset in spite of her best efforts to stay calm.

"You'll take care of each other, won't you? You'll watch out for each other?"

Mike turned to her at the door and put his arm solidly around her shoulder, squeezing her lightly. "I'll look after him like a brother," he promised solemnly and then, turning, he walked quickly out the door and left her alone with Garry.

Rita moved closer to her husband and hugged him tightly. "Promise me again you'll be careful," she said quietly, almost in a whisper.

Stepping back to look her in the face, Garry held her cheeks lightly with both his hands and said gently, "Hey little one, don't worry. We'll be careful. I promise."

And then in a lighter tone, he added, "Remember, I'm with Bude! Who better to look after me?"

These were more than words to comfort his wife; he meant it. Garry's own faith in his friend was unshakable. Together, nothing could happen to them.

They left Terrace in the dark, without fanfare, four hours after

Superintendent Bob Currie announced the call out. Paul Haugen, tight-lipped and tense, drove the ERT van, with Garry Rodgers, seated behind him, still sorting and checking equipment. Mike Buday followed closely behind in a station wagon with Trooper. They moved quickly along the ribbon of highway that hugged the Skeena River as it wound through the rugged Coast Mountain Range to Prince Rupert.

The night air in Prince Rupert was warm when they arrived, at least forty-five above, Fahrenheit. They paused for a moment outside, breathing deeply of it. The ocean mustiness mixed with the smells of seaweed and fish from the canneries and the gas and diesel from the docks only a few blocks away.

From the restaurants across the street, tantalizing odors of barbecuing steaks and Chinese cooking mixed with the sweet caramel smell from the granaries that were still shipping out last summer's wheat, enriching the night and awakening senses that an odorless winter in Terrace had left dormant for the past five months. From the darkness of the black sky above them, the wheeling cry of a sea gull drifted down to them like the screech of a nighthawk on a summer's night.

Murray Dreilich was waiting at the door of the darkened RCMP administration offices to let them in.

"Hey, what are you doing here?" Rodgers asked, surprised to see him.

"Hi!" Dreilich replied, smiling. His dark-ringed eyes, characteristically tired looking, showed the strain of a particularly difficult day.

Inside, the air was stale, the air-conditioning units having shut off automatically at 4:30, and the smell of cigarette smoke came faintly to them down the darkened hall from the conference room. They could hear muffled voices.

"I thought you were heading back to Smithers?" Rodgers asked. They all knew he wasn't an ERT member.

Dreilich was tense. "I did. Got back just in time to hear the news about Oros and then turn around and drive back again. O.C. asked me if I'd come along as the investigator on the case. Figured I might be able to add something as well. Fuckin' weird, eh. Just talking about him and now this."

They were glad to have him along. Inside the conference room, the much larger Rupert ERT team was gathered waiting for the arrival of the Terrace members.

Inspector Harry Wallace quickly called them to order.

"Alright, we haven't got much time. We got the Twin Otter and it should be landing in half an hour. We want to be ready to board when it does.

Just some brief introductions: I'm in over-all command of this operation and Staff Sergeant Forsythe—you all know Ollie—will be assisting me with any supply or logistics problems. Your team leader again is Ken Allen. Murray Dreilich is also coming out with us on this one. Everybody know Murray? He was in on the arrest of Oros in 1982 and he knows more about him than any of us. He'll brief us about Oros on the plane. You got any questions about the kind of guy we're going in after or what to expect, ask Murray. Alright, our first stop is Whitehorse. Once we get there, we'll have a more detailed briefing to work out final operational details but Ken'll brief you on what we know so far. Ken"

Ken Allen didn't need any introductions. The men had chosen him to act as their leader. He stood up and started to outline Oros' movements, and some tentative plans to try to contain him, using a pointer and a large sketch pad on which he had already prepared rough sketches of the lakeshores and the island Oros was camped on. Buday and Rodgers sat back, listening to the information they already knew, and watched Allen. They were pleased with the command. Wallace, the inspector, was a straight-thinking, levelheaded guy with a sense of humor, and Corporal Ken Allen's abilities as an ERT member were unquestioned. Like Buday, who was the next most qualified member in the room, Allen never made any mistakes, and was rated by the men he worked with as perhaps the top ERT leader in the entire country.

Allen was finishing the briefing when he was asked by one of the newer members why they didn't just leave Oros alone in the bush. Allen's response caught Rodgers' attention.

"Well, the short of it is we have no choice. He's committed some serious offenses. We know who he is and what he's done. So we have to arrest him. Simple as that. It's a police responsibility. Alright? But I want to make one thing absolutely clear here. Just because it's a police responsibility doesn't make it anybody's personal responsibility."

Allen paused and then dropped the bombshell. "I think Oros is going to have to be killed. And I think there's a good chance that one of us might get hurt or killed in the process."

He paused again to let that sink in and the room was as silent as though it were empty. Buday had said as much in Terrace but nobody had yet addressed the Rupert team in such absolute terms.

"You don't think we'll bring him in?" one of the Rupert members asked at last.

"Let me qualify that," Allen said.

"I don't think Oros will surrender to us, with or without a fight. It's not part of his character any more. But we're still going to give him the chance to give himself up. Maybe he will. I certainly hope he does but I can't see him doing it.... Anyway, the point here is that this is a very dangerous operation and I don't want anyone to feel you're committed to coming just because you're here now, or for any other reasons you're obligated to stay! This is a voluntary operation and if anybody has any bad feelings about it or for any other reasons at all you don't feel 100 percent about it, I want you out. No questions asked, no reasons, no discussion. Just let me know after the meeting and you're out. We can draw on the Yukon ERT team if we need more men, so we don't NEED anybody here."

"You pulling out, boss?" one of the men asked good-naturedly, kidding.

Allen didn't laugh. Instead, he looked at him seriously for a moment before continuing, answering him only obliquely.

"I don't want any hero stuff or macho bullshit or even the three musketeers let's-stick-together attitude! This is a personal decision for everybody and everybody has to make it on his own. And if anybody thinks this is going to be a picnic, forget it! The only scenario that comes close to this in our history is the Albert Johnson chase back in the '30s. If Oros takes off into the bush, it'll be a miserable, grueling, and dangerous job just trying to keep up with him. It's his world and he outclasses us in every category! Make no mistake about that!"

There was silence again until the tension levels became too high to sustain any longer. Buday suddenly cracked the room up when he asked in his most serious voice, "Why don't we just fly over and nuke the cocksucker?"

When the laughter died down, Allen was still grinning. Buday was a good friend and a valuable player on the team. His humor was one of the best safety valves they had, both to release tension and let off steam.

The procession of unmarked police vehicles, heavily loaded with gear, ground to a halt alongside the coast guard docks beside the CNR station where the coast guard cutter, *Point Henry,* was waiting to ferry them across the harbor to the island airport. With their gear piled up on its deck, the cutter left its moorings and turned out into the still harbor for the twenty-minute run to the island airport.

The crew running the ship weren't pleased with the cargo. Within minutes of boarding, Al Girard's dog Max broke free of its leash and attacked Trooper. In the confusion of snarling animals, men shouting and diving for cover, the galley was looted of all its cookies. Fistfuls of Dad's were passed out on the deck to the men watching the fight while betting on the outcome opened quickly.

Only Buday and Girard dared to enter the fray, the others being more inclined to let the dogs kill each other rather than risk injury to themselves. Amid cheers and hoots of encouragement, the two men dove into the fight and hauled their dogs away from each other with brute strength.

Their charges still snarling and straining to get at each other but securely lashed to the rails, Girard and Buday, almost as worked up, turned their attention to Rodgers. The sight of him happily munching cookies from the sidelines inspired another battle in which he vigorously resisted their attempts to throw him overboard while the rest of the group cheered and finished off their ill-gotten gains.

The first crisis happened at the airport. With all their gear piled on the tarmac beside the waiting plane, it was immediately apparent they had too much.

The pilot took one look at it and shook his head.

"You boys need a Hercules if you really want to take all this stuff with you," he said. Then he disappeared into the hangar for a smoke, leaving them to work out a solution.

"Alright!" Wallace yelled, getting everyone's attention. "Strip it down! Take only what you'll need for tomorrow and leave the rest. That means the clothes you're going to wear, one rifle per man, one set of snowshoes, and whatever else you feel you can't do without. Carry your guns now. There's no reason to keep them in their cases. Anything we leave behind, we'll fly up later—or steal out of Yukon's stores."

Buday packed the small orange aluminum snowshoes, leaving the spare set that Rodgers had insisted he take on the runway.

There were two portable repeaters in the pile. Rupert had brought out one of their own for backup in case the Terrace unit failed. It was too heavy a luxury. However, rather than taking just one and leaving the other, both sets were left behind. The information was wrong but the Whitehorse detachment had radioed that they had a setup there that the men could use.

In the darkness of the wet night, the men probed the gear with flashlights to sort out necessaries. The confusion and disarray became distressing. The M-16s were taken out of their cases and stacked together; then it became impossible to distinguish them one from the other; the slight variations that made up their individual shooting characteristics complicated the problem and the irritation of the men who had to use them increased.

Finally, the men and essential equipment still too heavy, they stripped out the seats and the plane's own survival kit to lighten the craft. Then they boarded, sitting wherever they could, their rifles resting on their gear, barrels pointing everywhere. The two dogs, still snarling at each other, were tied tightly to their handlers, who sat at opposite ends of the aircraft, Buday by the cabin and Girard in the tail.

In the narrow space of the cramped fuselage, the sound of loose bullets clattering over the metal floor as they bounced along, taxiing toward the runway, prompted a voice from the darkness.

"Somebody grab those little bastards before they pop off and I loose my nuts!"

They laughed and then they were airborne.

It was ten o'clock.

They climbed in silence. With a three-hour flight ahead of them, the men settled down to make themselves as comfortable as they could, watching the lights of Prince Rupert fall away below and then behind them as the plane banked to the north, leveled out, and continued climbing more slowly up to its cruising altitude. A few minutes later, they flew high over the coastal Indian village of Port Simpson, a small cluster of tiny flickering lights. Over the village, they left the coast to follow a compass bearing which took them almost due north. Ahead of them, from horizon to horizon, there was only the darkness of the night—unbroken by a single light for hundreds of miles.

Five hundred miles to the north of them waited the small city of Whitehorse, the capital of the Yukon, spread along the old banks of the Yukon River. Itself only a larger cluster of lights, there was nothing else beyond Whitehorse for another 1,000 miles. Absolute wilderness.

Buday gave Trooper to Rodgers to control and then stood up to take command of the situation. Pretending he was both the pilot of their aircraft and his own detachment commander at Terrace, an inspector, he started to perform for the men, entertaining them by exaggerating the familiar characteristics of his Terrace boss....

"Shit!... goddammit!" he yelled, madly pulling back on an imaginary flight stick and turning screws and shoving throttles as he pretended to be the inspector flying the plane. Peering out the window he jerked his head back in apparent anger and disgust at the sight of something. "Who the hell turned on that engine out there? We don't need two engines. One goddamned engine is enough. Turn it off. We're wasting fuel. Bloody fuel's expensive. We've got a budget to keep. Somebody's wasted fuel and I'll find out who it was."

The sound of the two engines sucking in air and pushing the heavily loaded plane through the icy blackness of space punctuated his ravings and made the men laugh even louder. They were all aware of an internal investigation in the Terrace detachment to locate the culprit who had stolen the inspector's personal nameplate off his door one night. The inspector had sworn to get to the bottom of it but, so far, nobody was talking. Least of all Mike Buday.

Pretending to be flying so low that he could see with his naked eyes and to save power by turning off the instruments, he had to react suddenly to obstacles which presented themselves to him unexpectedly. Whipping the steering wheel violently from side to side to avoid hitting mountains, he cursed loudly. Sitting in back of the plane, Inspector Wallace and Staff Sergeant Forsythe tried unsuccessfully to control their own laughter, Wallace biting his lip to keep from seeming to take sides in a dispute between the men and the brass. On an ERT exercise, Buday could say anything about anybody. And he was clearly enjoying himself.

"Goddamn it!" he suddenly roared again as he swerved angrily to avoid another mountain which had popped up in front of him. The men fell over on their sides laughing.

"Jesus," he said scratching his ear as he tried to think. "Maybe we should only send in one guy and call off all this bullshit...look at what this aircraft must be costing me! Look at all this goddamned overtime...and for what? Some two-bit thief. Jesus Christ this is expensive. My budget's ruined!"

Beneath it all, Buday was concerned. And he was concerned enough about the men to feel it necessary to entertain them to keep up their morale. Ken Allen's role as team leader made him responsible over-all for the men and the operation, but he couldn't afford to carry on the way Buday was, although that was exactly what the situation required and he appreciated Buday's leadership in that regard.

With their humor restored and the problems at the airstrip "behind them," Allen took his turn after Buday to continue his briefing, followed by Dreilich.

As Dreilich read aloud from his file, shouting to be heard above the noise of the engines, everybody listened attentively to the reports about the man they were on their way to try to capture.

"There's one theme you should know about that recurs over and over in his diaries, from as far back as 1975. And there's no reason to believe he's changed other than for the worse. Oros is totally paranoid about being attacked by teams of paramilitary men using helicopters, machine guns, and dogs. And those are HIS words. He's convinced they've been dispatched from time to time on search-and-destroy missions with the sole objective of killing him. His stated response to this threat is to fight back. To kill these people. In this case, you.

"This operation fits in so closely to his particular fear that we believe he'll react the way he's threatened to. Given the chance, he'll kill anybody he can who he thinks is after him."

Dreilich then turned to a page he'd marked in Oros' diary and continued.

"Here's one about us. It was written after we figure he killed the German, Gunter Lishy, and before he was arrested. He first says, 'The Mounties are trying to pull a fast one,' and then says:

I WILL KILL THEM!
MY BULLETS WANT TO EAT PORK!
Everyone knows there's nothing wrong with killing an enemy in battle. If you are attacked, you must defend yourself. Human blood is less sacred than other creature's blood.

"The diaries are full of this kind of shit. And remember, this was before he was arrested. Both Bomba and Bird figured we'd never arrest him again."

When he finished, Dreilich passed out the diaries to the men, to those who wanted to read from them themselves; then they all fell silent.

There was nothing to see out the windows, the only light in that immensity of space being the focused pencil beams from the reading lights and the occasional flashlight beam stabbing through the darkness of the cabin in search of something in the gear.

With the rhythmic drone of the engines flooding the cabin with sound, insulating the men from each other, they settled quietly into their own personal realities and secret thoughts.

The complexities of the situation were all internal, the fears private ones. Each confronted the possibility of his own death, thought of future hopes and love lost, of children and responsibilities. The visions and images, some painfully sweet, others terrible, drifted uncontrollably into mind and floated away again, the focus changing as rapidly as frames in an old movie.

Peter Robert paused again to stare out into the blackness before he finished writing on a small piece of paper he had balancing on his knee. Lifting it up close to his face and shining his flashlight on it, he examined the neat script, read it through slowly, and then carefully folded it up. Unbuttoning his shirt pocket, he tucked it inside and then buttoned the pocket down again over it, sealing it inside. He then shut off his flashlight, leaned back against the dark window, and closed his eyes. If he died in the morning, he knew they'd find the paper. On it, he had written out his will, and his last words to his family.

Sitting across from Peter Robert, Dennis O'Byrne also wrote out a will which he tucked secretly into his wallet.

Rodgers, tired from a day which had begun for him at 5:00 A.M., fell fast asleep. Even Buday, who was sitting beside him, nodded off, although some, like Ken Allen, didn't even try to rest. Instead, he remained in close conversation with Dreilich and continued to pour over Dreilich's files, occasionally turning white as he read some particularly disturbing fact.

The blast of inrushing cold air snapped Rodgers awake. All around him, the men were rising out of the baggage and making their way stiffly toward the open door. They were in Whitehorse. Right on time. It was shortly after one in the morning on March 19th.

Outside, the air, clear and crisp, was absolutely black between countless stars that filled the sky from horizon to horizon. Breathing deeply of it to expel the sponginess left by the ride in the closeted spaces of the aircraft, the men found it momentarily refreshing, like the initial burst of a cool shower, and then simply cold. Without wasting any time, they started unloading the gear from the aircraft into two RCMP suburbans which had been left parked there for them.

As they were working, Staff Sergeant Legassicke arrived and walked a little distance with Allen and Wallace to report to them in private. He had some good news. The Yukon ERT team was ready if necessary to relieve the B.C. team and he had also managed to round up most of the things they needed out of the Whitehorse supplies, things that had been left on the tarmac at the Prince Rupert airport.

Except for one item. And it was bad news. He couldn't get them a radio repeater. In fact, Legassicke said, "M" Division didn't even have one in their inventory. He was sorry.

Allen cursed. He couldn't blame Legassicke, who knew what it meant for them to be without it; but somebody had fucked up badly. They needed that repeater. Allen cursed again. If they waited for one to be flown up from Rupert or Vancouver, they'd miss their chance to get Oros out on the ice where he'd be most vulnerable. And after what he knew now about Oros, he wasn't at all sure they should even try to follow him if he disappeared into the bush. It was simply too dangerous. Well, they'd have to discuss the risks. He couldn't expect anyone to go in without a repeater.

The men finished loading the two vehicles and Allen briefly laid out the problem to them. Their decision wasn't changed. Without the repeater, the operation was even more dangerous but there might never be a better chance to get Oros than now. The operation was still on.

Forsythe and Dreilich each took control of one of the loaded suburbans and they left for the two-hour drive over the Yukon Highway to Teslin, 110 miles away. The rest of the men were driven to the Sheffield Hotel, where they'd been booked for the night.

As they filed in through the entrance, the civilized ambience of the lobby at this hour provided another sharp contrast to their feelings. Muscled, athletic, and clean-cut, they could have passed themselves off as a visiting hockey team, except for the intensity of their expressions and the general heaviness of their mood. To keep down costs, the men had been booked two to a room. As soon as Buday and

Rodgers walked into theirs, Buday vented a little pent-up anger at Allen's announcement.

"Well, that's fucking great! So now we go after that cocksucker without radios? Jesus what a mess!"

Buday then walked over purposefully to the TV, turned it on, and flipped through the channels looking for an all-night, satellite-broadcast blue-movie station. It wasn't clear what they were to do next except stay awake and wait for a telephone call.

While Buday sat on the edge of one of the beds watching TV, Rodgers opened the curtains and stood in front of the large plate window staring out into the cold night. As he watched, the wind picked up, whipping the snow on the parking lot into small whirlwind snow devils that chased each other around over the icy pavement. Rodgers wondered if Oros was sleeping tonight. Constable Warner's last report of him from the spotter plane before they flew to Teslin was that Oros had cut a mound of spruce boughs for a bed and for fuel for a fire he had lit. Even with a sleeping bag, it was a hell of a way to spend a night, but Rodgers knew that Oros must have spent thousands like it.

"Hey," Rodgers joked, turning away from the window. "We should have brought a crock with us for tomorrow!"

"Oh, Jesus!" Buday replied quickly. "I don't think it'll be any place for a jug."

Buday's response was so uncharacteristically serious that Rodgers turned and studied him carefully.

"We'll tie one on when we get back," Buday promised. He tightened up his face in a deliberate gesture to demonstrate that he had some considerable doubt about it, and finally broke out into a wide grin. He qualified his answer. "As long as we're not in the goddamned bush for two or three weeks."

He then shook his head and started laughing. "You know," he said slowly as he pretended to be changing his mind, "on second thought, maybe we should get a bottle. I don't think I can last that long without a drink."

They both laughed. And then the phone rang. Buday checked his watch as he picked up the receiver. It was almost 2:30, time for another briefing.

Allen wasted no time. The meeting was in his room and he had set up a large sketch pad on a tripod with rough scale maps drawn on a half dozen pages.

"We'll try to get photographs for you by tomorrow morning but until then these will have to do."

Allen pointed at an oval, tooth-shaped island he had drawn which was three miles north of The Narrows at the south end of Teslin Lake.

"He's camped here. At the north end of this island, Big Island. Obviously, he's expecting us to come down from the north over the ice. He's no dummy. We can't come in over him with helicopters or aircraft without risking them being shot down by him. We couldn't approach over the lake on snowmobiles because the snow's too deep. If we wanted to get him on the island, all we could do is walk over the snow in snowshoes. In short, he's put himself in the most defensible position possible. But he's not going to stay there. As soon as he realizes that we're not going to attack him in his fortress, he'll see that he's the one who's vulnerable and he'll try to get off the ice. We want to be in a position around the lake where we can watch the island and wait for him to leave it. With that heavy toboggan he's pulling, his rate of speed is only a mile an hour so we should have plenty of time to get in front of him and meet him when he tries to get to shore. You all know how dangerous this operation could be and now that we don't have a repeater, we won't have any communication with each other outside the radius of the headsets themselves—maybe 200–300 yards.

"Like I said in Rupert, this is a voluntary operation only and I don't want anybody along who's not 100 percent behind it.... We've already got word that we can use the Whitehorse ERT members if we need them, so we don't need anybody here. You're not jeopardizing the safety of the group or the operation by leaving and nobody here's going to hold it against anybody else for going. Nothing will ever be said about it."

Allen stopped talking again giving anybody the chance to speak up. With their heads down staring at the floor, they all waited in embarrassed silence for the moment to pass. If any one of them withdrew, it would only mean another man would have to step into his shoes to face the same risks. None of them had ever allowed that to happen before. Leaving the team altogether, quitting ERT, was one thing, but quitting an operation while they were on the team was something else entirely.

"Okay!" Allen said finally, ending the silence and announcing the next phase of the briefing. "We're going to split into three teams: team one is Rodgers, Buday, and Haugen; Robert, O'Donnell, and Girard on team two; and O'Byrne, Stiller, and myself are team three."

The only other person present and not assigned to one of the teams was Harry Wallace, who sat back on the edge of the bed listening as Allen continued.

"Each team has one marksman and teams one and two each have a dog." Allen flipped the sheet over to the next sketch, a much smaller scale drawing showing the south end of Teslin Lake with Big Island drawn the size of a quarter. "Oros will probably head south from the island but we can't say that for sure. He might just as well head straight for either shore, but he's not likely to come up closer to Teslin." He then pointed to the east shore of the lake directly across from Big Island to a location he had marked on the sketch with an 'X.'

"I think team one should be dropped here at the south side of the mouth of the Jennings River. There's an old abandoned settlement there with some buildings which are still standing and Oros might try to make for them. If he heads off for the east shore but moves down the lake instead of going right for the bush, then team one will also move south, keeping abreast of him but staying under cover. When he gets close enough to the shore to let you use your loudhailer, order his surrender. Everybody here knows the routine...get him to walk away from his supplies and have him lie down in the snow with his hands in the air. Maybe have him strip off his snowshoes as well and throw them aside. The marksman will keep him covered from the bush while the other two team members approach over the ice. If he makes any kind of hostile move at all, shoot him!"

He paused and looked at all their faces but nobody had any questions so he continued. On the opposite side of the lake, the west shore, he had drawn another 'X' and he pointed to it now.

"Team two will be dropped here so we'll have both shores covered. Like team one, if Oros keeps out to the ice but moves south, maybe back toward the Hase cabin, you'll move south with him, staying abreast of him. If he doesn't go to shore at all but stays out in the middle of the lake and heads south, both teams will be following him along in the bush and at this point, here, where the lake narrows, you can take him from either shore. He'll be close to both teams one and two if he heads through The Narrows. At any time he's close enough to hear the loudhailers, then confront him. Same drill after that."

The men all had their eyes on the third 'X,' the one placed at the southern edge of Big Island itself, but Allen ignored it for the moment.

"I'd like for all of us to go down the lake together in three choppers and, if we can arrange it, we will. But right now, all we got is two machines. "M" Division will work through the night trying to line up another one for the morning but it's not promising. If we do get a third one and if we can confirm Oros is still on the northern edge of Big Island in the morning, then we'll all fly down the lake together, split up by the island, team one to the east, two to the west, and three here!" And he tapped the tip of his pointer on the third 'X.' Right on Big Island. He smiled grimly and continued.

"Just in case Oros thinks he can wait us out by camping on the island till spring and forcing us to come to him, we'll be sitting right here on his ass making the island an unpleasant place for him to stay. He won't be able to keep a fire, cook his food, or even sleep if we're there. So, if he's decided to dig down on the island, we'll force him off."

Nobody had to tell him that being on the same island in heavy bush with Oros was a dangerous position for Allen's team. The reason he had taken it himself was because it was the most dangerous of all the locations and he didn't want to send anyone else there.

"And if we don't get a third chopper?" Buday asked.

"Then teams one and two go out first and take up your positions where you can watch the island. We'll come down on the first chopper that's back for us. At that point, we'll have to assess the situation. We've still got the Maule with Dreilich, who'll act as our spotter now. They'll be out over the island at first light watching Oros and will be reporting every movement he makes. If we can land safely on the island, we will. If not, we won't. It depends on what Oros does. You'll see our chopper so you'll know what we're doing. But we'll either get in front of him to confront him from cover or behind him to cut off his retreat and push him toward one of the other teams. Okay?"

There were still no questions. The basic approach had been worked out in the plane and they had all agreed it was the best action plan they had. The only thing Allen had decided on himself was who went where.

"Once we're all in place, Dreilich will return to Teslin and change places with Inspector Wallace, who'll then act as our eyes in the sky."

"Lot of good that'll do without radios!" one of the men said.

Allen shrugged his shoulders. There was no question the loss of the repeater was a serious problem. "Well," he said slowly, not making excuses but trying to make the best of a bad situation. "It's better than nothing. The headsets will still work to talk to the plane, only you gotta be real close to each other. If the plane's got something important to report, they'll be dropping down to tell us."

Allen looked over at Wallace to see if he wanted to add anything; but he didn't.

"As long as Oros isn't in firing range of the aircraft," the same member added, further, qualifying the spotter's usefulness.

"Of course," Allen agreed. There were no other questions or comments and Allen carried on. "Ollie, 'Staff,' will stay in Teslin at the airport beside the radio and will be in constant contact with the plane. If we need anything, the message will be relayed through the aircraft to Staff, who will deal with it. Okay?"

The briefing continued until 3:30 in the morning. The men were tired but mentally alert and, with a vision of superrealism that bordered on the surreal, there was again that sense of fatalistic inertia which was carrying them along like bodies on a raft drifting ahead through time toward the final act which now lay only hours away.

Chapter Twenty-One

Tuesday, March 19, 1985. Whitehorse: Their uneasy sleep ended with the phone ringing on the night table between their beds. Rodgers answered it. It was their wake-up call. Stumbling out of bed in the dark, he walked to the window. The blackness outside was relieved by the light of a single street lamp swinging over the frozen parking lot. Rodgers peered at his watch. It was 6:15.

Buday was still fast asleep and breathing heavily.

"Hey, Bude!" Rodgers called out. "Wake up!"

His adrenaline was rising. It was starting.

"Hey Bude, wake up!" Rodgers repeated a little louder.

Buday stirred.

"Bude!" Rodgers yelled, close to his head.

"What?" Buday asked painfully.

"It's morning, buddy!"

"Oh, fuck!" Buday groaned and then rolled over onto his stomach and buried his face in his pillow. In an instant his breathing grew heavy and he was sound asleep again.

Rodgers laughed. He knew his friend could go forever once he got going, but he was hard to start.

"C'mon, get up!" Rodgers said, shaking him to wake him again.

"Ah, fuck!" Buday complained. "Let me sleep!" His voice muffled from speaking straight into his pillow, without raising his head, he added, "Go and tell that asshole on the island to stay there for another day and we'll go and get him tomorrow."

Rodgers laughed again. "I hate to do this to you, buddy, but we ain't got much choice!"

Buday groaned, "Aughh, you know what really pisses me off about this? If that prick were half sane, he'd give himself up. He'd only get thirty days in the bucket. Then this whole fucking operation could be canceled and I could sleep."

Without shaving or showering, they dressed quickly and went straight out to the hotel's restaurant. A couple of the other men were already there drinking coffee.

"Who's running this show?" Buday asked as they entered.

"Well, we were just told to meet here," one of them reminded him.

Buday shrugged. "Might as well pull up a chair then and have breakfast. It might be a long day."

By the time they arrived at the airport, they were already behind schedule. Ready and anxious to be off to make up for the lost time, they still had to fly to Teslin. Tension levels were already high as they ran from their vehicles toward the hangar to meet their plane.

They were sure that Oros would abandon the island and would head for the forest at first light, and every minute counted. They had to get into place around the lake before Oros started moving.

Rushing into the hangar, they spotted their pilot. And their operations changed immediately.

He wasn't ready! And he wasn't about to be pushed around; whatever the urgency.

Ignoring their loud protests, he calmly poured himself a cup of coffee and settled himself down comfortably into a chair in the hangar's office.

A civilian member of the RCMP and past retirement age, he wasn't making personal compromises anymore. As the men stood around cursing him, he drained his first cup of coffee. Then, when he poured himself a second cup instead of starting up the plane, they went wild. Furious, Buday threatened to sic Trooper on him; but he ignored all their protests. Stubbornly focusing his eyes on some distant, imaginary point, he lit up a thick cigar and rooted himself into his chair to smoke it.

Firm in his resolve not to give in to them, he refused to forgo his morning routines for anything. Even Inspector Wallace, adding his insults and threats to the others, failed to budge him until, in his own time, the cigar finished, he finally got up to start the plane. So late.

The sun was already breaking over the horizon when they finally took off. It was 8:35 A.M. And they still had a thirty-minute flight to Teslin.

In the pale morning, the light reflected off the rolling, snowbound land in silvery, pink pastels. Except for the highway beneath them and a few short spur roads here and there that set off bravely from the pavement only to be quickly swallowed up by the immensity of the space, the earth stretched away, wild and unbroken, in every direction as far as they could see.

An ancient land, the mountains here were mere wrinkles on the face of the earth, squat, rounded folds that had been smothered by age.

"God, it's quite a space, isn't it?" Buday said, his voice breaking the relative quiet. "It's beautiful to look at but it must be sheer hell to live in."

Nobody else spoke much, the others spending these last few free minutes in personal and private reflections.

Two helicopters were waiting for them when they bounced to a stop on the hard snow-packed runway at Teslin. Their engines on, their blades turning slowly, they were warming up, ready for action.

At the sight of them, the tension became palpable. There was no turning back now.

Inside a garage nearby, they stripped down to change into their bush clothes and camouflage suits. Ken Allen, who'd been up most of the night with Inspector Harry Wallace, hovered around supervising the preparations.

The men rushed to get ready.

Dreilich had flown out at first light in the Maule aircraft to take up a spotter position in the sky high above Big Island and had been in constant radio contact since then.

They were late.

Maybe even too late!

Oros was already moving. As they feared, he'd left the island at first light. But he wasn't moving directly for the nearest forest. He was traveling south instead. Over the ice. Moving in the direction of Hutsigola.

The situation had changed. It was more dangerous now. Worse, the snow had hardened overnight with the freezing temperatures and Oros was now moving faster than ever over it. But Oros was still on the ice. Out in the open. If they could surround him, cut him off from the forest and contain him on the lake, exposed and vulnerable, they could force him to surrender. It was still their best plan. If they could only get into position in time.

They had to hurry.

Every moment counted.

One of the regular-duty police officers stationed in Teslin suddenly stuck his head into the garage. "Would everybody record your blood types and pass it up?"

Stone silence.

It was one of Allen's last-minute details and he held up his hands to draw their attention.

He had it!

"You guys know how dangerous this is. The possibility of one of us being shot or even killed is extremely high. If somebody gets hurt, we're going to do the best we can for him, but this isn't Vancouver. We're a long way from any hospital."

Allen then gave them their last chance to leave, swearing that nothing would ever be said about any one of them who backed out. Nobody spoke. Allen continued. "I know we can't do it," he said, "but I'd like to close in on him with the sniper rifles and blow him away. Unfortunately, we can't do that. We have to give him a reasonable opportunity to surrender—but I want to repeat what I said yesterday, if he makes any hostile move at all—you're to shoot him! Right away!"

"What's a hostile move?" one of the men asked.

"If he goes for a gun, that's hostile," Allen suggested, but raised his hands and explained. "Look, like any other situation, you'll have to make the call yourselves. There's no easy answer to that but the reality is that Oros is armed, dangerous, and, given the chance, will probably try to kill us."

Wallace quickly added the power of his rank to the very special message Allen was trying to give the men.

"We don't need any heros on this trip!" he said. "None of this he has to shoot first crap! If you wait till he shoots, you might be dead! So, if you think he's making any kind of a hostile move, shoot him! And I'll back you a 100 percent on that."

There was nothing more to be said.

Dreilich's next report came over the radio just as they were about to leave for the helicopters.

Oros had changed his direction. Instead of moving due south, he was now angling toward the west shoreline, moving in the general direction of the Hase cabin.

It now looked like team two, O'Donnell's team, was the one which would be confronting Oros instead of Allen's team.

O'Donnell, Robert, and Girard, with the dog Max tightly under control, climbed into their helicopter. It was 10:20 A.M. Hours late, they had missed their chance to get into their positions while Oros was still safely out on the island. With their thumbs up to the men watching, they lifted up into the sky and flew away over the town to the south.

Buday, Haugen, and Rodgers boarded their helicopter next. With the dog Trooper squeezed in between Rodgers and Buday in the back, and Haugen in the front beside their pilot, they exchanged the thumbs up with Allen, Stiller, and O'Byrne and then they, too, were airborne and away.

There were only two helicopters and so Allen's team was left behind. They were in no hurry now. It'd be an hour before one of the helicopters would be able to drop off Buday's team or O'Donnell's team and come back for them. Allen's team walked back to the office to listen to the radio and wait.

Acutely aware that somewhere ahead of them Oros was on the move, they spoke little.

It was so late.

Inside the helicopter, Buday's team blinked against the dazzling sunlight which reflected off the crust of deep snow covering the earth below. The sun was already so high that the temperature had risen to a snow-melting forty degrees above zero, Fahrenheit.

It would be hard going for all of them now.

The flights of the two helicopters took them over the town of Teslin and then above a bluff which rose up from the edge of the shore to a height with a view down the frozen lake. Along the rim of the bluff was an old Indian settlement. The line of simple, wood-frame houses stood exposed to the winds on the high, barren ground.

As the helicopters flew over the Indian village, eyes from inside those houses peered out fearfully and watched as they flew south.

The police weren't the only ones interested in Oros. The man the Indians knew as Sheslay Free Mike had threatened them for years. They had abandoned their own traplines for fear of him. He had kept them out of their own forest.

With their own radio sets tuned to the reports from the spotter aircraft for the past two days, the Indians knew almost as much as the police did about Oros' movements. But they knew something more, something the police didn't.

There'd be a killing soon. Oros was going to die today! And for reasons the police knew nothing about. At the very location where Oros had spent the night on Big Island, the last of their great shamans was buried. Although he had died 150 years ago, the rock pile covering his bones was still as it had been laid.

The island was sacred. It wasn't even to be passed by without an offering made to it. But Oros had violated it. He had slept on the grave of the shaman! And for that, he would die! Finally, after all these years, he would pay the price. The shaman would awake. And Oros would die.

Unaware of the excitement their activities were rousing in the villagers below them, Rodgers, Haugen, and Buday were watching the movement of the first helicopter far ahead and talking among themselves over their helicopter's closed-circuit system.

On hearing the news that Oros was heading west, while they were going east to Johnsontown, their own tension had relaxed dramatically. With the new development, there was almost no chance they'd have any contact with Oros.

"Boy," Buday said, his eyes fixed on the distant speck of O'Donnell's helicopter. "Am I ever glad I'm not those fucking guys! I'd hate to have to confront Oros in the bush!"

With their own course set safely for Johnsontown, their pilot was taking them across the lake toward the east shore. Flying into the sun, it was warm and, inside the bubble, almost summery.

"Nice day," Buday said.

"Yeah, we should have brought some suntan oil," Rodgers joked.

"Hey," Buday asked the pilot, "can you buy suntan lotion in Whitehorse this time of year?"

"I think you can buy a lot more than that if you got the money to pay for it," he said, grinning at them.

Buday laughed but his mind was focused on the dangers O'Donnell's team was going to have to face. Their own destination, Johnsontown, was going to be a holiday compared to that.

"I told you we should have brought a jug along," Rodgers joked. "Looks like Trooper needs a drink to calm his nerves!"

Uncomfortable in the cramped space and disturbed by the bird's eye view from their lofty perspective, Trooper wanted to be out and on the ground, and he was giving Buday a little trouble.

They flew over a large peninsula to the north of the mouth of Swift River and now were above the fast, open waters of Swift River itself.

Looking down over the Swift River, Rodgers imagined the same scene in the summer. It was a river that looked like it'd give a canoe a wild ride. He filed the image away with the thought that he might someday return here. The countryside below was certainly inviting enough. Along the shoreline and across open clearings in the bush, moose tracks were plainly visible, plowed through the deep snow like furrows in soft earth. It was an exciting land, powerful and moving. A trapper could still make a living off the land here, Rodgers thought. As long as he knew his business. Rodgers remembered enough from his childhood that he figured he could do it. If he had to.

The light that reflected off the varied ground surfaces filled their minds with a hundred visions, sparking thoughts that weren't fully articulated but were rather automatic responses to visual stimulation. Their real reactions were absent, temporarily suspended. The anticipation of deadly violence was too stressful to sustain indefinitely and the mind, in reaction, had relaxed its tight focus. It was the sight of Big Island creeping up on the horizon that brought their reality back into sharp focus again.

"I'm glad I'm not those guys!" Buday said once again. Rodgers agreed. Haugen, keeping his thoughts to himself, didn't say a word. Completely disciplined, Haugen never allowed himself the luxury of relaxing until the end of an operation when all responsibility was over. Under pressure, Haugen wouldn't let his emotions interfere in any decision he had to make and for that, the Terrace ERT team had made him their team leader.

O'Donnell's helicopter pilot had tried to stay out of sight of Oros and for the last few miles of their approach, he swung low over the forest to the west of the lake. They touched down on a small frozen pond 220 yards inland and hidden from the shore. From there, they intended to sneak out to the shoreline and follow Oros from the cover of the bush. Except, they completely misjudged Oros' location.

No sooner had they touched down than Dreilich raised them on the open radio frequency.

Everybody was listening.

"There's no point in landing there!" Dreilich radioed bluntly. From his position high over the lake in the fixed-wing, he had a superior vantage point. Oros was traveling fast. Much faster than he had yesterday.

"Oros is already 1,000 yards past your present position!" Dreilich informed them. "He's close to the trees. Only 200 yards out on the ice, moving south down the lake. And he's moving fast! If you stay where you are you'll never catch up to him!"

Moving even faster than any of them thought he could, Oros was also past the point where he could easily change direction.

There was a long, narrow strip of open water which paralleled the shore and stretched all the way south to The Narrows. Oros had already moved past the start of the open water and was traveling along the strip of ice between the water and the shore. With his toboggan in tow, he had to keep to the open ice and the only direction left to him was south. Toward The Narrows and Hutsigola. If he abandoned his toboggan, he could go west into the bush; but he couldn't go east.

Wherever else he was planning on going, he certainly wasn't going to Johnsontown.

O'Donnell confirmed over the radio that they'd skip over the forest and try to land closer to Oros. They didn't go far when they put down again in a bay on Teslin Lake out of Oros' sight. They were still far behind Oros but there were no closer places to land.

Still, O'Donnell was confident it was close enough. They'd catch up with Oros. Oros was, after all, under the handicap of dragging a heavy toboggan.

Inside their own helicopter, Buday looked at Rodgers. The men were stunned by the radio exchange they heard between Dreilich and O'Donnell. Before they could say anything, Dreilich raised them on the radio with the obvious.

"He's well past the point where he might have gone east, across the lake to Johnsontown." They didn't respond immediately and Dreilich, wanting to be sure there was no misunderstanding, added, "There's no reason for you to even go to Johnsontown now."

"Lovely!" Rodgers said on the private circuit as soon as Dreilich finished his radio transmission and left them to plan out their own course. "Just fucking lovely!"

The pressure was intense. There was no time for any calm deliberation. O'Donnell's team was already on the ground standing by their helicopter with its radio, waiting to know what Buday's team would do before releasing their own helicopter and, with it, their only communication link with Buday's team and the spotter aircraft.

Rodgers cursed again.

"Fuck, now what?"

Their pilot, understanding as well as the rest after the first radio exchange between O'Donnell and Dreilich that they'd be looking for a new landing site closer to Oros, had automatically flown them away from the east shore and out across the lake. Searching for Oros.

Silent throughout the latest radio exchange, he suddenly broke out excitedly.

"There he is! That's him! Look!"

Below them, down on the ice, they could see Oros clearly. At their approach, Oros had stopped pulling his toboggan and stood still. Watching them.

The harness of this toboggan strapped around his shoulders hung loosely. His dog stood behind him in his trail, also strapped into a harness and pulling a small sled.

The distance was closing rapidly. Any moment and they'd be within range of Oros' rifle.

"Jesus Christ!" Buday yelled at the pilot. "Keep this thing away from him! Get away from that prick! All we need is to get hit in this bucket!"

They pulled up sharply and swept out of danger. But their close look at the landscape ahead of Oros confirmed what they feared.

Ahead of Oros, the shoreline continued on, more or less smoothly, for another 1,000 yards to the south until The Narrows. Paralleling it for the entire distance was the strip of open water. There was nowhere either in front of Oros or behind him where they could land in safety in the forest and be in a position to confront him. He had already moved past Hase Creek, so they could forget the cabin there. But Oros was moving in a straight line south. And he was moving fast.

They'd have to get in front of Oros and confront him.

At The Narrows, there was a small, low peninsula which stuck out from the shore, almost touching the edge of the open water. If Oros stayed on the ice with his toboggan, he'd have to pass within 100 yards of that point.

There were no other choices. It was the only place to go.

Buday, Rodgers, and Haugen took off their headsets and set them aside for a private talk. Not even their pilot could hear them with his own set still on.

"This is fucking crazy!" Buday said, offering nothing more than his own opinion. There were no alternatives.

"We should think this through carefully," Rodgers said seriously. "Anybody that goes down there and gets in front of him on that point—that's suicide!" The point was covered in sparse growth but was otherwise open to Oros' view as he was approaching it.

"The only safe way to do this is to take off the doors and open up on him from the chopper." Rodgers knew when he said it, it was impossible. There was simply no safe way to confront Oros.

"Those other guys are already down there," Haugen said, the simple statement conveying both his decision and his rationale.

Buday shook his head. It had all changed so quickly. "Fuck!" he said, dismayed.

But, repressing his feelings, he made up his mind. "Okay! Let's go!" he said firmly.

They were all resolutely committed.

Haugen called O'Donnell over their helicopter radios. "We'll go down behind the point south of Oros' present position and cut him off. You might as well stay at your location but move down toward us and try to keep him from entering the bush. Team three will have to assess the situation when they get here. Dreilich can fill them in on our positions."

O'Donnell was pleased with the new plan. Oros would be squeezed between them. O'Donnell's men stepped away from their helicopter and it rose rapidly, heading back to Teslin to pick up team three.

O'Donnell tried raising team one with his ERT radio headset. He could see Buday's helicopter flying now in an arc toward the east in the direction of Johnsontown but, without a repeater, the signal was too weak to reach them.

They were on their own.

As planned, the fixed-wing aircraft with Dreilich inside also turned away now, flying back to Teslin to replace Dreilich with Inspector Wallace.

With trepidation, the men watched it go. Blind in the bush with no backup and no communication, they started to move.

The chase was on. But it was the kind of manhunt the police hadn't undertaken in modern memory.

With a gentle breeze blowing from the north, Girard separated from O'Donnell and Robert to move farther into the bush. If they got past Oros, or if he changed direction and moved north of them, there was a chance Max might wind him. And prevent an ambush.

Apart from the slight breeze, the day was calm and the sun, high in the sky, had warmed the snow. The upper surface was quickly turning into a soft mash, which fell in overtop their snowshoes with each step, weighing them down.

O'Donnell's team pushed south as quickly as they were able to but in the bush and with the snow conditions, it was slow going. With the aircraft gone, the stillness was almost disarming. It was a perfect day. Nothing, it seemed, could move near them without making noises they'd hear.

It was a false security.

Buday's team had flown east and were now over the location they had expected to be landing at until only a few minutes ago. Looking down at the ruins of Johnsontown, they saw a collection of old, collapsed buildings. Except for the occasional and transient visitor like Oros, the site was isolated and had remained undisturbed for years. A few miles south of there, they dropped down to treetop level and shot across the lake to the west shore.

Having swung around the lake out of Oros' sight, they approached the peninsula from the south side. Skimming the ice behind the cover of the trees, Oros would hear them but he wouldn't know for sure where they had put down. Under the circumstances, it was the only bit of surprise they could manage.

It was a dangerous landing. The snow was so soft it wouldn't support the weight of the helicopter on its skis and their pilot rocked the aircraft from side to side under full power to try to pack down the snow under them.

While the chopper rested precariously on its belly, its blade cutting the air near the snow, the men rolled out the side doors and the helicopter quickly took off, leaving them alone to deal with Oros.

There was no time to waste. Rodgers had fallen under the surface into the deep snow and had to swim more than walk to get above the snow, which was chest deep. Trooper, too, had fallen out of sight beneath the surface, floundering desperately, and Buday had to carry the dog. Forcing their way through the snow off the lake. The snow was more shallow and firmer at the shoreline. There, Trooper was able to move on his own.

Haugen broke away from Rodgers and Buday to take up his position out on the end of the point. It was an exposed spot but because of his camouflage suit and the cover of a few low shrubs, he hoped Oros wouldn't detect him. More importantly, the point offered a clear and unobstructed view up the lake and around all sides of the point, a good place to shoot from with the .308.

As Haugen left to take up his sniper's position, Buday insisted on a final weapons check with Rodgers before they parted company. Taking Rodgers' M-16, Buday examined it carefully to ensure it hadn't jammed up with snow and that it was charged and ready to fire. Satisfied, he handed it back to Rodgers. They were as ready as they'd ever be.

Still, Buday lingered.

"You know, if I don't make it out of here, you can have my chain saw."

He looked intently at Rodgers. His eyes, as clear as the blue sky, conveyed far more than his words.

Rodgers well remembered the night Buday used it to move in, but he couldn't think of a reply and smiled weakly instead.

Then with a final look at his friend, Buday pushed off through the snow with Trooper to take up his position in the heavier bush at the base of the peninsula where it joined with the main shoreline.

Rodgers' designated position was midway between Buday and Haugen and he too started working his way over the peninsula to find his best vantage point.

Haugen got in position first, and immediately spotted Oros, who was about 900 yards away and moving steadily toward them. So far, everything looked good. Oros was still hauling his toboggan, leaning heavily in the traces, with his dog close behind dragging the smaller sled. If Oros was going to abandon the sleds, Haugen thought, he would have done it by now. Haugen looked off to his right. The line of open water stretched just beyond his point. To keep to the ice, Oros would have to pass Haugen within a few dozen yards. But Haugen wasn't going to let him get that close. As soon as Oros got in hearing range of the bullhorn, Haugen would order his surrender.

Voices from hidden loudspeakers in the bush.

Haugen wondered what Oros would think about that? And how he would finally react. It was all so crazy. Oros. His nightmares. This operation.

Haugen turned his attention to his own position. He had taken one of his snowshoes off and was using it to lie on. With his lower body buried under the snow and his upper body clad in white and hidden by some scrubby willows, he felt well camouflaged.

His rifle rechecked and ready to fire, Haugen made several attempts at radio contact with O'Donnell's team; but it was hopeless. Somewhere to the north, making their way through the bush, O'Donnell's team was still too far away for the small sets. Haugen focused his concentration back on Oros, watching him through his powerful binoculars.

Haugen could hear Rodgers and Buday breaking bush still trying to get into their positions when he saw Oros do something completely unexpected.

Oros stopped out on the ice and shrugged out of the harness. Then, stepping up to the side of the toboggan, he pulled out a rifle.

Haugen quickly radioed his observations of Oros to Buday and Rodgers.

Carrying the rifle but leaving the toboggans and his dog out on the ice, Oros moved off directly toward the forest to the west. With long strides, he covered the distance quickly. And disappeared completely into the trees!

His anxiety soaring, Haugen tried again to raise O'Donnell's team. To warn them that Oros was off the ice. In the bush.

There was no response. Silence. Haugen tried again. Still nothing.

"Maybe he's gone in to test the snow conditions in the bush?" Rodgers offered hopefully.

It didn't make much sense to them for Oros to simply abandon his dog and all his supplies out on the ice. Not now. Not after he'd come all this way. But why had he left the ice?

Could Oros have heard O'Donnell's team? Haugen doubted it. The shoreline to the north continued on in a more-or-less smooth line for almost 2,000 yards before it dipped out of sight into a bay. Haugen studied it with the binoculars. That bay had to be the point where O'Donnell's team was dropped off. Too far for them to have gotten anywhere near Oros' position.

Unknown to everyone, while Rodgers and Buday scrambled to get into final position and Haugen continued to try to raise O'Donnell's team on the portable radios, Oros did the unthinkable.

Out of sight from the men on the point, under cover of the forest, Oros turned to the north—toward O'Donnell's team. He had watched the helicopters flying around. In the quiet winter's air, he had also heard them put down. And he had a good idea where they landed. And why.

Keeping to the more open forest nearer the shore but still under cover, Oros moved quickly. Faster than anyone could ever believe! North, in a straight line, directly to O'Donnell's team. Incredibly fast.

Within minutes, Oros snowshoed right up to O'Donnell's team. And quietly.

Forty-five yards away from O'Donnell and Robert, Oros stopped. And listened. Waiting. O'Donnell and Robert were moving noisily toward him. Girard with his dog, Max, was farther into the bush.

Off to the lake side from their line of travel, the men would pass right by Oros' position. And walk right into a deadly ambush. With his green and gray clothing, Oros was perfectly camouflaged in the bush, his form invisible. A few moments, a minute, and the men would step into sight. At almost point-blank range, killing them would have been easy.

But Oros didn't wait. The sounds of the shots would carry. Would alert the others. Oros had a different plan. A better one. Having confirmed the presence of men from the helicopter behind him, he now had another target.

A second helicopter had landed behind the point. To the south of him. In the direction he was heading. It, too, would have left men behind.

He would deal with those men first. Then, after that, he could kill these men.

Like a wild thing, Oros crept back, away from O'Donnell's team, and then, out of their hearing, raced back through the forest, retracing his steps.

O'Donnell's team, continuing their struggle through the heavy bush, trying to catch-up to Oros, never realized Oros had been there.

Ten minutes after he first disappeared from sight, Oros suddenly re-emerged at the same spot. Stepping boldly out of the bush, he walked back out across the ice to his sled and shoved his gun back into his load.

To Rodgers and Haugen, the sight was an immense relief. As they watched, Oros strapped on the harness and, leaning heavily, started moving the sled again. Directly toward their point! He had been gone for such a short time they didn't feel he had done anything threatening. He had been out of sight for only a few minutes. Long enough to defecate but not much more. Perhaps he was only checking the snow conditions in the bush to see if the snow was firmer in the trees, to figure out the easiest route back to Hutsigola. But whatever he did, they were confident that at least O'Donnell's team wasn't in any danger now. And Oros hadn't given any sign that he was aware of them. Or that he was the least bit alarmed.

In full sight of them, step by step, Oros approached. Another few minutes and he'd be close enough to challenge. Haugen was ready, the bullhorn by his side. As soon as Oros was within its range, he'd call out to him. Order him to surrender. Everything seemed to be working out.

Rodgers had dug himself down into the snow until he was standing on firmer ground. With a small clump of poplar shoots around him breaking his outline, he was satisfied with his cover.

But less than fifty yards away, he could still hear Buday moving around breaking branches as he tried to find a place to hide with Trooper. Rodgers called out to him through the bush without using the radio.

"Hey, Bude! Hurry up! Get into position!"

Although Oros was still almost 500 yards away, Rodgers was concerned that the snap of breaking branches would carry a long way through the winter air.

Buday finally found a deadfall large enough to hide under with Trooper. In the heavier forest at the base of the peninsula, his vision was limited to his immediate surroundings. Too far from the shoreline to see out over the ice, he was nevertheless satisfied.

He didn't need to see the lake. His role was to cover the bush.

Rodgers and Haugen could deal with Oros easily enough by themselves as long as Oros stayed out on the ice. But if Oros left the ice, if he got into the bush and moved around them, then Rodgers and Haugen would be in danger. Out on the point, they'd be exposed and vulnerable.

Buday was guarding their flank. Protecting their backs. With his gun cradled in both hands, he crawled under the fallen tree. With his bright snowshoes still on his feet, he lay down in the snow, facing off toward the northwest. He, too, was ready.

In silence the three men waited.

They didn't have to wait long!

Oros was covering ground rapidly. Very rapidly. With an energy he hadn't shown yesterday, he was moving over the snow toward them at twice the speed he had before.

Within minutes, he had closed the distance between them to 233 yards.

As easy a shot as it was for Haugen to make with the .308 rifle, he didn't consider it. To shoot Oros down on the lake in cold blood was murder. Oros still hadn't made any hostile moves. And until he did, there was no justification for any kind of violence.

Haugen was ready with the bullhorn instead. A few more yards, another minute, and Oros would be near enough to hear it. To understand he was under arrest. To give himself up.

But Oros came no farther! Stopping suddenly out on the ice, he slipped out of his harness and let it fall to the snow.

Rodgers and Haugen watched his every move carefully through their binoculars.

Oros had been carrying a pack on his back but now, standing beside his toboggan, he took it off and laid it on top of the toboggan. Then he dug out a pair of snowshoes, a spare set he had tucked into the side of his load. With his other hand, he picked up his rifle.

Carrying only the gun and the spare set of snowshoes, Oros left the toboggan. Without looking at them, or even at the peninsula they were hiding on, Oros turned toward the bush. Walking in rapid, long strides over the snow, he angled down the lake toward Buday's position. Entering the forest only 200 yards away.

Buday couldn't see anything. Relying instead on Haugen's detailed descriptions, Buday tried to assess Oros' actions.

Were they hostile?

Haugen caught sight of Oros again in the bush. Weaving through the trees. Heading straight for Buday!

"Looks like he's on a collision course with you!" Haugen radioed.

Buday was in an awful position. "Should I confront him?" he asked Haugen.

With no loudhailer, Buday would have to call out in his own voice. And he'd have to be near enough to Oros for them to hear each other. And see each other. Much too close! He'd have to wait to see if Oros made a hostile move. And then there'd be no time to react!

As with everything else, there was no choice.

Haugen confirmed it for him.

"You'll have to!" Haugen replied. The radio communicated none of his emotions.

It was a desperate situation. Out on the ice, in the open, they could deal with Oros. Confront him. Assess his reactions. Back each other up. But in the thick of the bush?

The worst thing imaginable was happening.

Now Buday would have to confront Oros. And Oros was in the bush. Under cover. And armed!

Rodgers spotted him this time. Keeping out of the heavier timber farther inland, Oros was in the thinner stands of poplar closer to the shore. Moving rapidly. Closing the distance quickly. Then, suddenly, he disappeared from sight again.

The air was dead calm. In the stillness, they strained their ears for the sound of a man moving through the trees. For the noise of breaking branches. For any sound at all. But nothing disturbed the silence.

Waiting. Breathlessly. Watching the bush. Intently. Oros was so near, Buday and Rodgers had put aside their binoculars.

Suddenly Rodgers spotted him.

"I see him!" Rodgers called out. Whispering into his mike. A flash. A movement. Still moving toward Buday. A mere glimpse. And then, he disappeared again. Oros was moving more slowly now. But he was very close.

Rodgers couldn't tell what Oros was up to. But he didn't believe Oros would actually turn on them. That Oros really wanted to kill them. The hunted turned hunter.

Oros' actions were certainly strange but they weren't overtly hostile. And Oros had already done the same thing farther up the lake, disappearing into the bush and then returning to the lake.

Buday had a different assessment of Oros. He had no misgivings about the dangers of confronting Oros in his home territory. Oros had sworn never to be taken again. Buday believed that.

Another minute passed. In absolute silence.

And another.

Time slowed down. And tensions soared. It was too long! Oros was up to something. At the speed he'd been going, Oros should have passed them by now. And he should have been making lots of noise.

Rodgers couldn't stand it any more.

"Bude!" His voice over the portable radio was a mere whisper in their ears from the tiny speakers but the urgency he felt wasn't lost. "I haven't seen him for a couple of minutes!" Rodgers said anxiously.

Oros was obviously hiding. And deliberately keeping quiet. They were all alarmed now.

"He might be coming around you," Rodgers warned him. "Watch your side."

"Yeah," Buday acknowledged. And then his familiar voice sounding so sure and confident, he added, "I got her under control."

Carefully so as not to give away his own position, Rodgers slowly shifted his body around until he was facing Buday's direction.

Scanning the bush rapidly back and forth with his eyes, he kept his head and his body still. It was almost always motion that exposed living things.

Like there! Off to the left!

Rodgers spotted something. A movement! From the south! Behind them! So slight it might only have been his imagination. His eyes playing tricks. But still he kept them riveted on the spot. Only there was nothing to see. Except bush. A gray tangled wash of poplar trunks and branches.

Whatever it was, if it was anything, there was nothing moving now. Yet Rodgers didn't quit. Staring at it so he wouldn't lose the spot.

And then, as he watched, he could almost see, or imagined he saw, the form of a man. Materializing, ghostlike, out of the gray background.

Rodgers continued staring, unsure whether his mind or his eyes were creating images.

But then it moved!

Slowly and deliberately, it moved!

Rodgers yelled immediately,

"Bude! He's right behind you!"

Oros had circled right around them through the bush and had snuck up on them from behind! Stalking them like a wild animal.

There was no time to react.

Instantly after Rodgers yelled, the sound of a rifle shot rang out.

CRACK!

They were all so close Rodgers couldn't tell where the sound had come from. Oros or Buday.

And then the figure moved again.

Rotating slightly, it faced Rodgers! The movement was mechanical. The change in posture almost imperceptible. Except Rodgers was now the focus of his attention!

Rodgers had the vague impression of dark green clothes. But it was only an impression. He couldn't see the body at all.

What he could see was Oros' face.

Shining brightly against the background of gray forest and white snow, it was almost luminous. Glowing brightly. Like a beacon.

And then it moved, jerking involuntarily to the hidden movements of his hands. Tilted forward, his face down, the beacon dulled. A pause.

In that instant, almost too late, Rodgers understood the movements. The tiny jerks of the head were in time to the necessary actions of reloading a rifle. A bolt action .303.

His head down, Oros was now aiming at Rodgers! Firing his second shot!

Instinctively, Rodgers snapped up his M-16 rifle, pointed it at Oros' face and fired a shot.

Far to the north, still struggling through the bush, O'Donnell stopped Robert and Girard with a radio command.

"I heard a shot!"

Drifting in through the forest, it had been muffled. And very faint.

And then came the sound of the second one. They all heard it.

Two shots. Down the lake. To the south. From Buday's team!

O'Donnell cursed. With no radio contact, there was no way of knowing what happened. Or what they were now getting themselves into. But one thing was certain. If shots were being fired, they were needed! Abandoning all caution, they raced on now, desperate to reach Buday's team as fast as possible.

Rodgers didn't know what to do. Exposed and vulnerable, he would have sprayed the bush with bullets if his rifle had been set up to fire automatically. But it had been modified for Canadian sensibilities and wasn't fully automatic.

The rifle up to his shoulder, the barrel pointing at the bush where he'd last seen Oros, he was on a hair-trigger. Waiting to be shot. Expecting Oros to kill him. Any second. Every second. Oros could shoot from anywhere. He had the cover!

The hunted turned hunter!

After Rodgers had fired, Oros' face had disappeared instantly, leaving only the gray wash of the winter's forest concealing everything within its amorphous mass—while Rodgers was stuck like a beacon out in the snow!

Intensely keyed. Ready to fire at the slightest motion, Rodgers maintained his vigilance. Crouching as low as he could into the snow. Behind him, out on the point, Haugen did the same.

It was another twenty minutes before O'Donnell's team finally broke through into radio contact with Haugen. They were now a quarter mile away.

Three hundred yards north of Oros' sleds and his dog, O'Donnell and Robert and Girard broke cover. Taking risks they knew they shouldn't, they moved out doggedly, single file, over the open ice.

Beyond Oros' sleds, farther to the south, they saw the peninsula for the first time. As Oros would have seen it. A low, tree-covered ridge of land that left the shore, hugging the ice, to peter out from trees to shrubbery to frozen lake.

Buday was in there somewhere.

Stopping at Oros' sleigh, O'Donnell stripped it of three other rifles, spinning them away in the air as far as he could throw them where they disappeared into the snow.

From there, they followed Oros' tracks.

It was a dangerous thing to do. But the surest way to find him. And now they wanted to get Oros.

Oros' tracks led them off the ice and into the bush. Weaving through the trees toward the base of the point, Oros' steps were wide and hurried.

Watching their progress through his binoculars, Haugen kept in constant radio communication with them as they approached Buday's position.

But then, suddenly, Oros' tracks changed direction. They turned away from the lake and stalked into the bush. Here, his strides became shorter. His steps carefully placed.

And here, too, his pursuers moved more cautiously, Girard and Robert in the lead. They moved forward one man at a time. From tree to tree. While the other two covered him. Watching for any movement.

Oros' steps then swung around again to the south in a wide arc around Buday's position. Almost as though Oros knew he was there. Or smelled him.

To the south of the point, well behind Buday, Oros had come out again to the edge of the bush. And there he had stood for a moment. His snowshoes rotated around in the snow as he first looked out over the ice studying the signs left there and then back at the peninsula beside him.

It was easy to see what he'd done. Oros had heard the helicopter. And had guessed what it meant. That the men were on the point.

In front of them, plainly visible in the snow, were the deep impressions left behind by the landing gear of the helicopter.

And leading away from the helicopter were the three sets of tracks left by Buday, Rodgers, and Haugen.

Oros had walked right out to them! Studying them. Making his plans. He was safely past them. He could have fled. On to Hutsigola.

Instead, he turned and stalked them. Followed them right to the edge of the peninsula. To the edge of its bush.

Here one set of tracks, Haugen's, left the other two and branched off, away along the south shoreline, out toward the end of the peninsula.

The other two led into the poplar. Crossing into the peninsula. The tracks of Buday and Rodgers.

Oros followed those.

The men were moving slowly now. Inching ahead. From cover to cover. Hunting the hunter. They had stayed outside Oros' tracks all the way around the peninsula. Oros was trapped. Inside their net!

He was close. The circle less than 200 yards wide.

Girard noted the wind. It was blowing here from the north. And Oros had come around from the west and the south. Buday's dog wouldn't have smelled him.

Girard tied Max down. The dog wasn't any help now. Even if he was smelling Oros, Girard was safer on his own. Watching the bush.

Waiting.

Moving ahead. One slow step at a time.

O'Donnell saw him first. And immediately had him in the center of his cross hairs. Ready to fire a bullet into him the moment he moved.

Covered by O'Donnell and Robert, Girard advanced, alone. Until he stood beside Oros and knew for sure the threat was over.

Oros was lying on his back with his knees bent and upraised. His feet in the snowshoes, still firmly planted in the snow. One arm was thrown out to the side and the other was resting almost casually over the stock of his .303 rifle. His eyes were wide open, staring up at the blue sky as though daydreaming on a midsummer's day. Only Oros would never move again. At the edge of his hairline in the center of his forehead a small trickle of blood gave evidence of a bullet's entry hole. The force of the shot from Rodgers' M-16 had knocked him over backward, killing him instantly. Oros was dead.

Girard looked ahead through the bush but he couldn't see Buday. Not at first. But beside him were Buday's tracks. Oros had fallen over them. Without moving, Girard followed them with his eyes. As Oros would have done. And then he saw him.

Only twenty-six yards away from Oros, he found the body of Michael Buday. Partially concealed under a deadfall that effectively hid him from view for anyone approaching from the north, he had been crouched until the end facing the north. His back to Oros.

He, too, had been killed instantly. The bullet had entered his head in his right ear as he turned his head toward Rodgers. He fell as he had been kneeling. He lay on his side, his clear blue eyes open, staring off toward his best friend.

Girard knelt down and closed his eyes gently before he returned to the others.

Epilogue

The men who survived the encounter with Oros were more than lucky. Oros knew three men had positioned themselves along the point. And he tracked them to kill them.

Standing where Oros stood, he had a clear view of both Buday and Rodgers. Buday was a mere twenty-six yards away. And Rodgers only forty-three. Had he killed them both, then Haugen was next. And, unprotected out on the point, Haugen presented an easy target.

After killing those three men, Oros knew there were others in the bush. And he knew exactly where they were. O'Donnell, Girard, and Robert would have walked into a trap. As he had done so often in the past, Oros would have circled around again in the bush to wait beside his own trail until O'Donnell's team came along.

Ken Allen's team, the third team, had no radio contact with the men on the ground. By the time they arrived, there might have been no one left alive. Except Oros. Waiting for them.

It wasn't skill which saved them. It wasn't Rodgers' quick reaction. He wasn't quick enough.

But Rodgers was right. Oros did reload after killing Buday. His gun was a bolt-action British army rifle with open iron sights. A gun Oros was familiar with. Oros had used the same model of rifle every day for years. And then he pointed the gun at Rodgers. Rodgers' own bullet hit Oros at the top of his forehead as Oros had his head down aiming along the sights at Rodgers.

But Oros didn't pause before firing. And Rodgers didn't fire first!

There was a live round in the chamber of Oros' rifle but it wasn't intact. Oros had pulled the trigger. The firing pin worked. It struck the bullet as it was meant to. The primer was even dented with the force of the impact. Only it didn't explode. For some reason, it failed to go off. And Rodgers' life was spared.

And Haugen's.

And the others'.

The misfire allowed Rodgers time to shoot back. To kill Oros.

The Tlingit Indians living along the windswept bluff at the northern shore of Teslin Lake weren't surprised. They knew Oros was going to die. And they were expecting it. But to them, it wasn't entirely a human affair.

They have their own secrets. And an old knowledge they don't wish to share, of things that are better left unsaid. Of spirits and power. Of forces beyond this world. Like those that are buried on Big Island. But Oros had crossed the line. Awakening sleeping giants.

The ancient shaman stopped Oros' bullet from killing Rodgers. And then, through Rodgers, the shaman killed Oros.

The Tlingit weren't alone in believing there was another force which intervened to save Rodgers. The sight of Buday's eyes fixed on his friend suggested it. That somehow Buday had saved him.

Loving Rodgers like a brother, Buday had sworn a solemn promise to keep him safe. And he never let him down. Ever.

The toboggan Oros had left out on the lake was heavy with supplies. Some of them, like the toboggan itself, belonged to Frank Hase. Inside Oros' pack, which had been left on top, was his last diary. Tucked into its pages was the note Hase had left for Oros at the cabin. The one that warned Oros his hideous crimes would be avenged.

Under the thick canvas tarpaulin covering the load were large chunks of moose meat. Raw and untreated, in various stages of rot, the meat had warmed up under the canvas in the sunshine. When the covers were pulled back, the maggots which had also been feeding on the meat were suddenly exposed, squirming uncomfortably in the colder air.

After the shootings, Michael Oros' body was flown to Prince George, in the exact condition it was found in the snow, for an autopsy by the pathologist Jennifer Rice.

Oros' upper body was covered first in a gray checked jacket, under which he had on a brown jacket, a brown shirt, and a gray woolen undershirt. In his shirt pockets were two 12-gauge shotgun shells and several .22 bullets. Covering his lower body were gray wool tweed pants. Under those, he was wearing jeans with a brown belt. Attached to the belt was a homemade leather sheath in which he had a hunting knife. Under the jeans he was wearing a pair of gray long johns. He was wearing bushpack-type boots on his feet, the boots having come from different pairs and both being for the right foot. He had several pairs of socks on each foot. Covering his head had been a gray toque, which was shipped loose with the body, accompanied by a note that it had been knocked off his head by the force of the bullet. All his outer clothing was of wool-like materials with colors and patterns that blended perfectly with the tangle of gray brush in which he made his final stalk. The only part of his body lacking camouflage was his face.

Under all his clothing, he wore a double-linked, yellow metal chain around his neck as well as a tight leather strap around his right wrist.

Naked, he appeared well nourished and well developed, with no signs of any natural disease processes. An examination of his genitalia showed them to be normal. Overall, his personal hygiene was poor. Microscopic examinations for the presence of disease were all negative. Blood, urine, and vitreous humor samples underwent rigorous toxicological examinations, all with negative results. There were no drugs present anywhere in his body. Physically, Oros was not suffering the effects of any chemical poisoning. He had been in perfect health. He was thirty-three.

Following the autopsy, his body was cremated in Prince George. There were no services for Michael Oros and no regrets at his passing. Instead, throughout the north, the mood was one of relief. Finally, after twelve years, it was all over. Sheslay Free Mike was gone. Even his ashes were quietly returned to the United States.

For the men, who Michael Buday left behind on Teslin Lake, there was no comfort other than the numbing emptiness of the frozen spaces. His death was felt across the country. His body was flown to his parents' home in the small farming community of Tilley, Alberta. The following day, in a service for him in the neighboring community of Brooks, over 2,000 mourners gathered at the small Roman Catholic Church with his family. Too many for the small church, they stood quietly outside under cold, gray skies and waited. The funeral procession wound its way for a half mile from the church to the cemetery. All along the route, people of southern Alberta lined the way, standing with their hats off. Behind the hearse bearing his body, 800 Mounted Police in their scarlet uniforms and high riding boots marched in front of nearly 1,000 other policemen who had come from across Canada and the United States to pay tribute.

Michael Buday's dog, Trooper, was sent to Innisfail, Alberta, where they had first worked together in the RCMP's dog training program. There, Trooper was assigned to another officer.

At Buday's funeral, his closest friends drank toasts to his life and then buried him with his own bottle.

More than a year later, on June 26, 1986, Garry Rodgers returned to the point on Teslin Lake where Michael Buday had been killed. There, Rodgers, some of the other members of the ERT team, and a small gathering of friends built a small rock cairn on the deserted shore. Inside the cairn they buried some soil from the land where Buday had grown up in Alberta and the bottle they had emptied toasting him. The cairn was fitted with a bronze plaque:

IN MEMORY Constable Michael Joseph Buday
Royal Canadian Mounted Police
Regimental No. 33631
Gave his life in the line of duty
on this location, March 19, 1985
MAINTIENS LE DROIT (MAINTAIN THE RIGHT)

It was something Michael Buday had believed in.

The one man whom almost everyone had forgotten after the funeral of Michael Buday was Gunter Lishy. The flurry of press stories that had appeared after the sudden disappearance of the German, all anticipating a dramatic and newsworthy breakthrough in the mystery in light of the massive search, had died completely with the acquittals in Terrace in the summer of 1982.

Although the press had lost interest then, the police hadn't. Quietly over the years, they were still digging, snooping through files, looking for clues, information, or hard evidence. Until the fatal shootings on Teslin Lake ended the life of the only person who knew what had happened to Gunter Lishy, there was still hope that one day Oros would slip. That one day he'd talk. But his death changed that. As unlikely as it now seemed that the Lishy case could ever be solved, RCMP policy required that the file remain open in the tiny Atlin RCMP detachment. Forever, if necessary. Even if it was no more than a curiosity for newly arrived members reading old files.

The detachment had gone through a complete staff rotation after Corporal Peter Bird finished his tour and before Corporal Barry Erickson arrived to take over the post. But Erickson was taken by the file. Determined to find something new, he made plans to carry on the investigation. On August 29, 1985, Erickson flew into Hutsigola Lake with Constable Warner from the Teslin detachment, who now also felt a personal need to continue the four-year-old search for Lishy for any clues which might help solve the case. They didn't expect to find much.

They landed on Hutsigola with a floatplane but the shallow, muddy shoreline around the lake didn't permit them to land in front of Oros' old cabin. Instead, they came to shore at a point about 200 yards south of the cabin. Jumping off the pontoons into the muck, they still had to wade through mud and water to get to shore. The bush here crowded the lake and, breaking through it, near the edge of the high water mark, they stepped into a more open forest carpeted in moss.

And there, at their feet, they discovered Gunter Lishy!

Laying in the moss, partially sunk into the ground and green with growth, was a human skull. Nearby, partially overgrown with roots and small plants, they found the lower jaw. The teeth in them were later compared by X-rays with Gunter Lishy's dental records, which Corporal Bird had seized years ago from Lishy's dentist in Whitehorse, and they confirmed that the remains found were those of the missing trapper.

There was yet a more exciting discovery to make. A trail followed the edge of the lake toward the south end of Hutsigola. And there Erickson found it. In the weeds of the water's edge, still partially buried under the mud, worn and dirty with age, was a large piece of heavy-duty plastic sheeting. Building material. Erickson knew immediately that Oros would have referred to it as a tarpaulin. As he had described so many years ago to a cell-plant in Terrace, it was the way he would dispose of a body. Here was Lishy's grave!

And beside it was the most important find of all. A large bone. The right shoulder blade of Gunter Lishy. Scattered around the watery grave site were other small pieces of bone, but it was the shoulder blade that excited him. Through one corner of the bone was a small, neat, circular hole!

Erickson knew at once it was a bullet hole. The same size a .303 bullet would make!

Dr. Mark Skinner from the archaeology department of Simon Fraser University in Vancouver confirmed Corporal Erickson's opinions. The bones were all human. From the nature and degree of decomposition of brain tissue still adhering to the inside of the skull, Skinner also confirmed the incomplete decomposition was due to a burial of the body in a wet environment.

Gunter Lishy's body had been rolled into the plastic tarp and buried beneath the shallow water in the mud at the southern edge of Hutsigola Lake.

Under water, preserved from rapid decomposition by the cold temperatures, hidden from view and odorless, it might never have been found, but for the fluctuating water levels. Constantly rising with each rain and falling with each drought, the body was slowly percolated up through the mud to the surface. There, exposed finally after years to the air and elements, it was scavenged by animals. Evidence of their feeding was left in the form of teeth marks in the bones, which were scattered through the area.

The final analysis was done by the RCMP Forensic Laboratory in Vancouver. They were interested in the right scapula. Lishy's shoulder blade.

Microscopic examination confirmed that the hole through the bone was, in fact, a bullet hole. More significantly, they were able to determine the direction the bullet had come from. And it had passed through the shoulder blade from the back to the front.

Here, finally, was the missing evidence which would have convicted Oros of the murder of Gunter Lishy in 1981.

The bones that washed ashore four years after his death told the final story. Lishy had been shot in the back by a bullet with the same dimensions as a .303-caliber bullet. The same kind of gun Oros had when he was arrested by the police in March of 1982. The same kind of gun he murdered Michael Buday with in March of 1985. The gun he had always preferred for its reliability.

All that remained was an official verdict.

It came almost a year later. On August 14, 1986. Five and a half years after Lishy's disappearance was first reported to Corporal Peter Bird by a breathless young pilot in Atlin, a public coroner's jury completed its review of all the evidence the police now had on the case. The Oros diaries which had always spoken so clearly to Bird of a concealed murder were finally supported by the physical evidence of Lishy's bones. Oros' own words, his thoughts, and his actions spoke to the jury from out of the diaries. The evidence against Oros was overwhelming.

Their verdict was a simple one.

Gunter Hans Lishy died as a result of a fatal gunshot wound to his chest having been shot in the back by Michael Oros.

At the request of his family, Lishy's remains were sent to Germany for burial. And the Atlin file was finally closed.

About the Author

Vernon Frolick was born in 1950 in Toronto and attended the universities of Toronto and Windsor, graduating with a Bachelor of Law degree in 1974. He commenced his practice of law in Kenora as an Assistant Crown Attorney and later worked as a defense lawyer in Toronto. Since 1982, when he moved to Terrace, British Columbia he has worked continuously as a prosecutor with the Attorney General's Office. He has traveled widely and has a special interest in the wilderness of northern British Columbia. He is married with two children and presently lives in Penticton. *Descent into Madness* is his first book.

More HANCOCK HOUSE *history & biography titles*

Alaska's Father Goose
G. Bodding & W. Cass
978-0-88839-651-8
5½ x 8½, sc, 176 pp

Back to the Barrens
George Erickson
978-0-88839-642-6
5½ x 8½, sc, 328 pp

Broken Arrow #1
John M. Clearwater
978-0-88839-596-2
5½ x 8½, sc, 160 pp

Discovery at Prudhoe Bay: Oil
John M. Sweet
978-0-88839-630-3
5½ x 8½, sc, 304 pp

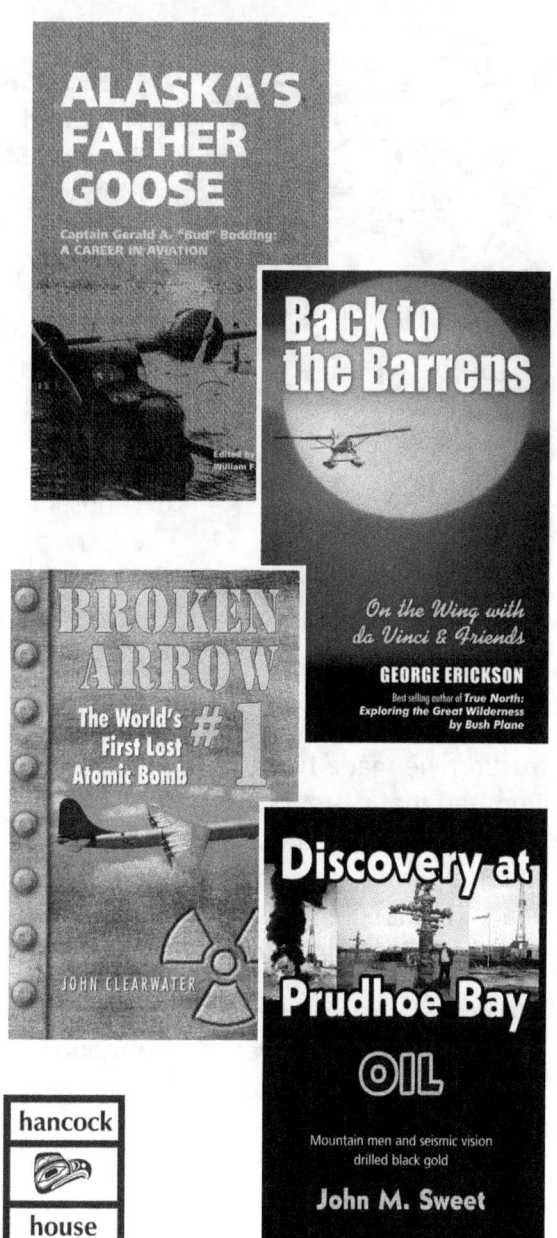

View all HANCOCK HOUSE *titles at* www.hancockhouse.com

More HANCOCK HOUSE history & biography titles

Remember Me
The Charles Morgan Blessing Story
Mervyn Dykes

Charles Morgan Blessing's last plea to his friend Wellington Delaney Moses was that he not be forgotten "if something should happen to me in this country."

Thousands of men slogged their way north from New Westminster in the 1860s in search of Cariboo gold. Some made their fortunes. Others left empty handed, or moved on to newer strikes still further north. But not Charlie Blessing. Shy and trusting, he made two classic mistakes at Quesnellemouth (now Quesnel) that were to cost him his life: he flashed his roll in a rowdy bar and he chose the wrong traveling companion. He ended up in the trailside bushes with a bullet in the back of his head. The details of his story vanished in time and were replaced by speculation and invention.

140 years later, intrigued by Blessing's story, author Mervyn Dykes set out to discover the truth and was shocked to find out how little was known about the murder victim who wanted to be remembered.

978-0-88839-627-3
5½ x 8½", sc, 104 pages
25 historical photos

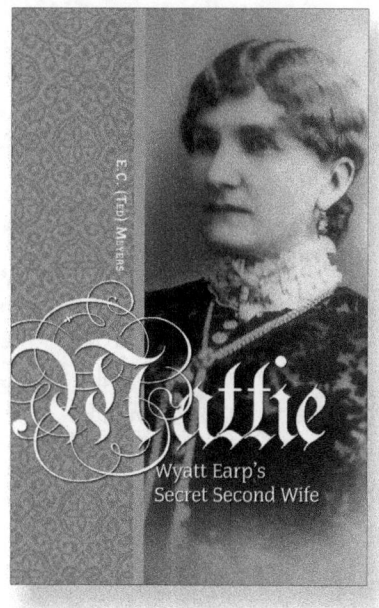

Mattie
Wyatt Earp's Secret Second Wife
E.C. (Ted) Meyers

Mattie Blaylock was Wyatt Earp's second wife and ultimately became his darkest secret. A runaway from a strict farming family, she was working in a brothel when she met and married the young, handsome—and, at the time, fugitive—Wyatt Earp in 1871, living a transient life with him for nearly eleven years before he deserted her.

Alcoholic, addicted to opium, and penniless, in 1888 Mattie committed suicide when she was just thirty-eight. As Wyatt Earp gained fame and fortune, he buried his association with Mattie, denying her very existence.

This heretofore-unknown story has been thoroughly researched and is heavily footnoted, with many fascinating historical facts and reproductions of historical documents.

978-0-88839-628-0
5½ x 8½", sc, 288 pages
25 historical photos / documents & court records

View all HANCOCK HOUSE *titles at* www.hancockhouse.com

More HANCOCK HOUSE *history & biography titles*

White Water Skippers of the North
The Barringtons
by Nancy Warren Ferrell

Occasionally, a family and its place in history are right for each other, and such was the case with the Barringtons. Two generations of mariners, fueled by gambling blood and gold fever, wove their own unique stories in an era of exploration and adventure.

White Water Skippers of the North: The Barringtons delivers an exciting taste of commercial riverboating in Canada and Alaska during the gold rush and into the 1900s.

Author Nancy Warren Ferrell recreates the exploits of the day as she chronicles the lives and livelihoods of the Barrington boys. Storytellers, gamblers, men of reckless daring, these adventurers, like their vessels, experienced a lusty existence marked with optimism, triumph and tragedy. They thought nothing of gambling with their own lives, and did it with the same ease as they gambled with their fortunes.

978-0-88839-616-7
5½ x 8½", sc, 216 pages
80 b/w photos

T.F. Godwin, MD, FRCP(C)

A Doctor's Notes
Taken from Both Sides of the Bedsheets
by T.F. Godwin, MD, FRCP(C)

Tom Godwin takes the reader through his sometimes-tumultuous career in medicine, beginning with his last year in high school when events in his life led to fortuitous meetings that set his sights on a medical career.

The stories of Tom's early medical training outline the enormous pressures placed on medical students. Patients' stories illustrate the problems attendant to their various illnesses. As a busy doctor attempting to do the best for his patients, Tom encountered many unbelievable frustrations, as well as many amazing successes. Some of the pitfalls of being a doctor are described, along with some foolhardy adventures. Sidebars throughout the book provide basic explanations of medical terminology and procedures.

The book is intended to both educate — to make the lay public more aware of the huge problems facing the profession today with a view to provoking lively discussion — and to entertain so that readers still laugh out loud at some of life's ridiculous moments.

978-0-88839-654-9
5½ x 8½", sc, 368 pages
38 photos, 15 illustrations

View all **HANCOCK HOUSE** *titles at* www.hancockhouse.com

The Incredible Gang Ranch
by Dale Alsager

Hardship, intrigue, humor, and tragedy went into author Dale Alsager's successful struggle to lasso The Incredible Gang Ranch, North America's largest cattle ranching empire and once the largest in the world at four million acres. Family squabbles, jealousies, and desperate financial hardship have gone into the continuing legal battle to keep it. The legendary million-acre ranch in central British Columbia is still worth more than $10 million today, even after having been broken up. Its colorful and dramatic 130-year history includes meddling government bureaucracies, absentee owners, and tough economic times.

978-0-88839-211-4
5½ x 8½", sc
448 pages

View all **HANCOCK HOUSE** *titles at* www.hancockhouse.com